Colossians
Second Edition

Colossians, Second Edition

© 2017 BEE World

Every attempt has been made to provide correct information. However, the publisher does not guarantee the accuracy of the book and does not assume responsibility for information included in or omitted from it.

All scripture quotations, unless otherwise indicated, are taken from the NET Bible®, ©1996-2006 by Biblical Studies Press, L.L.C. www.bible.org. All rights reserved. This material is available in its entirety as a free download or online web use at http://net.bible.org. Scripture quotations marked as NASB are taken from the New American Standard Bible, © 1960, 1995 by The Lockman Foundation. Used by permission. Scripture quotations marked KJV are taken from the King James Version. Scripture quotations marked (NIV) are taken from the Holy Bible, New International Version®, NIV®. Copyright © 1973, 1978, 1984, 2011 by Biblica, Inc.™ Used by permission of Zondervan. All rights reserved worldwide. www.zondervan.com The "NIV" and "New International Version" are trademarks registered in the United States Patent and Trademark Office by Biblica, Inc.™

All rights reserved. This publication is protected by copyright, and except for brief excerpts for review purposes, permission must be obtained from the publisher prior to any prohibited reproduction, storage in a retrieval system, or transmission in any form or by any means, electronic, mechanical, photocopying, recording, or likewise.

For information regarding permissions or special orders, please contact:

BEE World
International Headquarters
990 Pinon Ranch View, Ste. 100
Colorado Springs, CO 80907

ISBN: 978-1-937324-29-2

Second Edition

Printed in the United States of America

1 2 3 4 5 6 7 8 9 10 11 12

12012017

Contents

Course Introduction: Colossians 1
Unit One: A Foundation for Studying Colossians 3
Lesson 1: A Survey of Colossians 4
   Topic 1: How to Survey a Book of the Bible 5
   Topic 2: Researching the Historical Background of Colossians 10
   Topic 3: Making an Observational Chart of Colossians 15
   Topic 4: A Simplified Chart of Colossians 16
   Topic 5: A Theme Statement for Colossians 18
   Topic 6: The Contribution of Each Part of the Letter to the Whole 18
   Lesson 1 Self Check 22
   Lesson 1 Answers to Questions 24
   Lesson 1 Self Check Answers 26

Lesson 2: How to Study a Paragraph 27
Part I—Seeing the Paragraph as a Whole 27
   Topic 1: What is a Structural Diagram? 28
   Topic 2: How to Make a Structural Diagram 30
   Topic 3: How to Make a Structural Diagram—Identifying the Structure 33
   Topic 4: How to Summarize the Results of a Structural Diagram 38
   Lesson 2 Self Check 41
   Lesson 2 Answers to Questions 42
   Lesson 2 Self Check Answers 48

Lesson 3: How to Study a Paragraph, Part II—Detailed Analysis 49
   Topic 1: How to Examine the Details of a Paragraph 50
   Topic 2: How to Use a Commentary 56
   Topic 3: The Salutation (Col 1:1-2) 57
   Topic 4: Thanksgiving for Their Response to the Gospel (Col 1:3-8) 62
   Lesson 3 Self Check 71
   Lesson 3 Answers to Questions 72
   Lesson 3 Self Check Answers 75
   Unit One Exam: Colossians 76
   Unit 1 Exam Answers 79

Unit Two: Redemption Through Christ 80

Lesson 4: Prayer for Growth, Praise for Redemption—Colossians 1:9-14 81
    Topic 1: Prayer for Spiritual Growth (Col 1:9-12a) 82
    Topic 2: Praise for Redemption (Col 1:12b-14) 90
    Lesson 4 Self Check 97
    Lesson 4 Answers to Questions 98
    Lesson 4 Self Check Answers 101

Lesson 5: Christ, First in All Things—Colossians 1:15-20 102
    Topic 1: First in the Creation (Col 1:15-17) 103
    Topic 2: First in the New Creation (Col 1:18-20) 110
    Lesson 5 Self Check 117
    Lesson 5 Answers to Questions 119
    Lesson 5 Self Check Answers 122

Lesson 6: Paul's Message, Paul's Ministry—Colossians 1:21-29 123
    Topic 1: Reconciled to God (Col 1:21-23) 124
    Topic 2: Paul's Commission to Proclaim Christ (Col 1:24-27) 130
    Topic 3: The Goal of Paul's Ministry (Col 1:28-29) 136
    Lesson 6 Self Check 141
    Lesson 6 Answers to Questions 143
    Lesson 6 Self Check Answers 148
    Unit Two Exam 149
    Unit 2 Exam Answers 153

Unit Three: The Gospel Explained and Defended 154

Lesson 7: Paul's Goal for the Colossians (Col 2:1-8) 155
    Topic 1: Why Paul Writes This Letter (Col 2:1-5) 156
    Topic 2: Continue in the Path of Christ (Col 2:6-8) 163
    Lesson 7 Self Check 172
    Lesson 7 Answers to Questions 174
    Lesson 7 Self Check Answers 178

Lesson 8: The Theological Heart of the Letter—Colossians 2:9-15 179
    Topic 1: Made Full by Dying and Rising with Christ (Col 2:9-12) 180
    Topic 2: Made Alive with Christ (Col 2:13-15) 190
    Lesson 8 Self Check 196
    Lesson 8 Answers to Questions 198
    Lesson 8 Self Check Answers 202

Lesson 9: The False Teaching—Colossians 2:16-23 203
    Topic 1: Christ Fulfills the Ceremonial Law (Col 2:16-17) 204
    Topic 2: Those Who Claim to Have Visions (Col 2:18-19) 208
    Topic 3: Liberated from Ceremonial Rules (Col 2:20-23) 216
    Lesson 9 Self Check 225
    Lesson 9 Answers to Questions 227
    Lesson 9 Self Check Answers 232
    Unit Three Exam 233
    Unit 3 Exam Answers 237

Unit Four: The Gospel Applied to the Christian Life 238

Lesson 10: Set Your Minds on Things Above—Colossians 3:1-11 239
    Topic 1: The True Heavenly-Mindedness—Colossians 3:1-4 240
    Topic 2: Put off the Ways of the Old Man— Colossians 3:5-11 247
    Lesson 10 Self Check 256
    Lesson 10 Answers to Questions 258
    Lesson 10 Self Check Answers 262

Lesson 11: Walk as "New Men"—Colossians 3:12-21 263
    Topic 1: Put on the Ways of the "New Man" (Col 3:12-14) 264
    Topic 2: Let Christ Be All (Col 3:15-17) 269
    Topic 3: The Duties of Wives and Husbands (Col 3:18-19) 274
    Topic 4: The Duties of Parents and Children (Col 3:20-21) 278
    Lesson 11 Self Check 282
    Lesson 11 Answers to Questions 284
    Lesson 11 Self Check Answers 290

Lesson 12: Serve Christ and Closing Instructions—Colossians 3:22-4:7-18 291
    Topic 1: The Duties of Slaves and Masters (Col 3:22–4:1) 292
    Topic 2: Pray Persistently (Col 4:2-4) 299
    Topic 3: Act Wisely toward Non-Christians (Col 4:5-6) 303
    Topic 4: Closing Greetings and Instructions (Col 4:7-18) 306
    Lesson 12 Self Check 316
    Lesson 12 Answers to Questions 318
    Lesson 12 Self Check Answers 323
    Unit Four Exam 324
    Unit 4 Exam Answers 328

Course Introduction: Colossians

Colossians is a missionary letter. Paul wrote it to a small congregation of recent converts for the purpose of leading them to maturity in Christ. To accomplish this, Paul stressed the importance of understanding who Christ is, what he has accomplished for believers through his death and resurrection, and how they should conduct their lives as a result.

A real danger along their path to maturity was the presence in Colossae of a seductive false teaching. Consequently, Paul's emphasis on the person and work of Christ is shaped by his desire to demonstrate to these young believers the superiority of what they already have in Christ, in contrast to what these false teachers claimed to offer. This defense of the gospel is one of our earliest examples of Christian apologetics.

Therefore, Colossians is a book about how to live according to the gospel and how to avoid doctrines and practices that are contrary to the gospel. As such, it is a book about Christian growth and maturity. Moreover, Paul's goal with these young believers, his method, and his teaching provide the modern-day Christian with a model of how to lead others to maturity in Christ. The purpose of this course is to guide you in a study of this valuable and timely portion of God's Word.

Course Objectives

It is always important when beginning a study of any biblical topic to firmly understand the answers to these questions: Why you are taking time to do this? What difference will it make in your life? Why is it important? Identified below are the overall objectives you should keep in mind as you study the book of Colossians. When you have finished the Colossians course, you should be able to:

- Discuss the background, theme, and flow of thought of Colossians
- Exhibit a new confidence and skill in your ability to study the text of Scripture by using Bible study methods
- Explain God's plan of salvation as presented in Colossians, including how God desires his people to live as a result of his gift
- Exhibit a greater spiritual maturity and an enriched walk with the Lord
- Incorporate into your ministry principles of ministry found in Colossians
- Preach or teach a series of messages on Colossians
- Prepare and teach this course to others in your ministry setting

Course Organization

The lessons are grouped into four units:

Unit One: A Foundation for Studying Colossians

    Lesson 1: A Survey of Colossians

    Lesson 2: How to Study a Paragraph Part I—Seeing the Paragraph as a Whole

    Lesson 3: How to Study a Paragraph, Part II—Detailed Analysis

Unit Two: Redemption Through Christ

    Lesson 4: Prayer for Growth, Praise for Redemption (Col 1:9-14)

    Lesson 5: Christ, First in All Things (Col 1:15-20)

    Lesson 6: Paul's Message, Paul's Ministry (Col 1:21-29)

Unit Three: The Gospel Explained and Defended

    Lesson 7: Paul's Goal for the Colossians (Col 2:1-8)

Lesson 8: The Theological Heart of the Letter (Col 2:9-15)

Lesson 9: The False Teaching (Col 2:16-23)

Unit Four: The Gospel Applied to the Christian Life

Lesson 10: Set Your Minds on Things Above (Col 3:1-11)

Lesson 11: Walk as New Men (Col 3:12-21)

Lesson 12: Serve Christ (Col 3:22-4:6); Closing Instructions (Col 4:7-18)

Lesson Organization

Please give careful attention to every part of the lesson:
- Title
- Lesson Introduction
- Lesson Outline
- Lesson Objectives
- Lesson Assignments
- Lesson Development

The title, introduction, outline, and objectives provide a preview of the lesson. Your mind will be more alert and receptive, and you will learn better because of this preview.

The lesson assignments describe how and in what order to complete the lesson.

The lesson development follows the lesson outline. Its comments, suggestions, and questions all help you to reach the lesson objectives. Be sure to check your answers with the ones given for the study questions. These will fix your attention once more on the main points of the lesson. This procedure is designed to make your learning more effective and long lasting.

Unit One: A Foundation for Studying Colossians

The purpose of this first unit is to lay the foundation for our study of Colossians.

Lesson 1 is a survey of the entire book. Here, you will learn a five-step method for doing a book survey and then use it to survey Colossians.

Lessons 2 and 3 present a basic three-step method for studying paragraphs. We will use this method to study twenty-four paragraphs (all but Col 4:7-18). The first step is to observe the entire paragraph. This involves making a structural diagram and summarizing the results in an outline and theme statement. This is the subject of Lesson 2.

Lesson 3 covers the second and third steps. Step 2 is to make detailed observations with interpretation and application on the paragraph. Step 3 is to read a commentary. Lesson 3 will explain how to do these two steps (much of it will be review) and then you will begin using this three-step method on the first two paragraphs of Colossians.

Unit Outline

Lesson 1: A Survey of Colossians

Lesson 2: How to Study a Paragraph, Part I—Seeing the Paragraph as a Whole

Lesson 3: How to Study a Paragraph, Part II—Detailed Analysis

Unit One Objectives

When you have completed this unit, you should be able to:
- Demonstrate skill in doing a book survey
- Discuss the historical background of Colossians, its theme statement, and overall flow of thought
- Display a basic understanding of the structural diagram, paragraph theme statement, and outline
- Use these methods of observation, interpretation, and application with greater confidence and skill

Lesson 1: A Survey of Colossians

Lesson Introduction

The purpose of this lesson is to give you a broad overview of Colossians. We need to see the letter as a whole before we can begin a detailed study. There are two parts to this overview. The first is to examine the historical context of the letter. Who were the Colossians? What was their situation? Why did Paul write to them?

The second part of our task is to survey the text of the letter itself. What are its major parts? How does the thought flow through these parts from beginning to end? What is the overall theme of the letter? By answering these questions, we will lay a solid foundation for our verse-by-verse study in the remainder of the course.

Topic 1 explains a simple five-step method for performing a book survey. In the remainder of this lesson, we will follow these five steps to survey the book of Colossians.

Step 1 of the method is discussed in Topic 2, as you learn to examine the historical background of Colossians.

Next you will gain a quick overview of Colossians by reading the entire letter in a single sitting. This is step 2 of the book survey method.

In Topic 3, you learn how to make an observational chart of Colossians, which is step 3 of the survey method.

Topic 4 covers step 4. You will reduce your observational chart to a simplified chart. While this step is actually done for you, your task is to memorize this little "map" of Colossians. It will serve as a useful guide as you explore the details of the text later on.

You will learn to write a theme statement for Colossians in Topic 5. This is the fifth step of this book survey method.

Topic 6 is a summary that explains the flow of the argument and how the various parts of the letter fit together to make up its entire message.

Lesson Outline

Topic 1: How to Survey a Book of the Bible
- Step 1: Research the Background
- Step 2: Read the Book
- Step 3: Make an Observational Chart
- Step 4: Create a Simplified Chart
- Step 5: Write a Theme Statement

Topic 2: Researching the Historical Background of Colossians

Topic 3: Making an Observational Chart of Colossians

Topic 4: A Simplified Chart of Colossians

Topic 5: A Theme Statement for Colossians

Topic 6: The Contribution of Each Part of the Letter to the Whole

Lesson Objectives

When you have completed this lesson, you should be able to:
- Perform a basic five-step method for surveying a book of the Bible
- Explain the historical background of Colossians
- Have an overview of Colossians based on your own reading of it
- Make an observational chart of Colossians
- Reproduce from memory a simplified chart of Colossians
- State the unifying theme of Colossians
- Recognize how each part of Colossians contributes to the book as a whole

Topic 1: How to Survey a Book of the Bible

The study of a book should begin with an overview of its entire contents. We begin with the overview because it reveals the context of each part of the book. Context is vital to interpretation. To interpret a passage correctly, we must understand it in relation to the whole book of which it is a part. Thus, the overview comes first, then the detailed study of the parts.

This overview of the whole is called a book survey. Its basic task is to trace the flow of thought from beginning to end, identifying the major parts and how these fit together into a unified whole. We will use the following five-step procedure to do a survey of Colossians.

Step 1: Research the background

Step 2: Read the book

Step 3: Make an observational chart

Step 4: Create a simplified chart

Step 5: Write a theme statement

Step 1: Research the Background

Step 1 involves answering a set of questions regarding the author of the book and his original readers such as:
- Who wrote the book?
- When and where did the author write it?
- Under what circumstances was it written?
- Who were the original readers?
- What was their situation?
- What specific need or problem did the readers face that may have led the author to write this book?

The answers to some of these questions can often be found by a quick reading of the book to gain surface knowledge. Finding other answers may require some digging. A Bible dictionary or commentary can assist you in this. This lesson provides answers to these questions concerning the book of Colossians.

Step 2: Read the Book

Read the book quickly at one sitting. Do not pause to ponder individual paragraphs or difficult concepts. The purpose here is to get a quick overview of the contents—the major events and ideas, the general flow of thought and the organization of the book.

If possible, you should use a good modern translation (not a paraphrase) that divides the book according to paragraphs. This course includes a translation of Colossians made with the special needs of this course in mind. Most of the assignments, the commentary, and the answer sections follow this translation.

Step 3: Make an Observational Chart

A. Lay out the chart with a column for each chapter and a space for each paragraph.

Use a full sheet of paper and see the diagram below for an example of an observational chart. Notice the illustration has three chapters with four paragraphs in each chapter. (A paragraph consists of one or more sentences, deals with one point, and begins on a new line. The new line is usually indented or is separated from the previous paragraph by a blank line.)

Chapter 1	Chapter 2	Chapter 3
1-4	1-5	1-3
5-10	6-11	4-9
11-15	12-19	10-16
16-23	20-25	17-18

B. Write a summary of each paragraph.

As you read the book a second time, write a brief observational summary of each paragraph in the space allotted—as in this example of Colossians 1:1-8.

Colossians 1:1-8
1-2 Paul and Timothy to the Colossians —grace and peace
3-8 Thanksgiving for their faith and love, springing from hope in heaven heard in the gospel

Work quickly, jotting down what you see of the main points of the paragraph, and then move on to the next paragraph and the next. Beware of getting bogged down with details. Remember your purpose at this stage is to obtain a broad overview.

C. Identify relationships between paragraphs.

As you proceed through the book, observe how the author develops his case by linking the thought of one paragraph to the next and beyond. The task here is to recognize and label the logical relationships *between* paragraphs. There are many types of relationships to look for:

- Does one paragraph further explain a concept introduced in an earlier paragraph?
- Perhaps the explanation takes the form of an illustration, an application, or a conclusion.
- The relationship may be one of contrast, cause to effect, problem to solution, question to answer, a general principle to a specific case.
- A paragraph may be pivotal—concluding one section while introducing the next.
- There may be no apparent continuity between paragraphs except the introduction of a new subject.

The author often signals the nature of the relationship by introducing the paragraph with a connecting word such as "therefore," "for," "but," and "finally." Summarize the nature of the relationship between paragraphs in a word or two. Some find it helpful to draw and label an arrow from one paragraph to another.

Chapter 1	Chapter 2	Chapter 3
1-4 short summary of paragraph	1-5 **For** *explanation* short summary of paragraph	1-3 short summary of paragraph
new subject 5-10 short summary	6-11 *Cause to effect* short summary	*new subject* 4-9 short summary
contrast 11-15 **But** short summary	*conclusion* 12-19 **Therefore** short summary	*explanation* 10-16 short summary
new subject 16-23 short summary	*application* 20-25 short summary	17-18 short summary

D. Group the paragraphs into larger units of thought.

The final step in making an observational chart is to identify and label the larger units of thought in the book. The paragraph is the most basic unit of thought—the basic building block of the argument. The author has combined these basic units into larger units (sections and sub-sections), which function together like the parts of a machine to produce the overall message of the book. By identifying these larger parts, we are able to see more clearly what this overall message is and how each part contributes to it.

Begin by looking for places where two or more paragraphs share a common theme or subject. For example, the unifying subject of Colossians 1:24-29 and Colossians 2:1-5 (three paragraphs) is Paul's ministry. When you find a section like this, draw a horizontal line at the beginning and at the end to mark it off from the rest. It is also helpful if you can write a brief title at the beginning of the section—such as "Paul's ministry."

Similarly, you will often find that two or more of these smaller groups of paragraphs can be grouped together into a larger section on the basis of common subject matter. When you locate a section like this, mark it at the beginning and end with a heavy horizontal line.

Chapter 1	Chapter 2	Chapter 3
1-4 short summary of paragraph	1-5 **For** *explanation* short summary of paragraph	1-3 short summary of paragraph
5-10 *new subject* short summary	6-11 *Cause to effect* short summary	4-9 *new subject* short summary
11-15 **But** *contrast* short summary	12-19 **Therefore** *conclusion* short summary	10-16 *explanation* short summary
16-23 *new subject* short summary	20-25 *application* short summary	17-18 short summary

A final word of caution: some of these larger and smaller sections are quite easy to spot. Others are not so easy. At this stage, you will sometimes need to make educated guesses. The overall plan of the book will become clearer to you as you study the paragraphs in detail.

Summary of Step 3

To make an observational chart:
- Lay out the chart with a column for each chapter and a space for each paragraph.
- Write a summary for each paragraph.
- Identify relationships between paragraphs.
- Group the paragraphs into larger units of thought.

Step 4: Create a Simplified Chart

Your observational chart is a rough worksheet, which by this stage should look quite messy. The purpose of this step is to create a simpler and cleaner chart that displays, in columns, the larger units of thought that you identified on your observational chart. Begin by making a list in outline form of these larger units and sub-units (sub-sections) that you found within them—as in our illustration:

I. First Section—Colossians 1:1-4

II. Second Section—Colossians 1:5-15

III. Third Section—Colossians 1:16-29; Colossians 2; Colossians 3:1-3

    A. Sub-section Colossians 1:16-29; Colossians 2:1-11

    B. Sub-section Colossians 2:12-23; Colossians 3:1-3

IV. Final Section—Colossians 3:4-4:18

Next arrange these sections and sub-sections by column on your new chart, and write in a title for each, as shown in the following diagram. Within the columns themselves, you may write a title for each paragraph or, if you prefer, some other brief representation of that section's contents.

Descriptive Title for the Book				
Section Title	Section Title	Section Title		Section Title
		Sub-section Title	Sub-section Title	
paragraph title	1. paragraph title 2. paragraph title	1. paragraph title 2. paragraph title 3. paragraph title	1. paragraph title 2. paragraph title 3. paragraph title	1. paragraph title 2. paragraph title 3. paragraph title

Step 5: Write a Theme Statement

The task here is to identify the controlling theme of the book and to summarize it in a single sentence. The best way to do this is to answer the questions: What did the author intend to accomplish by writing this book? What was his objective, his purpose? What result was he seeking to bring about in the lives of the original readers? Each part of the book can then be understood as contributing to this single overall objective.

To illustrate, consider the way a bicycle works. It has a variety of parts; wheels, seat, frame, handlebars, pedals, chain, etc. Each part performs a different function, yet they all work together to accomplish a single purpose. The unity of the parts is seen in their common purpose. It is the same with a book of the Bible.

The aim of this step is to identify that unifying purpose. The correct answer will be the one that provides the most simple and direct explanation for the role of each part within the book. Ideally, the statement should include two things: (a) the need or problem faced by the original readers and (b) the solution offered by the writer—both his intended result and his means for accomplishing it.

A typical statement might run along these lines: The writer (Paul, John, etc.) wrote something to the readers faced with a certain situation so that they might respond in a certain way.

Here are three guidelines for identifying this controlling theme.
- First, look to see if the author himself makes a clear statement of his purpose for writing. John's purpose, for example, is written toward the end of his gospel, "that you may believe that Jesus is the Christ, the Son of God, and that by believing you may have life in his name" (Jn 20:31).
- Often you may infer the author's purpose from his exhortations and the applications he makes to the doctrinal parts of his book. Usually these will reflect his objective in writing.
- Finally, you may infer the controlling theme of the book by examining the themes of its various parts to see how they work together toward a common end. This approach may be compared to observing how each part of a device functions (a bicycle, for example) in order to discover what the entire device is designed to accomplish.

Summary of the Procedure for Doing a Book Survey

Step 1: Research the background.

Step 2: Read the book.

Step 3: Make an observational chart.

    A. Lay out the chart with a column for each chapter and a space for each paragraph.

    B. Write a summary for each paragraph.

    C. Identify relationships between paragraphs.

    D. Group the paragraphs into larger units of thought.

Step 4: Create a simplified chart that displays the larger units of thought in columns.

Step 5: Write a theme statement that reflects the purpose of the book.

In the remainder of this lesson you will be doing a survey of the book of Colossians by following this five-step procedure.

Topic 2: Researching the Historical Background of Colossians

Begin your survey of Colossians by researching the background. Read "The Historical Background of Colossians" carefully. Then answer the questions here in the lesson to test your comprehension.

> ### The Historical Background of Colossians
> ### The Founding of the Church (AD 52-55)
>
> During Paul's third missionary journey he stayed in the city of Ephesus for a period of three years (Acts 19:10; 20:31). From this strategic location, he directed a missionary outreach to the entire Roman province of Asia (the western part of modern Turkey). The seven churches of Asia described in Revelation 1-3 were likely founded at this time.
>
> One of Paul's co-workers in this outreach was a man named Epaphras. He was from the town of Colossae, about 120 miles (192 km) east of Ephesus. Paul sent Epaphras back to his home region where he preached the gospel and established churches in Colossae and in the neighboring towns of Laodicea and Hierapolis. These would have been relatively small congregations of not more than fifty persons. We know this because they met in private homes, and even the homes of well-to-do people could not have held many more than this. The Colossian congregation met in the home of Philemon (Phm 2). The church in Laodicea (or at least a portion of it) met in the home of Nympha (Col 4:15).

The Occasion of the Letter

Epaphras rejoined Paul and informed him of the situation in Colossae. He reports that the church is holding firm in its faith (Col 1:4; 2:5), but a significant problem has arisen. They had encountered in Colossae a teaching that was contrary to the gospel and threatened to seduce these young believers with its attractive arguments. Therefore, Paul writes a pastoral letter to strengthen them in their faith and prevent them from being taken captive by this false teaching.

At the time Paul writes, both he and Epaphras are in prison, although he expects to be released soon (Phm 1:22). Paul, therefore, commissions his co-worker, Tychicus, to carry the letter to Colossae. With Tychicus he also sends Onesimus, a runaway slave belonging to Philemon (Col 4:9). Paul encountered Onesimus while Onesimus was an escaped slave. Paul led him to faith in Christ and is now returning him to his master. In a separate letter, Paul appeals to Philemon to forgive Onesimus (Phm 1:17-21), and if possible to allow him to return to Paul that he might "serve me . . . during my imprisonment" (Phm 1:13-14).

The Place and Date of Writing

Paul's letters to the Colossians and to Philemon do not reveal the city from which he writes. We only know for certain that he writes from prison. We also know that he expected to be released soon, and that upon release he intended to visit Colossae ("Prepare a guest room for me, because I hope to be restored to you in answer to your prayers." Phm 22, NIV). The book of Acts records two extended periods when Paul was in prison: Caesarea (near Jerusalem) from AD 57 to 59 (Acts 24:27) and Rome from AD 60 to 62 (Acts 28:30-31). It is doubtful, however, that the events reflected in these two letters could have taken place during either of these imprisonments.

Caesarea can be eliminated for two reasons. First, it is highly unlikely that Onesimus would have fled to Palestine. Second, from Caesarea Paul's destination was Rome not Colossae, since he appealed his case to Caesar (Acts 25:12).

The theory that Paul wrote from Rome also presents many problems:

1. Rome to Colossae was a difficult journey of over 1000 miles (1600 km) by land and sea, requiring perhaps two months. Yet, the comings and goings between Paul and Colossae reflected in these two letters suggest a much shorter, easier journey. For example, if Paul were writing from Rome, would he have asked Philemon to send Onesimus back to him (a four–month round-trip journey) and then add that he expects to be released soon and to visit Colossae? What if Paul was gone by the time Onesimus finally returned? Such travel plans make a lot better sense if he was much closer when he made them, namely in Ephesus.

2. Second, Paul indicated in Romans 15:24 that after he reached Rome he planned to press on westward to Spain not eastward to Asia.

3. Third, in his farewell address to the elders of Ephesus in Acts 20, Paul solemnly says to his friends that they will not see his face again (Acts 20:25). But a trip to Colossae (Phm 1:22) following his release from Rome seven years later would almost certainly include a visit to nearby Ephesus. Paul's certainty in this context suggests it is due to the revelation he mentions earlier in Acts 20:23.

4. Fourth, it is argued that in order to avoid capture and punishment, Onesimus would have fled not to nearby Ephesus but to distant Rome where he could "disappear" within its vast population. But a fugitive slave would have been in great danger of being detected by the police on such a long journey, particularly when taking passage on a ship. Would Onesimus have risked his safety to make such a journey? Could he have evaded capture if he did? It seems more likely that he would have fled to Ephesus—itself a very large and prosperous city, the third largest in the Roman Empire after Rome itself and Alexandria in Egypt.

5. A fifth problem concerns Epaphras. It is difficult to understand why he would be arrested in Rome when visiting Paul. At that time, Paul was not in trouble with the Roman government. He was in custody there because of his appeal to Caesar, which he initiated after charges were made against him by Jews in Jerusalem. The official Roman opinion is summed up in Acts 26:32. "This man could have been released if he had not appealed to Caesar." Since Rome itself had nothing against Paul, why would they arrest his friend, Epaphras? Contrast, however, the situation in Ephesus where local pagan anger over Paul's missionary success erupted in mob violence in which two of Paul's co-workers were seized (Acts 19:23-41). Against such a background it is easy to see how Epaphras, returning from a successful church planting mission in the interior, would be targeted for arrest.

6. A sixth problem concerns Timothy, the co-sender of the letter (Col 1:1). We have no evidence that he was with Paul in Rome (unless, of course, Paul's letter to the Philippians of which Timothy is also the co-sender was written from Rome—but the evidence is against this as well). It is certain, though, that Timothy was with Paul in Ephesus (Acts 19:22).

7. Finally, Paul's letter to the Colossians gives the impression that the founding of the church was quite recent. This is seen both in his many references to their conversion (see especially Col 1:4-9) and in his strong emphasis on the need to grow to maturity. Yet, if Paul had written from Rome, the church would have been at least five years old.

The best solution would seem to be that Paul wrote these two letters while he was still nearby in Ephesus around the year AD 55. It is true that Acts does not mention an imprisonment during Paul's three-year stay in Ephesus. Yet we know from 2 Corinthians 6:5; and 2 Corinthians 11:23 that Paul experienced more hardships and imprisonments than are recorded in Acts. Most notably, in 2 Corinthians 1:8-9 Paul describes a time of violent persecution in Asia (the location of Ephesus) in which he and Timothy "so that we despaired even of living." It is likely that this persecution included imprisonment. We should also point out that, unlike our own day, imprisonment was used back then only to detain a person while he awaited trial or punishment. Those found guilty could be fined, flogged, exiled, enslaved or executed. As a rule though, they were not sentenced to a term in prison. This custom helps to explain how Paul could have experienced a number of relatively short stays in prison that are not recorded in Acts.

If this conclusion is correct, then the letter to the Colossians belongs to the period of intense evangelism and church planting which Paul and his co-workers carried out during his Ephesian ministry (see Acts 19:10). Epaphras had only recently established the church of Colossae, perhaps within the past year. The Colossians were growing in their faith, but they were also being confronted by a deceptive teaching. Epaphras then makes the short journey back to Ephesus to consult with the more experienced apostle regarding how to proceed. While conferring with Paul, however, Epaphras himself was arrested and imprisoned. Paul, therefore, put his response to this pastoral problem in a letter and sent it to the Colossians by the hand of his co-worker, Tychicus. It is within this context of a young congregation threatened by a subversive teaching that we are to understand Paul's emphasis in Colossians on the nature of salvation, spiritual growth, maturity, and stability.

The Nature of the False Teaching

While Paul wrote this letter in order to strengthen the Colossian Christians in the face of this threat, he never explains who these false teachers were, or what exactly they were teaching. The Colossians themselves knew quite well, so why should he explain? But we today must piece things together from Paul's various comments. This process may be compared to hearing only one side of a telephone conversation, and trying to discern from this what the other person is saying. It is a challenging task, requiring careful discernment.

The most important clues appear in Colossians 2:9-23. First of all, these false teachers practiced circumcision (Col 2:11) and celebrated the Sabbath (Col 2:16). In Paul's day, these two practices more than anything else marked a man as a Jew in the eyes of his non-Jewish neighbors. In addition, they kept the Old Testament rules regarding food and drink (Col 2:16). Paul acknowledges the biblical basis of these practices in Colossians 2:17 by saying, they "these are only the shadow of the things to come." Based on these clues alone, we could easily conclude that the false teachers were Jews. In fact, many other less direct clues support this identification. This conclusion, however, runs into difficulty with the rather un-Jewish sounding practices in Colossians 2:18; 23 —namely, their visions (Col 2:18), their "false humility achieved by an unsparing treatment of the body" (Col 2:23) and especially their "delights in . . . the worship of angels" (Col 2:18). Until recently, almost all scholars assumed that this last statement means the false teachers worshipped angels. And since Jews do not worship angels, the false teachers could not have been Jews. And thus, it was widely believed that the Colossian problem was some strange mixture of Jewish and pagan teachings.

But this interpretation also runs into difficulties. First, we find nothing else in the letter to indicate that the false teachers worshipped angels. Surely, Paul would have reacted more strongly to such a shocking violation of the first commandment (Deut 4:19; 5:7) and warned the Colossians accordingly (compare Rev 19:10). The fact that he did not, suggests there was no such violation. Second, historians of ancient Judaism do not know of any group that combined Jewish and pagan teachings in this way. They do, however, know a great amount about a movement within Judaism that fits all of the clues.

The Jews of this movement practiced fasting (which they called "humility") and other kinds of severe bodily discipline in order to attain visions in which they entered the heavenly temple and looked upon the worship of angels, or so they claimed. They would also join with the angels in their heavenly praise. When seen against this background, the key phrase "the worship of angels" in Colossians 2:18 is easily interpreted as a reference to worship that angels give to God—not worship they receive from men. These Jewish mystics would have formed an elite group of the super-spiritual within their local synagogue. As proof that their practices were not a departure from traditional Judaism, they could point to Scripture. Isaiah, they argued, experienced such a vision (Isa 6:1-3). So did Daniel (Dan 7:9-10) and Ezekiel (Ezk 1:4-28; Ezk 10:1-22). In fact, the movement eventually came to be called Merkabah mysticism after the heavenly chariot (*merkabah*) of Ezekiel's vision above which he saw God seated upon a throne (Ezk 1:26-28).

How then should we respond to this evidence? A growing number of scholars in recent decades have found it persuasive. They now believe that the puzzling clues of Colossians 2:18; 23 should be understood in terms of this mystical emphasis within Judaism. The writer of this course agrees. We will therefore proceed with the understanding that all of the clues in the letter regarding the nature of the false teaching lead to the same place: to the synagogue of Colossae. The deceptive teachers were Jews. They taught a traditional form of Judaism with the addition of their own special interest in super-spiritual experiences, in particular, heavenly visions of angelic worship.

History tells us that many thousands of Jews lived in the region of Colossae. Several hundred would have lived in Colossae itself. Their ancestors had moved there more than two centuries before from Babylonia. They were descendants of Jews Nebuchadnezzar had led away into exile centuries before (see 2 Kgs 24:14). These Jews were sent to the region of Colossae by the king as military colonists to pacify a rebellious area of his empire. By Paul's day the Jewish community of Colossae was large, well established, and prosperous. They claimed to worship the same God and to believe the same Old Testament Scriptures as the Gentile-born Colossian Christians.

We may imagine the encounters that must have taken place between these two groups in the marketplace of Colossae. The Christians would have told the Jews about their faith in Jesus as the Messiah and the salvation they had through him. The Jews would have replied that if Jesus were the Messiah, their leaders in Jerusalem would surely have told them. Rather, if these Gentile Christians truly wished to be saved—if they wished to be a part of God's people and to share their lot—they must become Jews. They must be circumcised and keep the Law of Moses.

Some of these Jews would have boasted to the Colossian Christians about their visions. It is not necessary to wait until death to experience the joys of heaven, they explained. This can be done even now in a visionary journey to heaven. Of course, such an experience (they claimed) can only be achieved by the most holy and righteous individuals. Moreover, to achieve a vision requires severe bodily disciplines including fasting and strict ceremonial purity. But the potential reward is great: a visionary experience of heaven, the place of eternal salvation, where one can look upon the angels in their worship before the throne of God and even join in their heavenly praise.

The Christians would have found all of this both disturbing and tempting. This was a seductive teaching that threatened to take them captive (Col 2:8). It is within this historical context that Paul writes to strengthen these young believers. The visions of these Jews are not genuine, he assures them, but merely the product of the human mind (Col 2:18). Their bodily disciplines, moreover, only gratify the flesh (Col 2:23). The blessings of salvation that Christians already have in Christ surpass in every way what these Jews claim to offer.

QUESTION 1

In what modern country does the site of ancient Colossae lie?

- A. Greece
- B. Spain
- C. Turkey
- D. Italy
- E. Syria

QUESTION 2

Who planted the church of Colossae?

QUESTION 3

What was the approximate size of the Colossian congregation?

- A. 25
- B. 50
- C. 100
- D. 200
- E. Several hundred

QUESTION 4

What was the approximate size of the group in Colossae to which the false teachers belonged?

- A. 25
- B. 50
- C. 100
- D. 200
- E. Several hundred

QUESTION 5

In whose house did the Colossian church meet?

QUESTION 6

What are the problems with the theory that Paul wrote his letter to the Colossians from Rome during his imprisonment there recorded in Acts 28?

QUESTION 7

When Paul wrote to the Colossians, how long had it been since the church was planted there?

    A. Less than a year

    B. Two years

    C. Five years

    D. Seven years

QUESTION 8

The group to which the false teachers belonged had been in Colossae for what length of time?

    A. Less than a year

    B. Twenty-five years

    C. One hundred years

    D. More than 200 years

QUESTION 9

Who were the false teachers?

    A. Jews

    B. Jewish Christians

    C. Greek philosophers

    D. Men who mixed Jewish and pagan teachings

QUESTION 10

According to Colossians 2:18, the false teachers took delight in the "worship of angels." Does this mean that they worshiped angels? Give reasons to support your answer.

Topic 3: Making an Observational Chart of Colossians

The second step in your survey is to read Colossians in one sitting. Read carefully but without stopping to take notes or ponder difficult issues. Remember the purpose of this step is to obtain a quick overview of the entire book—the general flow of thought and the organization of the book. Read the entire book of Colossians quickly but carefully at one sitting.

Step 3 is to make an observational chart of Colossians. Recall that the four-part instructions for this procedure appear in Topic 1. You may wish to refer back to these instructions. Begin your study by copying and filling in the "Observational Chart Worksheet." Work quickly and try to complete this step within an hour.

Worksheet for Step 3: Observational Chart of Colossians			
Chapter 1	**Chapter 2**	**Chapter 3**	**Chapter 4**
1-2	1-5	1-4	2-4
3-8	6-8	5-11	5-6
9-12a	9-12	12-14	7-9
12b-14	13-15	15-17	10-15
15-20	16-17	18-19	16-17
21-23	18-19	20-21	18
24-27	20-23	22-4:1	
28-29			

Topic 4: A Simplified Chart of Colossians

The fourth step in your survey is to reduce the observational chart to a simplified chart that displays the larger units and sub-units of the book. Instead of making your own simplified chart, study the one provided for you here. Your assignment is to commit this chart to memory. Think of it as a map. In future lessons, as we explore the landscape of Colossians, a mental map of the book can keep you from getting lost in the details. You will always know where you are, where you have been, and where you are going. Be prepared to demonstrate your knowledge of this chart in class.

Outline of the Main Parts of Colossians
- I. Salutation—Colossians 1:1-2
- II. Thanksgiving Section—Colossians 1:3-23
    - A. Paul's Prayers—Colossians 1:3-12a
    - B. Reason for Thanks—Colossians 1:12b-23
- III. Paul's Ministry—Colossians 1:24-2:5
- IV. Live According to the Gospel—Colossians 2:6-4:6
    - A. Introduction—Colossians 2:6-8
    - B. The Gospel Explained—Colossians 2:9-15
    - C. The Gospel Applied—Colossians 2:16-4:6
        - 1. To the False Teachers—Colossians 2:16-3:4
        - 2. To the Christian Life—Colossians 3:5-4:6
- V. Closing—Colossians 4:7-18

QUESTION 11

Copy the simplified chart of Colossians (provided above) in your Life Notebook. After you study the chart, make a copy of the chart on a separate paper, but leave out the section titles. Then without looking, try to fill in all the titles from memory. Next, check your answers with the copy you made. Keep doing this until you can reproduce the titles from memory. Once you have mastered the titles, work on reproducing the entire chart, lines and all, from memory. The goal of this exercise is for you to memorize the chart. It will greatly assist you in this course if you can keep a map of the book in your mind as you study its various parts.

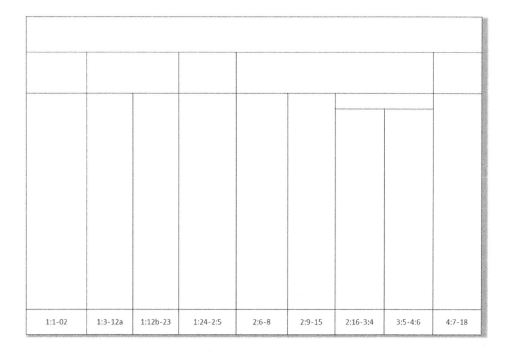

| 1:1-02 | 1:3-12a | 1:12b-23 | 1:24-2:5 | 2:6-8 | 2:9-15 | 2:16-3:4 | 3:5-4:6 | 4:7-18 |

Topic 5: A Theme Statement for Colossians

The fifth and final step in your survey of Colossians is to write a theme statement that reflects the purpose of the book. Again, this step has been done for you. Your assignment is to study and understand it so that you can reproduce it in your own words.

Paul's purpose in writing to the Colossians is reflected in his prayer of Colossians 1:9-10. The theme statement given is based on this prayer. Since this is the unifying idea of the letter, it is important that it be understood.

The Theme of Colossians

Theme Statement: "Paul writes to a young congregation confronted by a deceptive teaching, with the aim of bringing them to a mature knowledge of God's plan of salvation so that they might walk in accordance with it."

QUESTION 12

Open your Life Notebook. Based on what you have learned so far in this lesson, do you believe that this theme statement accurately describes the purpose of Colossians? If not, explain why. Please reflect on the statement, and then restate it (in your Life Notebook) in a way that will help you remember.

Topic 6: The Contribution of Each Part of the Letter to the Whole

We have seen the overall organization of Colossians in chart form and identified the unifying theme. Our purpose now is to explain briefly how the various parts of this book fit together to make up the whole. To do this we must bear in mind that Colossians is a letter. Paul organized it according to the customary rules of letter writing in his day. Thus, as we will see, these customary rules can serve as our guide to understanding how the parts of Colossians fit together. Please read carefully the following explanation and then answer the questions afterwards.

How Each Part of the Book Relates to the Whole

I. Salutation—Colossians 1:1-2

The salutation of Colossians, as in other ancient letters, introduces the letter. It identifies the senders, the recipients, and gives a brief greeting in the form of a prayer of blessing.

II. Thanksgiving Section—Colossians 1:3-23

The typical letter began on a religious note with a word of thanksgiving to the gods (or to God) for the well-being (usually the health) of the reader and a prayer for his continued well-being. Paul follows this basic custom but gives it fresh content.

A. Paul's Prayer—Colossians 1:3-12a

Paul tells the Colossians of his gratitude to God for their progress in their faith and of his prayers for their continued growth to full maturity. This prayer for continued growth to maturity is where Paul introduces the theme of the letter. He asks that God might fill them with the knowledge of his will so that they might walk in a manner worthy of the Lord (Col 1:9-10). God's *will* in this context refers to God's plan of salvation revealed in the gospel, including how he desires his people to live as a result. This prayer expresses the purpose of the letter.

B. Reason for Thanks—Colossians 1:12b-23

Paul closes this thanksgiving section with an extended explanation of why the Colossians should give thanks to God. The reason is his work of salvation through Christ. With this, Paul begins to carry out his purpose in writing—which is to bring his readers to a full or mature knowledge of God's will. This knowledge has two parts: (1) the doctrine, regarding the nature of God's saving work; and (2) the application, regarding how his people should walk as a result. Paul develops the doctrinal part here in Colossians 1:12b-23 and again in Colossians 2:9-15. These two doctrinal sections provide the basis for the application-based instruction of Colossians 2:16-4:6.

III. Paul's Ministry—Colossians 1:24-2:5

The thanksgiving section of ancient letters was followed by the actual "body" or message part of the letter. In the opening part of the body, the writer would explain his reason for writing. In the remainder of the body, he would discuss this matter in detail.

In Colossians 1:24-2:5, we see the opening part of the body of Colossians. It is here that Paul explains his reason for writing. God has commissioned him to make known the message of Christ among the nations, and in this task Paul labors with the goal of bringing everyone to maturity in Christ (Col 1:24-29). This is, therefore, his goal for the Colossians. It is the object of his prayers for them and the reason for this letter (Col 2:1-5). Paul's prayer of Colossians 1:9-10 expresses this same goal, only in different words.

IV. Live According to the Gospel—Colossians 2:6-4:6

This extended section is the main part of the body of the letter. Having explained his purpose for writing, Paul now directly undertakes to fulfill this purpose. The earlier parts of the letter have served as preparation; now comes the true substance of his message.

A. Introduction—Colossians 2:6-8

This introduction to the remainder of the body consists of an exhortation that again expresses the theme (including the purpose) of the letter. The Colossians must continue to walk in accordance with the message of Christ they received in the beginning as new believers. They must be built up further on that foundation and not allow themselves to be taken captive by a false teaching. What follows may be seen as a fresh exposition of the message they received in the beginning but with special attention to this false teaching. This exposition has two parts: (a) the doctrinal basis of the Christian life (the gospel explained) and, (b) how to walk in accordance with these truths (the gospel application).

B. The Gospel Explained—Colossians 2:9-15

This doctrinal exposition is the theological heart of the letter. Here Paul carries forward concepts introduced in the earlier doctrinal section, Colossians 1:12b-23, in order to explain the nature and benefits of Christ's saving death and resurrection.

C. The Gospel Applied—Colossians 2:16-4:6

Having explained the doctrinal basis of salvation, Paul now turns to the practical side of these truths: how to apply them to daily life.

1. To the False Teaching—Colossians 2:16-3:4

Paul begins by comparing the truth to the practices of the false teaching. His purpose is to show that Christians must walk in accordance with the salvation they have in Christ—and the practices of the false teachers are certainly not! They are of man and the world, and they only gratify the flesh.

2. To the Christian Life—Colossians 3:5-4:6

Paul now applies these saving truths to the Christian life in general. The central point is that Christians must conduct their lives in accordance with what God has made them, his redeemed people. This is his will. Paul's purpose in writing is that they might know God's will and walk in it.

V. Closing—Colossians 4:7-18

The letter closes in the customary manner with a mixture of personal greetings and final instructions. A part of this custom was to mention for a final time the reason for writing. Paul weaves this final mention into the greeting he sends from Epaphras. Paul reports that Epaphras strives continually for them in his prayers (Col 4:12) that they might "stand mature and fully assured in all the will of God." It is with this goal in mind that Paul has written to the Colossians. He announced it in the thanksgiving section in Colossians 1:9-10. He explained it more fully in Colossians 1:24-2:5. He sought to fulfill this goal in Colossians 2:6-4:6. And now, as a fitting part of the closing to this letter, he repeats it a final time.

The following outline can assist you in answering the questions below.

    I. Salutation—Colossians 1:1-2

    II. Thanksgiving Section—Colossians 1:3-23

        A. Paul's Prayers—Colossians 1:3-12a

B. Reason for Thanks—Colossians 1:12b-23

III. Paul's Ministry—Colossians 1:24-2:5

IV. Live According to the Gospel—Colossians 2:6-4:6

    A. Introduction—Colossians 2:6-8

    B. The Gospel Explained—Colossians 2:9-15

    C. The Gospel Applied—Colossians 2:16-4:6

        1. To the False Teaching—Colossians 2:16-3:4

        2. To the Christian Life—Colossians 3:5-4:6

V. Closing—Colossians 4:7-18

QUESTION 13

Each statement on the left describes a section of Colossians on the right. See if you can match them correctly.

Description of the Section	The Section
Paul explains his reason for writing	Colossians 3:5-4:6
The theological heart of the letter	Colossians 2:16-3:4
A large section containing the true substance of the letter	Colossians 1:24-2:5
The doctrinal truths of salvation are applied to the false teaching	Colossians 2:9-15
The first of the two doctrinal sections of the letter	Colossians 1:12b-23
Paul's prayer for the Colossians where he introduces the theme of the letter	Colossians 2:6-4:6
Application of the doctrinal truths of salvation to the Christian life in general	Colossians 1:3-12a

Important Facts to Remember about the Historical Background of Colossians

1. The town of Colossae was located 120 miles (192 km) east of Ephesus in what is today the western part of Turkey. Epaphras, a member of Paul's missionary team based in Ephesus, took the gospel to this area and planted churches in Colossae, Laodicea, and Hieropolis. The Colossian congregation met in the home of Philemon and, thus, probably numbered no more than fifty persons.

2. Not long after the founding of the church—perhaps within the first year—these young believers encountered a deceptive teaching that threatened to take them captive. Epaphras traveled to Ephesus to consult with Paul. It is with this threat in view that Paul, who is now in prison, writes to the Colossians.

3. The false teachers were actually Jews. Several hundred Jews lived in Colossae at this time. Their ancestors had moved to this area more than two centuries before.

4. These Jews taught that to be a part of God's redeemed people one must be circumcised and keep the Law of Moses. Some of them also boasted of visionary journeys to heaven where they joined the angels in their worship in the heavenly temple. The false teachers achieved this, they claimed, through personal righteousness and bodily disciplines including fasting.

5. Paul assures the Colossians that these visions are not genuine. They are the product of the human mind, and the bodily disciplines only gratify the flesh. But the salvation they have in Christ far exceeds what these Jews claim to offer.

6. Paul's prayer of Colossians 1:9-10 reveals the unifying theme of the letter, including its purpose. He desires that God might fill them with the knowledge of his plan of salvation in Christ so that they might walk in accordance with it.

7. Each of the major parts of the letter contributes to the fulfillment of this overall objective. These parts are displayed in the simplified chart that you were assigned to memorize.

Summary of the Contribution of Each Part of the Letter to the Whole

a. The salutation introduces the letter, while the closing section ends it.

b. The first part of the Thanksgiving Section "Paul's Prayers" (Col 1:3-12a) introduces the theme of the letter.

c. The second part of the Thanksgiving Section "Reason for Thanks" (Col 1:12b-23) gives doctrinal instruction regarding God's plan of salvation.

d. Paul opens the "body" of the letter "Paul's Ministry" (Col 1:24-2:5) by explaining his reason for writing.

e. Paul delivers the true substance of his message in the remainder of the letter's body "Live According to the Gospel" (Col 2:6-23, Col 3, Col 4:1-6). This section falls into three smaller parts.

f. The first part is an introduction (Col 2:6-8). It again spells out the theme of the letter.

g. Next is the central doctrinal message of the letter "The Gospel Explained" (Col 2:9-15). It explains more fully the nature of God's work of salvation through Christ.

h. The third section 'The Gospel Applied" (Col 2:16-23, , Col 3, , Col 4:1-6) applies this doctrinal message to the false teaching (Col 2:16-23, Col 3:1-4) and then to the Christian life in general (Col 3:1-5, Col 4:1-6).

QUESTION 14

Now that you have completed your survey of Colossians, take a few minutes to record in your Life Notebook some of your initial thoughts about the letter. First, what parallels do you see between the church of Colossae and the local assembly to which you belong? Second, briefly list the aspects of Paul's message to the Colossians that seem especially relevant to your church, to your ministry, or to your personal walk with the Lord. Finally, list any questions this survey has raised in your mind about the meaning of any statements in Colossians for which you hope to find answers in this course. Be prepared to discuss these questions in your next group meeting.

Lesson 1 Self Check

QUESTION 1
Which of the following is NOT one of the five steps for surveying a book of the Bible?
- A. Make an observational chart
- B. Research the background
- C. Trace the argument
- D. Write a theme statement

QUESTION 2
According to the historical background, where was Paul when he wrote to the Colossians?
- A. Ephesus
- B. Rome
- C. Corinth
- D. Caesarea

QUESTION 3
According to the historical background, how recent was the founding of the church in Colossae when Paul wrote his letter?
- A. less than a year
- B. Two years
- C. Five years
- D. Seven years

QUESTION 4
Which of the following activities did the false teachers NOT advocate?
- A. heavenly visions
- B. fasting
- C. worshiping angels
- D. circumcision

QUESTION 5
Who were the false teachers?
- A. men who mixed Jewish and pagan teachings
- B. Jews
- C. Jewish Christians
- D. Greek philosophers

QUESTION 6
LIST THE FIVE STEPS FOR SURVEYING A BOOK OF THE BIBLE.QUESTION 7

The theme statement of Colossians that we identified in Topic 6 is based on what text?
- A. Colossians 1:9-10
- B. Colossians 1:21-22
- C. Colossians 1:28
- D. Colossians 2:6-7

QUESTION 8

In what section of Colossians does Paul explain his reason for writing?
- A. Colossians 1:3-12a
- B. Colossians 1:15-20
- C. Colossians 1:24-2:5
- D. Colossians 2:9-15

QUESTION 9

Which section of Colossians is the theological heart of the letter?
- A. Colossians 1:15-20
- B. Colossians 1:24-2:5
- C. Colossians 2:9-15
- D. Colossians 2:16-3:4

QUESTION 10

In which section of Colossians does Paul apply the doctrinal truths of salvation to the false teaching?
- A. Colossians 2:9-15
- B. Colossians 2:16-3:4
- C. Colossians 3:5-4:6
- D. Colossians 1:24-2:5

Lesson 1 Answers to Questions

QUESTION 1
   C. Turkey

QUESTION 2: Epaphras

QUESTION 3
   B. 50

QUESTION 4
   E. Several hundred

QUESTION 5: Philemon

QUESTION 6: *Your answer should be similar to the following:*
The lesson identifies seven problems with this interpretation. First, from Rome to Colossae was a two-month journey of over 1000 miles (1600 km) by land and sea. Yet, the comings and goings between Paul and Colossae reflected in his letters to the Colossians and to Philemon suggest a much shorter, easier journey. Second, Paul indicates in Philemon 22 that he expected to be released from prison soon, and that upon release he intended to visit Colossae. Yet, we read in Romans 15:24 that after he reached Rome he planned to press on westward to Spain, not eastward to Asia. Third, Paul tells the elders of Ephesus in Acts 20:25 that he knows they will never see him again. Yet, if Paul wrote to the Colossians from Rome years later, then a trip to Colossae following his release from prison there would almost certainly include a visit to nearby Ephesus. Fourth, it is more likely that Onesimus would have fled to nearby Ephesus rather than distant Rome because of the danger of being caught on such a long journey. Fifth, the fact that Paul was not in trouble with the Roman government as such during his confinement in Rome makes it unlikely that Epaphras would have been arrested when visiting him there. The hostility of the pagans of Ephesus toward Paul (Acts 19) provides a much more likely explanation for this arrest. Sixth, we have no evidence that Timothy was ever with Paul during the imprisonment in Rome recorded in Acts. Finally, the letter to the Colossians gives the impression that the founding of the church was quite recent. Yet, if Paul wrote from Rome, the church would have been at least five years old.

QUESTION 7
   A. Less than a year

QUESTION 8
   D. More than 200 years

QUESTION 9
   A. Jews

QUESTION 10: *Your answer should be similar to the following:*
The lesson gave four reasons for interpreting the "worship of angels" as worship performed by angels. First, nothing else in the letter indicates that the false teachers worshiped angels. Second, everything else points to the conclusion that these false teachers were Jews—and the Jews did not worship angels. Third, historians do not know of any non-Jewish groups that worshiped angels but also engaged in Jewish practices such as those listed in Colossians 2:16. Fourth, there was a movement among the Jews known as Merkabah mysticism whose practices fit the description of Colossians 2:18. These Jews practiced fasting and other kinds of severe bodily discipline in order to attain visions in which they claimed to enter the heavenly temple and to see the angels worshiping God (the worship of angels).

QUESTION 11:

Your solution to this exercise should look similar to the following:

Colossians: Live According to the Gospel								
Salutation	Thanksgiving Section		Paul's Ministry	Live According to the Gospel				Closing
	Paul's Prayers	Reason for Thanks		Introduction	The Gospel Explained	The Gospel Applied		
						To the False Teachers	To the Christian Life	
1:1-02	1:3-12a	1:12b-23	1:24-2:5	2:6-8	2:9-15	2:16-3:4	3:5-4:6	4:7-18

QUESTION 12: *Your answer*

QUESTION 13

Description of the Section	The Section
Paul explains his reason for writing	Colossians 1:24-2:5
The theological heart of the letter	Colossians 2:9-15
A large section containing the true substance of the letter	Colossians 2:6-4:6
The doctrinal truths of salvation are applied to the false teaching	Colossians 2:16-3:4
The first of the two doctrinal sections of the letter	Colossians 1:12b-23
Paul's prayer for the Colossians where he introduces the theme of the letter	Colossians 1:3-12a
Application of the doctrinal truths of salvation to the Christian life in general	Colossians 3:5-4:6

QUESTION 14: *Your answer*

Lesson 1 Self Check Answers

QUESTION 1
   C. Trace the argument

QUESTION 2
   A. Ephesus

QUESTION 3
   A. less than a year

QUESTION 4
   C. worshiping angels

QUESTION 5
   B. Jews

QUESTION 6
   D. The New English Translation

QUESTION 7
   A. Colossians 1:9-10

QUESTION 8
   C. Colossians 1:24-2:5

QUESTION 9
   C. Colossians 2:9-15

QUESTION 10
   B. Colossians 2:16-3:4

Lesson 2: How to Study a Paragraph Part I—Seeing the Paragraph as a Whole

In Lesson 1, we saw that Colossians can be broken down into various sections, sub-sections, and paragraphs. Each of these parts displays a unifying theme, and together they make up the unified message of the letter. The smallest and easiest unit to work with is the paragraph. For this reason, Bible scholars recognize the paragraph as the basic unit of study. (Recall that a paragraph consists of one or more sentences, deals with one point, and begins on a new line that is indented or separated from the previous paragraph by a space.) For our more detailed study of Colossians, we will therefore focus on the paragraph. As we trace the meaning of each paragraph in sequence, the message of this letter in all its richness will unfold before us. In this course, we will use a three-step procedure for studying paragraphs:

Step 1: Observe the paragraph as a whole by making a structural diagram. Then, summarize your findings in an outline and theme statement.

Step 2: Make detailed observations with interpretation and application on the same page as the structural diagram.

Step 3: Read the commentary on the paragraph, then answer the various lesson questions.

The purpose of this lesson is to explain step 1, how to make a structural diagram. Steps 2 and 3 are the subject of the next lesson.

Topic 1 answers the question, "What is a structural diagram?" The structural diagram will be our basic method for getting an overview of each paragraph of Colossians.

The initial step in making a structural diagram is explained in Topic 2. It involves breaking the paragraph into its principal parts (which are lines of text) and laying them out on a page.

Topic 3 is the heart of the lesson. It explains how to trace the way these parts fit together to produce the message of the paragraph.

You will learn how to summarize the results of the structural diagram in an outline and theme statement in Topic 4.

Lesson Outline

Topic 1: What is a Structural Diagram?

Topic 2: How to Make a Structural Diagram—Laying Out the Text

Topic 3: How to Make a Structural Diagram—Identifying the Structure

    Label the Connecting Words

    Label the Descriptive Lines

    Label the Main Clauses

    Identify and Label the Sections

Topic 4: How to Summarize the Results of a Structural Diagram

    Make a Preliminary Outline

    Write a Theme Statement

Lesson Objectives

When you have completed this lesson, you should be able to:
- Describe a structural diagram and explain its value for observing a paragraph as a whole
- Begin a structural diagram by laying out the lines of the paragraph on a page
- Complete the structural diagram by analyzing the paragraph's structure
- Summarize the results of the structural diagram in an outline and theme statement

Topic 1: What is a Structural Diagram?

This topic focuses on:
- The study of Scripture
- The layout of a structural diagram

The Study of Structure

When studying Scripture, it is easy to become so focused on the details of a passage that you fail to understand its broader message. Because of this danger, it is helpful to begin with a broad overview. This will allow you to see how and where the various parts—the words, phrases, clauses, and sentences—fit into the broader whole. Once you have the big picture, you can turn your attention to a detailed study of these smaller elements. The task of this first step is to observe the broad *structure* of the passage.

Structure is the term Bible scholars use to describe the way a biblical author has arranged the various elements of writing to produce a unified argument. In other words, structure refers to how the parts of a passage fit together to make up the whole. An important first step in the study of any text of Scripture, therefore, is to understand its structure.

The task of observing the structure of a passage may be compared to observing a bicycle. Suppose a friend bought a new bicycle and invited you to come to his home to see it. When you arrived, you saw the parts of the bicycle scattered about on the floor. You saw some handlebars, a seat, a frame, two pedals, two wheels, a chain, and some other parts. Then your friend said to you, "What do you think of my new bicycle?" But you would surely say, "I don't know. I only see the parts of your bicycle. I still do not know what the bicycle itself looks like."

It is the same with studying a passage of the Bible. It is good to both see and understand the parts. But this is not enough. We need to see the parts in relation to the whole. We need to see how they fit together to produce the entire message. The structural diagram allows you to do this.

What a Structural Diagram Looks Like

The structural diagram is a relatively quick and easy method for observing the structure of a paragraph. The method involves breaking the passage into its constituent parts (or "lines"), arranging them on a single page to display as simply as possible the flow of thought, labeling these parts, and then marking off topics within the paragraph. Since this method is easier to illustrate than to explain, we will start with two simple examples.

Examples of Structural Diagrams:

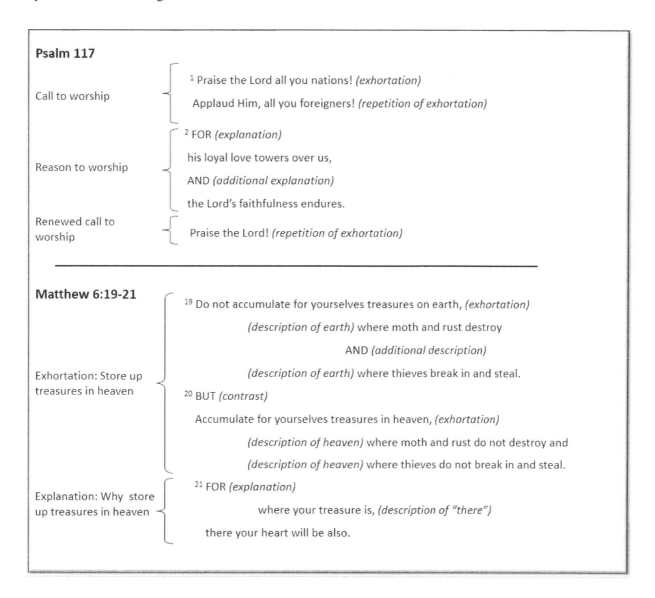

QUESTION 1

Explain briefly what we mean by the *structure* of a passage.

QUESTION 2

Based on what you have seen so far, how would you describe the actual method or steps for making a structural diagram?

QUESTION 3

What is the value of using a structural diagram to study a paragraph of Scripture?

Topic 2: How to Make a Structural Diagram

Guidelines for making a structural diagram fall under two headings: how to lay out the paragraph, and how to identify its structure. We will examine the first of these in Topic 2. The second will be the subject of Topic 3.

How to Lay Out the Lines of a Paragraph

1. Recognize three different types of "lines" in the paragraph: main clauses, connecting words, and descriptive lines. Write each on a separate line of the page.

    a. *Main clauses*. These include all independent clauses and all dependent clauses that are not "descriptive lines."

    Recall that a clause is a statement having both a subject and a verb. There are two types of clauses: independent and dependent (or subordinate). "The boy ran away" is an independent clause, because it can stand alone as a complete sentence. "Because he was afraid" is a dependent clause, since it cannot stand alone. It depends on another clause to make a complete sentence, for example, "The boy ran away, because he was afraid."

    b. *Connecting words*. These connect one clause to another. Examples are *but, and, therefore, since, because, that, so that, for*. Please note: Some of these words can do things in a sentence other than connect one clause to another. A word only becomes a "connecting word" when it serves to connect one *clause* to another.

    c. *Descriptive lines*. These are dependent clauses and extended phrases. Each descriptive line will describe in some way a word or phrase in another line. It will answer one of the basic observational *questions* (Who? What? When? Where? Why? How?) about this word or phrase. Consider, for example, the sentence "I am Jesus, whom you are persecuting." The words "whom you are persecuting" is a descriptive line that describes the word "Jesus." It answers the question, "Who is Jesus?" In the sentence "While we were still sinners, Christ died for us," the words "While we were still sinners" are a descriptive line that describes the action of the word "died." It answers the question, "When did Christ die for us?"

2. Write out all main clauses starting at the left-hand margin of your page.

3. Place all connecting words on a line by themselves. (It is helpful to emphasize these by capitalizing all the letters—such as BECAUSE.)

    The boy ran away

       BECAUSE

       he was afraid.

4. Begin each *descriptive line* under the word or phrase it describes (or above it if the descriptive line precedes it in the text) as in the following examples:

I am Jesus	While we were still sinners,
whom you are persecuting	Christ died for us

5. Arrange lists of items or other parallel phrases or clauses in vertical columns one under another for the sake of clarity.

The fruit of the Spirit is
love,
joy
peace
patience

6. Be flexible. This is a very simplified method. You will encounter things in the biblical text that do not fit neatly into this scheme. When in doubt, begin the line at the left-hand margin. This procedure is intended as an aid to your study, not an obstacle.

Summary of How to Lay Out a Paragraph

1. Recognize three kinds of "lines":
   a. <u>Main clauses</u> are independent clauses and dependent clauses that are not descriptive lines.
   b. <u>Connecting words</u> join one clause to another.
   c. <u>Descriptive lines</u> are dependent clauses and extended phrases that describe a single word or phrase in another line.
2. Main clauses begin at the left-hand margin of the page.
3. Connecting words go on a separate line.
4. Descriptive lines begin under (or above) the word or phrase they describe.
5. Lists and parallel clauses or phrases should be arranged in columns.
6. Be flexible. Not everything in the biblical text fits into this simple scheme.

QUESTION 4

Lay out the lines of the following sentence (Col 3:18):

Wives, submit to your husbands, as is fitting in the Lord.

QUESTION 5

Lay out the lines of the following sentence (Eph 6:17):

And take the helmet of salvation and the sword of the Spirit, which is the word of God.

QUESTION 6

Lay out the lines of the following sentence (Acts 16:38):

They were frightened when they heard Paul and Silas were Roman citizens.

QUESTION 7

Lay out the lines of the following sentence (Heb 12:3):

Think of him who endured such opposition against himself by sinners, so that you may not grow weary in your souls and give up.

Topic 3: How to Make a Structural Diagram—Identifying the Structure

Making a structural diagram is a two-part process: laying out the paragraph and identifying its structure. In Topic 2 you learned the first of these—how to break the paragraph into its basic parts or "lines" and lay them out on a page. These "lines" are the basic building blocks of the structure. The second part of the process is to identify how these parts fit together to produce the unified argument of the paragraph. The way to do this is to label each part to indicate its function and then mark off those lines that seem to belong to the same topic. There are actually four things to do:

1. Label the connecting words.
2. Label the descriptive lines.
3. Label the main clauses.
4. Identify and label the sections.

We will now explore how to do each of these.

Label the Connecting Words

The author has provided these connecting words as signposts to show the reader the logical path of his argument. The most common connectives and their "signpost" meanings are listed below:

a. **For, because, since** can indicate *explanation* or *reason*.

b. **Then, so, so then, and, therefore, that, so that** can indicate *result*.

c. **So that, that, in order that** can indicate *purpose*. Remember, a purpose is an intended result, while a result is often an achieved purpose.

d. **But, yet** indicate *contrast*.

e. **And, also, furthermore** are used to indicate something *additional*.

f. **That** can indicate the *content* of saying, knowing, praying, etc. ("I pray **that** . . .").

Label each connecting word to indicate its "signpost" meaning. For example, next to the word BECAUSE you would write *explanation* or *reason*.

QUESTION 8

Supply the correct label for the connecting word in the following verse.

Open my eyes THAT (_____) I may see wonderful things in your law.

QUESTION 9

In the following texts, match the connecting word on the left with the correct label on the right.

Connecting Word	Label
The Lord is far from the wicked BUT he hears the prayer of the upright.	Additional
Behold, I do not know how to speak BECAUSE I am a youth.	Purpose
In him was life AND the life was the light of men.	Result
A great storm developed on the sea SO THAT the waves began to swamp the boat.	Content
We pray for you always, THAT our God will make you worthy of his calling.	Contrast
I have hidden your word in my heart THAT I might not sin against you.	Explanation

QUESTION 10

Lay out the lines of the following text and label the two connecting words (Rom 6:23):

For the payoff of sin is death, but the gift of God is eternal life in Christ Jesus our Lord.

Label the Descriptive Lines

Typically, a descriptive line will describe either a noun (a person, place, or thing) or a verb (the action of a person or thing). Both types of lines appear in the example of Colossians 1:3 below. If the line describes a noun, such as the noun "God" in the example, you would write beside this line "description of God". Similarly, if the line describes the action of a verb, such as the verb "thank" in the example, you could write "description of thanking."

In the case of verbs, however, it is helpful if you can be more specific. Many of these lines clearly describe the **time**, the **manner** or the **means** of the action. Thus, in the example below, the line "when we pray for you" answers the question, *When?* in relation to the action of thanking God mentioned in the preceding main clause. So instead of writing "description of thanking" by the line, you could write "time of action," or better still, "time of thanking."

For example, Colossians 1:3 could be labeled this way:

We always give thanks to God,

       the Father of our Lord Jesus Christ, (*description of God*)

       when we pray for you (*timing of thanks*)

QUESTION 11

In the following sentence, identify the descriptive line, the word or phrase it describes, and the question it answers about that word or phrase. Then lay out the sentence and label the descriptive line. The sentence is, "And take the helmet of salvation and the sword of the Spirit, which is the word of God." (Eph. 6:17)

QUESTION 12

In the following sentence, identify the descriptive line, the word or phrase it describes, and the question it answers about that word or phrase. Then lay out the sentence and label the descriptive line. The sentence is, "They were frightened when they heard Paul and Silas were Roman citizens." (Acts 16:38)

Label the Main Clauses

These lines form the central thread or backbone of the argument. By observing what each line is saying and how it relates to its neighboring lines, you will be able to trace the flow of the argument.

a. Sometimes it is sufficient simply to label the line according to the kind of statement it makes: **assertion, question, command, exhortation, warning**.

b. Simple statements of fact often need no label at all.

c. If a connecting word precedes the line, such as FOR—which you have already labeled **explanation**—no additional label is necessary. The line is an explanation.

d. If a connecting word does not precede the line, ask yourself how this statement fits into the argument.

Does it describe someone in the previous verse? Does it explain, illustrate, or give a specific example of something in the previous verse? Perhaps it is the second point in a three-part explanation introduced by the connective FOR. Is it a conditional statement (introduced by if)? Does it introduce, conclude, or summarize an argument? Does it display a cause/effect relationship with another line or section of the paragraph? Does it repeat a point for emphasis? Whatever the function, summarize it in a short phrase such as, "second part of explanation" or "description of Christ."

Psalm 23:1, 2

The Lord is my shepherd,

I lack nothing. (*cause to effect*) or (*result*)

He takes me to lush pastures (*illustration*) or (*example*)

QUESTION 13

Lay out the lines of the following text and label them as needed (Heb 12:3):

"Think of him who endured such opposition against himself by sinners, so that you may not grow weary in your souls and give up."

QUESTION 14

Lay out the lines of the following text and label them as needed (Prov 16:26)

"A laborer's appetite works on his behalf, for his hunger urges him to work."

QUESTION 15

Lay out the lines of the following text and label them as needed (Col 3:18, 19):

"Wives, submit to your husbands, as is fitting in the Lord. Husbands, love your wives and do not be embittered against them."

Identify and Label the Sections

Once you have laid out the lines of the paragraph and labeled them, look over the entire text. Trace the flow of the argument in your mind. Use brackets to mark off those lines that seem to belong to the same topic. (See the examples in Topic 1 for the use of brackets.) Try to break each paragraph into at least two sections, but no more than three or four at the very most. Beside each bracket summarize as briefly as possible the topic of the section. This step can serve as the basis for your outline of the paragraph.

QUESTION 16

Lay out the lines of the paragraph below and label them as needed. Then use brackets to mark off those lines that seem to belong to the same topic, and write a brief summary beside each bracket.

"Wives, submit to your husbands, as is fitting in the Lord. Husbands, love your wives and do not be embittered against them." (Col 3:18, 19)

QUESTION 17

Lay out the lines of the paragraph below and label them as needed. Then use brackets to mark off those lines that seem to belong to the same topic, and write a brief summary beside each bracket.

"Come to me, all you who are weary and burdened, and I will give you rest. Take my yoke on you and learn from me, because I am gentle and humble in heart, and you will find rest for your souls. For my yoke is easy to bear and my load is not hard to carry." (Mt 11:28-30)

Topic 4: How to Summarize the Results of a Structural Diagram

Once you have completed the structural diagram, take a few minutes to summarize your findings in a preliminary outline and theme statement. It is **preliminary** because more detailed study may lead you to modify these earlier conclusions as the passage comes into sharper focus.

How to Make a Paragraph Outline

This exercise is valuable both as an aid to understanding and as a first step toward developing a teaching or preaching outline. For the main points of the outline (the Roman numerals), simply use the topics you have bracketed in your structural diagram. Similarly, the sub-points within these topics can serve as the sub-points of the outline. You need not use complete sentences in the outline. For the sake of clarity, however, you may wish to use fuller wording than what you put in the structural diagram.

Examples of Paragraph Outlines

1. Psalm 117

    I. All nations are called to worship the Lord — Psalm 117:1

    II. Reasons to worship him — Psalm 117:2a,b

        A. His great love toward us — Psalm 117:2a

        B. His enduring faithfulness — Psalm 117:2b

    III. Renewed call to worship — Psalm 117:2c

2. Matthew 6:19-20

    I. Store up treasures in heaven — Matthew 6:19-20

        A. Do not store them up on earth — Matthew 6:19

        B. Store them up in heaven — Matthew 6:20

    II. Explanation: Your heart will be where your treasure is — Matthew 6:21

Please note: A common mistake students make with outlines is to place only one sub-point under a heading. When using sub-points, you must have at least two. If you find that you have only one, simply make it a part of the main point.

How to Write a Theme Statement

Now that you have reduced the paragraph to an outline, the next step is to condense it to a single statement. The task is to capture the single, unifying idea or theme of the passage in a relatively short sentence. This requires thought. The challenge, so to speak, is to separate the trunk and the principal branches of the tree from the leaves and minor branches. If you have done the structural diagram and outline properly, these major features should be apparent.

Examples of Theme Statements

1. Psalm 117. All nations are called upon to worship the Lord for his love and faithfulness.

2. Matthew 6:19-21. Store up treasures in heaven, because your heart will be where your treasure is.

Please note: A common mistake students make in writing theme statements is to include too many details. Use the structural diagram and outline as your guide to the main thrust of the passage. Skill comes with practice.

QUESTION 18

Make a structural diagram, outline, and theme statement for Colossians 3:18-19:

"Wives, submit to your husbands, as is fitting in the Lord. Husbands, love your wives and do not be embittered against them."

QUESTION 19

Make a structural diagram, outline, and theme statement for Colossians 3:20-21:

"Children, obey your parents in everything, for this is pleasing in the Lord. Fathers, do not provoke your children, so they will not become disheartened."

QUESTION 20

Make a structural diagram, outline, and theme statement for the first paragraph of Colossians (Colossians 1:1-2):

"From Paul, an apostle of Christ Jesus by the will of God, and Timothy our brother, to the saints, the faithful brothers and sisters in Christ, at Colossae. Grace and peace to you from God our Father!"

QUESTION 21

Make a structural diagram, outline, and theme statement for the second paragraph of Colossians (Colossians 1:3-8). Because this paragraph is complex, we suggest that you lay it out in the following way:

(3) We always give thanks to God,
      the Father of our Lord Jesus Christ,
      when we pray for you

(4) **SINCE**
    we heard about your faith in Christ Jesus and the love that you have for all the saints.

(5) Your faith and love have arisen from the hope
      laid up for you in heaven,
  which you have heard about in the message of truth, the gospel
   (6) that has come to you.
  Just as in the entire world, this gospel is bearing fruit and growing,
      so it also has been bearing fruit and growing among you,
          from the first day you heard it and understood the
          grace of God in truth.

(7) You learned the gospel from Epaphras,
      our dear fellow slave,
      a faithful minister of Christ on our behalf -

(8) who also told us of your love in the Spirit.

Lesson 2 Self Check

QUESTION 1
What term refers to how the parts of a passage fit together to make up the whole? _____

QUESTION 2
The three different types of "lines" in a paragraph that you should recognize are called main clauses, connecting words, and dependent clauses. *True or False?*

QUESTION 3
The main clause in the sentence "While we were still sinners, Christ died for us" in Romans 5:8 (NIV) is "While we were still sinners." *True or False?*

QUESTION 4
Which of the following words cannot serve as a connecting word: that, then, they, but, for, since?
_____

QUESTION 5
What label would you write beside the connecting word "but"? _____

QUESTION 6
In the verse "The Lord is my shepherd, I lack nothing" which of the following best describes the phrase "I lack nothing"?

   A. main clause
   B. cause to effect
   C. illustration
   D. result

QUESTION 7
In a structural diagram, how would you label the second clause in the following sentence: "Endure your suffering as discipline; God is treating you as sons." _____

QUESTION 8
When making an outline based on a structural diagram, the main points (the Roman numerals) should be the topics you have _____.

   A. underlined
   B. placed on a line by themselves
   C. emphasized by capitalizing all the letters
   D. marked off with brackets

QUESTION 9
When making an outline, it is acceptable to have only one sub-point under a heading. *True or False?*

QUESTION 10
A common mistake in writing theme statements is to _____.

   A. include too many details
   B. fail to identify the theme correctly
   C. omit too many details
   D. make an incomplete sentence

Lesson 2 Answers to Questions

QUESTION 1: *Your answer should be similar to the following:*
The structure of a passage refers to how its parts fit together to make up the whole.

QUESTION 2: *Your answer should be similar to the following:*
(1) Break the paragraph into its constituent parts ("lines"), (2) arrange them on a single page to display the flow of thought, (3), label these parts, (4), and use brackets to mark off topics within the paragraph.

QUESTION 3: *Your answer should be similar to the following:*
It is a relatively quick and easy method that allows you to see the parts of a paragraph and how they fit together to produce the unified message of the paragraph.

QUESTION 4: *Your solution should look generally like this:*
  Wives, submit to your husbands,
      as is fitting in the Lord.

QUESTION 5: *Your solution should look generally like this:*
  AND
  take the helmet of salvation and the sword of the Spirit,
        which is the word of God.

QUESTION 6: *Your solution should look generally like this:*
  They were frightened
        when they heard Paul and Silas were Roman citizens.

QUESTION 7: *Your solution should look generally like this:*
  Think of him
      who endured such opposition against himself by sinners,
  SO THAT
  you may not grow weary in your souls and give up.

QUESTION 8: purpose

QUESTION 9

Connecting Word	Label
The Lord is far from the wicked BUT he hears the prayer of the upright.	Contrast
Behold, I do not know how to speak BECAUSE I am a youth.	Explanation
In him was life AND the life was the light of men.	Additional
A great storm developed on the sea SO THAT the waves began to swamp the boat.	Result
We pray for you always, THAT our God will make you worthy of his calling.	Content
I have hidden your word in my heart THAT I might not sin against you.	Purpose

QUESTION 10: *Your solution should look generally like this:*
  FOR (*explanation*)
  the payoff of sin is death,
  BUT (*contrast*)
  the gift of God is eternal life.

QUESTION 11: *Your solution should look generally like this:*
  The descriptive line is, "which is the word of God." The phrase it describes is "the sword of the Spirit." The question it answers is "What is the sword of the Spirit?"
  AND
  take the helmet of salvation and the sword of the Spirit,
      (*description of this sword*) which is the word of God.

QUESTION 12: *Your solution should look generally like this:*
The descriptive line is "when they heard Paul and Silas were Roman citizens." It describes the action of the verb "were frightened." It answers the question "When were they frightened?"
They were frightened
(*time of fright*) when they heard Paul and Silas were Roman citizens.

QUESTION 13: *Your solution should look generally like this:*
Think of him (*exhortation*)
      who endured such opposition against himself by sinners, (*description of "him"*)
SO THAT (*purpose*)
you may not grow weary in your souls and give up.

QUESTION 14: *Your solution should look generally like this:*
A laborer's appetite works on his behalf,
for his hunger urges him to work. (*explanation*)

QUESTION 15: *Your solution should look generally like this:*
Wives, submit to your husbands, (*command*)
(*explanation*)
as is fitting in the Lord.
Husbands, love your wives (*command*)
AND (*additional command: from general to specific*)
do not be embittered against them.

QUESTION 16: *Your solution should look generally like this:*

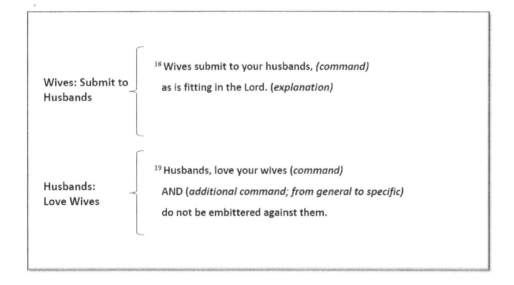

QUESTION 17: *Your solution should look generally like this:*

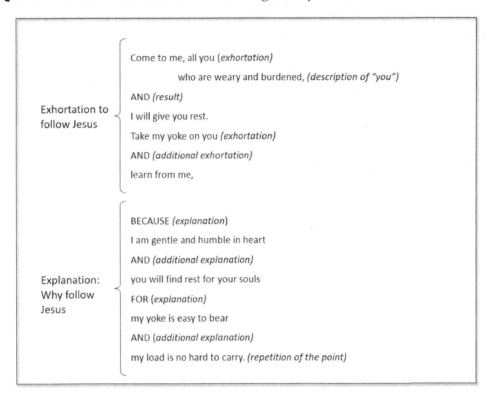

QUESTION 18: Your structural diagram, outline, and theme statement should look similar to what is shown below. Do not be discouraged if your answers do not quite match these. This does not necessarily mean that your analysis is wrong. Seldom will two good scholars arrive at the exact same results. Nevertheless, the answers given here are valid, and your answers should display the same basic understanding of the structure of the passage.

Outline of Colossians 3:18-19

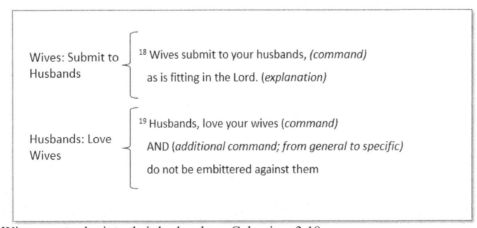

I. Wives must submit to their husbands — Colossians 3:18
    A. The command to submit — Colossians 3:18a
    B. The reason: It is fitting in the Lord — Colossians 3:18b
II. Husbands must love their wives — Colossians 3:19
    A. The command to love — Colossians 3:19a
    B. More specific command: Do not be harsh — Colossians 3:19b

Theme Statement for Colossians 3:18-19
Wives are to submit to their husbands, while husbands are to love their wives.

QUESTION 19: *Your structural diagram, outline, and theme statement should look similar to this:*

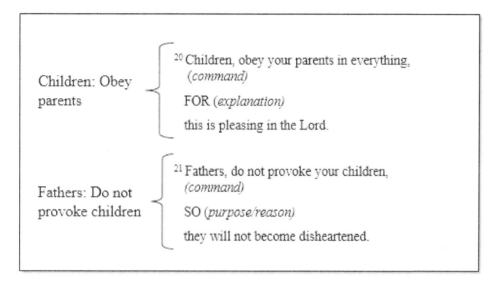

Outline of Colossians 3:20-21
I. Children must obey their parents — Colossians 3:20
    A. The command to obey — Colossians 3:20a
    B. Explanation: This pleases the Lord — Colossians 3:20b
II. Fathers must not provoke their children — Colossians 3:21
    A. The command not to provoke — Colossians 3:21a
    B. Reason: to avoid discouraging them — Colossians 3:21b

Theme Statement for Colossians 3:20-21
Children must obey their parents, while fathers must not provoke their children.

QUESTION 20: *Your structural diagram, outline, and theme statement should look similar to this:*

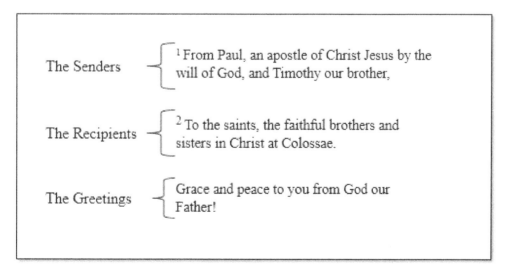

Outline of Colossians 1:1-2
I. The Senders of the Letter: Paul and Timothy
II. The Recipients: "The saints" in Colossae
III. The Greetings

Lesson 2 Answers to Questions

Theme Statement for Colossians 1:1-2
Paul and Timothy to the Colossians: Grace and peace.

Question 21: *Your answer should be similar to the following:*

Do not be discouraged if your answers do not quite match these. This does not necessarily mean that your analysis is wrong.

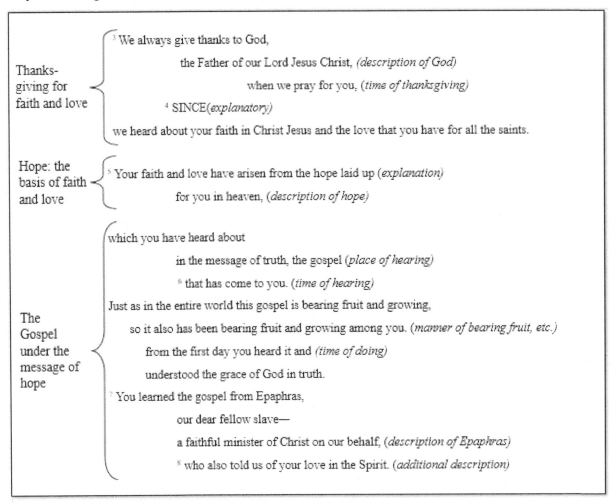

Outline of Colossians 1:3-8
I. Thanksgiving for faith and love — Colossians 1: 3-4
    A. Paul and Timothy thank God — Colossians 1:3
    B. Reason for thanksgiving: The faith and love of the Colossians – Colossians 1:4
II. Hope: The basis of faith and love — Colossians 1:5a-b
III. The gospel: the message of hope — Colossians 1:5c-8
    A. The Colossians heard of this hope in the gospel — Colossians 1:5c-6a
    B. The gospel produces faith and love everywhere it goes — Colossians 1:6b-d
    C. Epaphras: The messenger of the gospel — Colossians 1:7-8

Theme Statement for Colossians 1:3-8
Paul thanks God because the gospel's message of secure hope in heaven has borne the fruit of faith and love in the Christians of Colossae.

Lesson 2 Self Check Answers

QUESTION 1: Structure
QUESTION 2: False
QUESTION 3: False
QUESTION 4: they
QUESTION 5: contrast
QUESTION 6:
   D. result
QUESTION 7: explanation
QUESTION 8
   D. marked off with brackets
QUESTION 9: False
QUESTION 10
   A. include too many details

Lesson 3: How to Study a Paragraph, Part II—Detailed Analysis

A Study of the First Two Paragraphs—Colossians 1:1-8

In the first lesson of this course, you made a broad survey of Colossians. You examined the historical context, the overall theme and purpose of the letter, its major parts, and the flow of thought. In Lesson 2, you were introduced to a three-step method for studying the individual paragraphs of Colossians.

Step 1: Observe the paragraph as a whole by making a structural diagram, then summarize your findings in an outline and theme statement.

Step 2: Make detailed observations with interpretation and application on the same page as the structural diagram.

Step 3: Read the commentary on the paragraph, then answer the various questions about it in the lesson.

The focus of Lesson 2 was how to do step 1. Steps 2 and 3 are the focus of the present lesson. In this lesson, you will also begin to use this three-step method by applying it to the first two paragraphs of Colossians.

- Topic 1 explains step 2—the detailed examination of the paragraph using the method of observation, interpretation, and application.
- Topic 2 explains step 3—the value and use of a commentary. A verse-by-verse commentary on Colossians is provided in this course as a type of answer section to assist you in your study of this book.
- In Topic 3, you will use the three-step method to study the first paragraph of Colossians. This customary salutation identifies the senders and the recipients of the letter and gives a word of greeting.
- In Topic 4, you will apply the three-step method to the second paragraph of the letter (Col 1:3-8). In this opening paragraph of the thanksgiving section, Paul tells the Colossians of his gratitude to God for their response to the gospel. In doing this, Paul introduces the theme of his letter.

Lesson Outline

Topic 1: How to Examine the Details of a Paragraph

Topic 2: How to Use a Commentary

Topic 3: The Salutation (Col 1:1-2)

Topic 4: Thanksgiving for Their Response to the Gospel (Col 1:3-8)

Lesson Objectives

When you have completed this lesson, you should be able to:

- Explain the method of observation, interpretation, and application, and employ it in the detailed study of a passage of Scripture
- Understand the nature of a commentary, recognizing both its value and its shortcomings
- Define and discuss the following terms and concepts: apostle, saints, in Christ, grace, and God as our Father found in Colossians 1:1-2
- Identify and explain the principle regarding the relationship of understanding to Christian virtue in Colossians 1:4-5, and the principles of ministry regarding the work of an evangelist in Colossians 1:7

Topic 1: How to Examine the Details of a Paragraph

The purpose of this topic is to impart the understanding and skills necessary to do step 2 of our three-step procedure for studying a paragraph. This involves a review of the method of observation, interpretation, and application. To complete the topic, first read "How to Examine the Details of a Paragraph." Once you have read the material carefully, read and answer the questions that appear below.

How to Examine the Details of a Paragraph
A Review of Observation, Interpretation, and Application

I. The Study of Details

A. The Nature of Detailed Study

The purpose of Step 1 is to give a broad overview of the passage —to see the whole and how the parts fit together to make up the whole. The task of Step 2 is to examine these parts in detail. This will give you an even better understanding of the whole.

To use the analogy of the forest and the trees: In Step 1, you gain an idea of the size, the shape, the boundaries, and general characteristics of the forest; in Step 2, you turn your attention to the individual trees that make up the forest. Or to use the earlier image of a bicycle: In Step 1, you look at the entire bicycle fully assembled; in Step 2, you examine more carefully its various parts —the frame, wheels, seat, handlebars, pedals, chain, and so forth.

A detailed examination of the various parts of a paragraph means giving careful attention to each word, phrase, and clause, and how they fit together to produce the overall message of the passage. The goal is to understand more precisely what the writer, guided by the Holy Spirit, meant by these words, and what significance they have for our lives today.

B. The Dangers of Detailed Study

Becoming lost in the details and "missing the forest for the trees" is the first danger. Step 1 is offered as a way to avoid this problem. A second danger is closely related to the first. It arises from the fact that there is virtually no end to the amount of detailed study one can do on any given passage of Scripture. Such is the depth and richness of God's word. This is especially true when one is attempting to study an entire book. Often the student spends too much time on the opening passages seeking to mine all its richness and trace every issue. The experience itself is deeply rewarding, but he realizes that he could never have enough time to give this same depth of study to every paragraph of the book. And so his study of the book goes no further.

The problem may be compared to an athlete running a long-distance race. If he runs too fast early in the race, he will lose. To borrow the words of the apostle Paul: "Run in such a way as to win." To avoid this danger, we suggest —at least for this course —that you devote no more than one hour to the detailed study (Step 2) of each paragraph. You can always come back later for further study.

The challenge at this point is *to set a pace of study that you can maintain for the long run*. One of the goals of this course is to establish in you a method of studying through a book, paragraph by paragraph, that you can then employ with other books of the Bible. The course will have failed in this objective if the method proves impractical for future use because it is too time consuming.

II. Method for Detailed Study

Method means following certain steps in a certain order to achieve a certain result. For each desired result, there is the appropriate method. In order to grow and harvest a crop the farmer does not go about his work in a haphazard way. He follows a certain step-by-step procedure. The same is true of the cook making bread or the builder building a house. In the case of Bible study, the desired result is the application of the Scripture to life. The appropriate method for achieving this result is the three-step procedure of *observation, interpretation, and application.*

A. Observation

Observation may be defined as the act of *seeing*. Here you seek to answer the question, "What do I see?" What are the facts on the printed page? Observation is the basis of interpretation. Faulty interpretation and application are often the result of careless and inaccurate observation.

The first thing one should observe when studying a paragraph is its overall structure. The structural diagram is a means for doing this. Similarly, the book survey is a method for observing the overall structure of a book. Our concern at this point is with how to observe the parts or details of a paragraph.

An excellent way to do this is to probe the text with questions. Consider this little poem by a newspaper reporter that identifies six basic kinds of questions:

> I have six honest serving-men.
> They taught me all I knew.
> Their names are What and Why and When
> And How and Where and Who.

These "serving-men" are useful both for observation and for interpretation. Our concern for now is with observation —using these questions to help us *see* what the author has written.

Begin with the first verse, probing it with questions and writing down what you see. Observe the people who are mentioned (who?), the places (where?), the sequence of events and other references to time (when?). Notice any explanations that appear (how? why?). What concepts, events, actions are mentioned? What descriptions are given? Are there any promises, commands, warnings, figures of speech? What is the tone or atmosphere of the passage?

Discipline yourself to observe the grammatical features of each sentence. This is an excellent way to promote awareness of what the text is saying. Martin Luther said, "The science of theology is nothing else but the rules of grammar applied to the words of the Holy Spirit." Ask yourself, "What is the subject? What is the verb? What is the object of the verb?" Notice modifying words, phrases, and clauses. What questions do these answer?

To probe the text in this way, requires concentration, discipline, and time. The effect, however, is to saturate your mind thoroughly with the content of the passage so that your eyes are opened to see what you would not otherwise have seen. A second effect is that many questions (and some answers) will spring to mind regarding what the biblical author actually meant by the things you have observed. In this way, the process of observation turns quickly to the process of interpretation.

B. Interpretation

The task of interpretation is to answer the question, "What did the author mean by the words he used?" Because he wrote within a certain historical context with a certain audience in mind, there can be but one fixed and unchanging meaning to his words. The goal of interpretation is to determine that meaning. Once we understand this meaning, we will be in a position to consider the question of what it means for us today. This is the step of application.

Here are three general principles to help you determine the author's meaning.

1. Interpret According to the Normal Rules of Human Language and Usage

God speaks in the language of men. For the ancient rabbis, this was the first rule of biblical interpretation. Although the Bible is unique because it is inspired, the rules for interpreting it are otherwise the same as for any other piece of literature. We assume the normal, customary, socially accepted meaning of the words as the intended meaning. This is the normal way we think, speak, and write. And this is the way God's word is to be understood.

Thus, reason, common sense, and the everyday experience of ordinary people should play an important role in helping to uncover the meaning of the text.

Figurative language is very common in the Bible—just as it is in everyday speech today. Scripture tells us, for example, that we are to *bridle* our tongues, to *clothe* ourselves with kindness, and to *bear fruit* for God. Behind each of these figurative expressions stands a literal reality. The interpreter's task in each instance is to discern this literal meaning, relying on common sense and the context.

2. Interpret Contextually

The aim of interpretation is to understand what the author meant by what he wrote. Thus, there is no better guide to his meaning than other statements he made within the same context.

Each passage in a book should be understood within the broader framework of the original historical situation and the author's purpose in writing. In the case of Colossians, for example, Paul wrote to a house church of relatively new believers whose faith was threatened by a seductive, false teaching. His purpose in writing was to prevent them from being led astray by this false teaching and to strengthen them in their Christian walk through a fresh exposition of the gospel.

Each statement in the book should be interpreted in the light of its immediate context and other statements regarding the same subject elsewhere in the book.

3. Interpret in Light of the Divine Inspiration of Scripture

The Bible was written by approximately 40 human authors over a period of 1500 years. Yet behind each human author was the guiding hand of the Holy Spirit (2 Pet 1:21; 2 Tim 3:16). Hence, there is an underlying unity and harmony to the whole of Scripture. So, although we find different perspectives and emphases in Scripture (Psalms differs from Ecclesiastes, and James from Paul), and although we see many differences between the two testaments due to the progressive unfolding of God's plan of salvation from Genesis to Revelation, the Bible nevertheless presents a single unified story without contradiction.

Because of this unity, the entire Bible is the context and guide for understanding any particular passage of Scripture. Therefore, when faced with an interpretative problem we may look to other texts of Scripture for clarification. On the other hand, if our interpretation of a given text leads to direct conflict with the clear teaching of Scripture seen elsewhere, we should conclude we have misunderstood the text and seek an interpretation that is in harmony with the rest of Scripture.

A note of caution: A common source of misinterpretation is the practice of reading the meaning of familiar texts into texts with which we are unfamiliar. Each text must be examined in a fresh and objective manner and allowed to speak for itself. The inspiration of the Scriptures simply guarantees that each passage, when properly understood, will be harmonious with and complementary to every other passage.

C. Application

The third and indispensable aspect of Bible study is to translate our understanding of God's word into action. This is the ultimate aim of knowing spiritual truth. David prayed in Psalm 86:11, "O Lord, teach me how you want me to live! Then I will obey your commands. Make me wholeheartedly committed to you!" This basic principle, in fact, belongs to the very theme of Colossians. It is expressed in Colossians 1:9-10: "we . . . have not ceased praying for you and asking God to fill you with the *knowledge* of his will . . . so that you may *live worthily* of the Lord and please him in all respects" (italics added).

The process of application can be broken into four steps:

1. Know the interpretation.
2. Identify general application-based principles within the author's meaning.
3. Make specific application of the principle to your life.
4. Put the application into practice through prayer.

1. Know the Interpretation

The first step in translating Scripture into action is to understand what the author meant in the first place. In other words, interpretation is the essential foundation for application. Faulty application often results from faulty interpretation. Many, for example, have understood Paul's words in Romans 13:8, "Owe nothing to anyone" to mean that it is a sin to go into debt. It may indeed be unwise in many circumstances to incur debt. Careful examination of this passage, however, reveals that it does not forbid incurring a debt. Instead it simply means that Christians should faithfully repay any debt they incur (see Ps 37:21).

2. Identify General Application-based Principles within the Author's Meaning

Once you understand the author's meaning, the next step is to identify general truths or principles within this meaning that should lead to action. Often these principles are explicit and lie readily on the surface. Examples of this can be seen in the commands to honor our parents, love one another, and walk by the Spirit.

Frequently, however, principles for action lie beneath the surface, and need to be drawn out. For example, in 1 Kings 11:1-13 we read that Solomon had many foreign wives who turned his heart away from the Lord to follow other gods. A principle of action we may draw from this is that believers should not marry unbelievers.

A second example may be seen in Romans 15:30-32 with Paul's request for prayer for success and safety on his mission to Jerusalem. Paul is no longer in need of our prayers, but we may draw from this the application-based principle that Christians should pray for their missionaries. Similarly, missionaries should actively seek the participation of churches in their work in the form of prayer.

3. Make Specific Application of the Principle to Your Own Life

The question to answer now is, "How can I apply this principle to my life?" The following questions may help focus your thinking.

- Is there a command to obey?

- Is there a promise to claim?
- Is there a sin to confess and forsake?
- Is there an example to follow?
- Is there a truth to believe?
- Is there a prayer to express?
- Is there an attitude to adopt?

4. Put the Application into Practice

You have not applied until you have practiced. James wrote, "But be sure you live out the message and do not merely listen to it and so deceive yourselves." (James 1:22).

The practice itself will become an aid in helping you to understand the particular biblical principle. As you gain understanding, you will be able to teach it to others.

Remember, you cannot diligently apply everything, but you can apply some things. Ask God for wisdom in setting goals and carrying them out. James said of the conscientious doer of the word, "he will be blessed in what he does" (James 1:25).

III. How to Apply These Methods to the Study of a Paragraph

A. The Procedure for Detailed Study

1. Record Your Findings on the Structural Diagram

It is very important that you write out your observations, interpretations, and applications. Writing helps you think more clearly. Making a record of your findings is also essential if you intend to teach or preach from this passage. The weakest ink is more reliable than the best memory.

A simple way to do this is to use the structural diagram itself. Record your findings between the lines, beside the text and in the margins. You will need to write small. The end result may appear less than tidy, but there are advantages to this approach. First, the limitations of space will discipline you to limit the amount of time you spend analyzing the details. Second, this approach saves time, effort and paper since there is no need to copy the words and phrases of the text onto another page to record your findings. Finally, it is helpful to be able to see all of your findings together on a single sheet of paper. This will make it convenient when you wish to refer back to it later.

2. Proceed through the Paragraph Verse by Verse

Rather than making detailed observations on the entire paragraph before proceeding to interpretation, and then interpreting the entire paragraph before considering application, it is best to take an integrated approach. Begin by observing the first verse. This will lead naturally to questions about the author's meaning. Write down each interpretive question as it comes to mind. If the answer also comes to mind, write this down too. Otherwise, leave it for later. Similarly, insights regarding application may also come to mind during the process of observing and interpreting. Take time to record your insights here as well. Once you have observed the first verse, and considered issues of interpretation and application, move on to the next verse and so on through the paragraph.

3. Budget your Time

Be careful not to spend too much time on any single verse or issue. If you encounter a big issue requiring more attention, plan to come back to it after you have examined the rest of

> the passage. Spread your efforts evenly over all the parts of the paragraph, and limit the entire step of detailed study to one hour.
>
> ### B. Additional Suggestions Regarding Interpretative Questions
>
> - Write out the question whether you think you know the answer or not.
> - Simply expressing the question can be a helpful exercise in understanding.
> - The answer may come to you as you write out the question.
> - Turn the issue over in your mind by listing possible alternative answers.
> - Do not feel you must answer every interpretative question before moving on to the next point in the text. The answer may come to you later in your study of the paragraph or later in your study of the book.
> - You may find the answer to your question later when you consult a commentary. But the act of asking the question in your study of the passage and then pondering it will cause you to understand and remember the answer better once you find it in the commentary.
> - Given the time, you may wish to search out the answer later by doing a special study.

QUESTION 1

Use the six basic questions identified in this topic (who, what, why, when, where, how) to probe Colossians 1:1-2. Write out each question without taking time to answer it. These are questions of observation (What do I see?). You should also include questions of interpretation (What does it mean?). Ask the question whether you know the answer or not. Make it your goal to write at least ten questions and to finish in five minutes.

QUESTION 2

Now spend five minutes doing the same thing with Colossians 1:3-5a which includes the words "in heaven." This time, try to focus on the key questions related to the flow of thought.

QUESTION 3

The task of interpretation is to answer the question, "What does the text mean for us today?" *True or False?*

QUESTION 4

Colossians 1:4-5a contains a general principle of application. Can you identify it?

Topic 2: How to Use a Commentary

Step 3: Using a Commentary

The third, and final, step in your study of a paragraph is to read a commentary on this passage and answer the questions about it in the lesson.

What is a Commentary?

A good commentary provides a detailed, verse-by-verse interpretation of an entire book of the Bible. Good commentaries are written by experienced interpreters. These writers bring to their work knowledge of the historical background of the book, knowledge of the original language in which it was written, and an understanding of how it has been interpreted in the past.

What Is the Value of Consulting a Commentary?

There are several benefits to using a commentary. To be able to consult such a commentary after doing your own study is like having a teacher at your side who is an expert on the passage. The commentary can help you evaluate the results of your study. It can deepen your understanding of the passage and offer insights you may have overlooked. It can provide information from other sources about the historical and literary background of the passage. Finally, it can provide a good model for interpreting Scripture.

Is There a Negative Side to the Use of Commentaries?

The commentary should not take the place of personal study. Do your own study of the passage (steps 1 and 2) first, then consult the commentary. If you go to the commentary first, you will not learn as much. You will also deny yourself the joy of discovery.

Commentaries are not inspired. Two good commentaries may disagree on the interpretation of a passage. Nevertheless, good commentaries are the work of experienced scholars and usually offer reliable, though not infallible, guidance.

A Commentary on Colossians

A commentary on Colossians is included in this course. It is essential that you carefully read the commentary on each paragraph following your own personal study of that passage (steps 1 and 2). The commentary will function as the answer section for your interpretations.

QUESTION 5

How would you respond to the following argument? It is not necessary to look to a commentary or to any human teacher to assist us in the study of God's Word since we have the Holy Spirit as our Teacher.

Topic 3: The Salutation (Col 1:1-2)

Now that we have completed our survey of Colossians and established a three-step method for studying the paragraphs of this letter, we are finally in a position to begin our detailed study of each paragraph. Since Colossians is a letter, it begins with a customary salutation. In Paul's day, a person writing a letter would begin by identifying himself. Next, he would identify the person or persons to whom he was writing. Finally, he would add a word of greeting. A secular example can be seen in Acts 23:26. Often this greeting came in the form of a blessing or a wish for good health. Paul followed this basic pattern in all of his letters but adapted it to his own purpose. While his salutation to the Colossians is brief, the careful observer can find many valuable truths in it.

Begin your study by reading Colossians 1:1-2 and then reading the Worksheet on Colossians 1:1-2 (see next page). Copy it in your Life Notebook and complete Step 1: a structural diagram, outline, and theme statement. Even though you did this in the exercises for Lesson 2, it will be valuable to do it again since you will be following it this time with Steps 2 and 3. You can check your results by comparing them with the Answers for Colossians 1:1-2. Next, complete step 2 by recording your detailed observations, interpretations, and applications. For step 3, read the Commentary on Colossians 1:1-2 carefully. Then answer the questions based on the commentary.

Worksheet for Colossians 1:1-2

From Paul, an apostle of Christ Jesus by the will of God,

and Timothy our brother,

² to the saints, the faithful brothers and sisters in Christ, at Colossae.

Grace and peace to you from God our Father!

Commentary on Colossians 1:1-2
I. The Salutation—(Colossians 1:1-2)

Verse 1

From Paul, an apostle of Christ Jesus by the will of God. The second word of this letter identifies Paul as the author. He is writing from the large port city of Ephesus, 120 miles (192 km) to the west of Colossae, where he is confined in prison for preaching the gospel (Col 4:3). Paul had never met these Christians, but they knew of him through Epaphras and others.

The phrase "an apostle of Christ Jesus by the will of God" answers the question, "Who is Paul?" The word *apostle* in Greek means "one who is sent." In ordinary usage, it referred to someone who was sent on a mission with the authority to act on behalf of the sender—for example to negotiate a marriage (Jn 13:16). This ordinary use appears in Phil 2:25 where Paul describes Epaphroditus as a messenger (apostle) of the church of Philippi. The word is also used in a special sense of the Apostles of Christ. These were men commissioned by Christ and sent out with his authority to proclaim the gospel and establish the church. This group was made up of the original twelve disciples (minus Judas) along with certain others who were eyewitnesses of the resurrection, including Paul, and James—the Lord's brother (1 Cor 15:5-9).

We no longer have Apostles of Christ in the church today. Their mission was completed in the first century. In Ephesians 2:20 Paul pictures the church as a great temple with the apostles as the foundation and Christ as the cornerstone. Today this temple continues to grow on the same foundation, as new believers are added.

By identifying himself as an apostle of Christ in this opening verse Paul is signaling the official character of his letter. He writes with the authority of the One who sent him. Indeed, he adds that this authority was entrusted to him "by the will of God" (see also Col 1:25). What Paul writes to the Colossians is therefore a message from God. It is Scripture. And because it is Scripture, it is written for our instruction as well (see 2 Tim 2:16-17). Thus, through his letters Paul continues to serve the church today as "an apostle of Christ Jesus."

and Timothy our brother. This letter is also from Timothy. Paul often describes a fellow worker as "my brother" (1 Cor 1:1; Rom 16:23). It indicates their common spiritual kinship and the warmth of brotherly affection between them.

Paul had recruited Timothy when he was a very young man to help him in his missionary work (Acts 16:1-3). In time, Timothy became Paul's most cherished and important fellow-worker (Phil 2:20-22). Paul often sent Timothy on missions to various churches to sort out some problem (see for example 1 Thess 3:2-3). Thus, we could say that as Paul was an apostle of Christ, Timothy was an "apostle" of Paul. This helps to explain why Paul tells the Colossians that this letter is also from Timothy. Paul is saying, "What I say, Timothy also says. We work together." Paul further implies, "In my absence, Timothy speaks for me. Trust him."

Verse 2

to the saints, the faithful brothers and sisters in Christ, at Colossae. This letter is addressed to the Christians in the town of Colossae. Paul uses four terms to describe these people.

First, they are *saints*. This word means "holy ones." The term *holy* refers to that which is set apart from everyday use and dedicated to God. In the Old Testament the people of Israel, God's chosen covenant people, were often called "the saints." By describing these Gentile Christians in Colossae as saints, Paul is saying they now belong to the people of God. They are now fellow-heirs of God's promise of salvation. In spite of our imperfections, all believers are saints in this sense, not just a select few.

Second, the Colossians are *faithful*. The term means steadfast, firmly committed. Later in Colossians 2:5, Paul commends these young Christians for the steadfastness of their faith in the face of a seductive false teaching. His purpose in writing is to strengthen them further in their faith so that they might remain steadfast.

Third, Paul calls them *brothers and sisters*. As in Colossians 1:1 these words carry the idea of a common spiritual kinship and sibling affection. Paul is saying, "Even though I have never met you, you are as much brothers and sisters to me as Timothy."

Finally, they are *in Christ*. The words "in" and "at" designate locations. Paul is writing to people who are "in Christ" "at Colossae." But while "at Colossae" refers to a literal place, the phrase "in Christ" involves a figure of speech—a picture that communicates a spiritual truth. Paul is saying that Christ is the "place" or the person in whom salvation is present. We were all born "in Adam" (1 Cor 15:22). The new birth places us "in Christ."

Adam and Christ are the heads of two races of humanity. Adam, acting as the representative of his race, sinned and brought condemnation and death to all those descended from him. Christ, acting as the representative of a new human race, died and rose again to bring forgiveness and new life to all who trust in him. When a person believes the gospel, God includes him in the saving work that Christ accomplished on the cross. What was lost through Adam is restored through Christ. To be "in Christ" therefore means to be a partaker of this salvation accomplished through him (Rom 8:1).

Grace and peace to you from God our Father. In ancient letters the identification of the sender and receiver was followed by a word of greetings. Paul's greeting takes the form of a prayer of blessing. He is saying, "May God our Father grant you grace and peace."

Paul begins and ends all of his letters on the same note of grace (see Col 4:18). This is because he wishes everything he writes to be seen within the framework of God's grace—from beginning to end. The ordinary meaning of this word in Greek is "favor." But when we read of God acting in grace, it refers to his "undeserved favor" toward sinners. It is God's undeserved gift to men. The nature of grace is summarized clearly in Ephesians 2:8, "For by grace you are saved through faith, and this is not from yourselves, it is the gift of God." God acts in grace toward humans in many ways. The most basic is his gift of salvation that we received by faith. But we continue to experience this grace in the way he enables us to live the Christian life (Heb 4:16). It is for this enabling and sustaining grace that Paul prays here in Colossians 1:2.

The second part of Paul's prayer of blessing is for peace. Peace is not just the absence of disturbance or hostility. It includes the idea of well-being and harmony, especially in relationships. The Christian message is "the gospel of peace." Through Christ we have peace with God (Rom 5:1). Through Christ we also have true peace with our fellow Christians. He has made us members of one body. Paul's prayer is that this peace will continue, just as he writes later in Colossians 3:15, "Let the peace of Christ be in control in your heart (for you were in fact called as one body to this peace), and be thankful."

These two blessings of grace and peace come from "God our Father." What does it mean that God is our Father? First, we must see this as another reference to our salvation. He is not the Father of all. He is the Father of those he has redeemed and adopted as his sons and daughters through faith in Christ (Gal 3:26; Gal 4:5). Secondly, it means that his relationship to each believer is like that of a father to his child. He loves us. He watches over us. He is at work directing, enabling, and disciplining us that we might grow into a mature, Christian adulthood (Rom 8:29; Heb 12:7-10).

QUESTION 6

What is the basic meaning of the Greek word translated "apostle"?

   A. One who goes on long journeys
   B. One who plants churches
   C. One who is sent
   D. One who writes epistles
   E. One who is a witness of the resurrection
   F. One who proclaims good news

QUESTION 7

The word "saints" (holy ones) is used to describe those Christians who have progressed to an advanced level of spiritual maturity and holiness. *True or False?*

QUESTION 8

What does it mean to be "in Christ"?

QUESTION 9

God's grace is his _____ favor toward sinners.

QUESTION 10

In Colossians 1:2 Paul describes God as *our Father*. In what two ways should we understand this?

QUESTION 11

Consider the example of Paul and Timothy, his younger co-worker. How well would this type of team relationship between a mature Christian worker and a younger assistant work in your area?

QUESTION 12

Think of yourself in the role of Paul, the mature worker. How would you go about training your Timothy? How would you use him in your work? What responsibilities and experiences would you give him now if you knew that you must pass the torch of your ministry to him in three years (as Paul eventually did with Timothy)?

Important Facts to Remember about Colossians 1:1-2

1. The ordinary meaning of the Greek word translated "apostle" is one who is sent. This one sent was entrusted with the authority to act on behalf of the sender.

2. The word "saints" means holy ones. Those who belong to God's chosen, covenant people are his saints. All Christians are saints in this sense.

3. To be "in Christ" is the opposite of being "in Adam." Adam's sin brought condemnation and death to his descendants (all who are in Adam). Christ died and rose again to bring forgiveness and new life to a new race made up of all who trust in him (all who are in Christ.) When a person believes the gospel, God makes him a partaker of the salvation accomplished through Christ and thereby transfers him from Adam to Christ.

4. Grace is God's undeserved favor toward sinners.

5. Paul describes God as "our Father" because he has redeemed and adopted us as his sons and daughters, and his relationship toward us is like that of a wise and loving father toward his children.

Topic 4: Thanksgiving for Their Response to the Gospel (Col 1:3-8)

Paul began his letter in Colossians 1:1-2 with a customary salutation. Now in Colossians 1:3, we enter the part of the letter that we identified in Lesson 1 as the thanksgiving section (Col 1:3-23). It opens with the report of Paul's and Timothy's regular prayers of thanksgiving for the Colossians. Their gratitude is for the way the gospel that the Colossians learned from Epaphras has borne in them the fruit of faith and love. This statement sets the stage for the entire letter. It exhibits the basic principle that guides Paul's theme and purpose. This principle is that Christian virtue is the fruit of a proper understanding of the gospel—that is, of God's saving work toward us through Christ. Thus, Paul expresses his gratitude that the gospel has borne this fruit in them already, and he writes in order to impart an even better understanding of the gospel so that their fruit may abound all the more.

Begin your study by reading Colossians 1:3-8 and the reading the Worksheet on (see next page). Copy it in your Life Notebook and complete step 1: a structural diagram, outline, and theme statement. Even though you did this in the exercises for Lesson 2, it will be valuable to do it again since you will be following it this time with steps 2 and 3. You can check your results by comparing them with the Answers for Colossians 1:3-8. Next, complete step 2 by recording your detailed observations, interpretations, and applications. For step 3, read the Commentary on Colossians 1:3-8 carefully. Then answer the questions based on the commentary.

Worksheet for Colossians 1:3-8

³We always give thanks to God,

>   the Father of our Lord Jesus Christ,

> when we pray for you,

⁴since

we heard about your faith in Christ Jesus and

the love that you have for all the saints.

⁵Your faith and love have arisen from the hope

>   laid up for you in heaven,

which you have heard about

>   in the message of truth, the gospel

>   ⁶that has come to you.

Just as in the entire world this gospel is bearing fruit and growing,

>   so it has also been bearing fruit and growing among you

>   >   from the first day you heard it and understood

>   >   >   the grace of God in truth.

⁷You learned the gospel from Epaphras,

>   our dear fellow slave—

>   a faithful minister of Christ on our behalf—

>   ⁸who also told us of your love in the Spirit.

Commentary on Colossians 1:3-8
II. The Thanksgiving Section—(Col 1:3-23)

In most of Paul's letters, a thanksgiving section follows his opening salutation. The thanksgiving section is Colossians 1:3-23. This section works in two ways to prepare the Colossians for what Paul has to say later in the letter. The first concerns his personal and pastoral relationship with them. The church is facing certain dangers. It is a young congregation with weaknesses and in need of strong exhortation. The account of Paul's sincere prayers in Colossians 1:3-12 serves to assure them of his good will and his confidence in their progress. As a wise teacher, Paul knows that this assurance should cause them to receive his later exhortations and warnings with greater openness. (There is a principle of application here for everyone.) The second function of this section is to introduce important subjects that Paul will develop later in the letter.

> The thanksgiving section falls into five paragraphs. First, in Colossians 1:3-8 is a report of Paul's prayer of thanksgiving for the Colossians. Next in Colossians 1:9-12a is a description of his intercessory prayer for them. This prayer concludes on a note of thanksgiving that moves seamlessly into a description in Colossians 1:12b-14 of the salvation that God, the Father, has provided for them through Christ. This description in turn leads to a hymn or a poem in praise of Christ in Colossians 1:15-20. The final paragraph, Colossians 1:21-23, concludes the section by applying the reconciling work of Christ described in Colossians 1:15-20 to the Colossian Christians.

A. Paul's Prayers for the Colossians—(Col 1:3-12a)

1. Thanksgiving for the Colossians' Response to the Gospel—(Col 1:3-8)

Paul begins by sharing with his readers his heart-felt gratitude to God for his work of grace in their lives. Specifically, he thanks God for how the gospel's message of hope has produced in them the virtues of faith and love (Col 1:4-5). This statement introduces the theme of the letter. It is not the complete theme. Instead it is the spiritual principle upon which the theme is based. The principle is this: godly conduct is the fruit of a proper understanding of God's saving work toward us through Christ. The complete theme of the letter (including its purpose) appears in Colossians 1:9-10. Paul desires these young Christians to gain a full understanding of God's saving work so that they may "live worthily of the Lord and please him in all respects."

Verse 3

We always give thanks to God. Paul writes "we" instead of "I" because he is writing on behalf of Timothy, who also prays regularly for the Colossians. Later in the chapter, Paul will switch to the first person "I" when he takes up the subject of his special commission as an apostle to the Gentiles (Colossians 1:23). The word "thanks" means to express gratitude for something received. It is a form of praise. By giving thanks to God for the faith and love of Colossians, Paul is acknowledging that these qualities are ultimately the result of God's grace at work in their hearts.

The Father of our Lord Jesus Christ. This One to whom Paul offers thanks is "the Father of our Lord Jesus Christ." God the Father is revealed to us in his unique Son whom he sent into the world (Heb 1:3; Jn 1:18). We know the Father because we know the Son. Jesus said in John 14:9 (NASB) "He who has seen Me has seen the Father."

> The words "our Lord Jesus Christ" served as a confession of faith in the early church. The one who used these words acknowledged that the man Jesus is both Lord and Christ. The term "Christ" ("anointed one") identifies him as the Messiah, the coming king of Israel, promised in the Old Testament, who would establish in the end-time a world–wide reign of peace and righteousness (Isa 9:6-7 and Isa 11:1-9).

> The term "Lord" identifies him as the one to whom God has delegated power and authority to rule this kingdom. The Messiah's elevation to this position is reflected in Psalm 110:1 (NASB): "The LORD says to my Lord, 'Sit at My right hand until I make your enemies a footstool for Your feet'" (also Dan 7:13-14). Jesus now sits enthroned as Lord at the right hand of the Father in heaven (Acts 2:32-36; Col 3:1). Christians are those whom God has rescued from the dominion of darkness and transferred into the kingdom of his Son (Col 1:13). Therefore, they confess the Son as "our Lord Jesus Christ."

When we pray for you. This clause answers the question, when do Paul and Timothy thank God? Paul is saying, "Each time we pray for you, we always thank God." We may observe from this statement that Paul prayed for the Colossians on a regular basis. According to Colossians 1:9, he prayed for them frequently. We learn from Colossians 2:1-2 that these times of prayer were a vital part of his apostolic labor for the Colossians.

Verse 4

since. This word signals the beginning of an explanation that answers the question, why do Paul and Timothy give thanks to God?

we heard about your faith in Christ Jesus and the love that you have for all the saints. Paul gives two reasons for his gratitude. The first is the Colossians' faith in Christ Jesus. The biblical idea of faith is basically that of trust (reliance upon, confidence in). Through the preaching of Epaphras the Colossians placed their trust in Christ. Ever since then, they have made Christ the focus and directing authority of their lives. Earlier in Colossians 1:2 Paul made special note of their faithfulness in Christ—that is, the steadfastness of their faith. Now in Colossians 1:4 he thanks God for this faith, and thus acknowledges that this is the result of God's grace at work in them.

The second reason Paul gives thanks is the love that the Colossians have shown toward all the saints. Christian love is based on the divine love demonstrated in Christ's death for us (Rom 5:8; 2 Cor 5:14-15; 1 Jn 4:9-10). It manifests itself in active concern for others, even to the sacrifice of one's own personal interests. Such love is the mark of genuine faith and the chief fruit of the Spirit (Gal 5:22). The Colossians had demonstrated this love not only among themselves but toward "all the saints"—that is, toward other Christians wherever they met them.

Verse 5

Your faith and love have arisen from the hope. Their faith and love are the product of hope. Hope is an attitude of the heart, the expectation of an unseen future blessing. Sometimes, however, "hope" refers to the object of that expectation—the thing hoped for itself. This is the meaning here in Colossians 1:5. The object of their hope, as the remainder of the verse states, is "laid up for you in heaven." Later in Colossians 1:23 Paul refers to this expectation as "the hope of the gospel that you heard." In Colossians 1:27 it is "the hope of glory." **laid up for you in heaven.**

By describing this hope as "laid up for you in heaven," Paul is saying that the salvation they await in the future is already present in heaven. In the same way, Peter describes it as "an inheritance imperishable, undefiled, and unfading. It is reserved in heaven for you" (1 Pet 1:4). Both of these statements stress the *certainty* of salvation. It is secure in heaven where no power, human or otherwise, can touch it. This heavenly hope is centered on Christ himself who is now seated at God's right hand in heaven (Col 3:1). Because this hope is now hidden in heaven, the New Testament often refers to the end-time coming of salvation as its revelation or "unveiling" (Rom 8:18-19; 1 Pet 1:5,13). This will take place when Christ is revealed from heaven at his second coming (Col 3:4). Believers who die physically before this great event enter immediately into heaven to be with Christ (2 Cor 5:6; Phil 1:23). Yet, the fullness of salvation (which includes the redemption of our bodies) must await Christ's return (Phil 3:20-21).

This raises an interpretative question: How did the knowledge of this secure hope in heaven produce faith and love in the Colossians? Indeed, how does it produce faith and love in us? First, Paul is not saying that the hope of heavenly rewards motivated them to earn them by works of faith and love. This inheritance is the gift of God's grace. Instead, Paul is saying that their understanding of this gift produced in them the confidence to trust God with every aspect of their lives, and to express this faith in acts of love toward others (1 Cor 15:58; Gal 5:6).

We see here a vital principle of Christian living. It is this: A proper understanding of our future inheritance and the confident expectation of it bears the fruit of faith and love. We should, therefore, prayerfully seek to understand this future inheritance more deeply (see Eph 1:18) and to conduct our daily lives in the light of it.

This principle plays a central role in Paul's message to the Colossians. We mentioned earlier that it is the function of the thanksgiving section (Col 1:3-23) to introduce important subjects that will be developed later. The most basic of these subjects is this spiritual principle that we see here in Colossians 1:4-5. The principle, to state it more simply, is that *Christian virtue is the fruit of the gospel*. In other words, godly Christian conduct results from a proper understanding of God's saving work toward us through Christ. The theme of the letter is based on this principle (see Col 1:9-10). The outline of the letter reflects the two aspects of the principle: A fresh exposition of God's saving work (Col 1:12b-23; Col 2:9-16) followed by instruction to walk in accordance with these truths (Col 2:16-4:6).

which you have heard about in the message of truth, the gospel. Paul devotes the remainder of this paragraph, Colossians 1:5c-8 to a description of the gospel—that is, to the message of hope that produced the faith and love for which he gives thanks (Col 1:3-5b). He begins by reminding them of where and when they heard about this hope. They heard of it in the gospel when it was first proclaimed to them. This tells us that an essential element in the proclamation of the gospel is not only what Christ has accomplished in the past through his death and resurrection, and the peace with God that this offers in the present. It also includes a promise about the future: a secure inheritance presently laid up in heaven, with the final fulfillment of it to be revealed on earth at Christ's return.

Paul goes on to describe the gospel as "the message of truth." The Old Testament uses these same words to describe God's word, which is his revealed will for his people (Ps 119:43). The word "truth" in the Old Testament indicates not only that something is real and correct, but also that it is completely reliable. Like God himself, his word is completely reliable. This description of the gospel as "the message of truth" suggests a contrast with the seductive teaching that threatened the Colossian church. In Colossians 2:8 Paul refers to this rival teaching as "hollow and deceptive." Central to Paul's purpose in writing to the Colossians is to point out the errors of this false teaching by reminding them of the truths of the gospel.

Verse 6

that has come to you. On the face of it, this clause answers the simple question, when did the Colossians hear about this hope? Two additional observations can be made. First, the gospel is the subject of the verb "has come," as if the gospel could act of its own will and power. When the Bible speaks of God's word doing something, this is simply a vivid way of describing God acting through his word (Isa 55:11). Similarly, in the remainder of Colossians 1:6 Paul's image of the gospel as bearing fruit and growing refers to God's saving activity through the gospel (see Rom 1:16). Our second observation is that the gospel did not simply come and then depart. It remained with these Christians and continued to exercise its transforming power, as the final part of this verse makes clear.

Just as in the entire world this gospel is bearing fruit and growing. Paul now moves from the specific to the general. Not only has the gospel produced faith and love among the Colossians, it does this everywhere it goes. Their experience is not unusual. It is the norm. By saying this, he is also reminding them that they are a part of a larger movement that is spreading throughout the Roman Empire and beyond.

Paul uses a metaphor here to describe the gospel. It is like a tree that bears fruit and grows. How are we to interpret this comparison? If fruit is what a tree produces, what does the gospel produce? In Colossians 1:4-5 this fruit is the faith and love of the Colossians. How then should we understand the *growth* of the gospel among them? In Acts 6:7 the image of the gospel "growing" refers to successful evangelism. In Colossians, however, the image refers to the work of the gospel in causing believers to grow spiritually.

We see this in Colossians 1:10 where Paul uses the same two words to describe Christians "bearing fruit in every good deed, growing in the knowledge of God" It is true that the two images are slightly different. In Colossians 1:6 the gospel is likened to a tree, while in Colossians 1:10 it is Christians that are like trees. Yet, the basic truth remains the same: God works through the gospel to transform lives. The idea of evangelism is, nevertheless, present in Colossians 1:6. The saving activity of the gospel begins with the unconverted. It bears fruit first by awakening them to saving faith. It then continues to bear fruit in them while steadily spreading its influence in their thoughts and actions.

among you from the first day you heard it and understood the grace of God in truth. Now in the final part of the verse Paul returns from the general experience of Christians "in the entire world" to the specific experience of the Colossians. This same process of growth and fruit bearing that the gospel displays everywhere has been happening among the Colossians since the day of their conversion. Two observations here call for comment. First, the gospel is the basis of all true spiritual growth. It is as Christians grow in their understanding and application of the gospel that they bear the fruit of godliness, and they progress toward Christian maturity. By contrast, this fruit does not come by other means. Certain men, for example, were telling the Colossians that fasting and visions of heaven would produce godliness. Not so, says Paul: It is the power of God working through the gospel that achieves this.

The second observation is that Paul refers to the gospel here as "the grace of God." Earlier in Colossians 1:5 he described it as "the message of truth." In Colossians 1:25 he calls it "the word of God." Each description emphasizes a different aspect of the gospel. By referring to it in Colossians 1:6 as "the grace of God," Paul emphasizes that salvation is the free gift of God bestowed upon the undeserving (see the comments on Colossians 1:2). By contrast, the seductive teaching in Colossae was not grace but rules and regulations; it was not of God, but of man and the world (Col 2:20-23).

Verse 7

You learned the gospel from Epaphras. This clause tells how the Colossians heard and understood the gospel of the grace of God. Epaphras was a native of Colossae (Col 4:12). He apparently encountered Paul during his long stay in Ephesus (Acts 19:8-10) and was converted through the apostle's preaching. It was Paul's missionary strategy to concentrate his own efforts in major cities, while sending out missionaries to plant churches in the smaller towns of the region. Paul invited Epaphras to become a fellow worker in this missionary effort and sent him as an evangelist to the Lycus Valley. There he planted churches in Laodicea, Hierapolis, and Colossae.

> The verb translated "you learned" identifies Epaphras as a teacher. This verb means "to learn through instruction from a teacher." In other words, Paul is not simply referring here to the evangelistic message that Epaphras preached to win the unconverted. He is also referring to the systematic instruction that Epaphras imparted to the Colossians after their conversion in order to nurture them in the faith. The work of an evangelist is not simply to win the unconverted. He must also instruct new converts systematically and thoroughly in the meaning of the gospel—both its doctrinal content and its application to daily living.

The evangelist's task is spelled out in the Great Commission of Matthew 28:18-20. The disciples had been with Jesus for three years learning from him as their teacher. The Greek word for "disciple" is based on the verb "to learn" used here in Colossians 1:7. A disciple is a learner, a pupil, a follower. Thus, in Matthew 28:19 when Jesus commissioned these men to "go" and "make disciples" He was appointing them not just to win converts, but to instruct these converts even as they themselves were instructed by Jesus—"teaching them to obey everything I have commanded you" (Matt 28:20). Epaphras carried out this commission among the Colossians. He made them disciples of Jesus by instructing them in the gospel. In fact, much of this letter to the Colossians—namely the doctrinal and application–based sections—should be seen as a reminder of what Epaphras had taught them.

Three important principles of ministry can be seen here:

1. *Every new convert* should receive systematic instruction in the meaning of God's work of salvation through Christ.

2. It should be given by someone like Epaphras. That is, he should be a faithful servant of Christ, who understands these truths and is able to teach others (2 Tim 2:2).

3. The exact content of this instruction is the gospel of Christ—understood in a broad sense. It answers such basic questions as: What was God's original intention for the human race? What went wrong? What is man's condition apart from Christ? What is the nature of salvation? Who is Jesus Christ? What is the meaning of his death and resurrection? What must I do to be saved? What happens to a person at conversion? Is salvation forever? How should Christians conduct their lives? Most of these questions find answers in the book of Colossians. This is because Colossians is a book about the gospel. Paul wrote it to remind these new Christians of what Epaphras had taught them, and to help them understand it better.

Our dear fellow slave. Both Paul and Epaphras were "slaves," that is, servants of Christ. By calling Epaphras his fellow slave, Paul is emphasizing that they serve a common master and are co-workers in a common task. Paul is also emphasizing his confidence in Epaphras. He is assuring the Colossians that the gospel they learned from Epaphras is the true apostolic gospel and not some confused version of it.

a faithful minister of Christ on our behalf. This clause continues Paul's assurance regarding Epaphras. "Minister" is very similar to the term "slave." Both refer to one whose duty is to offer humble service to a superior. ("Minister" for example was often used of one who waited on tables, as in Acts 6:2.) The description of Epaphras as "faithful" points to his sustained commitment to Christ in his service. The words "on our behalf" indicate that Epaphras had ministered among them as Paul's representative. The teaching of Epaphras, says Paul, came to you with the seal of my authority.

Verse 8

who also told us of your love in the Spirit. Epaphras had recently traveled to Ephesus and informed Paul about the situation in Colossae. While this report included some disturbing news—news that Paul will deal with presently—his purpose at this stage of the letter is to dwell on those qualities in the Colossians for which he praises God. The phrase "your love in the Spirit" refers to a love that has been awakened and sustained in them by the Holy Spirit. This is the second mention of their love (see Col 1:4). Paul does this to emphasize his gratitude for this genuine fruit of the Spirit among them.

This second mention of the Colossians' love raises an important interpretative question. Earlier Paul indicated that their love was the fruit of their understanding of the gospel. Now in Colossians 1:8 he says it is the fruit of the Spirit. Is this a contradiction? Or, are there two separate ways that love is produced? In fact, the two are one and the same. The Spirit of God illumines the hearts of believers to understand his work of salvation, and he leads and empowers them to apply these truths in their daily lives. To put it more simply: God's word is a part of God's means for making us holy.

QUESTION 13

Colossians 1:3-8 introduces what section of the letter?

- A. The prayer section
- B. The introductory section
- C. The thanksgiving section
- D. The greetings section

QUESTION 14

What phrase served as a confession of faith in the early church?

- A. *Our Lord Jesus Christ*
- B. *Love for all the saints*
- C. *The message of truth, the gospel*
- D. *Hope, prepared for you in heaven*

QUESTION 15

The statements in Colossians 1:5 and 1 Peter 1:4 regarding what lies prepared for the believer in heaven stress the _____ of salvation.

QUESTION 16

In what two verses does Paul introduce the spiritual principle upon which the theme of the letter is based?

- A. Colossians 1:3-4
- B. Colossians 1:4-5
- C. Colossians 1:5-6
- D. Colossians 1:6-7

QUESTION 17

State briefly the basic principle upon which the theme of the letter is based. You may put it in your own words.

QUESTION 18

The task of an evangelist is simply to win the unconverted. He must then move on to fresh fields and leave the task of instruction and nurture to others. *True or False?*

QUESTION 19

Summarize briefly the three principles of ministry observed in the commentary in relation to Epaphras' work as an evangelist.

QUESTION 20

There are two separate ways that love is produced in the believer: (a) through understanding the gospel and (b) through the Spirit. *True or False?*

QUESTION 21

Re-read the principles of ministry in the Commentary on Colossians 1:7a (refer to this Article placed earlier in the lesson). Assume you wish to follow the example of Epaphras by preparing a short course for new converts. The title of this short course will be, "What Every Christian Should Know about Salvation." Take a moment right now to sketch out a list of topics you would wish to cover in such a course. Try to be more specific than the questions listed in the third principle. Record your answer in your Life Notebook.

QUESTION 22

What truths about salvation do you find in Colossians 1:3-8 that should be included in this course? You will be asked this same question in most of the remaining paragraphs of Colossians. By the end of the course you should have in hand the basic ingredients for teaching your own course on what every Christian should know about salvation. Record your answer in your Life Notebook.

Important Facts to Remember about Colossians 1:3-8

1. In Colossians 1:4-5 Paul introduces the spiritual principle on which the theme of the letter is based: Godly Christian conduct is the fruit of a proper understanding of God's saving work toward us through Christ.

2. In his work as an evangelist, Epaphras not only led the Colossians to faith in Christ, he also gave them systematic instruction in the meaning of the gospel—in both its doctrinal and application-based aspects. Much of Paul's letter to the Colossians serves as a reminder of this earlier instruction that they received from Epaphras.

Lesson 3 Self Check

QUESTION 1
Which of the six basic questions is missing from this list: *what, why, when, where, who* and _____?

QUESTION 2
The task of interpretation is to determine what the text means for us today. *True or False?*

QUESTION 3
It is best to read a commentary on a passage before studying it personally since this will help to alert you to the important issues. *True or False?*

QUESTION 4
It is possible for two good commentaries to disagree on the interpretation of a passage. *True or False?*

QUESTION 5
The basic meaning of the Greek word translated apostle is "one who is _____."

QUESTION 6
To be in Christ is the opposite of being in _____.

QUESTION 7
God's grace is his _____ favor toward sinners.

QUESTION 8
Paul introduces the spiritual principle that forms the basis of the theme of Colossians in what passage?
- A. Colossians 1:2-3
- B. Colossians 1:3-4
- C. Colossians 1:4-5
- D. Colossians 1:6-7

QUESTION 9
Simply stated, the principle referred to in Question 8 is that of Christian virtue being the fruit of the gospel. *True or False?*

QUESTION 10
Systematic instruction in the nature of God's saving work through Christ should not be given to every new convert but only to those who demonstrate a more advanced level of spiritual commitment and understanding. *True or False?*

Lesson 3 Answers to Questions

QUESTION 1: *Your answer should be similar to the following:*
Who is Paul? What is an apostle? Who is Jesus Christ? What does the term "in Christ" mean? What does it mean to be an apostle of Christ Jesus? Who decided that Paul should become an apostle of Christ? Who is Timothy? What does it mean that Timothy is Paul's brother? What does the word "saints" mean? Where is Colossae? And so forth.

QUESTION 2: *Your answer should be similar to the following:*
The key questions relating to the flow of thought are as follows: When did Paul and Timothy thank God? What is significant about the fact that they prayed for the Colossians? Why did they give thanks for the Colossians? What was the source of the Colossians' faith and love? What is this hope that lies prepared for them in heaven? How did the knowledge of this hope produce faith and love?

QUESTION 3: False [Deciding what the text means for us today is the task of application.]

QUESTION 4: *Your answer should be similar to the following:*
Since the knowledge of the hope that lies prepared for them in heaven produced in the Colossians faith and love, we can see in this a truth that is valid for all Christians. Stated rather specifically, this principle is that knowledge of the hope that lies prepared for believers in heaven should produce in them faith in Christ and love for all the saints. But the principle can also be stated in a more general way as follows: Christian virtue is the fruit of a proper understanding of God's saving work toward us through Christ.

QUESTION 5: *Your answer*

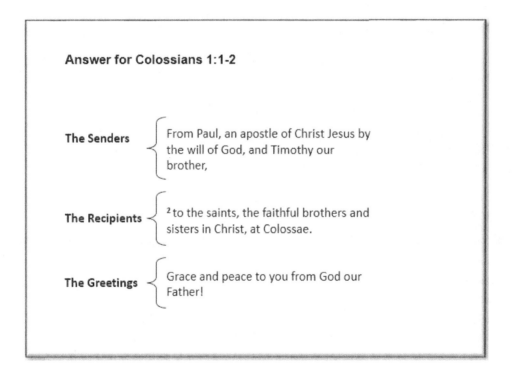

Textual Outline of Colossians 1:1-2

I. The Senders of the Letter: Paul and Timothy

II. The Recipients: "The Saints" in Colossae

III. The Greetings

Theme Statement of Colossians 1:1-2

Paul and Timothy to the Colossians: Grace and peace.

QUESTION 6
    C. One who is sent
QUESTION 7: False
QUESTION 8: *Your answer should be similar to the following:*
To be in Christ is the opposite of being in Adam. Those who are in Adam share in the condemnation and death that his disobedience brought upon the race descended from him. Christ came as a new Adam to restore what was lost through the original Adam. Acting as the representative of a new race, Christ died and rose again to bring forgiveness and new life to those who trust in him. To be in Christ therefore means one is no longer in Adam, but is a partaker of this salvation that Christ accomplished.
QUESTION 9: undeserved
QUESTION 10: *Your answer should be similar to the following:*
First, it refers to the fact that we are saved. He has redeemed us and adopted us as his sons and daughters through faith in Christ. Second, it refers to his fatherly care. his relationship to each believer is like that of a wise and loving father to his child.
QUESTION 11: *Your answer*
QUESTION 12: *Your answer*

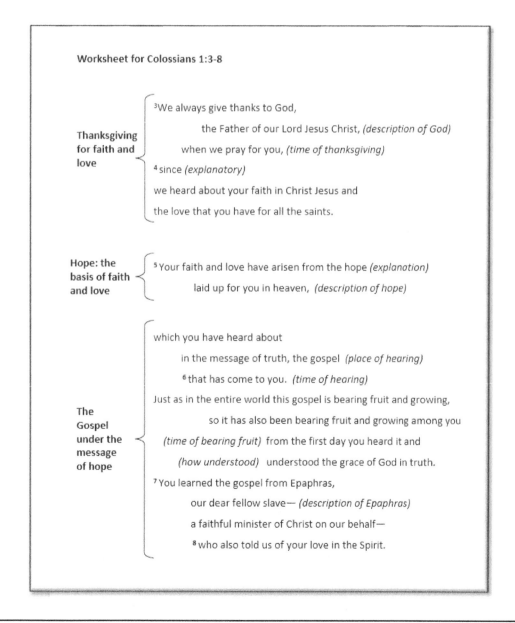

Lesson 3 Answers to Questions

Textual Outline of Colossians 1:3-8

I. Thanksgiving for faith and love. (Col 1:3-4)

    A. Paul and Timothy thank God. (Col 1:3)

    B. Reason for thanksgiving: The faith and love of the Colossians (Col 1:4)

II. Hope: The basis of faith and love. (Col 1:5a, b)

III. The Gospel: The message of hope. (Col 1:5c-8)

    A. The Colossians heard of this hope in the gospel. (Col 1:5c-6a)

    B. The gospel produces faith and love everywhere it goes. (Col 1:6b-d)

    C. Epaphras: The messenger of the gospel. (Col 1:7-8)

Theme Statement for Colossians 1:3-8

Paul thanks God because the gospel's message of secure hope in heaven has borne the fruit of faith and love in the Christians of Colossae.

QUESTION 13
    C. The thanksgiving section

QUESTION 14
    A. *Our Lord Jesus Christ*

QUESTION 15: certainty

QUESTION 16
    B. Colossians 1:4-5

QUESTION 17: *Your answer should be similar to the following:*
The principle was stated in a variety of ways in the commentary. The basic idea to remember is that godly Christian conduct results from a proper understanding of God's saving work toward us through Christ.

QUESTION 18: False [The work of an evangelist is not simply to win the unconverted. He must also instruct new converts systematically and thoroughly in the meaning of the gospel—both its doctrinal content and its application to daily living.]

QUESTION 19: *Your answer should be similar to the following:*
(1) Every new convert should receive systematic instruction in the meaning of Christian salvation. (2) The instructor should be a faithful servant of Christ who understands these truths and is able to teach others (2 Tim 2:2). (3) The exact content of this instruction is the gospel of Christ—understood in a broad sense.

QUESTION 20: False [Their love was the fruit of their understanding of the gospel. It is also the fruit of the Spirit. The two are one and the same. The Spirit of God illumines the hearts of believers to understand his work of salvation, and he leads and empowers them to apply these truths in their daily lives. To put it more simply: God's word is a part of God's means for making us holy.]

QUESTION 21: *Your answer*

QUESTION 22: *Your answer*

Lesson 3 Self Check Answers

QUESTION 1: how
QUESTION 2: False
QUESTION 3: False
QUESTION 4: True
QUESTION 5: sent
QUESTION 6: Adam
QUESTION 7: undeserved
QUESTION 8
    C. Colossians 1:4-5
QUESTION 9: True
QUESTION 10: False

Unit One Exam: Colossians

QUESTION 1
Which of the following is NOT one of the five steps for surveying a book of the Bible?
- A. Make an observational chart
- B. Research the background
- C. Trace the argument
- D. Write a theme statement

QUESTION 2
According to the lesson, Paul wrote to the Colossians from the city of _____.

QUESTION 3
According to the lesson, how recent was the founding of the church in Colossae when Paul wrote his letter?
- A. less than a year
- B. 2 years
- C. 5 years
- D. 7 years

QUESTION 4
Who were the false teachers?
- A. men who mixed Jewish and pagan teachings
- B. Jews
- C. Jewish Christians
- D. Greek philosophers

QUESTION 5
LIST THE FIVE STEPS FOR SURVEYING A BOOK OF THE BIBLE.QUESTION 6

In what passage does Paul express the theme and purpose of his letter to the Colossians?
- A. Colossians 1:9-10
- B. Colossians 1:21-22
- C. Colossians 1:28
- D. Colossians 2:6-7

QUESTION 7
In the simplified chart of Colossians, where does the subsection "The Gospel Explained" belong?
- A. Under the section entitled "Paul's Ministry"
- B. Under the section entitled "The Gospel Proclaimed and Defended"
- C. Under the section entitled "Live According to the Gospel"
- D. Under the section entitled "Thanksgiving Section"

QUESTION 8
Which section of Colossians is the theological heart of the letter?
- A. Colossians 1:15-20
- B. Colossians 1:24-2:5
- C. Colossians 2:9-15
- D. Colossians 2:16-3:4

QUESTION 9
In which section of Colossians does Paul apply the doctrinal truths of salvation to the false teaching?
- A. Colossians 2:9-15
- B. Colossians 2:16-3:4
- C. Colossians 3:5-4:6
- D. Colossians 1:24-2:5

QUESTION 10
The term referring to how the parts of a passage fit together to make up the whole is _____.

QUESTION 11
The three different types of "lines" in a paragraph that you should recognize are called main clauses, connecting words, and descriptive lines. *True or False?*

QUESTION 12
While we were still sinners is the main clause in the sentence *While we were still sinners, Christ died for us.* *True or False?*

QUESTION 13
The label you would write beside the connecting word *but* is _____.

QUESTION 14
In the verse "The Lord is my shepherd, I lack nothing" which of the following best describes the phrase "I lack nothing"?
- A. main clause
- B. cause to effect
- C. illustration
- D. result

QUESTION 15
In a structural diagram, how would you label the second clause in the following sentence? *Endure your suffering as discipline; God is treating you as sons.* _____

QUESTION 16
When making an outline based on a structural diagram, the main points (the Roman numerals) should be the topics you have _____.
- A. Underlined
- B. Placed on a line by themselves
- C. Emphasized by capitalizing all the letters
- D. Marked off with brackets

QUESTION 17

A common mistake in writing a theme statement is to _____.

    A. Include too many details

    B. Fail to identify the theme correctly

    C. Omit too many details

    D. Write an incomplete sentence

QUESTION 18

Which of the six basic questions is missing from this list? *What, why, when, where, who* _____.

QUESTION 19

It is the task of *application* to determine what the text means for us today. *True or False?*

QUESTION 20

It is best to read a commentary on a passage before studying it personally since this will help to alert you to the important issues. *True or False?*

QUESTION 21

To be in Christ is the opposite of being in _____.

QUESTION 22

God's grace is his _____ favor toward sinners.

QUESTION 23

Paul introduces the spiritual principle that forms the basis of the theme of Colossians in what passage?

    A. Colossians 1:2-3

    B. Colossians 1:3-4

    C. Colossians 1:4-5

    D. Colossians 1:6-7

QUESTION 24

The spiritual principle that forms the basis of the theme of Colossians is that Christian virtue is the fruit of the gospel. *True or False?*

QUESTION 25

The work of an evangelist is simply to proclaim the gospel to the lost. The task of instructing new converts belongs to pastors and teachers. *True or False?*

Unit 1 Exam Answers

QUESTION 1
   C. Trace the argument

QUESTION 2: Ephesus

QUESTION 3
   A. less than a year

QUESTION 4
   B. Jews

QUESTION 5
   D. The New English Translation

QUESTION 6
   A. Colossians 1:9-10

QUESTION 7
   C. Under the section entitled "Live According to the Gospel"

QUESTION 8
   C. Colossians 2:9-15

QUESTION 9
   B. Colossians 2:16-3:4

QUESTION 10: structure

QUESTION 11: True

QUESTION 12: False

QUESTION 13: Contrast

QUESTION 14:
   D. result

QUESTION 15: explanation

QUESTION 16
   D. Marked off with brackets

QUESTION 17
   A. Include too many details

QUESTION 18: how

QUESTION 19: True

QUESTION 20: False

QUESTION 21: Adam

QUESTION 22: undeserved

QUESTION 23
   C. Colossians 1:4-5

QUESTION 24: True

QUESTION 25: False

Unit Two: Redemption Through Christ

Unit One laid the foundation for your study of Colossians. You made a survey of the book, learned a three-step method for studying its individual paragraphs, and applied this method to the first two paragraphs. Unit Two will take you through the next six paragraphs, Colossians 1:9-29.

Lesson 4 covers Colossians 1:9-14. In Colossians 1:9-12a, you will examine Paul's prayer for the Colossians' continued growth to spiritual maturity. This prayer announces the theme of the letter. Paul's purpose in writing is to lead them to maturity in Christ. Paul begins to implement this purpose in the next paragraph, Colossians 1:12b-14. He does this by reminding them of what God the Father already accomplished: He has qualified them to share the heavenly inheritance of his people, the saints. Proof of this is seen by God rescuing them out of the domain of darkness and transferred them into the kingdom of his Son.

Colossians 1:15-20 is the subject of Lesson 5. This is probably the best known and most studied passage in Colossians. It focuses on the person of Christ and answers the question, Who is this One through whom we were redeemed and into whose kingdom we have been transferred? Finally, in Lesson 6 you will study the three paragraphs of Colossians 1:21-29. These passages deal with the application of Christ's reconciling work to the Colossian church (Col 1:21-23), Paul's commission to proclaim this message of reconciliation among the Gentiles (Col 1:24-27), and his goal of bringing every convert to maturity in Christ (Col 1:28-29).

Unit Outline

Lesson 4: Prayer for Growth, Praise for Redemption—Colossians:1:9-14

Lesson 5: Christ, First in All Things—Colossians 1:15-20

Lesson 6: Paul's Message, Paul's Ministry—Colossians 1:21-29

Unit Objectives

When you have completed this unit, you should be able to:

- Discuss the meaning of Paul's prayer in Colossians 1:9-12b for knowledge of God's will that results in a walk worthy of the Lord, and the value of this prayer for your own ministry.
- Explain what it means that God rescued believers out of the domain of darkness and transferred them into the kingdom of his Son (Col 1:12b-14).
- Understand what it means that Christ is God's agent in both creation and new creation, and the role of his death and resurrection in renewing the creation (Col 1:15-20).
- Explain the believer's former state of alienation, and the nature, purpose, and condition of reconciliation (Col 1:21-23).
- Describe the nature of Paul's commission to proclaim the gospel, and discuss the role of suffering in his ministry in relation to the suffering you experience in your ministry (Col 1:23-29).
- Identify the goal of Paul's ministry and evaluate your own ministry in light of this goal (Col 1:28-29).

Lesson 4: Prayer for Growth, Praise for Redemption—Colossians 1:9-14

Lesson Introduction

In the last lesson, you began your detailed study of the individual paragraphs of Colossians by using the three-step method explained in Lessons 2 and 3. The salutation in Colossians 1:1-2 introduced you to some important concepts that we will meet again in Colossians. These include the terms "apostle" and "saints," and what it means to be "in Christ" versus "in Adam." The second paragraph, Colossians 1:3-8, begins the thanksgiving section of the letter. Here Paul tells these new Christians of his thankful prayers to God for how the knowledge of the hope that is prepared for them in heaven has borne in them the fruit of faith and love. This statement introduces the basic principle upon which Paul bases the theme of his letter. The principle is: The knowledge of God's saving work toward us in Christ bears the fruit of godly conduct. Lesson 4 shows how Paul develops this basic principle in two ways.

Topic 1 covers Colossians 1:9-12a. Paul incorporates this principle into his prayer for the Colossians to be filled with the knowledge of God's will so that they might walk in a manner worthy of the Lord. This prayer expresses the theme and purpose of the letter.

Topic 2 covers Colossians 1:12b-14. This paragraph focuses on the second element of the principle: the knowledge of God's saving work toward us. We can be certain that he has qualified us to share the heavenly inheritance of the saints because already he has rescued us out of darkness and transferred us into the kingdom of his beloved Son.

Lesson Outline

Topic 1: Prayer for Spiritual Growth (Col 1:9-12a)

Topic 2: Praise for Redemption (Col 1:12b-14)

Lesson Objectives

There are two major objectives in this lesson. By the end of this lesson, you should be able to:

- Explain the concepts of illumination and sanctification, the meaning and importance of knowing God's will (Col 1:9), what it means to walk worthy of the Lord (Col 1:10), and how Colossians 1:9-10 expresses the theme of the letter.
- Define and discuss the following concepts from Colossians 1:12b-14: the inheritance of the saints in the light, the dominion of darkness, the kingdom of God's Son, and rescue out of the darkness and into the kingdom as God's act of redemption through Christ.

Memory Verse

In this lesson, you are to memorize Colossians 1:9-10a. This passage expresses the theme and purpose of the letter. Be prepared to quote it from memory in your next group meeting.

> "For this reason we also, from the day we heard about you, have not ceased praying for you and asking God to fill you with the knowledge of his will in all spiritual wisdom and understanding, so that you may live worthily of the Lord and please him in all respects"

Assignments

Follow the three-step procedure outlined below for each of the paragraphs of Colossians covered in this lesson.

Step 1:

    (a) Make a structural diagram of the passage on the worksheet provided.

    (b) Summarize the results in an outline and theme statement.

    (c) Compare your conclusions with those in the answer section.

Step 2:

    Examine the details of the paragraph. Record your observations, interpretations, and applications on the worksheet.

Step 3:

    (a) Read the commentary on this passage of Colossians.

    (b) Answer the questions in the lesson.

    (c) Pay special attention to the *Important Facts to Remember*.

Topic 1: Prayer for Spiritual Growth (Col 1:9-12a)

Paul's message to the Colossians opens on a note of thanksgiving. He tells them of his gratitude to God that the gospel's message of secure hope in heaven has borne the fruit of faith and love in their lives (Col 1:3-8). Now in Colossians 1:9-12a, he turns from thanksgiving to intercession. His constant prayer is that this knowledge of God and his saving work will grow to full maturity so that it might produce in them an even more abundant harvest of Christian virtue. This prayer of intercession expresses the theme of the letter. Paul's concern is for the Colossians to be firmly established in their understanding and commitment to the gospel of Christ so that they might "live worthily of the Lord and please him in all respects." (Col 1:10)

Begin your study by reading Colossians 1:9-12a, and then by reading the Worksheet on Colossians 1:9-12a below. Copy it in your Life Notebook and complete step 1: a structural diagram, outline, and theme statement. You can check your results by comparing them with the Answers for Colossians 1:9-12. Next, complete step 2 by recording on the worksheet your detailed observations, interpretations, and applications. For step 3, carefully read the Commentary on Colossians 1:9-12a. Next, answer the questions, taking special note of the *Important Facts to Remember*.

Worksheet for Colossians 1:9-12a

⁹ FOR THIS REASON WE ALSO,

    from the day we heard about you,

have not ceased praying for you and asking God

to fill you with the knowledge of his will

    in all spiritual wisdom and understanding,

¹⁰ SO THAT

you may live worthily of the Lord and please him in all respects—

    bearing fruit in every good deed,

    growing in the knowledge of God,

    ¹¹ being strengthened with all power according to his glorious might

    FOR

    the display of all patience and steadfastness,

    joyfully ¹²giving thanks to the Father.

Commentary on Colossians 1:9-12a

2. Prayer for Knowledge Resulting in Godly Conduct—Colossians 1:9-12a

Paul's message to the Colossians opened on a note of thanksgiving. He told them of his gratitude to God that the gospel's message of secure hope in heaven had borne the fruit of faith and love in their lives (Col 1:3-8). Now in Colossians 1:9-12a, he turns from thanksgiving to intercession. His constant prayer is that this knowledge of God and his saving work will grow to full maturity so that it might produce in them an even more abundant harvest of Christian virtue. This prayer of intercession expresses the theme of the letter. Paul's concern is for the Colossians to be firmly established in their understanding and commitment to the gospel of Christ so that they might "live worthily of the Lord."

Verse 9

For this reason we also. The prayer in Colossians 1:9-12 comes in response to the encouraging news from Epaphras regarding the Colossians' faith and love. It is for this reason that Paul and Timothy have been interceding for them. The word "also" links this statement with Colossians 1:3, "We always give thanks to God."

from the day we heard about you, This line tells when they began praying. The wording echoes Colossians 1:6. Just as the gospel has been bearing fruit in the Colossians since the day they heard it, so Paul and Timothy have been praying for them since the day they heard about them.

have not ceased praying for you and asking. Paul and Timothy not only thank God for the Colossians, they also continually intercede for them. As in Colossians 1:3, these prayers are not literally unceasing and uninterrupted. Rather, they were frequent and regular. These times of prayer were a vital part of Paul's ministry toward the Colossians (see Col 2:1-2). Later in Colossians 1:28-29 he explains that the goal of his ministry is to bring each and every person to maturity in Christ. The prayer of Colossians 1:9-12 expresses this goal.

God to fill you with the knowledge of his will. These words introduce the content of Paul's prayer. It has two parts. The first is a request for the Colossians to be filled with the knowledge of God's will (Col 1:9c,d). The second states the purpose of this knowledge. It is that they might walk in a manner worthy of the Lord (Col 1:10-12a). God's will in this context refers to his saving will. By this we mean his plan of salvation as revealed in the gospel (Gal 1:4; Eph 1:5, 9). It is God's overall plan to redeem his fallen creation. It includes what he has done in the past, what he will do in the future, and how he desires his people to conduct themselves in the light of these truths.

Epaphras taught the Colossians these things in the beginning. They had embraced this message by faith and it had borne the fruit of godly conduct in their lives. Yet their knowledge remained imperfect. Therefore, Paul prays that God will bring them to a full and mature understanding of these truths. And it is to help them achieve this understanding that Paul is writing to them.

Why is this knowledge so important?

1. It is the object of faith. Faith does not rest on ignorance but on knowledge. Faith means belief and trust. It includes commitment. To grow in the knowledge of God's will means to grow in faith and commitment to these truths.

2. It is the basis for action. Its purpose is for believers to walk in a manner worthy of the Lord (Col 1:10). What a person believes and thinks determines the decisions he makes. The one who understands God's will and trusts him is able to choose the right path. The opposite of knowing God's will is a life of foolishness (Eph 5:18).

3. It is a means of spiritual growth. As believers grow in their understanding and application of God's will, they progress toward Christian maturity. We will have more to say on this subject as the passage unfolds.

4. It is a safeguard against false teachings. Those who have a mature understanding of God's truth will not easily be taken captive by false teachings (Col 2:8).

Knowledge of God's saving work is foundational to the Christian walk. We must know and understand it in order to act correctly. For this reason, all Christians should seek to grow in their understanding of God's plan of salvation as revealed in the gospel. It is a central responsibility of pastors and Christian workers to impart this understanding.

Finally, notice that this prayer request (Col 1:9) together with its purpose (Col 1:10) expresses the theme of the letter. As we saw earlier, Paul introduced this theme in Colossians 1:4-5. This passage displays the basic principle that godly Christian conduct is the fruit of a proper understanding of God's saving work toward us. Now in Colossians 1:9-10, Paul makes this principle the basis of his prayer that the Colossians might be filled with the knowledge of God's saving will so that they might walk worthy of the Lord. This prayer expresses the theme and purpose of this letter. Paul writes to instruct them in these matters so that they might walk accordingly.

in all spiritual wisdom and understanding. How are they to be filled with this knowledge? Knowledge of the gospel requires human teachers (such as Epaphras). However, it is only through the enabling ministry of the Holy Spirit that believers can have the wisdom to understand and properly apply God's truth. This enabling ministry is called *illumination* (see Eph 1:18; 2 Cor 4:6).

The work of illumination is needed because the human mind—including the will and desires—has been darkened by Adam's fall. Sin is rooted in the human mind, in its thinking (Gen 6:5). Apart from Christ all live in moral and spiritual darkness (Col 1:13; Eph 4:18). To the natural man the things of the Spirit of God are foolishness; he cannot understand them (1 Cor 2:14). When a person turns to Christ, the light comes on. He now sees with eyes of faith. What was previously foolishness to him, he now recognizes as the wisdom of God.

But the effects of the Fall are not removed all at once. The believer still needs to have his mind further renewed, his will, thinking, and desires further changed. This is why Paul refers to the process of spiritual growth as "the renewing of your mind" in Romans 12:2. Similarly in Colossians 3:10, he describes the believer as "being renewed in knowledge according to the image of the one who created it." This work of renewal goes forward as the Holy Spirit enables believers to understand and apply God's Word. This divine work of renewal, which begins with the new birth, is called "sanctification." The term is based on a word that means holy. Sanctification is the process of being made holy.

Because of the remaining effects of the Fall, Christians are not able by themselves to understand and apply God's word properly. Therefore, we must look to God daily in prayerful dependence to illuminate his Word (see Ps 86:11; 119:34).

Verse 10

<u>**So that**</u>. These words introduce the second part of Paul's prayer of intercession. It explains the purpose of this knowledge of God's will.

you may live worthily of the Lord and please him in all respects. The purpose of this knowledge is that they might conduct their lives in accordance with it. The Old Testament frequently describes a person's conduct in terms of how he **lives or walks** (Prov 2:20; Ps 1:1). This metaphor appears three other times (Col 2:6; 3:7; 4:5). "The Lord" in this context refers to Christ (Col 1:3). It is through him that God is carrying out his plan of salvation. Paul's meaning here is the same as in Philippians 1:27 where he exhorts his readers to "conduct yourselves in a manner worthy of the gospel of Christ."

The word "worthy" means in keeping with or in a corresponding way. Paul's prayer is for the Colossians to be filled with an understanding of God's saving work through Christ so that they might conduct their lives in a corresponding way.

The logic of this statement appears repeatedly in Paul's letters. Let your actions correspond to what he has done for you. It is not, "Do these things so that you may earn salvation." Rather, it is, "Because he has already graciously blessed you with salvation, live in accordance with it." For example, Paul writes in Colossians 3:13, "Just as the Lord has forgiven you, so you also forgive others." Here we see that the knowledge of what God has done for us in Christ leads to a corresponding action. To walk worthy of the Lord, therefore, means to live out the gospel of Christ.

The final words of Colossians 1:10a explain the aim of this conduct. It is to please the Lord in every way. In short, this is the aim of the Christian's life (2 Cor 5:9). It is not to please ourselves. Not even Christ pleased himself (Rom 15:3). As the redeemed servants of Christ, our goal is to please him. This verse leaves no doubt regarding how to do this. It is by walking in a manner worthy of the Lord—that is, by leading a life that corresponds to the truth of the gospel.

This verse contains one of the most basic principles of Christian living. God desires his people to conduct themselves in a way that corresponds to what he has done for them through Christ. First of all, this means they must understand his saving work. Studying the book of Colossians is a good way to gain this understanding. Secondly, it means applying these truths in the various situations of daily life.

Bearing fruit in every good deed. This is the first of four statements that explains more about the nature of living a life that is worthy of the Lord and pleasing to him. Earlier in Colossians 1:6, Paul used the phrase "bearing fruit and growing," which suggests the image of a fruit tree to describe the powerful action of the gospel to produce the fruit of faith and love in their lives. Now in Colossians 1:10, he again takes up this image. His prayer is that a greater knowledge of the gospel will produce in them an even more abundant harvest of godly virtues demonstrated "in every good deed." This statement also illustrates the place of good deeds in the Christian life. No one can earn salvation by doing good works (Rom 3:20). Rather, those who have received the gift of salvation should do good works in response to God's work for them.

Growing in the knowledge of God. Paul continues with the suggested image of a tree to explain this aspect of the Christian walk. Not only does the tree produce a harvest of fruit, it continues to grow putting forth new shoots in preparation for the next crop. So it is with the Christian life. Just as the knowledge of God's will produces godly conduct, so the response of obedience is followed by a fresh growth of knowledge. Knowledge leads to application, application to deeper knowledge, faith, and commitment. By contrast, Romans 1:18-32 describes the downward spiral into deepening darkness and sin of those who reject the knowledge of God (compare Eph 4:22). This spiral is reversed in those who have embraced the knowledge of God in the gospel. By growing in the knowledge of God, they are being made more and more like Christ (Col 3:10). This is the process of *sanctification*.

Verse 11

being strengthened with all power according to his glorious might. The third characteristic of this worthy walk is that God's power is at work within Christians enabling them to live in this way. We do not have the strength in ourselves to do it. Jesus said, "apart from me, you can accomplish nothing" (Jn 15:5). The Christian life must be lived in dependence upon God's sustaining empowering grace.

for the display of. These words introduce the purpose of this strengthening.

> **all patience and steadfastness**. The purpose of this strength is to give believers patience and steadfastness to persevere in this worthy walk in spite of every kind of obstacle. The two Greek words translated "patience" and "steadfastness" mean very nearly the same thing. Paul uses them together to emphasize the single idea that the Christian life requires patient and steadfast endurance. Patient endurance is a quality of faith (Heb 6:12-15; 12:1-3; Jas 5:10-11).
>
> There are two aspects of this quality; one concerns the future, the other the present. It means (1) maintaining a confident expectation of the future fulfillment of God's promise ("the hope of the gospel") while (2) enduring patiently the trials and temptations of the present. The Colossians demonstrated this quality of steadfast faith up until that time. Paul gives thanks for this in Colossians 1:3-4. His concern now is that God might further strengthen them so that they will continue steadfastly to follow Christ.
>
> *Verse 12*
>
> **joyfully giving thanks to the Father**. This fourth characteristic of the "worthy life" must be seen in connection with the third. It is one thing to bear trials and hardships with patient endurance. It is another to do so with joyful thanksgiving. This truly demonstrates God's sustaining power! We see an example of this with Paul and Silas "singing hymns of praise to God" after being beaten and thrown into the town jail (Acts 16:25, NASB). The experience of joy was common among the early Christians (Acts 2:46; Phil 4:4; 1 Thess 5:16), especially in the midst of suffering (1 Thess 1:6; Heb 10:34). We saw earlier that conduct worthy of the Lord is conduct that corresponds to what the Lord has done to bring salvation. One very important way to do this is to praise God joyfully for this wonderful gift.
>
> These verses provide a model of intercessory prayer. As a minister of the gospel seeking the spiritual welfare of the Colossians, Paul made this his regular prayer. He recognized that what they needed most was to grow in their knowledge of God and his saving will so that they might live in a way that pleases him. Those who minister God's Word today can do no better than to follow Paul's example.

QUESTION 1

In Colossians 1:9, Paul tells the Colossians of his constant prayers for them to be filled with the knowledge of God's will. What does Paul mean by "God's will" in this context?

QUESTION 2

Why is the knowledge of God's will so important to the Christian life? Give four reasons using four short sentences.

QUESTION 3

Paul prays for the Colossians to be filled with the knowledge of God's will so that they might live **worthily** of the Lord (Col 1:10). Give a definition of the term "worthily," and then use it to clarify the meaning of Paul's prayer for the Colossians to live worthily of the Lord.

QUESTION 4

The term used to describe the work of the Holy Spirit that enables believers to understand and apply God's truth is _____.

QUESTION 5

The theological term for the process of spiritual growth or renewal is _____.

QUESTION 6

Paul prayed regularly for the Christians under his care. He prayed that God would cause them to grow to a full and mature understanding of his plan of salvation including how to live in accordance with it. He prayed that this knowledge would bear fruit in conduct worthy of the Lord. What does this tell you about the priorities and aims of Paul's ministry? In what ways does your ministry reflect these priorities? In what ways are they different? Can you think of things you could do in the future to bring the aims and priorities of your work more into line with the ones we see in Colossians 1:9-12a? Record your response in your Life Notebook.

QUESTION 7

What truths do you see in Colossians 1:9-12a that should be included in your course, *What Every Christian Should Know about Salvation*? If you need to refresh your memory regarding the nature and content of this course, reread question 21 in Lesson 3 and the principles of ministry in the Commentary on Colossians 1:7a (provided below).

> *Verse 7*
>
> **You learned the gospel from Epaphras**. This clause tells how the Colossians heard and understood the gospel of the grace of God. Epaphras was a native of Colossae (Col 4:12). He apparently encountered Paul during his long stay in Ephesus (Acts 19:8-10) and was converted through the apostle's preaching. It was Paul's missionary strategy to concentrate his own efforts in major cities, while sending out missionaries to plant churches in the smaller towns of the region. Paul invited Epaphras to become a fellow worker in this missionary effort and sent him as an evangelist to the Lycus Valley. There he planted churches in Laodicea, Hierapolis, and Colossae.
>
> The verb translated "you learned" identifies Epaphras as a teacher. This verb means "to learn through instruction from a teacher." In other words, Paul is not simply referring here to the evangelistic message that Epaphras preached to win the unconverted. He is also referring to the systematic instruction that Epaphras imparted to the Colossians after their conversion in order to nurture them in the faith. The work of an evangelist is not simply to win the unconverted. He must also instruct new converts systematically and thoroughly in the meaning of the gospel—both its doctrinal content and its application to daily living.
>
> The evangelist's task is spelled out in the Great Commission of Matthew 28:18-20. The disciples had been with Jesus for three years learning from him as their teacher. The Greek word for "disciple" is based on the verb "to learn" used here in Colossians 1:7. A disciple is a learner, a pupil, a follower. Thus, in Matthew 28:19 when Jesus commissioned these men to "go" and "make disciples" He was appointing them not just to win converts, but to instruct these converts even as they themselves were instructed by Jesus—"teaching them to obey everything I have commanded you" (Matt 28:20). Epaphras carried out this commission among the Colossians. He made them disciples of Jesus by instructing them in the gospel. In fact, much of this letter to the Colossians—namely the doctrinal and application–based sections—should be seen as a reminder of what Epaphras had taught them.
>
> **Three important principles of ministry can be seen here:**
>
> 1. *Every new convert* should receive systematic instruction in the meaning of God's work of salvation through Christ.
>
> 2. It should be given by someone like Epaphras. That is, he should be a faithful servant of Christ, who understands these truths and is able to teach others (2 Tim 2:2).
>
> 3. The exact content of this instruction is the gospel of Christ—understood in a broad sense. It answers such basic questions as: What was God's original intention for the human race? What went wrong? What is man's condition apart from Christ? What is the nature of salvation? Who is Jesus Christ? What is the meaning of his death and resurrection? What must I do to be saved? What happens to a person at conversion? Is salvation forever? How should Christians conduct their lives? Most of these questions find answers in the book of Colossians. This is because Colossians is a book about the gospel. Paul wrote it to remind these new Christians of what Epaphras had taught them, and to help them understand it better.

Important Facts to Remember about Colossians 1:9-12a

1. Paul's prayer request in Colossians 1:9-10 expresses the theme and purpose of the letter. His request is for the Colossians to be filled with the knowledge of God's will so that they might walk in a manner worthy of the Lord. What Paul prays for the Colossians, he seeks to accomplish through his instruction in this letter to them.

2. In this context "God's will" refers to his saving will, his plan of salvation revealed in the gospel. It is his overall plan to redeem his fallen creation. It includes what he has done in the past, what he will do in the future, and how he desires his people to live in the light of these truths. The aim of this letter is to remind the readers of "God's will" so that they might walk in accordance with it.

3. This knowledge is important because it is the object of faith, the basis of action, a means of spiritual growth, and a safeguard against false teachings.

4. It is through the enabling ministry of the Holy Spirit that believers can properly understand and apply these truths. This enabling ministry is called illumination.

5. God's Spirit illuminates these truths in order to renew our minds. This work of renewal is necessary because of the remaining effects of the Fall. Spiritual growth is the process of renewal in which God is at work to renew us according to his image (Col 3:10). This process is called sanctification.

6. The purpose of knowing God's will (his plan of salvation revealed in the gospel) is that we might "**live *worthily* of the Lord**" (emphasis added). The term "worthily" means in keeping with or in a corresponding way. Therefore, to live worthily of the Lord means to conduct ourselves in a way that corresponds to God's will. It means to live in accordance with the gospel.

7. Colossians 1:9-12a provides a model of how to pray for others.

Topic 2: Praise for Redemption (Col 1:12b-14)

In the previous paragraph, Paul informed the Colossians of his continual prayers for their spiritual growth. He prays that they might be filled with the knowledge of God's will—that is, with the knowledge of God's plan of redemption including how he desires his people to live—so that they might walk in a manner worthy of the Lord. Paul ended his prayer in Colossians 1:12a by describing this manner of life that is worthy of the Lord as one of joyful thanksgiving to the Father. Now in Colossians 1:12b, Paul proceeds to explain **why** they should give thanks to the Father. This shows the proper connection between thanksgiving and knowledge. Our understanding of God's gift of salvation should go hand in hand with a joyful response of praise. Paul starts by explaining what God did for them in conversion. He qualified them to share the inheritance of the saints in the light. Proof of this is seen in the fact that he has already rescued them out of darkness and transferred them into the kingdom of his beloved Son.

Begin your study by reading Colossians 1:12b-14, and then by reading the Worksheet on Colossians 1:12b-14 (see next page). Copy it in your Life Notebook and complete step 1: a structural diagram, outline, and theme statement. You can check your results by comparing them with the Answer section for Colossians 1:12b-14. Next, complete step 2 by recording on the worksheet your detailed observations, interpretations, and applications. For step 3, carefully read the Commentary on Colossians 1:12b-14. Next, answer the questions, taking special note of the *Important Facts to Remember*.

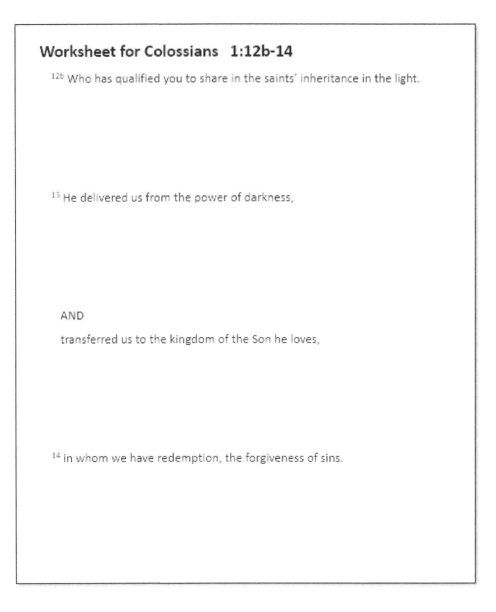

Commentary on Colossians 1:12b-14
B. Reason for Giving Thanks: Redemption Through Christ—Colossians 1:12b-23

In the previous paragraph, Paul informed the Colossians that he had been praying for their spiritual growth from the day he heard of their conversion. He prays that they might be filled with the knowledge of God's will—that is, with the knowledge of God's plan of redemption, including how he desires his people to live—so they might walk in a manner worthy of the Lord. This prayer expresses the theme of the letter. It also expresses its purpose. Paul writes to instruct these young believers in the nature of God's gift of salvation and how they should live in the light of these truths.

To carry out this purpose, Paul proceeds in Colossians 1:12b-23 to give an overview of God's work of salvation through Christ. This is the first of two major sections in Colossians devoted to the nature of God's saving work. The second is Colossians 2:9-15. Paul uses the first section to introduce various subjects which he then develops in more detail in the second. After explaining the nature of salvation in these two sections, he goes on in Colossians 2:16-4:6 to explain how believers should conduct themselves on the basis of these truths.

1. An Inheritance Among God's People—Colossians 1:12b-14

Paul ended his prayer in Colossians 1:12a by describing the Christian life as one of joyful thanksgiving to the Father. Now in Colossians 1:12b, he begins to explain why they should thank him. This shows the proper connection between thanksgiving and knowledge. Our understanding of God's gift of salvation should go hand-in-hand with a joyful response of praise. Paul begins by explaining what God did for them in conversion. He brought them out of darkness into the light, from Satan's kingdom into his Son's, where they share in the blessings He has allotted to his holy people through Christ.

Verse 12

giving thanks to the Father who has qualified you to share in the saints' inheritance in the light. Recall that in Colossians 1:2, Paul addressed the Colossians Christians as "saints." Now in Colossians 1:12 he returns to this topic. He is reminding them of what it means to be a saint so that they might praise God for this blessing. As we learned earlier, the word "saints" means holy ones, people set apart by God and for God. The saints are the covenant people of God in all ages, the community of salvation. In the era of the old covenant, Israel was God's holy people (Ex 19:6). Now that the promised Messiah has come, God has established a new covenant with his people. He is drawing Jews and Gentiles together into a single people on an equal basis through faith in Christ. It is this great truth that underlies Paul's statement here (see also Eph 2:11-3:6). God has included the Gentile-born Colossians among his saints. They are now "the elect of God, holy and dearly loved" (Col 3:12).

Paul does not say in this verse how God qualified the Colossians to be saints and to share their inheritance. This will come later (see Colossians 1:14, 20-22; 2:11-15). The important point is simply that he did it. The Colossians did not qualify themselves. Moreover, they need not bow to the pressure of the local Jews who taught that circumcision and obedience to the Law of Moses are what qualifies a person for membership in God's people. Paul's point is that God has already qualified them. He did it at the time of their conversion. This was an act of grace, and for it they should give thanks.

What does it mean to share in the inheritance of the saints in the light? The statement refers to the blessings of salvation believers receive at the time of conversion. But to illustrate this, Paul uses language drawn from the exodus, a well-known story in the Old Testament. When Israel came forth from Egypt, God gave them the land of Canaan as their inheritance. Each tribe and family received a portion of land as their share in the inheritance. By using this language, Paul paints a small picture that helps his readers understand the nature of their own inheritance. As God's people of the old covenant received a share of the inheritance of the land of Canaan, so his people of the new covenant have received a share in the inheritance of a new realm—the realm of light.

The words "in the light" describe the location or environment of the allotted blessings. It is a place characterized by light. The Colossians have entered this place and now share its blessings together with the rest of the saints. That the Colossians themselves are now in the light is evident from the following explanation in Colossians 1:13, "He delivered us from the power of darkness." Many passages emphasize this truth that conversion means passage from darkness to light (Acts 26:18; Eph 5:8; 1 Pet 2:9). Coming to the light means repenting of evil and embracing the truth of the life-giving gospel (2 Cor 4:4; Jn 8:12).

The light thus symbolizes salvation. It is the domain ruled by Christ and characterized by goodness and truth.

Verse 13

He delivered us from the power of darkness. Paul switches from "you" (Col 1:12) to "us" in this verse because he wishes to make clear that what he says about the Colossians holds true for all believers. The Colossians are now in the light where they share in the blessings of God's people because he rescued them out of the darkness and transferred them into the realm of light—namely, the kingdom of his beloved Son. In order to enter the realm of light, it was first necessary for God to rescue us out of the realm of darkness. The "power of darkness" is the sphere of authority characterized by the absence of light and ruled by Satan (see Acts 26:18; Jn 12:31; 2 Cor 4:4; 1 Jn 5:19). Darkness symbolizes not only evil and falsehood, but also the condition of those under judgment. All those outside of Christ are held under this dominion. Later in Colossians 2:13, Paul describes this condition as one of spiritual death resulting from sin (see also Eph 2:1-3).

Christ came to liberate Satan's captives and to bring them into his own kingdom (1 Jn 3:8). His work of liberation began during his earthly ministry (see Lk 11:14-22). In the events of Christ's betrayal, arrest, and execution Satan appeared to gain the upper hand (Jn 13:2; Lk 22:53). But through his death and resurrection, Christ won the victory over the powers of death, sin, and Satan, and thereby opened the way of deliverance from the dominion of darkness. When a person responds in faith to the message of the gospel, God applies to him the saving work of Christ. He thereby rescues him out of Satan's dark domain and transfers him into the realm of light, the kingdom of God's beloved Son.

And. This word introduces the second part of Paul's explanation of why Christians now **"share in the saints' inheritance in the light."**

transferred us to the kingdom of the Son he loves. Our present existence "in the light" is the result of a two-part act of salvation. (1) God rescued us out of the darkness of Satan's domain. (2) He transferred us into a new sphere of authority, the kingdom of his beloved Son. Thus, the kingdom of God's Son is simply another way of describing the realm of light where we now share the inheritance of the saints. By describing our entry into the light of salvation as deliverance from one sphere of authority and entry into another, Paul is emphasizing that conversion means a transfer of lordship. Satan, the former tyrant who held us captive, no longer has any claim on us. We have a new Lord and King, "our Lord Jesus Christ" (Col 1:3).

This leads to an important point of application. We observed earlier that Paul's basic principle for applying the truth of the gospel is that our conduct should correspond to what God has done for us. What then is the proper response to the deliverance and transfer of dominions described in Colossians 1:13? Stated simply, we should trust and obey our new Lord. We should no longer live as though we still belonged to the old master—following in the ways of darkness. Instead, we should submit in loving obedience to Christ. We should allow him to shape all of our thinking, relationships, and actions.

Colossians 1:13 raises an important theological question. It clearly states that Christians have already entered Christ's kingdom and already share in its blessings (see also Rom 14:17). Other passages, however, clearly state that the kingdom of God and its inheritance remain in the future (Mt 25:34; 1 Cor 15:50; Gal 5:21). It will be established at Christ's return. How are we to understand this? Are there two kingdoms—one present called the kingdom of God's Son, and the other future called the kingdom of God? No. These statements simply reflect two different stages of the same kingdom. It is variously called the kingdom of God, the kingdom of his Son, and, on one occasion, the kingdom of Christ and God (Eph 5:5). It is God's kingdom which he has entrusted to Christ, his incarnate Son, to rule in order to restore his fallen creation ("Sit at my right hand until I put your enemies under your feet"; Mk 12:36; Acts 2:34-36; 1 Cor 15:25-28).

> The first stage of the kingdom is the present era in which Christ rules from heaven (Mk 16:19; Eph 1:20-22; Col 3:1). During this period, those who believe "the good news about the kingdom of God" (Acts 8:12) are being rescued out of the dominion of darkness and transferred into the kingdom. The second stage will begin when Christ returns in glory and establishes the kingdom on earth (Mt 25:31-34). At that time, the people of God will experience in full measure the kingdom and its inheritance. Nevertheless, we have already begun to experience these things in part. We have already entered the kingdom in its present stage. And the blessings we now share "in the light" are a foretaste and pledge of the salvation that is now laid up in heaven and will be revealed at Christ's coming (Col 1:5; 3:4; 1 Pet 1:4-5).
>
> *Verse 14*
>
> **in whom we have redemption, the forgiveness of sins**. This brief statement explains the role of Christ, the Son, in the deliverance described in Colossians 1:13. Our deliverance was accomplished through the forgiveness of sins that he won on our behalf, and which we receive when we believe in him. This statement about Christ's role in salvation serves as a transition to an expanded explanation in Colossians 1:15-23 and is taken up again in Colossians 2:11-15.
>
> Paul uses the word "redemption" here to describe our deliverance. To redeem something means basically to recover it by the payment of a price—to buy it back. It came to be used of deliverance from some great adversity (such as oppression, captivity, slavery) and the cost required to achieve this deliverance. The premier example from the Old Testament is the Exodus, in which God redeemed his people Israel out of bondage in Egypt (Ex 6:6-7). Similarly, when God delivered us out of bondage in Satan's domain, it was an act of redemption.
>
> While Paul does not mention the price of our redemption, other texts make it clear that the price was Christ's atoning death (Mk 10:45; Eph 1:7; 1 Pet 1:18-19; Rev 5:6). It was our sin that brought us into bondage under Satan's authority, and thus it is only by paying the price of our sins that we could be delivered. Christ's death on the cross paid that price. And by paying it, He redeemed us. We have therefore been bought with a price (1 Cor 6:19-20; 7:22-23) and belong to a new Lord and Master. But does this imply that the price of our redemption was paid to Satan, our captor? No, this would be reading more into the image than Paul intended. The Bible never teaches such a doctrine. The point is simply that our deliverance was costly. While it cost us nothing, it cost the Father very much indeed (Jn 3:16).

QUESTION 8

What parallel can be drawn between a well-known event that occurs early in the Old Testament and the blessings of salvation described in Colossians 1:12b?

QUESTION 9

The transfer of believers into the kingdom of God's Son serves as proof that God has qualified them to share in the inheritance of the saints when Christ returns. *True or False?*

QUESTION 10

In what Old Testament passage is the language of inheritance used to describe what the righteous will receive following the resurrection?

- A. Isaiah 25:8
- B. Isaiah 60:19
- C. Jeremiah 31:33
- D. Daniel 12:13
- E. Hosea 6:1

QUESTION 11

The dominion of darkness is simply the prison of ignorance and sorrow into which men cast themselves through their own sin and folly. *True or False?*

QUESTION 12

What are the **two stages** of God's kingdom described in the commentary?

QUESTION 13

The basic meaning of the word "redeem" in the Old Testament is to recover something by offering a sacrifice at the temple. *True or False?*

QUESTION 14

In the Old Testament, the premier example of a deliverance that is described as God's act of redemption is the _____.

QUESTION 15

This question concerns your personal testimony. In what ways did you experience your life before Christ as confinement in the dominion of darkness? In what ways did you experience your conversion as deliverance from this domain of darkness and transfer into Christ's kingdom of light? Record your answer in your Life Notebook.

QUESTION 16

This paragraph (Col 1:12b-14) begins the first doctrinal section of Colossians 1:12-23 which is especially rich with the type of material that should be included in your course, *What Every Christian Should Know about Salvation*. What truths do you find in Colossians 1:12b-14 that belong in this course? Notice especially the answers it supplies to the questions, What is man's condition apart from Christ? What happens to a person at conversion?

Important Facts to Remember about Colossians 1:12b-14

1. The inheritance that God the Father has qualified all believers (the saints) to share is the fullness of the end-time salvation which is presently laid up for them in heaven (Col 1:5), and which they will receive at the time of Christ's return.

2. Proof that God has qualified them to share this inheritance is seen in the fact that he has already rescued them out of the dominion of darkness and transferred them into the kingdom of his Son. This deliverance is the foretaste and pledge of the inheritance which guarantees that they will receive the fullness of it on the last day.

3. God has entrusted his kingdom to his incarnate Son in order to restore his fallen creation. This kingdom has two stages. The first is the present era in which Christ rules from heaven. Believers are transferred into it at conversion. The second will begin with Christ's return when he will establish his kingdom on earth.

4. Our deliverance out of Satan's domain was an act of "redemption." To redeem means to recover by payment of a price. The price of our redemption was the atoning death of Christ. Since sin had brought us into a state of bondage, it was by paying the penalty for our sins that he redeemed us. This does not mean the price was paid to Satan, but simply that our deliverance was costly.

Lesson 4 Self Check

QUESTION 1

In which passage does Paul express the theme and purpose of his letter to the Colossians?
- A. Colossians 1:9-10
- B. Colossians 1:10-11
- C. Colossians 1:11-12
- D. Colossians 1:13

QUESTION 2

In Colossians 1:9 "God's will" refers primarily to _____.
- A. His eternal plan of predestination
- B. His plan for believers to lead holy lives
- C. His plan of salvation revealed in the gospel
- D. His choice of Paul to be an apostle

QUESTION 3

The commentary lists four reasons why the knowledge of God's will is of foundational importance for the Christian life. Which of the following is **not** on that list?
- A. It is the basis for action.
- B. It is the object of faith.
- C. It is the basis for religion.
- D. It is a means of spiritual growth.

QUESTION 4

What is the term used to describe the work of the Holy Spirit that enables believers to understand and apply God's truth? _____

QUESTION 5

The theological term for the process of spiritual growth or renewal is _____.

QUESTION 6

According to the definition given in the commentary, "so that you may live worthily of the Lord" means to follow Christ's example of humility. *True or False?*

QUESTION 7

That Christians have already received their "inheritance in the light" (Col 1:12) is proved by the statement of Colossians 1:13 that God has rescued them out of the dominion of darkness and transferred them into the light of Christ's kingdom. *True or False?*

QUESTION 8

The commentary describes two stages of Christ's reign over the kingdom of God: one present, the other to begin at Christ's return. *True or False?*

QUESTION 9

In the Old Testament, the premier example of a deliverance that is described as God's act of redemption is the _____.

QUESTION 10

The price of our redemption from the dominion of darkness was paid to Satan, the ruler of this domain. *True or False?*

Lesson 4 Answers to Questions

WORKSHEET FOR COLOSSIANS 1:9-12A

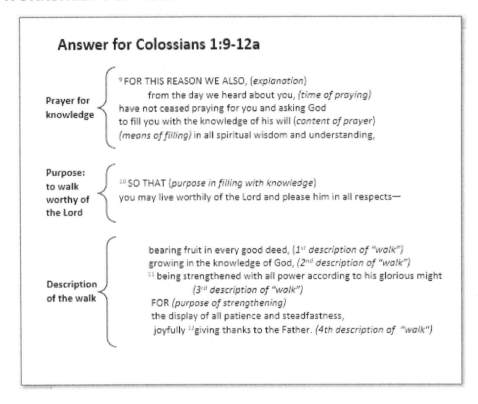

Textual Outline of Colossians 1:9-12a

I. Prayer request for knowledge (Col 1:9)

    A. Paul and Timothy pray persistently. (Col 1:9a)

    B. Their request: Knowledge of God's will (Col 1:9b)

II. Purpose of this request: To walk worthy of the Lord (Col 1:10a)

III. Description of walking worthy of the Lord (Col 1:10b-12a)

    A. A harvest of good deeds (Col 1:10b)

    B. Growth in the knowledge of God (Col 1:10c)

    C. Strength for endurance (Col 1:11)

    D. Joyful thanksgiving (Col 1:12b)

Theme Statement for Colossians 1:9-12a

Paul prays for the Colossians to be filled with the knowledge of God's will so that they might walk in a manner worthy of the Lord.

QUESTION 1: *Your answer should be similar to the following:*
He refers here to God's saving will. By this we mean his plan of salvation as revealed in the gospel. It is God's overall plan to redeem his fallen creation. It includes what he has done in the past, what he will do in the future, and how he desires his people to conduct themselves in the light of these truths.

QUESTION 2: *Your answer should be similar to the following:*
(1) It is the object of faith. (2) It is the basis for action. (3) It is a means of spiritual growth. (4) It is a safeguard against false teaching.

QUESTION 3: *Your answer should be similar to the following:*
The word worthily means "in keeping with" or "in a corresponding way." Paul's prayer is for the Colossians to be filled with the knowledge of God's saving work through Christ so that they might conduct their lives in a corresponding way.

QUESTION 4: illumination
QUESTION 5: sanctification
QUESTION 6: *Your answer*
QUESTION 7: *Your answer*

WORKSHEET FOR COLOSSIANS 1:12B-14

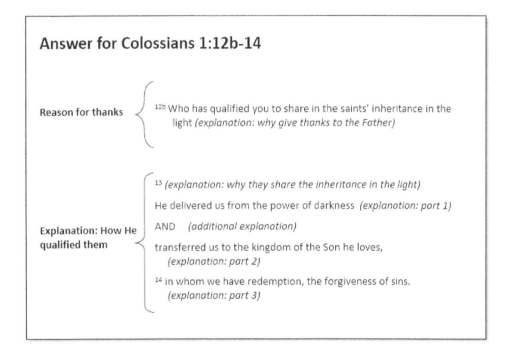

Textual Outline of Colossians 1:12b-14

I. Reason for thanks: God qualified them to share the inheritance of the saints. (Col 1:12b)

II. Explanation: He transferred them into the kingdom of his Son. (Col 1:13-14)

    A. Rescued out of the dominion of darkness (Col 1:13a)

    B. Transferred into the kingdom of his Son (Col 1:13b)

    C. In him they have this redemption, through forgiveness. (Col 1:14)

Theme Statement for Colossians 1:12b-14

We share the inheritance of the saints in the light because God rescued us out of darkness and transferred us into the kingdom of his Son.

QUESTION 8: *Your answer should be similar to the following:*
As God's people of the old covenant received a share in the inheritance of the land of Canaan, so his people of the new covenant receive a share in the inheritance of a new realm—the realm of light.

QUESTION 9: True

QUESTION 10
   D. Daniel 12:13

QUESTION 11: False [The dominion of darkness is much more than this. It is the sphere of authority ruled by Satan and inhabited by those under God's judgment because of their sin.]

QUESTION 12: *Your answer should be similar to the following:*
The first is the present era in which Christ rules from heaven. Believers are transferred into it at conversion. The second will begin with Christ's return when he will establish God's kingdom on earth.

QUESTION 13: False [Paul uses the word "redemption" here to describe our deliverance. To redeem something means basically to recover it by the payment of a price—to buy it back. It came to be used of deliverance from some great adversity (such as oppression, captivity, slavery) and the cost required to achieve this deliverance. The premier example from the Old Testament is the Exodus, in which God redeemed his people Israel out of bondage in Egypt (Ex 6:6-7). Similarly, when God delivered us out of bondage in Satan's domain, it was an act of redemption.]

QUESTION 14: Exodus

QUESTION 15: *Your answer*

QUESTION 16: *Your answer*

Lesson 4 Self Check Answers

QUESTION 1
    A. Colossians 1:9-10

QUESTION 2
    C. His plan of salvation revealed in the gospel

QUESTION 3
    C. It is the basis for religion.

QUESTION 4: Illumination

QUESTION 5: sanctification

QUESTION 6: False

QUESTION 7: True

QUESTION 8: True

QUESTION 9: Exodus

QUESTION 10: False

Lesson 5: Christ, First in All Things—Colossians 1:15-20

In Lesson 4, we first examined Paul's prayer in Colossians 1:9-12a for the spiritual growth of the Colossians. He prays for these young Christians to be filled with the knowledge of God's will so that they might walk in a manner worthy of the Lord. We saw that "God's will" in this context refers to his plan of salvation revealed in the gospel, including how he desires his people to conduct themselves in the light of these truths. This prayer, therefore, sets the agenda for the entire letter because its purpose is to give a fresh exposition of God's saving work and to exhort the readers to live in accordance with these truths.

We then examined Colossians 1:12b-14 where Paul begins to fulfill this purpose by explaining what God the Father has already accomplished for them. He rescued them out of the dominion of darkness and transferred them into the kingdom of his beloved Son where they now share in the blessings of salvation he has allotted to his people. Moreover, it is through his Son that he accomplished this act of redemption.

This brings us to Colossians 1:15-20, the subject of the present lesson. It is one of the best-known and most important passages in the Bible on the person of Jesus Christ. It answers the question, "Who is this One into whose kingdom we have been transferred and through whom we have been redeemed?" The answer has two parts: He is first in honor and authority in all things—first in the creation and first in the new creation.

Topic 1 covers the first part (Col 1:15-17). Here Paul describes Christ in relation to the creation as a whole. He is worthy of the highest place of honor and authority over the creation because all things were created through him and for him, and he now sustains all things.

Topic 2 covers the second part (Col 1:18-20). Here Paul describes Christ in relation to the new creation—the restoration of the fallen creation. He is worthy of the highest place of honor and authority here as well, because God purposed to restore the fallen creation through him. Christ's exalted position is seen in the fact that he is the firstborn from the dead and, thus, the head of the church.

Lesson Outline

Topic 1: First in the Creation (Col 1:15-17)

Topic 2: First in the New Creation (Col 1:18-20)

Lesson Objectives

There are two major objectives in this lesson. When you have completed it you should be able to:
- Explain how Colossians 1:15 describes Christ as the supreme Lord over the creation and why, according to Colossians 1:16-17, he is worthy of this exalted position.
- Discuss what it means that Christ is head of the church, how this relates to his resurrection, the meaning of God's fullness dwelling in Christ, and God's plan to reconcile all things to himself through Christ.

Assignments

Our normal procedure is to cover a single paragraph of Colossians with each topic. This lesson is the exception. Here we are devoting two topics to one paragraph. The reason for the extra attention is the great theological importance of this passage. Our procedure will be as follows. In Topic 1, you will make a structural diagram of the entire paragraph together with an outline and theme statement. In addition, you will do a detailed analysis of the first half of the paragraph, Colossians 1:15-17, on a separate worksheet. Then read the commentary on these verses and answer the questions in Topic 1. For Topic 2 you will do a similar study of the second half of the paragraph, Colossians 1:18-20.

Topic 1: First in the Creation (Col 1:15-17)

The subject of Colossians 1:15-20 is the person of Christ. The first three verses explain who he is in relation to the creation. Paul describes him in Colossians 1:15 as "the image of the invisible God" and "the firstborn over all creation." Together these phrases identify him as the incarnate and resurrected Lord of the creation. The reason he holds this exalted position follows in Colossians 1:16-17. It is because before his incarnation, all things—the entire universe including humans and angels—were created through him and for him, and he now sustains all things.

Begin your study by reading Colossians 1:15-20 and then reading Worksheet A on Colossians 1:15-20 (see next page). Copy it in your Life Notebook and complete a structural diagram, outline, and theme statement. You can check your results by comparing them with the Answer Section for Colossians 1:15-20. Next, read Worksheet B on Colossians 1:15-17. Complete step 2 by recording on a copy of the worksheet your detailed observations, interpretations, and applications. For step 3, carefully read the Commentary on Colossians 1:15-17. Then answer the questions, taking special note of the *Important Facts to Remember*.

Worksheet A: Structural Diagram of Colossians 1:15-20

¹⁵ He is the image of the invisible God,

    the firstborn over all creation.

¹⁶ FOR

all thing in heaven and earth were created by him—

    all things, whether visible or invisible,

        whether thrones or dominions, whether principalities or powers—

all things were created through him and for him.

¹⁷ He himself is before all things

AND

all things are held together in him.

¹⁸ He is the head of the body, the church,

AS WELL AS

the beginning, the firstborn from among the dead,

SO THAT

He himself may become first in all things.

¹⁹ FOR

God was pleased to have all his fullness dwell in the Son,

²⁰ and through him to reconcile all things to himself,

    by making peace through the blood of his cross—

  whether things on the earth or things in heaven.

Worksheet B: Structural Diagram of Colossians 1:15-17

¹⁵ He is the image of the invisible God,

    the firstborn over all creation,

¹⁶ FOR

  all things in heaven and on earth were created by him—

    all things, whether visible or invisible,

      whether thrones or dominions,

      whether principalities or powers—

all things were created through him and for him.

¹⁷ He Himself is before all things

  AND

all things are held together in him.

Commentary on Colossians 1:15-17

2. Christ: First in Creation, First in Reconciliation—Colossians 1:15-17

Recall that Paul's purpose in writing to the Colossians was to bring them to a mature understanding of God's will—that is, his plan of salvation—so that they might walk in accordance with it (Col 1:9-10). In Colossians 1:12b-23 we see the first of two major doctrinal sections devoted to this plan of salvation. The first paragraph of this section explains how God, the Father, has rescued believers from the dominion of darkness and transferred them into the kingdom of his beloved Son, through whom we have this redemption.

The second paragraph, Colossians 1:15-20, answers the question, who is this one into whose kingdom we have been transferred and through whom God has redeemed us? It is one of the grandest passages in the Bible on the person of Christ. Colossians 1:15-17 explains his relationship to all creation. He is first in honor and authority in the creation because all things were created through him and for him, and he now continues to sustain the creation. Colossians 1:18-20 explains his relationship to reconciliation. He is first in honor and authority here as well because through his death and resurrection the Father has undertaken to restore the fallen creation. Thus, as Paul summarizes in Colossians 1:18c, Christ is "first in all things."

Finally, we should note that the language and style of this paragraph is different from the rest of the letter. It is poetry. The words appear to be those of a hymn. In fact, this passage is often called the *Colossians hymn*. In Colossians 3:16, Paul exhorts the Colossians to use psalms, hymns, and spiritual songs to teach and admonish one another. This is what Paul is doing here in Colossians 1:15-20. He has composed a hymn with the dual purpose of instructing believers about Christ while lifting their hearts in worship to God.

Verse15

He is the image of the invisible God. This description of Christ must be seen in immediate connection with Colossians 1:13. The statement that God transferred us into the kingdom of his beloved Son identifies the resurrected and exalted Christ as our **king**. Colossians 1:14 adds that it is through him that God accomplished this work of redemption. Now in Colossians 1:15, Paul takes up the subject of what it means that Christ is our king. By describing him as "the image of the invisible God" and "the firstborn over all creation," Paul draws on two concepts from the Old Testament regarding the nature of the coming Messiah, the King of kings.

The first concept concerns Adam. The phrase "the image of the invisible God" echoes the language of Genesis 1:26-27. Here we read that Adam was created as the image of God so that he might rule over the creation, as God's representative. In the ancient world, kings used to set up images of themselves in their dominions as a sign of their royal authority. Thus, as God's image, Adam served as the sign and representative of the divine authority on earth. Adam, in other words, was appointed king on the earth. He ruled on behalf of the unseen heavenly King. Because of Adam's fall, he and his descendants failed to carry out the role God intended for them. But the Old Testament looked to a future day of salvation when God would renew the creation by restoring the conditions he intended from the beginning (Isa 11:6-9). In Israel's future king, the promised Messiah, God's representative would once again rule the creation (Ps 2:8; 72:8; 110:1). He would be the Adam of the new creation. Christ has fulfilled this expectation. God has enthroned him as Lord over all things (Phil 2:9-11; Eph 1:20-22). As the image of the unseen God, he rules the creation with the authority of the Father. He is the new Adam (1 Cor 15:45).

In Colossians 3:10, Paul applies the truth of this text to the subject of Christian growth (sanctification). As the new Adam, Jesus Christ displays the pure image that God intended men to be from the beginning. Christian growth is the process of being renewed to this same image (Col 3:10). It means being conformed to the image of Christ (Rom 8:29; 2 Cor 3:18).

The firstborn over all creation. This second phrase of Colossians 1:15 further describes Christ in his position as King and supreme ruler of the creation. Before examining it directly, we should note that this text was the scene of a famous battle in the ancient church. The Arians (followers of Arius, a church leader in North Africa) used it to teach that God's first act of creation was to create his Son, the pre-incarnate Christ. The Son of God is, therefore, the most exalted being in the creation, but he is not truly God. "There was a time when he was not." This teaching led many astray. Indeed, it took over large portions of the church before the true teaching of Scripture finally prevailed. This controversy led, in AD 325, to the first general council of leaders representing the entire Christian world since the council of Jerusalem in Acts 15. It was called the Council of Nicaea after the town in western Asia where they met. The council condemned the teachings of Arius and affirmed that the Son is truly God, not created, but equally eternal with the Father. Its official statement, known as the Nicene Creed, is one of the most important doctrinal statements in the history of the church. It is the common teaching of all three principal branches of historic Christianity (Catholic, Protestant, Orthodox) and serves as a boundary marker between true Christian belief and heresy. It is rejected by all the cults. Indeed, the Jehovah's Witnesses are modern-day Arians. They consider Arius a forerunner of their founder Charles Taze Russell (1852-1916).

At first glance, however, the Arian interpretation of Colossians 1:15 would seem to be correct. In ordinary usage, the term "firstborn" designates the one born first in a family. But in ancient Israel the firstborn son also held the place of honor among the offspring. He inherited twice as much as any other son. He also inherited the authority of the father. Thus, the word came to be used in a figurative way (a metaphor) of one who held the top position among others, the foremost rank. For example, in Exodus 4:22 God calls Israel his firstborn son. More significant is God's declaration regarding Israel's ideal king in Psalm 89:27: "I will appoint him to be my firstborn son, the most exalted of earth's kings" (compare 2 Sam 7:12-14 and Heb 1:5-6). Indeed, the description of Christ in Colossians 1:15 as "the firstborn over all creation" is undoubtedly based on Psalm 89:27. Paul uses it to declare that Jesus is Israel's ideal king. He fulfills God's promise of the coming Messiah who would be the King of kings. Indeed, as the resurrected and exalted Messiah, he holds the place of highest honor in the creation—as Adam did in the beginning.

Both statements in Colossians 1:15 focus on the humanity of Christ. He is the Adam of the end time; he is the ultimate heir of the throne of David. In his incarnation (the term means "to take bodily form") the eternal Son of God became fully man without ceasing to be fully God (Jn 1:1-3, 14). He is the unique God-man: two distinct natures—one divine, one human—united in one person. While each statement in Colossians 1:15-20 is true of the person of Jesus Christ, some focus on his humanity while others focus on his deity. Only in regard to his humanity can it be said that he belongs to the creation (Col 1:15b). Only in regard to his deity can it be said that he created all things (Col 1:16). Both statements, however, are true of the person of Christ. The Arians failed to understand this distinction.

Verse 16

For. This word introduces a three-part explanation of why Christ is worthy of the foremost place of honor and authority within the creation: (1) All things were created through him and for him (Col 1:16); (2) He existed before the creation (Col 1:17a); and (3) He now sustains the creation (Col 1:17b). In other words, the resurrected Christ is worthy to occupy the foremost place within the creation because before becoming part of the creation (when "the Word became flesh"— Jn 1:14), he existed eternally with the Father, he created all things, and now continues to sustain all things.

all things in heaven and on earth were created by him - all things,. The verb translated "created" is only used in the Bible for actions done by God (Gen 1:1; 1 Tim 4:3). This fact suggests that to create means to do something only God can do. The clear implication is that Jesus Christ is God. He is the eternal Son, the second person of the Trinity. Paul uses the passive voice of the verb to indicate that God the Father created the universe through the Son (see Heb 1:2; Jn 1:3, 10; 1 Cor 8:6). This point is brought out more clearly in the last line of this verse. The Son was the agent of the creation in the beginning. Therefore, as the incarnate and exalted Lord, he is worthy to occupy the place of supremacy in the creation.

whether visible or invisible,. This line and the next explain in more detail what Paul means by "all things" in the previous line. His words recall Genesis 1:1 (NASB) "in the beginning God created the heavens and the earth." They leave no doubt that Paul means everything without exception: the entire universe, including every living creature, came into being through Christ. The word "**visible**" refers to the entire material universe including people. The word "**invisible**" refers to the world of spirits which is the subject of the next line.

whether thrones or dominions, whether principalities or powers. These terms may designate various orders of angels, probably the highest orders. The names indicate that these angels exercise power and dominion in the heavenly or spiritual realm. "Thrones", for example, refers to angels who sit on heavenly thrones (compare the enthroned elders in Rev 4:4). All of the angels were created by Christ in the beginning. Some of them later rebelled against God. These are the evil "rulers and authorities" of Colossians 2:15 and Ephesians 6:12. God's work of reconciliation (or new creation) through Christ includes the defeat and pacification of these powers (see Col 1:20; 2:10, 15). The point here in Colossians 1:16, however, is that all of these angelic powers, along with the rest of the creation, owe honor and allegiance to Christ. It was through him and for him they were created. His name is above every name in heaven and on earth (Phil 2:9-10).

All things were created through him and for him. The final line of the verse repeats the message of the first line. This is done for the sake of emphasis. This repetition belongs to the poetic style of the paragraph. Yet two differences can be observed. First is the phrase "through him." It is parallel in meaning to "by him" in Colossians 1:16a, only it makes plain the point that the pre-existent Christ was the agent by whom the Father created all things. The other difference is the additional phrase "for him." Christ is the purpose of universe. The creation finds its ultimate aim and purpose in giving glory and service to him. Paul says the same thing about God the Father in 1 Corinthians 8:6 (see also Rom 11:36 and Heb 2:10). But there is no contradiction. In this connection, what is true of the Father is true of the Son.

Verse 17

He himself is before all things. This line is the second of Paul's three-part explanation of why Christ holds the foremost place of honor and authority in the creation. It is because in his deity Christ existed before anything was created. It does not mean, as the Arians claimed, that he was simply the first to be created, before all else. Instead, it means that he existed eternally with the Father (Jn 1:1-2; 8:58; 17:5). There was never a time when he was not. Thus, as the incarnate Lord, he is worthy of the highest place in the universe.

And. This word introduces the third and final part of Paul's explanation of why Christ holds the highest place of honor in the creation.

all things are held together in him. That which Christ created in the beginning, he continues to maintain in the present (Heb 1:3). In the beginning, God did not simply start up the universe like some great machine and then leave it to run on its own. This is the teaching of *Deism*. Instead, Christ continues to sustain the creation. Apart from this sustaining work, the universe would fall apart. The created order would return to a state of chaos.

This means, for example, that every person is dependent upon Christ for his existence from one moment to the next. No one is self-sufficient. From the godly servant of Christ to the one who opposes his rule and persecutes his followers—all owe their daily existence to him. This is what theologians call "common grace." Common grace refers to the undeserved blessings that God freely bestows on all mankind without distinction. "causes the sun to rise on the evil and the good, and sends rain on the righteous and the unrighteous" (Mt 5:45).

To summarize, Colossians 1:16-17 explains why the resurrected Christ is worthy of the highest place of honor and authority in the creation (Col 1:15). It is because all things were created through him and for him and are now sustained by him. Having shown that he is first in the creation, Paul now turns in Colossians 1:18-20 to show that he is also "first" in the new creation, that is, in God's saving work of reconciling the fallen creation to himself.

QUESTION 1

Christ is described as the image of God here because, as the incarnate and resurrected Son, he is the Adam of the new creation who fulfills the mission from which Adam turned aside. *True or False?*

QUESTION 2

In Colossians 3:10 Paul applies the truth of Christ being the image of God to the subject of Christian _____.

QUESTION 3

The official statement of the Council of Nicaea is called the Nicene Creed. *True or False?*

QUESTION 4

With which of the following statements would an Arian NOT agree?
   A. Christ was the first being that God created.
   B. God created all things through Christ.
   C. Christ existed from all eternity with the Father.
   D. Christ rose from the dead.
   E. Christ is the head of the church.

QUESTION 5

The phrase "the firstborn over all creation" describes Christ, not in his pre-incarnate state, but as the incarnate and exalted Messiah who fulfills the promise of Psalm 89:27. *True or False?*

QUESTION 6

The words "whether thrones or dominions, whether principalities or powers" in Colossians 1:16 are used to indicate that Christ created _____.
   A. all human authorities
   B. all of the angelic orders
   C. all human and angelic authorities
   D. only those angels who never rebelled

QUESTION 7

What is the teaching that God created the universe in the beginning and then left it to run on its own?
   A. Universalism
   B. Common grace
   C. Creationism
   D. Deism
   E. The Machine Theory of the Universe

QUESTION 8

What reasons are given in Colossians 1:16-17 to explain why Christ is worthy to occupy the place of highest honor and authority in the entire creation?

QUESTION 9

Consider the fact that every person—righteous and unrighteous—was created by Christ (Col 1:16). Moreover, each person continues to exist from one moment to the next only because he sustains them (Col 1:17b). What does this tell you about his attitude toward those he created? What does this tell you about the attitude you, as a Christian, should have toward those who oppose or persecute you? See especially what Jesus said on this subject in Matthew 5:43-48.

Important Facts to Remember about Colossians 1:15-17

1. The description of Christ as the image of God in Col 1:15a uses the language of Genesis 1:26-27 to portray him as the Adam of the new creation. He now fulfills the mission from which Adam turned aside: He rules the creation as God's representative. Moreover, as the new Adam, Christ displays the pure image that God intended man to possess from the beginning. Christian growth means being renewed to this same image (Col 3:10).

2. The Arians used Col 1:15b to teach that God's first and greatest act of creation was to create his Son, the pre-incarnate Christ. The Son is, therefore, not truly God but a part of the creation. The Council of Nicaea condemned this teaching and affirmed in the Nicene Creed that Christ is truly God, equally eternal with the Father.

3. "The firstborn over all creation" in Colossians 1:15b describes not the pre-incarnate Son, as such, but the incarnate and resurrected Messiah (see Ps 89:27). It means that he holds the foremost place of honor and authority within the creation—as Adam did in the beginning.

4. Christ holds the first rank within the creation because before his incarnation (John 1:14), all things were created through him and for him, he existed before all things, and he now sustains all things Col 1:16-17.

Topic 2: First in the New Creation (Col 1:18-20)

In the first half of this Colossian hymn, Paul sets forth Christ's relationship to the creation. Christ holds the place of highest honor and authority in the creation because in the beginning he was God's agent in creating all things, and he now sustains all things. In the second half of the hymn, Paul turns to the topic of Christ's relationship to the new creation—the creation as it has been reconciled to God following its rebellion against him. He is worthy of the place of highest honor and authority here as well, because God purposed to restore the fallen creation through him. Christ's exalted position is seen in the fact that he is the firstborn from the dead and thus, the head of the church.

Begin your study by reading Colossians 1:18-20 and then reading Worksheet C (see next page). Copy it in your Life Notebook. Since you have already done step 1 for the entire paragraph of Colossians 1:15-20, you need only do steps 2 and 3 for Colossians 1:18-20. Complete step 2 by recording on the worksheet your detailed observations, interpretations, and applications. For step 3, carefully read the Commentary on Colossians 1:18-20. Next, return to this page. Answer the questions, taking special note of the *Important Facts to Remember*.

Worksheet C: Structural Diagram of Colossians 1:18-20

¹⁸ He is the head of the body, the church,

as well as the beginning,

the firstborn from among the dead,

SO THAT

He himself may become first in all things.

¹⁹ FOR

God was pleased to have all his fullness dwell in the Son,

²⁰ and through him to reconcile all things to himself

    by making peace through the blood of his cross—

through him, whether things on earth or things in heaven.

Commentary on Colossians 1:18-20

Verse 18

He is the head of the body, the church. In Colossians 1:15-17, Paul described Christ's relationship to all creation. Now he describes Christ's special relationship to the church. It is like that of the head to the body. This One who is supreme in all the creation, is himself also the head of the body, the church. In 1 Corinthians 12:12-27 and Romans 12:4-5, Paul uses the image of the church as a body to illustrate the relationship of believers to one another. In Colossians, he uses it to illustrate their relationship to Christ. In the Bible, the head is considered to be the most important and honored member of the human body. God signified this by placing it on top of the body, as its highest member. Moreover, the head is the **governing** member of the body. It is the command center from which all the members are directed, coordinated, and maintained (Col 2:19).

We can observe a direct parallel between Christ's relationship to the church and his relationship to all creation (Col 1:15-17). In both cases, he holds the foremost rank: He is ruler and sustainer. But in the case of the church, the relationship exists on a new and completely different level. The church is the redeemed people of the new creation, rescued out of the midst of the old fallen creation. They share the life of their redeemer and depend on him as the members of the body depend upon the head.

as well as the beginning, the firstborn from among the dead. The words "beginning" and "firstborn" were used among the Jews to describe the founder of a people (see Gen 49:3). The new people or race that Christ founded is the church. The church, in this context, refers not only to every local assembly but to the universal church made up of all believers of all lands throughout the centuries. Together they make up the redeemed people of God. The founding event of this new race is not Christ's birth but his resurrection. He was the first to make this passage from death to new life. The church is made up of those whom God has made alive with Christ (Col 2:13), as we will explain in more detail presently.

Why is Christ's resurrection so important? We must understand that Paul is thinking of salvation here in terms of new creation—the restoration of what was lost in the Fall. Thus, when he describes Christ as the founder of a new race through his resurrection, he is again comparing Christ to Adam. Adam was the founder of the race descended from him. He was its beginning—the firstborn. But Adam, through his disobedience, brought his race under the reign of sin and death (Rom 5:17-21). Christ came to deliver men from this tyranny. To do this he became one with Adam's race and died their death—bearing in himself the penalty of God's judgment for their sins. Christ's resurrection was a victory over death in which God delivered him from its reign (Rom 6:9) and bestowed on him the immortal existence that God intended for man from the beginning (1 Cor 15:42-45). This was an act of new creation in which Christ, as the first to rise, became the Adam of the new human race, its founder and head.

How does one become a member of this new race? We entered the race of Adam through the process of natural birth. We enter the race of Christ through the process of resurrection. As God established this new race when he raised Christ from the dead, so we enter it by becoming partakers of Christ's resurrection. Baptism symbolizes this spiritual event (Col 2:12). At conversion, the believer passes from death to life, from the old creation to the new, from the fallen race of Adam to the redeemed race of Christ—which is the church.

So that. This expression introduces an explanation of the result of Christ being both the firstborn of all creation (Col 1:15a) and the firstborn from among the dead (Col 1:18b).

He himself may become first in all things. This line serves as a summary statement of what Paul has said up to this point in the paragraph. In fact, as we will see, it also sums up the remainder of the paragraph. The word "first" in this context refers to the foremost place of honor and greatness. In the first half of the hymn (Col 1:15-17), Paul declares that Christ holds the foremost place in relation to the entire creation. This is because before his incarnation he created all things, and he now continues to sustain the creation. In the second half, Paul takes up the subject of God's work of new creation through Christ. This is his work of reconciling the fallen creation to himself. The goal is to restore it to the conditions that God intended from the beginning. As the first to rise, Christ became the founder and head of the new redeemed race—the Adam of God's new creation. Thus, Christ has become first in everything: first in creation, first in new creation.

Verse 19

For. This word introduces an additional explanation of why Christ "became first in all things." Paul's flow of thought is this: God was pleased to have all his fullness dwell in Christ (Col 1:19) so that all things could be reconciled through his death on the cross (Col 1:20) with the result that he became first in the new creation—and thus first in everything.

God was pleased to have all his fullness dwell in the Son. What is God's fullness? Paul uses the longer phrase "the fullness of deity" in Colossians 2:9. Greek writers used this word to describe that which is completed or made full. For example, a ship with a full crew is said to have its "fullness." The fullness of God, therefore, describes the sum total of attributes of which God is full. It is the divine nature itself. God was pleased to have all the fullness of the divine nature dwell (make its permanent home) in Christ.

When did this indwelling begin? It was in the event of the incarnation, when "the Word became flesh and dwelt among us" (Jn 1:14, NASB). The meaning is not that God indwelt Jesus in the same sense that the Holy Spirit indwells Christians. Instead, this verse refers to the unique event in which the divine nature was united with human nature in the person of Jesus Christ. And it is because all the fullness of God dwelt in Christ—the unique God-man—that he could accomplish fully the work of reconciliation. "God was in Christ reconciling the world to himself" (2 Cor 5:19 NASB).

Verse 20

And through him to reconcile all things to himself. This line begins the second part of Paul's explanation of why Christ "became first in **all things**". The verb "to reconcile" means to make peace (Eph 2:14-17). It means that a state of conflict and hostility is overcome and peace is restored. The conflict, for example, could be between a husband and a wife (1 Cor 7:11), a man and his brother (Mt 5:24), or between Jews and Gentiles (Eph 2:11, 16). Most important, it is used of the peace that is restored between God and men (Rom 5:10). Here in Colossians 1:20, however, Paul uses it in a very broad way to speak of the reconciliation of "all things." This statement assumes that the original harmony in which God created all things, according to Colossians 1:16, gave way at some point to conflict. Thus, before we can determine what it means for God to reconcile all things to himself, we need to ask how this state of hostility developed between God and his creation.

Paul does not provide an answer to this question in Colossians. He simply assumes his readers already know. The original harmony of the creation was destroyed by sin. This rebellion of sin began among the ranks of the angels and swept away a portion of them. It then spread to mankind through the sin of Adam. Indeed, as a result of Adam's fall, the whole of creation was "subjected to futility" and "the bondage of decay" (Rom 8:20-21). The message of Colossians 1:20 is that God has undertaken to end this conflict and to restore the conditions of peace and harmony he intended from the beginning. But what, to be more precise, does it mean for God to reconcile *all things* to himself?

by making peace through the blood of his cross. This line explains the means of God's reconciling work. It is through the event of Christ's death. Paul uses two words to describe this death. *Blood* refers to a life taken by violence (Mt 23:35; Rev 6:10). The *cross* reminds us of the shame and humiliation of this Roman form of execution by which he died (Phil 2:8). The incarnation alone was not enough (Col 1:19). It was necessary for Christ to die if the creation was to be restored and men saved. It was sin that destroyed the peace of the creation. Therefore, it was to deal with sin that Christ died. Paul will explain in more detail in Colossians 2:14-15 how Christ's sacrificial death resulted in victory over the hostile "principalities or powers" and forgiveness for believers. The point to understand here is that Christ's sacrificial death on the cross is God's means of making peace. It is his means of reconciling the fallen creation to himself.

> **through him whether things on earth or things in heaven**. This line spells out the extent of God's reconciling work by defining more clearly the meaning of "all things" in Colossians 1:20a. Notice the parallel with Colossians 1:16: As all things were created through Christ—things in heaven and on earth, including the angelic powers—so all things (these same things) are the object of God's reconciling work in Colossians 1:20. In other words, God's work of reconciliation extends to everything he created. Does this mean that in the end every descendant of Adam will be saved? Does it mean that even the devil and his angels will be saved? The belief that all humans will be saved regardless of their attitude toward Christ is called "Universalism." Scripture, however, is very clear on this point. Neither unbelievers (Mt 25:46) nor the fallen angels will be saved (Rev 20:10). Paul is not speaking here about universal salvation. Rather, he is speaking of the removal of conflict from the universe and the restoration of the harmony that God intended for his creation from the beginning.
>
> In the case of the human race, this reconciliation means forgiveness and salvation for all who believe (Col 1:21-23), but eternal punishment for those who reject Christ. In the case of the devil and his angels, it means their subjugation (Col 2:15; Phil 2:10-11) and eternal punishment (Rev 21:10). In the case of the remainder of the creation, it will mean a transformation to a state of perfection (Rom 8:21; Rev 21:22). Thus in the end, the entire creation will once again be in the state of harmony that God intended from the beginning. It is in this sense that it will be a new creation, and all things will be reconciled to God.

QUESTION 10

Paul describes Christ as the head of the body, the church, in Colossians 1:18 because in the human body the head is the governing member. *True or False?*

QUESTION 11

Paul uses the words "beginning" and "firstborn" in Colossians 1:18 to indicate that Christ is the _____ of a new people—the redeemed people of God.

QUESTION 12

How did Christ's resurrection from the dead establish him as the founder and head of the church, the new redeemed people of God (Col 1:18)?

QUESTION 13

Which statement best summarizes the message of Colossians 1:15-20?

- A. Christ is the firstborn of all creation.
- B. Christ is the firstborn from the dead.
- C. Christ in you, the hope of glory.
- D. Christ is the head of the body, the church.
- E. Christ is first in everything.
- F. Christ is the reconciler of all things to God.

QUESTION 14

What is meant by "all his fullness" in Colossians 1:19, and when did this "fullness" begin to dwell in Christ?

QUESTION 15

As all things were created through Christ—things in heaven and on earth, including the angelic powers—so all things (these same things) are the object of God's reconciling work in Colossians 1:20. In other words, God's work of reconciliation extends to everything he created. *True or False?*

QUESTION 16

The belief that every person will be saved regardless of his or her attitude toward Christ is called _____.

QUESTION 17

This question concerns the fact that Paul presents the lofty teaching of Colossians 1:15-20 in the words of a hymn of worship. This tells us that worship and theological truth go hand in hand. It also tells us that hymns can be an effective method of teaching these truths. How can you use the example of Paul's teaching method in Colossians 1:15-20 in your own ministry? The procedure is, first, to consider the basic concepts that you desire those in your care to grasp. Then, think of some modern-day hymns that communicate those concepts. Suppose, for example, you are planning to give a message on the resurrection of Christ. What are two or three hymns that celebrate and teach this truth? Now consider a message on the person and work of Christ in general. What are two or three hymns that would be appropriate for this subject?

QUESTION 18

If Christ is first in everything, Colossians 1:18, he should be first in our hearts. Can you think of a recent situation in your personal life (relating to your time, money, or family) where you made a choice that showed he is first in your life? Is there an area in your life, either now or in the past, where you have struggled to make Christ first? Record your answer in your Life Notebook.

QUESTION 19

What truths do you find in this paragraph that belongs in your course, *What Every Christian Should Know about Salvation*? Notice especially the answers it supplies to the questions: Who is Jesus Christ? What is the meaning of his death and resurrection? What is the nature of salvation? Record your answer in your Life Notebook.

Important Facts to Remember about Colossians 1:18-20

1. Paul describes Christ as "the head of the body, the church" in Colossians 1:18a because the head is the governing member of the human body and its most honored part (see Col 2:19). Thus, as Christ holds the foremost rank in the creation (Col 1:15-17), so also does he hold the foremost rank in the church, the redeemed people of the new creation.

2. That Christ is "the beginning, the firstborn from among the dead" (Col 1:18b) means he is the founder and head of this new redeemed people which is the church. His resurrection was the founding event of this new race, because, as the first to rise, he became the first to experience deliverance from the judgment of death and entry into the immortal existence that God intended for men from the beginning. The new race is made up of those God has raised up with him. He is, therefore, the new Adam who restores what was lost through the first Adam. Resurrection with Christ is symbolized in baptism (Col 2:12).

3. All the fullness of God in Colossians 1:19 refers to the sum total of the attributes of God. It is the divine nature itself. The divine nature made its permanent home in Jesus Christ in the unique event of the incarnation. This was necessary so that God could reconcile all things to himself through Christ's death.

4. The reconciliation of *all things* to God in Colossians 1:20 does not mean that every person will be saved (the doctrine of Universalism). It means God will end the conflict that entered the creation because of sin and restore the peace and harmony he intended from the beginning. In this context, then, "to reconcile" means "to make peace" in a broad sense. For humans, this means salvation for all who believe. For the evil angels, it means pacification by conquest followed by eternal punishment.

Lesson 5 Self Check

QUESTION 1

Christ is described as "the image of the invisible God" in Colossians 1:15 because, as the incarnate and resurrected Son, he is the Adam of the new creation who fulfills the mission from which Adam turned aside. *True or False?*

QUESTION 2

According to the commentary, Paul uses the phrase "the firstborn over all creation" in Colossians 1:15b to describe Christ, not in his pre-incarnate state, but as the incarnate and exalted Messiah who fulfills the promise of Psalm 89:27. *True or False?*

QUESTION 3

Which of the following does **not** appear in Colossians 1:16-17 as a reason why Christ is worthy to hold the place of highest honor and authority in the universe? *(Select all that apply.)*

- A. He existed before all things.
- B. He created all things.
- C. He sustains all things.
- D. He rules all things.
- E. He reconciles all things.

QUESTION 4

The teaching that God created the universe in the beginning and then left it to run on its own is called _____?

QUESTION 5

The head is the **governing** member of the church. *True or False?*

QUESTION 6

Paul uses the words "beginning" and "firstborn" in Colossians 1:18 to indicate that Christ is the _____ of a new people—the redeemed people of God.

QUESTION 7

What was the founding event of this new people?

- A. Christ's birth
- B. His baptism
- C. His death
- D. His resurrection
- E. His act of sending of the Holy Spirit on the day of Pentecost

QUESTION 8

Which statement best summarizes the message of Colossians 1:15-20?

    A. Christ is the firstborn of all creation.
    B. Christ is the firstborn from the dead.
    C. Christ in you, the hope of glory
    D. Christ is the head of the body, the church.
    E. Christ is first in everything.
    F. God was pleased for all his fullness to dwell in Christ.

QUESTION 9

God's fullness in Colossians 1:19 refers to the fullness of the Holy Spirit which dwelt in Christ. *True or False?*

QUESTION 10

The teaching that every person will be saved regardless of his or her attitude toward Christ is called _____.

Lesson 5 Answers to Questions

Answer for Colossians 1:15-20

Christ: First in creation
- ¹⁵ He is the image of the invisible God,
  - the firstborn over all creation.
- ¹⁶ FOR
  - all things in heaven and on earth were created by him—
    - all things, whether visible or invisible,
      - whether thrones or dominions, whether principalities or powers—
    - all things were created through him and for him.
- ¹⁷ He Himself is before all things,

AND

Christ: First in reconciliation
- all things are held together in him.
- ¹⁸ He is the head of the body, the church,

  AS WELL AS

  the beginning, the firstborn from among the dead,

  SO THAT

  He himself may become first in all things.
- ¹⁹ FOR

  God was pleased to have all his fullness dwell in the Son,
- ²⁰ and through him to reconcile all things to himself,
  - by making peace through the blood of his cross
  - whether things on the earth or things in heaven.

Textual Outline of Colossians 1:15-20.
I. Christ is first in the creation. (Col 1:15-17)
    A. He is the image of the unseen God. (Col 1:15a)
    B. He is the firstborn of all creation. (Col 1:15b)
    C. Explanation: Why he is the firstborn of all creation. (Col 1:16-17)
        1. All things were created by him and for him. (Col 1:16)
        2. He is before all things. (Col 1:17a)
        3. All things hold together in him. (Col 1:17b)
II. Christ is first in reconciliation. (Col 1:18-20)
    A. He is the head of the body, the church. (Col 1:18a)
    B. The reason: He is the firstborn from the dead. (Col 1:18b)
    C. The result: He became first in everything. (Col 1:18c)
    D. Explanation: Why he became first in everything. (Col 1:19-20)
        1. All God's fullness dwelt in Christ. (Col 1:19)
        2. God was pleased to reconcile all things to himself through Christ. (Col 1:20)

Theme Statement for Colossians 1:15-20.
Christ is first in everything because he is the Father's agent both in creating all things and in reconciling all things to himself.

QUESTION 1: True [Christ is described as "the image of the invisible God" in Colossians 1:15 because, as the pre-incarnate Son, he was the original image according to which Adam was created in the beginning.]

QUESTION 2: *Your answer should be one of the following:*
growth, sanctification

QUESTION 3: True

QUESTION 4
    C. Christ existed from all eternity with the Father.

QUESTION 5: True [According to the commentary, Paul uses the phrase "the firstborn over all creation" in Colossians 1:15b to describe Christ as the pre-incarnate divine Lord of the creation.]

QUESTION 6
    C. all human and angelic authorities

QUESTION 7
    D. Deism

QUESTION 8: *Your answer should be similar to the following:*
Christ is worthy of this position because all things were created through him and for him, he existed before all things, and he now sustains all things.

QUESTION 9: *Your answer*

QUESTION 10: True

QUESTION 11: founder

QUESTION 12: *Your answer should be similar to the following:*
These events must be understood within the framework of salvation as new creation—the restoration of what was lost in the Fall. Adam was the founder and head of the race that descended from him. God intended them to live eternally in fellowship with him. Instead, through his disobedience, Adam brought his race under the reign of sin and death. Christ came to redeem men from this tyranny. Christ identified himself with Adam's race and died their death to pay the penalty for their sins. Christ's resurrection was a victory over death in which God delivered him from its reign and bestowed on him the immortal existence that God intended for man from the beginning. This was an act of new creation in which Christ, as the first to rise, became the Adam of the new human race, its founder and head. As God established this new race when he raised Christ from the dead, so we enter it by becoming partakers of Christ's resurrection at conversion when we are raised with him.

QUESTION 13
    E. Christ is first in everything.

QUESTION 14: *Your answer should be similar to the following:*
"All his fullness" in Colossians 1:19 refers to the sum total of the attributes of God. It is the divine nature itself. The divine nature made its permanent home in Christ in the unique event of the incarnation.

QUESTION 15: True [In the statement regarding God's plan to reconcile all things to himself (Col 1:20), the phrase "all things" is limited to good angels and humans who believe in Christ.]
QUESTION 16: Universalism
QUESTION 17: *Your answer*
QUESTION 18: *Your answer*
QUESTION 19: *Your answer*

Lesson 5 Self Check Answers

QUESTION 1: True
QUESTION 2: True
QUESTION 3
    D. He rules all things.
    E. He reconciles all things.
QUESTION 4: Deism
QUESTION 5: True
QUESTION 6: founder
QUESTION 7
    D. His resurrection
QUESTION 8
    E. Christ is first in everything.
QUESTION 9: False
QUESTION 10: Universalism

Lesson 6: Paul's Message, Paul's Ministry—Colossians 1:21-29

Paul was a man with a mission. He had a *message* to proclaim, a *commission* from God to proclaim it, and a *goal* to achieve. These three aspects of his mission are the subject of this lesson.

In some ways Paul's ministry was unique, since he was an apostle. Nevertheless, the same basic principles apply to Christian ministry today. The minister of the gospel today has the same basic mission. He has a **message** to proclaim, a *commission* from God to proclaim it, and a *goal* to achieve. These are the lessons to be learned in Colossians 1:21-29.

Topic 1 deals with Paul's message of man's fallen condition and alienation from God and how God has reconciled believers to himself, in the hope they will ultimately be presented "mature" before Christ (Col 1:21-23).

Topic 2 deals with Paul's commission to proclaim this message (Col 1:24-27). God entrusted Paul with the stewardship of making known this previously hidden truth among the Gentiles. This task involves suffering, but it is necessary for the realization of God's purpose of salvation for the world.

Topic 3 deals with the goal of Paul's ministry, which is to bring every convert to maturity in Christ (Col 1:28-29).

Lesson Outline

Topic 1: Reconciled to God in Hope of Being Presented "Mature" (Col 1:21-23)

Topic 2: Paul's Commission to Proclaim Christ (Col 1:24-27)

Topic 3: The Goal of Paul's Ministry (Col 1:28-29)

Lesson Objectives

When you have completed this lesson, you should be able to:

- Describe the believer's prior state of alienation from God (Col 1:21)
- Explain how God has reconciled believers in the hope that they will ultimately stand before Christ holy, unblemished, and beyond reproach (Col 1:22)
- Define *justification* and *sanctification*, and evaluate the role of faith in regard to both (Col 1:23)
- Discuss how Paul's sufferings in the service of the church could help complete what is still lacking in "the sufferings of Christ" (Col 1:24)
- Explain what it means that the gospel is a mystery (Col 1:26-27)
- Appreciate the significance of the fact that God entrusted Paul with the special stewardship of making known the mystery of the gospel among the nations (Col 1:25-27)
- Recognize that the goal of Paul's ministry was to present every convert mature in Christ, explain what Paul meant by maturity in Christ, and describe the means that Paul used to bring believers to maturity (Col 1:28)

Memory Verse

In this lesson you are to memorize Col 1:28. This verse summarizes the goal and philosophy of Paul's ministry. Be prepared to quote it from memory in your next group meeting.

> We proclaim him by instructing and teaching all people with all wisdom so that we may present every person mature in Christ.

Assignments

In this lesson, you will follow a three-step procedure for each of the paragraphs of Colossians covered in this lesson (Col 1:21-23, (Col 1:24-27), and (Col 1:28-29).

Step 1:

    (a) Make a structural diagram of the passage on the worksheet provided.

    (b) Summarize the results in an outline and theme statement.

    (c) Compare your conclusions with those in the answer section.

Step 2:

    Examine the details of the paragraph. Record your observations, interpretations, and applications on the worksheet.

Step 3:

    (a) Read the commentary on this passage of Colossians.

    (b) Answer the questions in the lesson.

    (c) Pay special attention to the *Important Facts to Remember*.

Topic 1: Reconciled to God (Col 1:21-23)

This topic covers the third and final paragraph of the doctrinal section begun in Colossians 1:12b. As we have seen, Paul's task in this section is to give an overview of God's work of salvation through Christ. In the first paragraph, (Col 1:12b-14), he focused directly on the Colossians' own experience of salvation. God, the Father, rescued them out of the dominion of darkness and transferred them into the kingdom of his beloved Son where they now share in the blessings he has allotted his holy people. Next, in Colossians 1:15-20 Paul focused on Christ, the one through whom they have received this salvation. It is through him that God created and now sustains all things. And it is through him that God is also reconciling the fallen creation to himself. Therefore, Christ is supreme in everything. In the final paragraph, Colossians 1:21-23, Paul returns to the Colossians' experience of salvation. Formerly, they were alienated from God, but he has reconciled them to himself through Christ's death. They are now able to have the relationship with God for which he created them. Furthermore, they will one day be presented mature in Christ—assuming, of course, that they remain steadfast in the faith.

Begin your study by reading Colossians 1:21-23. Then read the Worksheet on Colossians 1:21-23. Copy it in your Life Notebook and complete the tasks described in step 1 of the Assignments section. Check your conclusions by comparing them with the Answer Section for 1:21-23. Next, complete step 2 by recording on the same worksheet your detailed observations, interpretations, and applications. For the third and final step, carefully read the Commentary on Colossians 1:21-23. Then answer the questions, taking special note of the *Important Facts to Remember*.

Worksheet for Colossians 1:21-23

²¹ You were at one time strangers

              and enemies in your minds as expressed through your evil deeds,
²²BUT

  now he has reconciled you

       by his physical body through death
TO

present you holy, without blemish, and blameless before him—

²³ IF INDEED

  you remain in the faith, established and firm,

       without shifting from the hope of the gospel that you heard.

This gospel has also been preached in all creation under heaven

      AND

  I, Paul, have become its servant.

Commentary on Colossians 1:21-23

3. Reconciled to God—Colossians 1:21-23

This is the third and final paragraph of the doctrinal section begun in Colossians 1:12b. Paul's task in this section is to give an overview of God's work of salvation through Christ. The first paragraph, Colossians 1:12b-14, focuses directly on the Colossians' own experience of salvation. God, the Father, rescued them out of the dominion of darkness and transferred them into the kingdom of his beloved Son where they now share in the blessings he has allotted his holy people. In Colossians 1:15-20, Paul focuses on Christ, the one through whom they have received this salvation. It is through him that God created and now sustains all things. It is also through him that God is reconciling the fallen creation to himself. Christ is, therefore, supreme in everything: first in the creation, first in the new creation. The final paragraph, Colossians 1:21-23, returns to the subject of the Colossians' experience of salvation. Formerly, they were alienated from God, but he has reconciled them to himself through Christ's death. Furthermore, they will one day be presented mature in Christ--assuming, of course, that they remain steadfast in the faith.

Verse 21

And you were at one time strangers. What Paul has just said about the reconciliation of the entire creation in Colossians 1:20, he now applies to the Colossians. The text, therefore, moves from the general to the specific. Before conversion they too were a part of the fallen, rebellious creation. God created them for fellowship with himself. But sin had spoiled this plan. They had become strangers to him. This is the condition of everyone outside of Christ. To be strangers to God means to be separated from him, excluded from his fellowship and service. It is the opposite of being at peace with him. It is what Paul describes later in Colossians 2:13 as being spiritually dead.

and enemies in your minds as expressed through your evil deeds. This line further describes the Colossians' former state of being strangers. There were two aspects to this state. In their minds, they were actively hostile to God, and this hostility expressed itself outwardly in evil actions. Paul describes these evil deeds in Colossians 3:5-9. The word "mind" means essentially the same thing as the word "heart" (see Heb 8:10; 10:16). It is the organ of our thinking, our emotions, and our will. Because of the Fall the human heart was corrupted. The mind was darkened. Paul writes in Romans 8:7, "because the outlook of the flesh is hostile to God, for it does not submit to the law of God, nor is it able to do so."

Verse 22

But. This word introduces a contrast between the Colossians' former state of alienation and their present state of reconciliation.

Now he has reconciled you. The Colossians are no longer in this state of enmity with God. His reconciling work corresponds to the two aspects of their former state. He has forgiven their sins and taken the hostility from their hearts (compare Jer 31:33-34; Heb 10:16-17). Paul describes this saving event later in Colossians 2:11 as a circumcision made without hands, and in Colossians 2:13 as forgiveness resulting in their passage from death to life. They now have peace with God (Rom 5:1). They are a new creation (2 Cor 5:17). They have entered the relationship with God that he intended for mankind from the beginning. It is important to observe here that God is the One who acted to restore this relationship. Indeed, it only could be restored by him.

by his physical body through death to present you holy, without blemish, and blameless before him. The means of this reconciliation was Christ's death. The background of this statement is found in the sin offering of the Old Testament. When an Israelite sinned, his relationship with God was broken, and he was deserving of death. But the Law provided a means of atonement (reconciliation) through the sacrifice of an animal that was holy and unblemished. The animal served as the substitute and representative of the sinner so that its death paid the penalty for his sin and thus rendered him once more "**holy, without blemish**" before God. Paul's point here is that Christ is the true and perfect sacrifice—"as a lamb unblemished and spotless" (1 Pet 1:19, NASB)—whose death has paid the penalty for their sins and reconciled them to God.

The words "**by his physical body**" emphasize the reality of Christ's humanity and his identification with those for whom he came to die. The words "**physical body**" refer to his earthly body. By taking a body like ours, Christ fully identified himself with unredeemed man (Rom 8:3; 2 Cor 5:21; Gal 3:13). Only in this way could he represent us before God and bear in himself the penalty for our sins. Only by dying our death in this way could he reconcile us to God.

Paul has thus far explained the *means* of our reconciliation. Now he sets out and explains its *purpose*. At issue here, is not arrival in heaven but whether or not we will arrive there holy, blameless, and beyond reproach. This is the goal toward which Paul labors. This is a goal of sanctification, not salvation. (Sanctification refers to the work of the Holy Spirit in our lives to conform us to the image of Christ, a work that is "in progress." When the believer eventually meets Christ after this life, he will be completely sanctified . . . what theologians refer to as "ultimate sanctification"). Throughout the New Testament we are told of a time in which believers will be presented before their King. At that time, some will be revealed as faithful and others as unfaithful servants (Lk 19:16-19).

Probably the major reason that some would understand this passage as referring to salvation is that the words "holy," "blameless," and **"without blemish"** are taken absolutely. Yet this is not the best interpretation of these terms. Elsewhere in the New Testament, the terms are used to describe imperfectly holy and imperfectly blameless Christians. Elders of the church, for example, are to be "blameless" (Tit 1:6). When the 144,000 stand before the throne, they are declared blameless, not because of their justification but because of their experience. There was no deceit in their mouth (Rev 14:5). A believer is elsewhere exhorted to be holy in both body and spirit ((1 Pet 1:15; cf., 1 Cor 7:34). This obviously refers to an imperfect experiential holiness, not absolute justification.

Furthermore, the notion of being "blameless" in the sense of being experientially righteous and good is grounded in the Old Testament. "How blessed are those whose way is blameless, Who walk in the law of the Lord" (Ps 119:1, NASB). The Hebrew word for "blameless" was translated into Greek in the LXX as *amomos*, the same word which Paul uses in Colossians 1:23. When the Psalmist refers to a man who is blessed because his ways are blameless, he refers to the man's lifestyle, i.e. a person who will "do no wrong" (Ps 119:3), "observe his rules," and he will "seek him with all their heart" (Ps 119: 2). This is not the absolute blamelessness of justification, but the experiential and relative blamelessness of one who is mature and who walks in God's ways.

In substantiation of this consider Paul's own explanation of this conditional clause:

> *that we may present every person mature [Gk. telios] in Christ. Toward this goal I also labor* (Col 1:28-29).

Most interpreters of the New Testament understand Paul's use of **telios** to refer to maturity. This is the completeness to which James referred when he said we must endure trials joyfully so that we will be " *perfect and complete, not deficient in anything*" (Jas 1:4). This is the "mature man" to which Paul refers elsewhere when he says:

> *until we all attain to the unity of the faith and of the knowledge of the Son of God - a mature [Gk. telios] person, attaining to the measure of Christ's full stature. So we are no longer to be children, tossed back and forth by waves and carried about by every wind of teaching . . . But practicing the truth in love, we will in all things grow up into Christ.* (Eph 4:13-15).

In other words, he does not strive to produce perfect Christians. He knows that is impossible. But he does labor to produce mature Christians, that is, Christians who are relatively holy, relatively blameless, and relatively beyond reproach.

Paul develops a different image in Colossians 2:13-15 to explain how God made believers alive with Christ. As the judge in this law-court, God blotted out the indictment against them because Christ suffered the penalty of death in their place. He declared them "not guilty"—"free from accusation" before him. This is the verdict of the final judgment announced in advance. The theological term for this act is *justification*. (The opposite of justification is *condemnation*.) This verdict is not based upon steadfast faith or continuing in the faith; it is a declaration of God based solely on the finished work of Christ. Those who receive this verdict of justification are made alive with Christ. They enter the eternal life of fellowship with God that he intended from the beginning. The message of Colossians 1:22 is different. Having already been justified and declared blameless before

God through faith in Christ, they are now to live this out and become blameless in their daily life so that they can be blameless before men.

Continuing in the faith (Col 1:23) is the means of living a blameless life. Paul's point here is to establish the condition of a future presentation before God. Only by faithful obedience can they arrive at full maturity and hear the Master say, "Well done."

Verse 23

If indeed. These words introduce a condition. Paul is saying, "You will be presented mature and blameless before God *assuming of course that* you continue steadfast in the faith." Those Christians who do not continue steadfast in faith will face divine discipline in time and will suffer loss at the judgment seat of Christ (2 Cor 5:10). They will be "saved" but saved through the fire (1 Cor 3:15), and will experience a sense of "shame" when they stand before him (1 Jn 2:28).

You remain in the faith. Paul is not suggesting here that they will lose their salvation if they lose their faith. Rather, to "remain" is the means of living a blameless life. Paul's point here is to establish the condition of a future presentation before God, only by faithful obedience can they arrive at full maturity and hear the Master say, "Well done." The Bible consistently teaches that salvation is forever because God sustains and protects those who are his (Jn 10:27-29; Rom 8:38-39; 1 Cor 1:8-9). Instead, Paul's point is that only those who are faithful disciples will arrive at a mature state and be blameless before men.

established and firm, without shifting from the hope of the gospel. Paul now explains what is involved in continuing in the faith. The man who continues in the faith is like a building erected on a firm foundation. He is like a wise man who built his house upon the rock (Mt 7:25). Because of its firm foundation, the house is stable. When the storms of life come—with temptations and "every wind of doctrine" (Eph 4:14, NASB)—the house remains steadfast and unmoved. This firm foundation from which the faithful believer is unmoved is the hope promised in the gospel which they heard in the beginning (Col 1:5). An exhortation lies just below the surface of this statement. In the face of a false teaching that threatened to turn the Colossians away from this hope, Paul is emphasizing the importance of remaining steadfast to the message they believed in the beginning.

This gospel has also been preached. The final part of the verse describes further the gospel in order to underscore the importance of holding fast to it. First, Paul stresses that this is the message they heard in the beginning. This message of hope was the means of their conversion, and through God's power it bore in them the fruit of love and faith (Col 1:4-5). It is this life-changing teaching to which they must hold fast.

in all creation under heaven. Second, Paul reminds them that this is the same life-changing message that is being proclaimed and received throughout the world (Col 1:6). We may observe here that the words "all creation" and "heaven" recall the message of the hymn (see Col 1:15, 16, 20). Because God has acted in Christ to reconcile all creation to himself, the message of reconciliation must be proclaimed in all creation. The proclamation, of course, is directed to humans only.

and I, Paul, have become its servant. Finally, Paul points out that he is among those who are proclaiming this message throughout the world. A servant of the gospel is one who preaches and teaches the gospel (2 Cor 3:16; 1 Cor 3:5). It includes both evangelism and the nurture of new believers. Paul devotes the next major section of the letter (Col 1:24-2:5) to an explanation of his work as a servant of the gospel. This final line of Colossians 1:23 serves as a transitional statement to that new subject.

QUESTION 1
The opposite of being at peace with God is to be _____ from him.

QUESTION 2
In what passage of Colossians does Paul describe the "evil deeds" (Col 1:21) of the Colossians during their former state of alienation from God?
- A. Colossians 2:18-19
- B. Colossians 2:21-23
- C. Colossians 3:5-9
- D. Colossians 4:5-9

QUESTION 3
What is meant by the phrase in Colossians 1:22 "now he has reconciled you"?
- A. He has forgiven their sins
- B. He has taken the hostility from their hearts
- C. They have entered the relationship with God that he intended for mankind from the beginning
- D. God is the One who acted to restore this relationship
- E. All of the above responses are correct.

QUESTION 4
The theological term for God's act of declaring believers "not guilty" is _____.

QUESTION 5
Colossians 1:23 teaches that those who lose their faith lose their salvation. *True or False?*

QUESTION 6
According to Colossians 1:22, God's purpose in reconciling sinners to himself through the death of Christ is to present them before himself holy, unblemished, and free from accusation. Based on your study of this passage, how would you answer the following questions? Record your responses in your Life Notebook.
- When does this presentation take place—at conversion, maturity, or Christ's return?
- What are some of the practical ways that you can respond to God in the light of this truth? Consider, for example, Romans 6:13, 2 Timothy 2:15 and Hebrews 10:19-22.

QUESTION 7
This paragraph concludes the first major doctrinal section of Colossians 1:12b-23. What truths do you find in Colossians 1:21-23 that belong in your course, *What Every Christian Should Know About Salvation*? Notice especially the answer it provides to the following questions:
- What is man's condition apart from Christ?
- What happens to a person at conversion?
- What must a person do to be saved?

- Is salvation forever?

Important Facts to Remember About Colossians 1:21-23

1. Everyone outside of Christ is alienated (separated) from God and hostile to him. But God has reconciled believers to himself through the death of Christ.

2. God's purpose in reconciling sinners to himself through Christ's death is for them to progress in godly living so that when they stand before him, they will be holy, unblemished, and beyond reproof (Col 1:22). The commentary argued that this act should be understood in terms of *progressive sanctification* and those believers who remain steadfast in faith can expect to be so regarded when they stand before Christ.

3. The response of faith to the message of the gospel is the condition of reconciliation. Those who are genuinely reconciled are encouraged in this passage not to become lukewarm in their faith (Col 1:23) but rather to aspire to being presented "mature" at the judgment seat of Christ.

4. God's act of declaring believers "not guilty" before him is called justification.

Topic 2: Paul's Commission to Proclaim Christ (Col 1:24-27)

The letter has now reached a major turning point. Paul has completed the "thanksgiving section" (Col 1:3-23), and he now begins the actual body or message part of the letter (Col 1:24-4:6). The opening section of the body, Colossians 1:24-2:5, concerns the nature of Paul's ministry. The purpose of this section is to explain **why** he is writing the letter. It is because God has entrusted him with the task of making known the message of Christ among the nations (Col 1:24-27) with the goal of bringing every convert to maturity in Christ (Col 1:28-29). Paul is therefore writing to the Colossians in order to fulfill this God-given ministry by bringing them to maturity (Col 2:1-5).

In Colossians 1:24-27 we see the first step of Paul's explanation of why he is writing to the Colossians. This first step concerns the overall nature of his ministry. God has given him a special stewardship of service for the sake of the church. The gospel is a previously hidden mystery, and God has entrusted Paul with the task of making it known among the nations.

Begin your study by reading Colossians 1:24-27. Then read the Worksheet on Colossians 1:24-27. Copy it in your Life Notebook and complete step 1 of the "Assignments." Check your conclusions by comparing them with the Answer Section for Colossians 1:24-27. Next, complete step 2 by recording on the same worksheet your detailed observations, interpretations, and applications. For the third and final step, carefully read the Commentary on Colossians 1:24-27. Then answer the following questions, taking special note of the *Important Facts to Remember*.

Worksheet for Colossians 1:24-27

²⁴ Now I rejoice in my sufferings for you,

AND

I fill up in my physical body—

for the sake of his body, the church—

what is lacking in the sufferings of Christ.

²⁵ I became a servant of the church according to the stewardship from God—

> given to me for you—in order to complete the word of God,

²⁶ that is, the mystery

> that has been kept hidden from ages and generations,

> but has now been revealed to his saints.

²⁷ God wanted to make known to them the glorious riches
of this mystery among the Gentiles,

which is Christ in you, the hope of glory.

Commentary on Colossians 1:24-27
III. Paul's Ministry—Colossians 1:24-2:5

The letter has now reached a major turning point. Paul has completed the "thanksgiving section" (Col 1:3-23), and he now begins the actual body or message part of the letter (Col 1:24-4:6). In the opening section of the body, Colossians 1:24-2:5, Paul explains why he is writing this letter. It is because God has entrusted him with the task of making known the message of Christ among the nations (Col 1:24-27) with the goal of bringing everyone to maturity in Christ (Col 1:28-29). Therefore, Paul is writing to the Colossians in order to fulfill this God-given ministry by bringing them to maturity (Col 2:1-5).

A. Paul's Commission to Proclaim Christ: Colossians 1:24-27

Paul's explanation begins with the broader framework. He is carrying out God's business. The gospel is a previously hidden mystery, and God has entrusted him with the stewardship of making it known among the nations.

Verse 24

Now I rejoice in my sufferings for you. Paul's sufferings are those that have resulted from his work of proclaiming the gospel to the Gentiles (see 2 Cor 11:23-33). When Christ commissioned Paul to preach the gospel among the Gentiles, he told him that it would involve much suffering (Acts 9:16). This suffering is for the sake of the Colossians in the sense that if Paul had not exposed himself to the hardships of missionary work, they would probably still be unreached and unsaved (Phil 2:17). Thus, for Paul, proclaiming the gospel meant traveling the path of hardship. But this path led to great spiritual blessing for the church. And because of this, Paul rejoices.

and I fill up in my physical body - for the sake of his body, the church - what is lacking in the sufferings of Christ. What are "the sufferings of Christ"? In what sense are they not complete? And how could Paul's sufferings serve to complete them? First, we must understand that there is nothing incomplete about the atoning work of Christ on the cross. He paid the penalty for our sins in full. What is still lacking is the toil and hardship required to proclaim this message of forgiveness throughout the world. These hardships are "the sufferings of Christ." As Christ suffered death to establish the gospel, so Paul suffers hardship to proclaim it.

As the nineteenth–century English theologian J. A. Beet explained: "When Christ breathed his last upon the cross, all the sufferings needed for the complete establishment of the kingdom of God had not yet been endured. For the full realization of the purposes of God it was needful, not only that Christ should die for the sins of the world, but that the gospel should be preached to all nations. This involved, owing to the wickedness of men, hardship to the preachers. This hardship Paul willingly endured to save men."

What was true of Paul is true of every servant of the gospel (Col 1:23). Every Christian who toils and suffers to advance the gospel is helping to fill up "what is lacking" in the hardships necessary to complete the worldwide proclamation of the gospel. And for this reason they too should rejoice in their sufferings.

Paul emphasizes that his sufferings and Christ's are for the sake of the church. In both cases, the suffering is endured for the sake of another. Paul suffered to spread the gospel, not to atone for our sins. However, like Christ, he endures suffering for the benefit of the church, which is Christ's body (see Col 1:18a). The same is true of Christian workers today. To suffer in the work of the gospel is Christ-like suffering.

Verse 25

I became a servant of the church according to the stewardship from God - given to me for you. Paul suffers these hardships in the service of the church because God entrusted him with this responsibility. Paul uses many images to describe the nature of his ministry. The minister of the gospel is like a farmer, a builder, a soldier, an athlete, an ambassador. Here he uses the image of a steward (see also 1 Cor 4:1).

A steward was a chief slave or servant who was placed in charge of the entire household or even the entire property of the master. A well-known example is Joseph in Genesis 39:3-6. Potiphar made him overseer of his household and all that he owned. The duties and responsibilities of a steward are called his stewardship. To be a steward, one must be trustworthy and sensible (Lk 12:42). The steward carries out his duties with the authority of the owner, and in accordance with his instructions. This is Paul's point here in

Colossians 1:25. God has entrusted him with a great responsibility. It is the task of proclaiming the gospel as the remainder of this passage makes clear.

Paul is speaking here of his commission to be an apostle. In this sense, his stewardship is unique. Apostles belong only to the foundational period of the church. Nevertheless, there is a sense in which all pastors and Christian leaders should be stewards (Tit 1:7). God has entrusted them with the responsibility of serving the church. This is their stewardship.

in order to complete the word of God. This line answers the question: What was Paul's stewardship? "[T]he word" in this context means the gospel. Paul described it earlier in Colossians 1:5 as "the message of truth." The task God entrusted to Paul to fulfill was the proclamation of the gospel of salvation through Christ among the Gentiles (see Rom 1:5; 15:15-16; Gal 1:15-16; Eph 3:8). In Romans 15:19, Paul states that he has fulfilled this task of preaching the gospel from Jerusalem westward as far as Illyricum (in Paul's day a Roman province to the east of Rome; today this is part of southeastern Europe). By this he means he has established churches in key areas between these two points. He goes on to explain in Colossians 1:28 that his goal in proclaiming the gospel is not just to win converts but to bring every one of them to maturity in Christ.

Verse 26

that is, the mystery. The message God commissioned Paul to preach is now described more specifically as a mystery. The term mystery does not refer to something hard to understand. Instead, it means a secret. Jews of Paul's day used this word to describe a secret aspect of God's purposes that could not be discovered unless God revealed it (see Dan 2:27-28). The gospel is a divine secret in this sense. It is the account of the fulfillment of God's purpose to reconcile his fallen creation through Christ. This purpose which was long hidden has now been revealed in the gospel. This mystery is, therefore, now an open secret.

that has been kept hidden from ages and generations, but has now been revealed to his saints. Here Paul emphasizes the previous hidden nature of the mystery. Ages are periods of human history. Generations are groups of people born and living at about the same time. This secret remained hidden to all those who lived in the past. This does not mean that the Old Testament says nothing about God's final plan of salvation through Christ. Indeed, many pieces of the puzzle appear there yet the overall picture remained veiled in mystery (Mt 13:17; 1 Pet 1:10-12). But in the gospel the full picture is revealed (Eph 3:5, 9).

The mystery was disclosed "to his saints." As we have seen, saints is a term that applies to all Christians (see the comments on Col 1:2). In this context, however, the meaning is not that God disclosed the mystery directly to all believers. Rather, he disclosed it to a select group of saints—namely the apostles—and entrusted them with the task of proclaiming it to the world. That this is Paul's meaning here can be seen by comparing it with the parallel statement in Ephesians 3:5 where he explains that this previously hidden mystery "has now been revealed to his holy apostles and prophets by the Spirit" (see Col 1:9; Gal 1:11-12, 15-16).

Verse 27

God wanted to make known to them the glorious riches of this mystery among the Gentiles. God chose certain individuals to be the stewards of the mystery of the gospel. He disclosed the long-hidden secret of his plan of salvation to them and commissioned them to make it known in all creation. Paul's special assignment was to proclaim it among the Gentiles (non-Jewish people; see Gal 1:16; 2:9). As he explains in Ephesians 3:8, (NASB) "to me, the very least of all the saints, this grace was given to preach to the Gentiles the unfathomable riches of Christ" (see Rom 15:15-16).

> **which is Christ in you, the hope of glory**. Paul now summarizes the content of the mystery. Already he has identified the mystery with the word of God—namely the gospel—which God commissioned him to make known among the Gentiles. Now Paul simply clarifies his meaning. The mystery is the fact that the gospel of Christ is being proclaimed "among the Gentile" readers of this letter. This statement picks up the thought of Colossians 1:6 where Paul refers to how the gospel is "bearing fruit and growing, so it has also been bearing fruit and growing among you from the first day you heard it and understood the grace of God in truth." Paul frequently uses the word "Christ, among you from the first day you heard it and understood the grace of God in truth." or the equivalent, as a shorthand way of saying "the message about Christ" (Col 1:28; 2:6; 4:3; 1 Cor 1:23; 2 Cor 1:19; Gal 1:16; Phil 1:17; 1 Tim 3:16).
>
> Next, Paul further clarifies that the content of this message is "the hope of glory" that awaits them. Twice already Paul has described the gospel in terms of hope (Col 1:5, 23). The gospel of Christ that the Colossians received and which bore fruit in their lives is the message of a secure hope that lies prepared for them in heaven (Col 1:5) and an inheritance of glory at Christ's return (Col 3:4).
>
> An essential aspect of this mystery is the way God is bringing these Gentiles into his covenant people, the church. he does not require them to become Jews in order to be saved. They need not keep the ceremonial law of the Old Testament. He accepts them on an equal basis with Jewish believers. There is no distinction. Jew and Gentile alike are saved by faith (Rom 3:27-30). Thus in Ephesians 3:5-6, Paul can say that the mystery is the fact that "the Gentiles are fellow heirs, fellow members of the body, and fellow partakers of the promise in Christ Jesus" (see Eph 2:11-19).

QUESTION 8

What are the "sufferings of Christ" in Colossians 1:24?
- A. The suffering Christ endured on the cross
- B. The sufferings Christians must endure to atone for sins committed after conversion
- C. The hardships required to proclaim the gospel
- D. The afflictions with which God disciplines us that we may share his holiness

QUESTION 9

The duties and responsibilities of a steward are his _____.

QUESTION 10

What well-known person in Genesis served as a steward? _____.

QUESTION 11

What is the meaning of the word "mystery"?
- A. Something that is hard to understand
- B. Something that is impossible to understand
- C. Something that only mature believers can understand
- D. Something that is a secret until revealed
- E. Something only an apostle could reveal

QUESTION 12

According to Colossians 1:25-27, what is the mystery that God commissioned Paul to make known?

A. The rapture of the church
B. The gospel
C. The indwelling of Christ in all believers, Jew and Gentile alike
D. The incarnation

QUESTION 13

An essential part of Paul's stewardship was to make known the fact that God is receiving what group of people into the church on an equal basis with Jewish believers? _____.

QUESTION 14

Colossians 1:24 expresses a profound (and sometimes misunderstood) truth about the value of the hardships endured by those who labor in the service of the gospel. Consider the hardships you have endured in your own ministry. In what ways can this verse give you a renewed outlook on these hardships? How can it help you to find a new joy in the midst of them? Record your answer in your Life Notebook.

QUESTION 15

Each Christian leader has a stewardship from God. Take a moment to read Titus 1:7-9, and then answer the following questions by recording them in your Life Notebook.

1. What are the specific responsibilities of your stewardship (be brief and general)?

2. In what ways can you be more faithful and sensible in fulfilling these tasks?

3. Consider especially Paul's statement in Titus 1:9 that the overseer "must hold firmly to the faithful message as it has been taught, so that he will be able to give exhortation in such healthy teaching." Can you think of ways that you can be more diligent in holding firmly to this teaching?

Important Facts to Remember About Colossians 1:24-27

1. Colossians 1:24-2:5 is the opening section of the body (the message part) of the letter. Paul's purpose in this section is to explain to the Colossians his reason for writing to them.

2. The "sufferings of Christ" in Colossians 1:24 are the toils and hardships required to proclaim the gospel of Christ in the world. They will remain incomplete as long as the missionary task of proclaiming the gospel is incomplete.

3. Jews of Paul's day used the word *mystery* to describe a secret aspect of God's purposes that could not be discovered unless God revealed it.

4. The gospel is a divine secret in this sense. God revealed it to Paul and other apostles, and entrusted them with the stewardship of making it known to the world.

5. An essential aspect of this mystery (the gospel) is that God is receiving the Gentiles into the church on an equal basis with Jewish believers (Col 1:27; Eph 3:5-6).

Topic 3: The Goal of Paul's Ministry (Col 1:28-29)

Our third topic is the brief but very important paragraph of Colossians 1:28-29. Its importance is seen in the fact that Paul summarizes here the goal of his ministry. Indeed, we see here a summary of his philosophy of ministry.

This is the second paragraph of the opening section of the body—the actual message part of the letter. Paul's purpose in this section is to explain why he is writing this letter. In the first paragraph, Colossians 1:24-27, he informed the Colossians of his special stewardship from God to proclaim Christ among the Gentiles. Now in Colossians 1:28-29 he tells them of the goal for which he strives in this work of proclamation. It is to present everyone mature in Christ.

Begin your study by reading Colossians 1:28-29. Then read the Worksheet on Colossians 1:28-29. Copy it in your Life Notebook and complete step 1 of the "Assignments." Check your conclusions by comparing them with the Answer Section for Colossians 1:28-29. Next, complete step 2 by recording on the same worksheet your detailed observations, interpretations, and applications. For the third and final step, carefully read the Commentary on Colossians 1:28-29. Then answer the following questions, taking special note of the *Important Facts to Remember*.

Worksheet for Colossians 1:28-29

[28] We proclaim him

    by instructing and teaching all people with all wisdom,

    SO THAT

    we may present every person mature in Christ.

[29] TOWARD THIS GOAL

    I also labor

    struggling according to his power that powerfully works in me.

Commentary on Colossians 1:28-29
B. The Goal of Paul's Ministry—Colossians 1:28-29

This is the second paragraph of the opening section of the body—the actual message part of the letter. Paul's purpose in this section is to explain why he is writing this letter. In the first paragraph, Colossians 1:24-27, he informed the Colossians of his special stewardship from God to proclaim Christ among the Gentiles. Now in Colossians 1:28-29 he tells them of the goal for which he strives in this work of proclamation. It is to present everyone mature in Christ.

Verse 28

We proclaim him. The verb "proclaim" is used frequently in the New Testament to refer to the missionary preaching of the gospel (Acts 4:2; 13:5, 17:3; 1 Cor 9:14). The term, however, does not always refer simply to the work of evangelizing non-Christians. It can include the work of instructing new believers. That this is the meaning here in Colossians 1:28 can be seen from the fact that Paul is proclaiming Christ as the **means** of bringing people to maturity in him.

What does Paul mean by "him" (referring to Christ) in this statement? As we saw in our study of Colossians 1:27, this is simply a shorthand way of saying "the message about Christ." But what, to be more specific, does Paul mean by "the message about Christ"? Broadly defined it is the gospel. The form and application of this message, however, depend on the audience. If the hearers are non-Christians, then it is a message aimed at leading them to saving faith. If, however, the hearers are new converts, then it is a message about Christ aimed at leading them to Christian maturity.

What then was this instruction that was delivered to new converts and was the means of their spiritual growth? Stated briefly, it contained two parts: one doctrinal, the other application-based. The doctrinal part concerned God's overall plan of salvation revealed in the gospel. It focused on who Christ is and the nature of his work as Redeemer. The second part focused on how Christians are to live in accordance with these truths.

instructing and teaching all people with all wisdom. The two verbs "**instructing**" and "teaching" serve to explain further the activity of proclaiming Christ. Proclamation is the broader activity. It includes the work of instructing and teaching. For people to understand and embrace the gospel, they must be exhorted, corrected, and warned regarding their misguided beliefs and conduct. This is the work of admonition. In addition, they must be instructed in a new way of life based on a new knowledge and understanding of Christ. This is the work of teaching. These two kinds of instruction are inseparable. They are like two sides of the same coin.

Notice how Paul uses the word "all" twice, and "every" once, in Colossians 1:28. He does this to emphasize a point. A similar emphasis appears in 1 Thessalonians 2:11-12 (NASB). Here Paul reminds the Thessalonians of the way he ministered among them when they were new converts. "We were exhorting and encouraging and imploring each one of you, as a father would his own children, so that you would walk in a manner worthy of the God who calls you into his own kingdom and glory." This is the point Paul wishes to underscore in Colossians 1:28. He gives personal attention and care to each and every individual in order to bring them to Christian maturity.

The words "with all wisdom" describe how Paul admonishes and teaches each person. He does it with God-given wisdom. It requires wisdom from above to know how to tailor the message of Christ to the needs of each person in each situation.

so that. These words introduce the purpose and ultimate goal of Paul's labor of proclaiming, admonishing, and teaching.

we may present every person mature in Christ. This is the principal statement of the paragraph. It sums up the goal of Paul's efforts described in the first two lines of Colossians 1:28. He further states in Colossians 1:29 that it is "toward this goal" that he labors.

This statement in Colossians 1:28c is especially important because it summarizes the purpose and goal of Paul's ministry. If this was the goal of Paul's ministry, it should be the goal of our ministry today. This statement, therefore, deserves special attention.

First, what is this presentation to which Paul refers? God had commissioned him to proclaim the gospel among the Gentiles (Col 1:25). Thus, he wishes to present to God as the fruit of his obedient labors those who have responded in faith and grown to maturity in Christ. Paul had previously used the concept of believers being presented before God in Col 1:21-23. (In the original language, the same word for "present," *paristēmi*, is used in both Col 1:22 and 1:28. It is also used in Rom 14:10 of "standing before the judgment seat of Christ"). Every believer will one day be *presented before God* at the judgment seat of Christ, at which time he will give an account of himself to the Lord, and his works will be examined for the purpose of determining what reward he should receive (2 Cor 5:9-10; 1 Cor 4:5). This will take place following the "return" of the Lord Jesus Christ (1 Thess 2:19).

Second, what does it mean to be mature in Christ? The word "mature" means to be full grown, an adult. When a person responds to the gospel with saving faith, he is "born again." He is now a babe in Christ. He requires admonition and instruction to grow from this state of spiritual infancy to maturity in Christ.

What then are the qualities of a mature Christian? To answer this question, we may begin by observing that Paul does not define maturity for us in this passage. He does, however, mention the **means** of bringing people to maturity and this opens a window for understanding the meaning of maturity itself. First, we see that maturity comes as the result of instruction (proclamation, admonition, teaching). Second, the content of this instruction is Christ—that is, the message about Christ. This message, as we stated earlier, focuses on the nature of salvation in Christ and how to live out this salvation in the world. From these two observations, we may infer that to be mature in Christ means to have a thorough understanding of the message of Christ, a firm faith in its truthfulness, and to walk in accordance with it (see further Eph 4:13-16). For those who grow to maturity, their lives are described in Col 1:22 as "holy, blameless, and beyond reproach."

This definition of Christian maturity, in fact, reflects the structure of the book of Colossians. In our survey of the entire letter, we saw that Paul constructs it along two lines. First, he gives a fresh exposition of the gospel (or the nature of Christian salvation). This exposition is found chiefly in Colossians 1:12b-23 and Colossians 2:9-15. Second, he exhorts and instructs the Colossians to conduct their lives on the basis of these truths. This application-based material is found in Colossians 2:16-4:6.

This leads to an important observation about the relation of Colossians 1:28 to the entire letter. In this verse, Paul outlines his basic philosophy of ministry: proclaiming Christ in order to bring everyone to Christian maturity. And it is precisely this philosophy of ministry that we see in action in Paul's letter to the Colossians. He writes to young Christians. They are being tempted by a seductive, false teaching. He writes to reinforce their understanding of the gospel, to show them the proper response to this false teaching (Col 2:16-3:4) and how to live out the gospel in daily life (Col 3:5-4:6). His goal for them is a strong, confident Christian adulthood (see also Col 4:12). This shows the special value of Colossians as a tool for Christian ministry today. It serves as a model of how to bring believers to maturity in Christ.

Verse 29

Toward this goal. The goal of Paul's labor is to present everyone mature in Christ.

I also labor, struggling. The Greek verb translated "labor" refers to intense labor or toil resulting in weariness (see Mt 11:28; Phil 2:16). The labor Paul refers to is, first of all, his evangelistic and pastoral efforts in proclaiming, admonishing, and teaching. But it goes beyond this to include all the labor and hardship he endures in order to carry out the commission God gave him (1 Thess 2:9; 2 Thess 3:8; 2 Cor 11:27).

The verb translated "struggling" does not refer to a separate activity. Rather, it further characterizes Paul's labor. Originally it meant "to compete in an athletic contest" such as a wrestling match or a foot race. It clearly has this meaning in 1 Corinthians 9:25. Through common usage, it came to be used in a figurative sense of any kind of struggle or conflict (see Jn 18:36). Behind each usage is the image of the disciplined athlete who strives with all his energy to attain a specific goal. Paul used this image of the striving athlete in other contexts to describe the toil of his ministry (1 Cor 9:24-27; Gal 2:2; Phil 2:16; 1 Thess 2:19). Near the end of his life, he chose this verb and a related noun to sum up his entire Christian life and ministry: "I have *fought* the good *fight*" (2 Tim 4:7, NASB, emphasis added).

in reliance upon the energy that he powerfully generates within me. This final line describes the means of Paul's toil and striving. He carries out his ministry using the energy that Christ supplies. It is important to observe the balance displayed here between man's toil and God's power. The two are complementary, not contradictory. One could reason that if Christ powerfully supplies the energy for Paul's work, there would be no wearisome toil or striving on his part. Paul's work would be effortless. By this line of reasoning, for Paul to toil and strive would indicate that he is attempting to serve God in the power of the flesh. Scripture, however, does not reason in this way. Rather, this passage illustrates the biblical balance between human effort and divine empowerment. God supplies the strength, and in that strength Paul labors and strives. (See also 1 Cor 15:10 and Phil 2:12-13.)

QUESTION 16

The instruction Paul gave to new converts in order to bring them to maturity in Christ contained two parts. What were they?

A. One dealt with justification, the other with sanctification

B. One was doctrinal, the other application-based

C. One was basic, the other advanced

D. One was for Jewish Christians, the other for Gentile converts

QUESTION 17

What passage in 1 Thessalonians illustrates Paul's emphasis in Colossians 1:28 on giving personal attention to every individual in order to bring them to maturity in Christ?

A. 1 Thessalonians 1:11-12

B. 1 Thessalonians 2:1-2

C. 1 Thessalonians 2:11-12

D. 1 Thessalonians 2:19-20

QUESTION 18

Our study of Colossians 1:28 led us to a definition of maturity in Christ. What is this definition? You may summarize it in your own words, but try to state it in a single sentence.

QUESTION 19

According to the commentary, this definition of Christian maturity reflects the structure of which book of the New Testament?

- A. John
- B. 1 Corinthians
- C. Galatians
- D. Colossians
- E. 1 Peter

QUESTION 20

In what verse of Colossians does Paul outline the goal and the basic philosophy of his ministry?

- A. Colossians 1:24
- B. Colossians 1:26
- C. Colossians 1:28
- D. Colossians 1:29

QUESTION 21

In Colossians 1:28 Paul summarizes both the goal of his ministry and his means for achieving that goal. The goal is to present every one mature in Christ. The means is proclaiming Christ —that is, preaching and teaching the message about Christ. Compare Paul's approach to ministry with yours. In what ways are you now seeking to reach the same goal as Paul? In what ways are you using the same means? Can you think of some specific ways to bring the goal and means of your ministry more into line with Paul's? Record your answer in your Life Notebook.

Important Facts to Remember about Colossians 1:28-29

1. The goal of Paul's ministry was to bring every person to maturity in Christ (Col 1:28).

2. To be mature in Christ means to have a thorough understanding of the message of Christ, a firm faith in its truthfulness, and to walk in accordance with it.

3. The means of bringing believers to maturity is instruction in the nature of salvation through Christ and how to live in accordance with this salvation (Col 1:28).

Lesson 6 Self Check

QUESTION 1
The opposite of being at peace with God is to be _____ from him.

QUESTION 2
God's act of restoring us to fellowship with himself through Christ's death for our sins is called _____.
- A. redemption
- B. justification
- C. sanctification
- D. reconciliation

QUESTION 3
The theological term for God's act of declaring believers "not guilty" is _____.

QUESTION 4
Colossians 1:23 teaches that those who lose their faith lose their salvation. *True or False?*

QUESTION 5
What are the "sufferings of Christ" in Colossians 1:24?
- A. The suffering Christ endured on the cross
- B. The sufferings required for Christians to atone for sins committed after conversion
- C. The hardships required to proclaim the gospel
- D. The afflictions with which God disciplines us that we may share his holiness

QUESTION 6
According to Colossians 1:25-27, what is the mystery that God commissioned Paul to make known?
- A. The rapture of the church
- B. The indwelling of Christ in all believers, Jew and Gentile alike
- C. The incarnation
- D. The gospel

QUESTION 7
An essential aspect of the mystery is the fact that God is receiving what group of people into the church on an equal basis with Jewish believers?

QUESTION 8

The "message of Christ" that Paul proclaimed to new converts in order to bring them to maturity in Christ contained two parts. What are they?

- A. One was doctrinal, the other application-based
- B. One was basic, the other advanced
- C. One was for Jewish Christians, the other for Gentile converts
- D. One dealt with justification, the other with sanctification

QUESTION 9

To be mature in Christ means to have a thorough _____ of the message of Christ, a firm faith in its truthfulness, and to walk in accordance with it.

QUESTION 10

In what verse of Colossians does Paul outline the goal and the basic philosophy of his ministry?

- A. Colossians 1:24
- B. Colossians 1:26
- C. Colossians 1:28
- D. Colossians 1:29

Lesson 6 Answers to Questions
WORKSHEET FOR COLOSSIANS 1:21-23

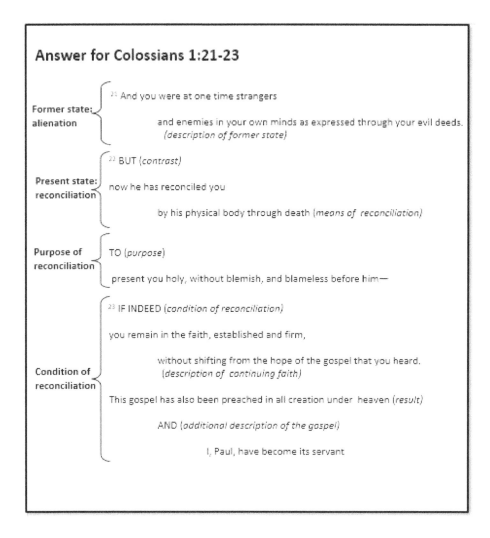

Textual Outline of Colossians 1:21-23.
I. Former state: alienation (Col 1:21)
    A. Strangers and enemies (Col 1:21a)
    B. As expressed through evil deeds (Col 1:21b)
II. Present state: reconciliation by Christ's physical body through death (Col 1:22a)
III. Purpose of reconciliation: by presentation (Col 1:22b)
    A. As holy (Col 1:22b)
    B. Without blemish (Col 1:22b)
    C. Blameless (Col 1:22b)
IV. Condition of reconciliation (Col 1:23)
    A. Remain firm in the faith (Col 1:23a)
    B. Without shifting from the hope of the gospel (Col 1:23b)
    C. Gospel has been preached in all creation (Col 1:23c)
    D. Paul has become the Gospel's servant (Col 1:23d)

Theme statement
Although all people were strangers and enemies of God, Christ has reconciled us, presenting us blameless before God, provided we remain firm in the faith.

QUESTION 1: alienated
QUESTION 2
    C. Colossians 3:5-9
QUESTION 3
    E. All of the above responses are correct.
QUESTION 4: justification
QUESTION 5: False
QUESTION 6: *Your answer*
QUESTION 7: *Your answer*

WORKSHEET FOR COLOSSIANS 1:24-27

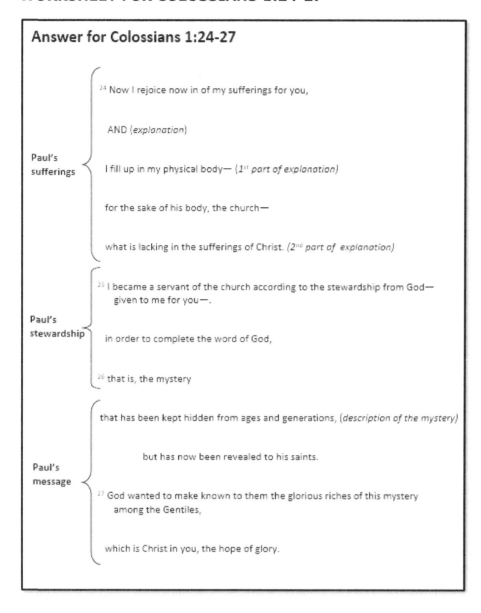

Textual Outline of Colossians 1:24-27.
I. Paul's sufferings (Col 1:24)
    A. Joy in suffering for the church (Col 1:24a)
    B. Explanation: He fills up what is lacking in the afflictions of Christ. (Col 1:24b,c)
II. Paul's stewardship (Col 1:25)
    A. A stewardship given by God for the Colossians' benefit (Col 1:25a)
    B. The task: To proclaim God's word (Col 1:25b)
III. Paul's message (Col 1:26-27)
    A. The mystery formerly hidden but now disclosed (Col 1:26)
    B. The recipients of the message: the Gentiles (Col 1:27a)
    C. The message itself: Christ, the hope of glory (Col 1:27b)

Theme Statement for Colossians 1:24-27.
Paul's stewardship from God is to proclaim the previously hidden mystery of the gospel among the Gentiles.

QUESTION 8
    C. The hardships required to proclaim the gospel
QUESTION 9: stewardship
QUESTION 10: Joseph
QUESTION 11
    D. Something that is a secret until revealed
QUESTION 12
    B. The gospel
QUESTION 13: Gentiles
QUESTION 14: *Your answer*
QUESTION 15: *Your answer*

WORKSHEET FOR COLOSSIANS 1:28-29

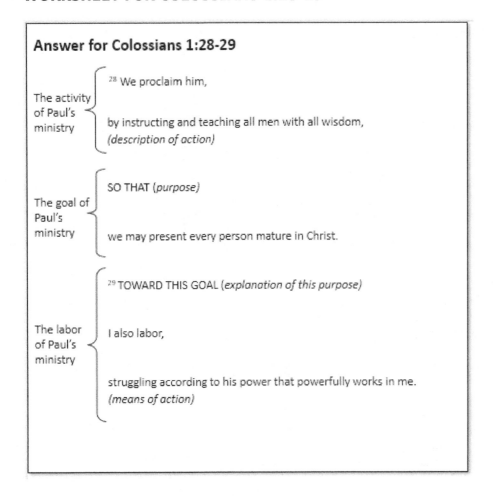

Textual Outline of Colossians 1:28-29
I. The activity of Paul's ministry (Col 1:28a,b)
    A. Proclaiming Christ (Col 1:28a)
    B. Description of activity: Admonishing and teaching everyone with wisdom (Col 1:28b)
II. The goal of Paul's ministry: To present everyone mature in Christ (Col 1:28c)
III. The labor of Paul's ministry (Col 1:29)
    A. He labors towards this goal. (Col 1:29a)
    B. The means of Paul's labor: Reliance upon the power Christ supplies (Col 1:29b)

Theme Statement for Colossians 1:28-29
Paul labors to proclaim Christ in order to present everyone mature in Christ.

QUESTION 16
    B. One was doctrinal, the other application-based

QUESTION 17
    C. 1 Thessalonians 2:11-12

QUESTION 18: *Your answer should be similar to the following:*
To be mature in Christ means to have a thorough understanding of the message of Christ, a firm faith in its truthfulness, and to walk in accordance with it.

QUESTION 19
    D. Colossians

QUESTION 20
    C. Colossians 1:28

QUESTION 21: *Your answer*

Lesson 6 Self Check Answers

QUESTION 1: alienated
QUESTION 2
   D. reconciliation
QUESTION 3: justification
QUESTION 4: False
QUESTION 5
   C. The hardships required to proclaim the gospel
QUESTION 6
   D. The gospel
QUESTION 7: Gentiles
QUESTION 8
   A. One was doctrinal, the other application-based
QUESTION 9: understanding
QUESTION 10
   C. Colossians 1:28

Unit Two Exam

QUESTION 1

Paul's prayer for the Colossians to be filled with the knowledge of God's will in Colossians 1:9-10 so that they might walk worthy of the Lord expresses the theme of the letter because its purpose is to give them a fresh explanation of God's will so that they might walk worthy of the Lord. *True or False?*

QUESTION 2

In Colossians 1:9, *God's will* refers primarily to _____.
- A. His eternal plan of predestination
- B. His plan for believers to lead holy lives
- C. His plan of salvation revealed in the gospel
- D. His choice of Paul to be an apostle

QUESTION 3

The theological term for the work of the Holy Spirit that enables believers to understand and apply God's word is _____.

QUESTION 4

The theological term for the process of spiritual growth or renewal is _____.

QUESTION 5

The "saints' inheritance in the light" in Colossians 1:12 is simply another way of describing "the hope laid up for you in heaven" mentioned earlier in Colossians 1:5. *True or False?*

QUESTION 6

What story from the Old Testament best illustrates the statement in Colossians 1:12b that God has qualified believers to share the inheritance of the saints in the light?
- A. God's promise to Abraham that in him all the nations would be blessed
- B. Israel's restoration to the land after the Babylonian captivity
- C. Israel's entry into the land following their deliverance from Egypt
- D. Noah's return to dry land after the waters of the flood had receded
- E. God's gift of the Garden of Eden to Adam and Eve before the Fall

QUESTION 7

The commentary describes *two* stages of Christ's reign over the kingdom of God: one present, the other to begin at Christ's return. *True or False?*

QUESTION 8
What is the basic meaning of the word *redeem* in the Old Testament?
- A. To find something that was previously lost
- B. To deliver someone from an enemy
- C. To restore a broken relationship by an act of humility
- D. To recover something by the payment of a price
- E. To forgive and remarry a wife who was previously divorced for unfaithfulness

QUESTION 9
Christ is described as "the image of the invisible God" in Colossians 1:15 because, as the pre-incarnate Son, he was the original image according to which Adam was created in the beginning. *True or False?*

QUESTION 10
According to the commentary, Paul using the phrase "the firstborn over all creation" in Colossians 1:15 describes Christ as the pre-incarnate divine Lord of the creation. *True or False?*

QUESTION 11
What is the teaching that God created the universe in the beginning and then left it to run on its own?
- A. Universalism
- B. Common grace
- C. Creationism
- D. Deism
- E. The Machine View of the Universe

QUESTION 12
According to Colossians 1:16-17, why is Christ worthy to occupy the place of highest honor and authority in the entire creation?
- A. He is the firstborn over all creation.
- B. He is the creator and sustainer of all things.
- C. He is the Head of the church.
- D. All the fullness of deity dwells in him.
- E. He died to reconcile all things to God.
- F. He is the first to rise from the dead.

QUESTION 13
Paul describes Christ as the head of the body, the church, in Colossians 1:18 because in the human body the head is the *governing* member. *True or False?*

QUESTION 14

What was the founding event of the church, new people of God, of which Christ is the Head (Colossians 1:18)?

- A. Christ's birth
- B. His baptism
- C. His death
- D. His resurrection
- E. His enthronement in heaven at the right hand of the Father
- F. His act of sending of the Holy Spirit on the day of Pentecost

QUESTION 15

What is the fullness of God that dwelt in Christ (Colossians 1:19)?

- A. The fullness of the Holy Spirit
- B. The fullness of God's revelation
- C. The fullness of God's love and saving power
- D. The fullness of God's authority
- E. The fullness of all that God intended for man to be from the beginning
- F. The fullness of the divine nature itself

QUESTION 16

In the statement regarding God's plan to reconcile all things to himself (Col 1:20), the phrase "all things" is limited to good angels and humans who believe in Christ. *True or False?*

QUESTION 17

The theological term for God's act of making peace with those who are alienated from him is _____.

QUESTION 18

The theological term for God's act of declaring believers "not guilty" is _____.

QUESTION 19

According to Colossians 1:23, those who have been reconciled to God but later lose their faith also lose their salvation. *True or False?*

QUESTION 20

What is meant by the expression, "the sufferings of Christ," in Colossians 1:24?

- A. The sufferings that Christ endured on the cross
- B. The sufferings Christians must endure to atone for sins committed after conversion
- C. The hardships that must be endured in order for the gospel to be proclaimed
- D. The afflictions with which God disciplines us that we might share his holiness
- E. The sufferings Christ continues to experience through his Body, the church, since to persecute the church is to persecute Christ

QUESTION 21

The Bible uses the term *mystery* to describe something that is very difficult to understand. *True or False?*

QUESTION 22

The mystery that God commissioned Paul to proclaim is the indwelling of Christ in all believers—Gentiles as well as Jews. *True or False?*

QUESTION 23

The message about Christ that Paul proclaimed to new converts in order to bring them to maturity in Christ had two parts. What were they?

- A. One was doctrinal, the other application-based.
- B. One was basic, the other advanced.
- C. One was for Jewish Christians, the other for Gentile believers.
- D. One concerned justification, the other sanctification.
- E. One concerned the old covenant, the other the new covenant.

QUESTION 24

To be mature in Christ means to have a thorough _____ of the message of Christ and to walk in accordance with it.

QUESTION 25

This definition of maturity in question 24 reflects the structure of which book of the Bible?

- A. John
- B. Acts
- C. 1 Corinthians
- D. Colossians
- E. 1 Peter

Unit 2 Exam Answers

QUESTION 1: True
QUESTION 2
   C. His plan of salvation revealed in the gospel
QUESTION 3: illumination
QUESTION 4: sanctification
QUESTION 5: False
QUESTION 6
   C. Israel's entry into the land following their deliverance from Egypt
QUESTION 7: True
QUESTION 8
   D. To recover something by the payment of a price
QUESTION 9: False
QUESTION 10: False
QUESTION 11
   D. Deism
QUESTION 12
   B. He is the creator and sustainer of all things.
QUESTION 13: True
QUESTION 14
   D. His resurrection
QUESTION 15
   F. The fullness of the divine nature itself
QUESTION 16: True
QUESTION 17: reconciliation
QUESTION 18: justification
QUESTION 19: False
QUESTION 20
   C. The hardships that must be endured in order for the gospel to be proclaimed
QUESTION 21: False
QUESTION 22: False
QUESTION 23
   A. One was doctrinal, the other application-based.
QUESTION 24: understanding
QUESTION 25
   D. Colossians

Unit Three: The Gospel Explained and Defended

You have now reached the halfway mark of the course. Six lessons are completed; six more remain. The three lessons of this unit will take you through the entire second chapter of Colossians.

You will examine Colossians 2:1-8 in Lesson 7. In the first five verses Paul explains that he is writing this letter to lead the readers to maturity in Christ. In the final three verses, he sets about this purpose in earnest by first exhorting them to continue in the truths they received in the beginning and not to allow a false teaching to lead them astray. This exhortation introduces the section of the letter that sets forth the true substance of its message—Colossians 2:6-4:6.

Lesson 8 covers Colossians 2:9-15. This is the theological heart of the letter. Here Paul shows the superiority of the gospel to the false teaching. He does this by reminding the Colossians of the blessings of salvation that are already theirs through their union with Christ in his death, burial, and resurrection.

Colossians 2:16-23 is the subject of Lesson 9. In those verses, Paul applies the truths to the claims of the false teachers. Paul explains the fullness of spiritual experience is found in a relationship with Christ, not in the empty practices of these Jews with their claims of private mystical experiences.

Unit Outline

Lesson 7: Paul's Goal for the Colossians—Colossians 2:1-8

Lesson 8: The Theological Heart of the Letter—Colossians 2:9-15

Lesson 9: The False Teaching—Colossians 2:16-23)

Unit Objectives

When you have completed this unit, you should be able to:
- Recognize how Paul sets forth the specific purpose of his letter to the Colossians in Colossians 2:1-5, and particularly what he means by his goal "that they may have all the riches that assurance brings in their understanding of the knowledge of the mystery of God, namely, Christ."
- Explain the relationship of Colossians 2:6-8 to Colossians 1:9-10 and how this paragraph forms the introduction to the extended section of the letter that contains the true substance of its message
- Discuss how Paul uses this doctrinal section of Colossians 2:9-15 to explain why the Colossians should reject the claims of the false teachers—in particular how their union with Christ in his death, burial, and resurrection fits into this explanation
- Describe Paul's critique of the false teaching in Colossians 2:16-23 and identify methods and principles in this critique that can be used in combating modern day false teachings

Lesson 7: Paul's Goal for the Colossians (Col 2:1-8)

Lesson 6 began with a study of Colossians 1:21-23. In this final paragraph of the first doctrinal section of the letter, Paul focuses on the doctrine of reconciliation. Formerly the Colossians were alienated from God, but he has reconciled them to himself through the death of his son so that they can now enjoy the relationship with him that he intended from the beginning.

Then Lesson 6 dealt with Paul's explanation in Colossians 1:24-29 of the nature of his mission. God has entrusted him with the stewardship of making known among the nations the previously hidden mystery of the gospel (Col 1:24-27). The goal for which Paul strives is to bring each and every convert to maturity in Christ (Col 1:28-29).

Now in Lesson 7, you will examine two paragraphs that together form a transition in the structure of the letter. The first, Colossians 2:1-5, concludes Paul's explanation of the nature of his mission. The second, Colossians 2:6-8, introduces that section of the letter which contains the real substance of his message.

Topic 1 covers Colossians 2:1-5. In this paragraph, Paul states his goal for his readers and hence the purpose of this letter. It is for them to come to a mature faith and understanding of God's plan of salvation revealed in the gospel and to continue to stand firm and not fall prey to deceptive arguments.

Colossians 2:6-8 is the foundation for Topic 2. Here Paul introduces the final major section of the letter by repeating its theme in the form of an exhortation. He urges them to continue steadfastly in the teachings about Christ that they received in the beginning and to be on guard against those who seek to lead them away from this path.

Lesson Outline

Topic 1: Why Paul Writes This Letter (Col 2:1-5)

Topic 2: Continue in the Path of Christ (Col 2:6-8)

Lesson Objectives

When you have completed this lesson, you should be able to:
- State the specific purpose of the letter as explained in Colossians 2:1-5
- Describe the nature of Paul's striving for the Colossians
- Explain what it means to truly know God's mystery
- Differentiate between what the Jews taught about the treasures of wisdom and knowledge and what Paul instructed
- Discuss the condition of the Colossians' faith and how Paul was able to be present to encourage them
- Discuss the role of Colossians 2:6-8 in the overall structure of the letter
- Explain in what sense the Colossians formerly "received Jesus" as stated in Colossians 2:6
- Recognize the importance of laying the right foundation of instruction with new believers according to Colossians 2:6-7
- Define "the traditions of men" and "the elements of the world" in Colossians 2:8

Assignments

For each of the paragraphs of Colossians covered in this lesson follow this three-step procedure:

Step 1:

(a) Make a structural diagram of the passage on the worksheet provided.

(b) Summarize the results in an outline and theme statement.

(c) Compare your conclusions with those in the Answer Section.

Step 2:

Examine the details of the paragraph. Record your observations, interpretations, and applications on the worksheet.

Step 3:

(a) Read the commentary on this passage of Colossians.

(b) Answer the questions in the lesson.

(c) Pay special attention to the *Important Facts to Remember*.

Topic 1: Why Paul Writes This Letter (Col 2:1-5)

This is the third and final paragraph of the opening section of the body of the letter, Colossians 1:24-2:5. Paul's purpose in this section is to state his reason for writing. In the first paragraph, Colossians 1:24-27, he tells how God commissioned him to proclaim the message of Christ among the Gentiles. In Colossians 1:28-29 he explains that the goal of his preaching and teaching is to present everyone mature in Christ. This, he now explains in Colossians 2:1-5, is likewise his goal for the Colossians. With this purpose in mind, he is writing to them.

Begin your study by reading Colossians 2:1-5. Then read the Worksheet on Colossians 2:1-5. Copy it in your Life Notebook and complete step 1 of the "Assignments." Check your conclusions by comparing them with the Answer Section for Colossians 2:1-5. Next, complete step 2 by recording on the same worksheet your detailed observations, interpretations, and applications. For the third and final step, carefully read the Commentary on Colossians 2:1-5. Then answer the questions, taking special note of the *Important Facts to Remember*.

Worksheet for Colossians 2:1-5

¹ FOR

I want you to know

how great a struggle I have for you, and for those in Laodicea,
and for those who have not met me face to face.

² MY GOAL IS THAT

their hearts, having been knit together in love,
may be encouraged,

AND THAT

they may have all the riches that assurance brings in their understanding
of the knowledge of the mystery of God,

namely, Christ.

³ in whom are hidden all the treasures of wisdom and knowledge.

⁴ I SAY THIS SO THAT

no one will deceive you through arguments that sound reasonable.

⁵ FOR

though I am absent from you in body,

I am present with you in spirit,

Rejoicing to see your morale and the firmness of your faith in Christ.

Commentary on Colossians 2:1-5
C. Paul's Goal for the Colossians—Colossians 2:1-5

This is the third and final paragraph of the opening section of the body of the letter, Colossians 1:24-2:5. To review, Paul's purpose in this section is to state his reason for writing. In the first paragraph (Col 1:4-27), he told how God commissioned him to proclaim the message of Christ among the Gentiles. In Colossians 1:28-29 he explained that the goal of his preaching and teaching is to present everyone mature in Christ. This, he now explains in Colossians 2:1-5, is likewise his goal for the Colossians. And it is with this aim in mind that he is writing to them.

Verse 1

For. This word introduces an explanation of why Paul told them all of this in Colossians 1:24-29 about his calling, the aim of his ministry and how he strives to accomplish this goal. It is because his ministry includes them. He is striving on their behalf to bring them to maturity in Christ.

I want you to know. Expressions like this were commonly used by letter writers in Paul's day to introduce some matter of special importance (see Rom 1:13; 11:25; 1 Cor 10:1; 2 Cor 1:8; Phil 1:12). Paul uses it here to introduce a concise statement of the specific reason for this letter.

how great a struggle I have for you, and for those in Laodicea, and for those who have not met me face to face. In Colossians 1:28-29, Paul spoke of his toil and struggle to bring everyone to maturity in Christ. Now he moves from the general to the specific. He is presently striving on behalf of the Colossians and other believers in that area. His struggle for these young believers was inward. He wrestled in prayer for them (Col 1:9-10; 4:12). He was deeply concerned about their spiritual well-being—particularly because of the danger they faced from the deceptive teaching (see 2 Cor 11:28-29). No doubt he thought long and hard about the seductiveness of this teaching and the best way to refute it. This letter, in fact, is the result of his Spirit–guided meditations. In addition to these things, there was the hardship caused by his imprisonment.

This is the first mention of Laodicea in the letter (see Col 4:13-16). Laodicea was a large town twelve miles (19.3 km) to the west of Colossae where Epaphras had also established a church. This verse plainly indicates that Paul had never visited these churches. But does it also tell us that he had never set foot in these towns? Interpreters usually assume that it does. This interpretation is reflected in the many Bible atlases that show Paul passing to the north of Colossae on his third missionary journey when he traveled west from Antioch through the Galatian region and Phrygia and then to Ephesus (Acts 18:22-19:1). But this may be a misreading of both the text and the geography of the region.

The Galatian region and eastern Phrygia lie on the great central plateau of Asia Minor, which is 3,000 to 5,000 feet (900-1500 meters) above sea level. Between the sea and the plateau is a low-lying coastal region that consists mainly of river valleys separated by great mountain ridges that extend from the central plateau. Roads that descend from the plateau into the coastal lowlands to the west follow these valleys. There were two such valley roads available to Paul as he headed for Ephesus: a northern route and a southern one. The first passed to the north of Colossae and approached Ephesus through the valley of the Cayster River. This road was steep and rugged and not heavily traveled. It is the one shown in many Bible atlases. The other road descended through the valley of the Lycus River and passed through Colossae and Laodicea. It was by far the easier and more heavily traveled route. It has been called the great Eastern Highway. This is because it was the principal trade route from Ephesus eastward to the Euphrates valley and beyond. A reasonable assumption is that Paul used it too, and thus he passed through Colossae and Laodicea on his way to Ephesus. This conclusion is entirely consistent with our verse. It tells us that Paul had not visited these churches (indeed, they had not yet been planted), not that he had never visited these towns.

Verse 2

My goal is that their hearts, having been knit together in love, may be encouraged. With these words, Paul begins to explain the purpose of his efforts for them. It is to impart strength and encouragement, particularly in the face of the deceptive teaching (Col 2:4) that threatened the congregation. Paul's concern is not simply for the Colossians as a collection of individuals. The words "knit together in love" (or "held together in love") show he is concerned for the unity and well-being of the church as a whole. As the church is united by love, its members grow towards maturity in Christ (compare Col 2:19).

and that they may have all the riches that assurance brings in their understanding. The intended result of this encouragement and unity of the body is growth in understanding of the gospel leading to a firm and settled confidence in its truthfulness. In Colossians 1:28-29, we saw that Paul's efforts were directed towards bringing believers to maturity in Christ. Here in Colossians 2:1-2, we see more specifically what Paul means by maturity. It is, first of all, a clear-sighted understanding of God's plan of salvation revealed in the gospel. Secondly, it means a rich confidence in the truthfulness of the gospel and in Christ its author. Implied in this, thirdly, is the living out of this confidence and understanding in daily life. Paul first introduced this theme in Colossians 1:9-10 in his prayer for knowledge and spiritual understanding that they might walk worthy of the Lord. Now in Colossians 2:2, he equates this outcome with Christian maturity and identifies it as the goal of his efforts for his readers. This, in fact, is the purpose of the letter to the Colossians.

of the knowledge of the mystery of God, namely, Christ. Paul restates the goal of his efforts for emphasis on what he wishes them to understand and have confidence. In doing so, he sums up the nature of Christian maturity as simply **knowing Christ**. This is very compressed language. It is as compressed as when Paul said in Colossians 1:28 that his ministry consists of **proclaiming Christ**. Both of these compressed statements must be understood in the context of Paul's emphasis in Colossians on the need for believers to understand the gospel and to walk accordingly (see Col 1:9-10). Thus, as we saw earlier, proclaiming Christ means—in the case of converts—instructing them in God's overall plan of salvation through Christ, including how to live in accordance with it. In the same way, knowing Christ in this verse means attaining a thorough understanding of these truths. Moreover, understanding these truths is inseparable in Paul's mind from believing them and walking accordingly. Therefore, in this context to understand "the knowledge of the mystery of God, namely, Christ" means the same thing as to be mature in Christ.

Verse 3

in whom are hidden all the treasures of wisdom and knowledge. Paul now explains why knowing Christ—that is, understanding God's plan of salvation through Christ—is the goal of his labors for them. It is because all the resources they need are found in Christ. All we need to know about God, his purposes, and how he desires us to live can be found in the crucified and risen Christ who is the focus of Paul's preaching and teaching.

The false teachers were telling the Colossians otherwise. The Jews of Paul's day taught that all the treasures of wisdom and knowledge are laid up in heaven. The righteous would inherit them after the judgment in the age to come. The false teachers, however, claimed that through fasting and keeping the Law they had achieved visionary journeys to heaven where these treasures of knowledge were open to them. And with such claims they sought to lure the Colossian Christians into seeking the same mystical experiences. This verse can therefore be seen as Paul's reply to such claims. The believer already has access to God's treasury of wisdom and knowledge. These treasures are found in Christ —not in mystical journeys to heaven.

Verse 4

I say this so that. These words introduce a reason for what Paul just said in Colossians 2:2-3. But these two verses simply summarize the purpose for the entire letter. The purpose is to impart to the readers a clearer knowledge and understanding of God's plan of salvation through Christ so that they might walk worthy of the Lord and become mature in the faith. Thus, when Paul says, "I am saying this," he is referring not just to Colossians 2:2-3 but to the entire point of the letter. And since the letter's aim is to bring them to maturity in Christ, this includes warning them against deceptive false teachings that would lead them away from this path to Christian maturity.

no one will deceive you through arguments that sound reasonable. This is the first direct statement in the letter regarding the presence of a deceptive teaching in Colossae and the danger it posed for the church. An argument that "sound[s] reasonable" is an argument that may seem superficially good, however, closer examination shows it to be false and misleading. The enemy often attacks young converts in this way. He uses clever, fine-sounding arguments that are close enough to the truth to appear acceptable (often quoting Scripture), but in reality, they are contrary to the gospel. It was with such arguments that the Jewish mystics of Colossae sought to persuade these young Christians. Young converts lack the stability and discernment of more mature believers and are more easily deceived. The best defense against such deception, says Paul, is a clear and mature understanding of the truth (see Eph 4:13-14).

Verse 5

For. In this final verse, Paul explains how he can warn and instruct them as he is doing here, including how he can do it with a knowledge of their specific needs.

though I am absent from you in body, I am present with you in spirit. In order to fulfill his stewardship in regard to the Christians of Colossae, Paul faced a great obstacle. He had never met them. Moreover, he was unable to be present with them now. He was in prison over a hundred miles away. How was he to instruct and admonish without being present? How was he to tailor his instructions to their specific needs? The answer, of course, is through a letter.

It was understood in the ancient world that a letter served as a substitute for the personal presence of the writer. Thus, the expression "absent in body, present in spirit" was often used of a writer's presence through his letter. Epaphras had informed Paul of the nature of the false teaching and how the church was holding up against this threat. Paul was therefore able to carry out his apostolic ministry among the Colossians—and tailor his instruction to their specific needs—by means of this letter. Through it he was present among them. And through it he continues to minister among us to this day.

rejoicing to see your morale and the firmness of your faith in Christ. In this second part of Paul's explanation of how he is able to be present (in spirit) with the Colossians and helping to nurture them in their faith, he tells them how they appear to him. He sees (having heard from Epaphras) that they are in good shape, and in this he rejoices. The church is in a well-ordered condition—unlike the Corinthians (1 Cor 14:40). The Colossians' faith in Christ remains firm and steadfast. They have not yet fallen captive to the deceitful teaching. Thus, Paul's warnings regarding the false teaching are aimed not at restoring those who have fallen prey to error (as happened with the Galatians), but at keeping them in the path of truth.

QUESTION 1

In Colossians 2:1-5, Paul explains the specific purpose of his letter to the Colossians. State briefly this purpose.

QUESTION 2

Which of the following was **not** a part of Paul's striving for the Christians of Colossae and Laodicea (Col 2:1)?

- A. His prayers for them
- B. His deep concern for their spiritual well-being
- C. His efforts to raise money because of the famine
- D. His letter to them

QUESTION 3

What is clear from Colossians 2:1 is that Paul had not visited the churches in these towns. It is likely, however, that he passed through the towns on his way to Ephesus before the churches were planted. *True or False?*

QUESTION 4

According to Colossians 2:2, Paul's goal was for each of his readers to truly know God's mystery, namely Christ. Explain briefly what it means in this context to "know Christ."

QUESTION 5

According to the Jews of Paul's day, where are all the treasures of wisdom and knowledge to be found?

- A. The Scriptures
- B. Heaven
- C. The Messiah
- D. The temple
- E. The scribes and wise men of Jerusalem

QUESTION 6

In the ancient world, the expression "absent in body, present in spirit" was often used of a writer's presence through his _____.

QUESTION 7

Paul praises the Colossians for the firmness of their faith in Colossians 2:5 because it was customary to say only positive things in the early part of a letter. Further on in the letter, however, it becomes clear that many of the Colossians had in fact been taken captive by the fine-sounding arguments of the false teachers. *True or False?*

QUESTION 8

What were the most significant influences that God used to lead you toward maturity in Christ? These could be people, books, sermons, experiences, etc. What role did the understanding of God's plan of salvation through Christ play in this process (Col 2:2)? Record your thoughts in your Life Notebook.

QUESTION 9

What "arguments that sound reasonable" (Col 2:4) did you find attractive as a young Christian? In what ways did a better understanding of God's word allow you to see through this deception? Record your thoughts in your Life Notebook.

QUESTION 10

What are the two most significant insights into the nature of Christian ministry that you gained from Colossians 1:24-2:5?

Important Facts to Remember About Colossians 2:1-5

1. In Colossians 2:1-5 Paul states that the specific purpose of his letter is to bring the readers to maturity in Christ.

2. In Colossians 2:2 Paul uses very compressed language to summarize the goal of his efforts for the Colossians. It is that they might truly know God's mystery, namely Christ. In this context to know Christ means the same thing as to be mature in Christ (compare Col 1:28).

3. While the false teachers claimed that "the treasures of wisdom and knowledge" are in heaven and available to those who gain heavenly visions, Paul assured the Colossians that these treasures are in fact found in Christ.

4. Paul looked upon his letter to the Colossians as a substitute for his personal presence and ministry among them (Col 2:5).

5. Although the deceptive teaching posed a threat to the Colossians, they remained firm in their faith.

Topic 2: Continue in the Path of Christ (Col 2:6-8)

In Colossians 1:24-2:5, Paul explains to the Colossians why he is writing to them. God has commissioned him to proclaim the message of Christ among the Gentiles with the goal of bringing every convert to maturity in Christ. And it is with this goal in mind that he is writing to them. In Colossians 2:6-8, Paul takes up this task in earnest by introducing the section of the letter that presents the true substance of his message (Col 2:6-4:6). He does this by repeating the theme of the letter first announced in Colossians 1:9-10. The Colossian Christians must steadfastly continue in the teachings they received in the beginning, being built up on that foundation, and not allow a false teaching to lead them astray.

Begin your study by reading Colossians 2:6-8. Then read the Worksheet on Colossians 2:6-8. Copy it in your Life Notebook and complete step 1 of the "Assignments." Check your conclusions by comparing them with the Answer Section for Colossians 2:6-8. Next, complete step 2 by recording on the same worksheet your detailed observations, interpretations, and applications. For the third and final step, carefully read the Commentary on Colossians 2:6-8. Then answer the questions, taking special note of the *Important Facts to Remember*.

Worksheet for Colossians 2:6-8

⁶ THEREFORE,

just as you received [the message of] Christ Jesus as Lord,

continue to live your lives in him,

    ⁷ rooted

    AND

    built up in him

    AND

    firm in your faith, just as you were taught

    AND

    overflowing with thankfulness.

⁸ Be careful

not to allow anyone to captivate you

    through an empty, deceitful philosophy

        that is according to human traditions

        and the elemental spirits of the world,

        and not according to Christ.

Commentary on Colossians 2:6-8

IV. Live According to the Gospel—Colossians 2:6-4:6

We have now completed the first major section of the body of the letter, Colossians 1:24-2:5. As we saw, Paul explains here his reason for writing. God has commissioned him to proclaim Christ among the Gentiles with the goal of bringing every convert to maturity in Christ. Hence, this is his goal for the Colossians as well. It is the object of his prayers (Col 1:9-10) and the purpose of his letter (Col 2:1-5).

Having stated his purpose for writing, Paul now devotes the remainder of the body of the letter, Colossians 2:6-4:6, to fulfilling this purpose. It is here that we meet the true substance of the letter. This remaining section of the body divides into two principal parts. The first part, Colossians 2:9-15, gives a fresh exposition of the doctrinal basis of the Christian life. The second part, Colossians 2:16-4:6, explains how to walk in accordance with these truths—particularly in light of the deceptive teaching that threatened the congregation. The opening paragraph, Colossians 2:6-8, introduces this entire two-part section.

A. Introduction: Continue in the Gospel as You Began—Colossians 2:6-8

This introduction takes the form of an exhortation that once again expresses the theme and purpose of the letter. Paul exhorts the Colossians to continue to walk in accordance with the teachings about Christ that they received in the beginning. Having been firmly rooted in Christ, they are to grow and develop towards Christian maturity. They must not allow themselves to be led away from this path and taken captive by a deceitful teaching.

Verse 6

Therefore. These words introduce a result (a conclusion) that follows from the last part of Colossians 2:5, where Paul commends the Colossians for the firmness of their faith in Christ. So then, says Paul here in Colossians 2:6, continue in this steadfast way of life—just as you were taught from the beginning.

just as you received [the message of] Christ Jesus as Lord. These words explain how the Colossians are to carry out the exhortation of the second half of this verse: "continue to live your lives in him." They are to continue to walk in the path they were taught in the beginning.

The words "the message of" do not appear in the Greek text. They are added here to clarify Paul's actual meaning. The verb translated "received" was commonly used in the early church to refer to instruction delivered by a teacher and received by students (1 Cor 11:23; 15:3; Phil 4:9; 1 Thess 4:1). Thus, when Paul reminds the Colossians of when they received Jesus, he is referring to the teaching about Jesus that they received. We saw this same manner of expression in Colossians 1:27, 28 where proclaiming Christ actually means proclaiming the message about Christ (see also Col 2:2 and Phil 1:17).

In the comments on Colossians 1:7, we noted that the teaching about Jesus that the Colossians received was not just the evangelistic message that Epaphras preached in order to lead them to Christ. It included also the systematic instruction that he delivered to them as new believers in order to establish them in the faith and set them on the path of spiritual growth. He taught them who Jesus is as the Messiah and Lord, and how Jesus brought redemption to this fallen world. A second aspect of this instruction focused on how Christians should conduct themselves in the light of these truths.

continue to live your lives in him. In the first half of the verse, Paul identified the true and right path. It is the one delivered to them in the beginning by Epaphras. Now Paul exhorts them to remain steadfastly on this path. In the words of Isaiah, "This is the way; walk in it" (Isa 30:21, NASB). They must not allow a false teaching to turn them aside from the road on which they have started.

The Bible frequently uses the metaphor of **walking** or **living** to describe a person's conduct or way of life. Paul used it earlier in Colossians 1:10 in his prayer for the Colossians to be filled with the knowledge of God's saving will so that they might live in a manner worthy of the Lord. This prayer expressed the theme and purpose of the letter. Now in Colossians 2:6 he uses the same metaphor to express the same basic idea. Both texts express Paul's objective for his readers: a life lived in accordance with the gospel. This is the object of Paul's intercession for them in Colossians 1:10 and the object of his exhortation in Colossians 2:6. This shows how intercession and exhortation—prayer and action—go hand in hand. Paul obviously looked upon his exhortation and instruction as part of the means God would use to answer his prayer.

Verse 7

rooted and built up in him and firm in your faith. In this verse, Paul now uses a series of four verbs to describe the nature of this continuing walk in Christ: "rooted," "built up," "firm," and "overflowing," with thankfulness. It is interesting to observe that Paul used a very similar series of four verbs to describe the nature of the walk that was "worthy of the Lord" in Colossians 1:10-12: "bearing fruit," "growing," "being strengthened," and "giving thanks." Each series begins with the suggestion of an image of a fruit tree. Then follows the notion of development, then strengthening, and finally thanksgiving.

The similarity between these two passages is striking. It is obviously there for the sake of emphasis. But to understand this emphasis properly we need to explore the similarity further. We already noted that each set of describing verbs follows a statement of the theme and purpose of the letter (Col 1:9-10; 2:6). The statement of the theme and purpose in Colossians 1:9-10 introduces the letter as a whole. The four descriptive verbs then lead directly into the first of the two doctrinal sections of the letter (Col 1:12-23). This pattern repeats itself starting with Colossians 2:6. Paul has arrived at that point in his letter where he intends to set forth the true substance of his message. He therefore restates his theme in Colossians 2:6 together with the four verbs that describe this walk of faith in Colossians 2:7. Then, following a warning in Colossians 2:8 concerning those who would lead them astray from this path, he launches into the second doctrinal section of his letter (Col 2:9-15). These observations demonstrate the great importance of Colossians 2:6-8 as a structural feature in the landscape of Colossians. These verses pick up the theme of the letter from Colossians 1:9-10, reminding the readers once again of its central purpose, and thus provide a fitting introduction to Colossians 2:6-4:6, the section in which we meet the true substance of the letter.

The first of these four descriptive verbs, "rooted," pictures these young believers as a newly planted tree that has extended its roots deeply into the soil. The tense of the verb points to a time in the past when the rooting took place. It further indicates that they have remained rooted up to the present time. The verb is also passive. They did not root themselves. Someone else did it. Paul is referring here to the ministry of Epaphras. He planted them when they trusted Christ, and through his ministry of teaching, they became firmly rooted. But behind the labors of Epaphras was the supernatural working of God causing the growth. As Paul wrote to the Corinthians, "I planted, Apollos watered, but God caused it to grow" (1 Cor 3:6).

What is the point of this comparison of the Colossians with a tree? When Paul compared them to a tree in Colossians 1:10, the point was fruitfulness and growth. Now in Colossians 2:7 the point is being **built up**. As a tree continues steadfastly it will be sustained and grow from the same roots that it developed when it was newly planted, so also must the Colossians. They must continue to grow by conducting their lives on the basis of what they were taught in the beginning.

In this second description of their continuing walk in Christ ("built up"), Paul takes up a new image. They are to be like a building under construction, which rises on its foundation. (The roots in the first image have become the foundation in this second image.) The point of this new image is **development**. They are to progress and develop in Christ, and they are to do it in accordance with the foundation that was laid for them in the beginning. Maturity in Christ is the goal of this development (Col 1:28).

and firm in your faith just as you were taught. The third descriptive verb ("firm") further describes this process of development. As they are being built up, they are to be strengthened (established and reinforced) in the faith. The building should not simply grow bigger. It must also grow in strength and durability. The term "faith" in this context refers to the object of faith. The words "as you were taught" indicate that the object of their faith is the teaching they received from Epaphras. What then does it mean to be strengthened in this teaching? It means being strengthened by God in our spiritual understanding, commitment and application of these truths in daily life. In this context it has special reference to being strong in order to resist the temptation and deception of the false teaching (see Col 2:5, 8).

Observe that each of these descriptions of the Christian life relates to the instruction the Colossians received in the beginning. It is the path they must walk. It established their roots and the foundation for all subsequent growth and development. Growth, in fact, means becoming stronger in it. All of this shows the vital importance of laying the right foundation of instruction with new Christians.

and overflowing with thankfulness. The fourth and final description of this way of life that should characterize Christians is "overflowing with thankfulness." Thankfulness is an expression of gratitude to God. Another word for thankfulness is praise. Thankfulness is an essential part of faith because by thanking God we acknowledge that he is the source of all things. He is creator, sustainer, and redeemer. Most importantly, we should thank God for the salvation he has freely granted us through Christ (Col 1:12-22). Thankfulness is our response to God. As the result, he is glorified. Growth in our understanding of God and his grace should produce a growing response of abundant, overflowing praise. Giving praise to God is one way that we serve him.

Verse 8

Be careful not to allow anyone to captivate you. Colossians 2:6-7 focus on the foundational instruction about Christ that the Colossians received from Epaphras. This is the path they must walk. Now in Colossians 2:8, Paul warns them against those who would lead them astray from this path.

This warning suggests immediate danger. He first mentioned this danger in Colossians 2:4 where he warned of their fine-sounding but deceptive arguments. Now he warns the Colossians against being taken captive by these arguments. The image is drawn from the realm of warfare. It pictures soldiers carrying away captives as the spoils of war in order to enslave them. Thus, Paul warns, to watch out lest someone carry you away from the truth into the slavery of error.

through an empty, deceitful philosophy. This line answers the questions, "How could they be taken captive?" "What methods would they use?" The term "philosophy" originally meant love of wisdom. It is a high–sounding term which many groups applied to their teachings. One Jewish writer explained that Judaism is "the philosophy of Moses." An early Christian leader described Christianity as "the true philosophy." The false teachers apparently made a similar claim about their doctrines. Paul's point then is not to condemn all philosophy. It is to expose this one as false. He describes it as hollow or empty. It has the "appearance of wisdom" (Col 2:23), but only the appearance. It is therefore "deceptive." It is a sham, a fraud, seductive, and misleading. By contrast, the gospel is "the message of truth" (Col 1:5), and in Christ "are hidden all the treasures of wisdom and knowledge" (Col 2:3).

that is according to human traditions. This line and the next describe further this "empty, deceitful philosophy." Here Paul identifies the source of the false teaching: the traditions of **men**. The word "tradition" refers to an authoritative teaching that has been handed down from earlier teachers in the past. Jesus used the same phrase in Mk 7:8 to describe the detailed rules of conduct that the scribes and Pharisees imposed on the people. Their intention was to build a fence around the Law by adding detailed rules to God's commands, which in fact went far beyond these commands. For example, where Scripture simply required a person to wash his hands, the tradition added detailed rules about how to do it: how to hold the hands, and exactly how much water was required. These interpretations were viewed as nearly equal in authority to Scripture. Some even claimed that Moses received them from God on Mount Sinai, and they were handed down by word of mouth from his day to their own. But Jesus rejected these rules as a human invention. God did not require them. They are traditions of men.

Paul is saying basically the same thing here. The false teachers were Jewish. They used the Scriptures to support their claims. But like the Pharisees they added many rules that went far beyond the Scriptures. Like the Pharisees they also claimed the authority of Scripture for these rules. Such claims are false, says Paul. These teachings depend on the traditions of men. They are not from God.

A regrettable part of human nature is the tendency to add to God's commandments. Eve did it in the Garden of Eden (Gen 3:3). The ancient Pharisees did it. Modern–day cults do it. And some Christian leaders do it. This is a form of **legalism**. The task of the Christian leader is not to twist, distort, or add to God's commandments. If he is to speak with the authority of God, he must "not go beyond what is written" (1 Cor 4:6).

and the elemental spirits of the world. These words further describe the basis and nature of the deceptive teaching. The expression "the elemental spirits of the world" was commonly used among the Greeks to describe the basic elements or building blocks of which all physical things are composed. Paul uses it as a general designation for ceremonial rules and practices—whether Jewish or pagan. His point is that such practices are concerned with merely physical things, whereas the gospel of Christ concerns spiritual realities. The Jews for example insisted on physical circumcision. But Paul assures the Colossians in Colossians 2:11 that they have received a better circumcision—a circumcision made without hands. The Jews also insisted that one's relationship with God depended on keeping rules that prohibited handling, tasting, and touching certain things (Col 2:21). But such things are all destined to perish with use, says Paul (Col 2:22). They are material, fleshly, earthly (Heb 9:10). At best, they served as symbols and shadows of the new era of salvation that Christ would bring (Col 2:16). Christians have been freed from these "elemental spirits of the world" because they no longer belong to the world (Col 2:20). Instead they belong to the realm above (Col 3:1)—that is, to the new era of salvation which Christ introduced through his death and resurrection.

In Galatians 4:3, 9, Paul refers to ceremonial laws as the "basic forces" of the world. The Galatian Christians were formerly pagans, but now certain men were telling them that they must also keep the ceremonial laws of Judaism to be saved. In response to this false teaching, Paul compared these laws to the guardians and managers to which a child had to submit until he reached the age when he could inherit his father's estate. Before that age, he was no different than a slave. Afterwards, he was free of these managers and able to enjoy the full privileges of a mature son (Gal 4:1-7). So it is with the Christian, says Paul. Formerly we were as children, held in bondage under the "elemental spirits of the world"— ceremonial rules and regulations. Now we are free as mature sons and heirs. Therefore, do not turn back to the bondage of childhood by submitting again to ceremonial rules (Gal 4:9).

> These are the concepts that underlie Paul's warning to the Colossians here in Colossians 2:8. The false teachers were telling these young Christians that keeping their ceremonial rules and regulations would lead to an advanced spiritual experience. On the contrary, says Paul. It would be a step backwards—from the spiritual to the material, from maturity to childhood, and from freedom to bondage.
>
> **and not according to Christ**. This final criticism of the false teaching is the most important: it is not based on Christ. By this Paul means it is contrary to the instruction about Christ they received in the beginning. In other words, it is contrary to the gospel. The biblical teaching about Christ must be the standard by which we judge every teacher and every doctrine. Whatever fails this test must be rejected.

QUESTION 11

Explain briefly the role of Colossians 2:6-8 in the overall structure of Colossians.

QUESTION 12

The translation of the word "received" in Col 2:6 was commonly used in the early church to refer to instruction delivered by a teacher and received by students. Thus, the reference is to the instruction about Christ that they received in the beginning from Epaphras. They are to continue to walk in this path. *True or False?*

QUESTION 13

In Colossians 2:7 Paul compares the Colossians to a tree that has been "rooted." What is the point of this comparison?

   A. Fruitfulness
   B. Mystery
   C. Growth
   D. Steadfastness

Use the following graphics for reference as you answer Question 14

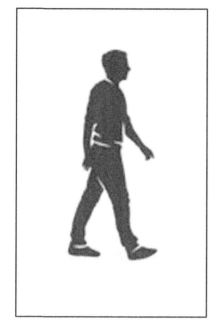  

QUESTION 14

Explain briefly how Paul uses the image of (a) living (or walking) in Colossians 2:6a, of (b) a tree and (c) a building in Colossians 2:7 to emphasize the importance of the teachings the Colossians received from Epaphras in the beginning.

QUESTION 15

The term "philosophy" originally meant "love of _____."

QUESTION 16

The term "human traditions" in Colossians 2:8 was used to describe the Jewish practice of adding detailed rules of conduct to God's commands. *True or False?*

QUESTION 17

What are "elemental spirits of the world" in Colossians 2:8?

    A. Worldly philosophies

    B. Ceremonial rules and practices

    C. Spirits that exercise authority in the world

    D. All the laws of Judaism

    E. Things of the world that tempt believers to sin

QUESTION 18

In Colossians 2:7 Paul describes the Colossians' progress in the Christian life in terms of a young tree and a new building under construction. The instruction about Christ they received in the beginning established the roots for this new tree; it laid the foundation for the new building. Each image emphasizes the importance of the starting point to ensure the strength and quality of what proceeds from it (what grows from the roots, what is built on the foundation).

    a. What does this tell you about the importance of the instruction that is given to new converts?

    b. What does it tell you about what the content of this instruction should be?

    c. Consider what you were taught as a new convert. Did it provide you with a solid foundation? In what ways could it have been improved?

    d. Consider your course *What Every Christian Should Know About Salvation*. What insights from this passage can you use to make this course better?

QUESTION 19

Is there a false teaching that threatens to take captive those to whom you minister? In what ways does this teaching resemble the description that Paul gives in Colossians 2:8 of the Colossian false teaching?

Important Facts to Remember About Colossians 2:6-8

1. In Colossians 2:6-8 Paul introduces the principal part of the body of the letter (Col 2:6-4:6). Here he again expresses the theme and purpose of the letter by urging the Colossians to continue walking the path of instruction about Christ they received in the beginning. They must not allow a false teaching to lead them astray from this path.

2. This instruction laid out the path to Christian maturity. It established the roots and the foundation for all their subsequent growth (Col 2:7). This illustrates the vital importance of laying the right foundation of instruction for new Christians.

3. The expression "human traditions" in Colossians 2:8 refers to the Jewish practice of adding detailed rules and regulations to God's commandments.

4. In ordinary Greek usage "the elemental spirits of the world" refers to physical things. Paul uses this expression in Colossians 2:8 as a designation for ceremonial rules and practices—both Jewish and pagan—because they are concerned with physical, earthly things, unlike the gospel which is concerned with spiritual, heavenly matters. These ceremonial rules enslave all who are under them.

Lesson 7 Self Check

QUESTION 1

In Colossians 2:1-5 Paul explains that the specific purpose of his letter is to bring the readers to maturity in Christ. *True or False?*

QUESTION 2

In Colossians 2:1 Paul mentions how hard he was striving for the Christians in the area of Colossae. Which of the following was **not** a part of Paul's striving?

    A. His letter to them

    B. His concern regarding the false teaching

    C. His anxieties over the persecution they faced

    D. His prayers for them

QUESTION 3

To have the "knowledge of the mystery of God, namely, Christ" (Col 2:2) means to have a thorough understanding of God's plan of salvation through Christ, including how to live according to it. *True or False?*

QUESTION 4

The Jews of Paul's day were teaching the Colossians that "the treasures of wisdom and knowledge" are stored in heaven. *True or False?*

QUESTION 5

In the ancient world, the expression "absent in body, present in spirit" was often used to describe a writer's presence through his letter. *True or False?*

QUESTION 6

Which of the following is **not** true of the paragraph Colossians 2:6-8?

    A. In it Paul repeats the theme and purpose of the letter.

    B. It displays striking similarities with Colossians 1:9-10.

    C. It introduces the final major section of the body of the letter, Colossians 2:6-4:6.

    D. It summarizes the saving benefits of Christ's death and resurrection.

QUESTION 7

The term "received" refers to instruction received from a teacher. To receive Jesus in this context refers to the message about Jesus that the Colossians received in the beginning. *True or False?*

QUESTION 8

The images of a tree and a building in Colossians 2:7 both illustrate the importance of instruction in the life of the new convert. *True or False?*

QUESTION 9

The expression "human traditions" describes the Jewish practice of adding detailed rules of conduct to God's commands. *True or False?*

QUESTION 10

What are "elemental spirits of the world" in Colossians 2:8?
- A. Things of the world that can tempt believers to sin
- B. The Jewish Law in general
- C. Spirits that exercise authority in the world
- D. Teachings of worldly philosophers
- E. Ceremonial rules and regulations

Lesson 7 Answers to Questions

WORKSHEET FOR COLOSSIANS 2:1-5

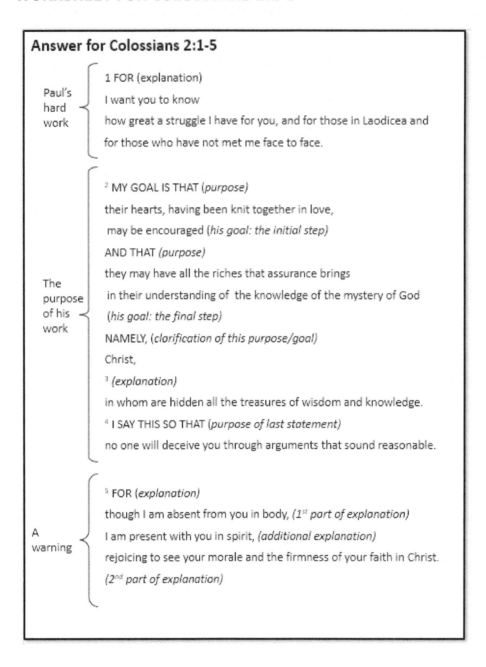

Textual Outline of Colossians 2:1-5
I. Paul's hard work on behalf of the Colossians and others (Col 2:1)
II. The purpose of Paul's hard work (Col 2:2-3)
    A. His goal, the initial step: Encouragement and unity in love (Col 2:2a)
    B. His goal, the final step: Full conviction that understanding brings (Col 2:2b)
    C. The goal clarified: To truly know God's mystery, Christ (Col 2:2c)
    D. Explanation: All wisdom and knowledge is found in Christ. (Col 2:3)
III. A warning (Col 2:4-5)
    A. Purpose of the last statement: To keep them from being deceived (Col 2:4)
    B. Explanation: How Paul can instruct and warn them (Col 2:5)

Theme Statement for Colossians 2:1-5.
Paul strives to bring the Colossians to a true knowledge of Christ and to prevent them from being deceived by false teachers.

QUESTION 1: *Your answer should be similar to the following:*
The purpose was to bring them to maturity in Christ. In the two previous verses (Col 1:28-29), Paul explained that the goal for which he labors with all the Gentiles to whom he carries the gospel is to bring everyone to maturity in Christ. In Colossians 2:1-5, he simply moves from the general to the specific. This is also his goal for the Colossians. This letter belongs to his overall effort to bring them to maturity in Christ.

QUESTION 2
    C. His efforts to raise money because of the famine

QUESTION 3: True

QUESTION 4: *Your answer should be similar to the following:*
To know Christ in this context refers to having a thorough understanding of God's plan of salvation through Christ, including how to live in accordance with it. Therefore, in this context, to truly know Christ means the same thing as to be mature in Christ.

QUESTION 5
    B. Heaven

QUESTION 6: letter

QUESTION 7: False [The Colossians' faith in Christ remains firm and steadfast. They have not yet fallen captive to the deceitful teaching. Thus, Paul's warnings regarding the false teaching are aimed not at restoring those who have fallen prey to error (as happened with the Galatians), but at keeping them in the path of truth.]

QUESTION 8: *Your answer*

QUESTION 9: *Your answer*

QUESTION 10: *Your answer*

WORKSHEET FOR COLOSSIANS 2:6-8

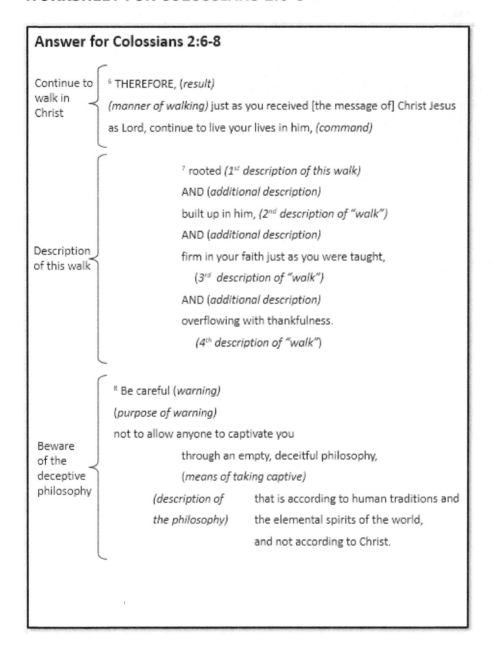

Textual Outline of Colossians 2:6-8.
I. Continue to walk in Christ. (Col 2:6)
II. Description of this walk (Col 2:7)
    A. Staying firmly rooted in him (Col 2:7a)
    B. Being built up in him (Col 2:7b)
    C. Growing stronger in the faith they were taught (Col 2:7c,d)
    D. Overflowing with thanksgiving (Col 2:7e)
III. Beware the deceptive philosophy. (Col 2:8)
    A. Warning: Guard yourselves. (Col 2:8a)
    B. Purpose of warning: To avoid capture (Col 2:8b)
    C. The means of capture: A deceptive philosophy (Col 2:8c)
    D. Description the philosophy: Of man and the world rather than Christ (Col 2:8d-f)

Theme Statement for Colossians 2:6-8.
The Colossians must continue to live according to the message of Christ they received in the beginning.

QUESTION 11: *Your answer should be similar to the following:*
In Colossians 2:6-4:6 we meet the true substance of the letter. This section is devoted to fulfilling the purpose of the letter that Paul first expressed in his prayer of Colossians 1:9-10. The role of Colossians 2:6-8 is to introduce this extended section.

QUESTION 12: True

QUESTION 13
    D. Steadfastness

QUESTION 14: *Your answer should be similar to the following:*
(a) These teachings about Christ and the Christian life are the path, the way of life, that they must continue to follow. (b) As a newly planted tree becomes established by extending its roots into the soil, and as it continues to grow from these roots, so the Colossians must continue steadfastly in the way of life they were taught in the beginning. (c) As a building under construction rises on its foundation, so their lives must be built on the foundation that was laid for them by Epaphras.

QUESTION 15: wisdom

QUESTION 16: True

QUESTION 17
    B. Ceremonial rules and regulations

QUESTION 18: *Your answer*

QUESTION 19: *Your answer*

Lesson 7 Self Check Answers

QUESTION 1: True

QUESTION 2
    C. His anxieties over the persecution they faced

QUESTION 3: True

QUESTION 4: True

QUESTION 5: True

QUESTION 6
    D. It summarizes the saving benefits of Christ's death and resurrection.

QUESTION 7: True

QUESTION 8: True

QUESTION 9: True

QUESTION 10
    E. Ceremonial rules and regulations

Lesson 8: The Theological Heart of the Letter—Colossians 2:9-15

In Lesson 7, you examined Colossians 2:1-8. Together, these two paragraphs act like a hinge upon which the letter turns—concluding one section and introducing the next. The first paragraph concludes Paul's explanation of his mission. It is to proclaim Christ among the Gentiles. His goal is to bring every convert to maturity in Christ, and it is with this goal in mind that he is writing to the Colossians. The second paragraph (Col 2:6-8) introduces the section of the letter most directly concerned with reaching this goal (Col 2:6–4:6). The introduction repeats the theme of the letter first set forth in the prayer of Paul (Col 1:9-10). The Colossians must continue to walk in accordance with the message of Christ they received in the beginning. This is the path to Christian maturity. They must be further built up on that foundation and not allow themselves to be taken captive by a deceptive teaching.

What follows in Colossians 2:9– 4:6 is a fresh exposition of this message they received in the beginning, but with special attention to the deceptive teaching. This exposition has two parts: the doctrinal basis of the Christian life in Colossians 2:9-15 (the gospel explained), and how to walk in accordance with these truths in Colossians 2:16– 4:6 (the gospel applied).

The doctrinal exposition is the subject of Lesson 8. In these two paragraphs Paul explains why the Colossians should reject this deceitful teaching by reminding them of the blessings of redemption they already possess through Christ. This doctrinal section is the theological heart of the letter.

Colossians 2:9-12 is the basis for Topic 1. Paul begins by assuring them that contrary to the claims of false teachers, there is nothing inferior or lacking in the salvation Christ brings. Through their union with him in his death, burial, and resurrection, they have received the circumcision of the heart promised by the prophets and entered the life of the new creation.

Topic 2 covers Colossians 2:13-15. In this second paragraph Paul explains the implications of what it means for Christ to have died for us on the cross. Because Christ paid the penalty for our sins, God has blotted out the indictment against us, declaring us not guilty and granting us eternal life with Christ. As a result, those who believe the gospel go from being spiritually dead to being spiritually alive.

Lesson Outline

Topic 1: Made Full by Dying and Rising with Christ (Col 2:9-12)

Topic 2: Made Alive with Christ (Col 2:13-15)

Lesson Objectives

When you have completed this lesson, you should be able to:
- Explain how believers have been *made full* in Christ (Col 2:9).
- Identify the Old Testament background of the circumcision of the heart and show how this relates to Colossians 2:11.
- Understand the meaning of the Christian's death and resurrection with Christ in Colossians 2:11-12.
- Discuss the symbolism of water baptism and its relationship to saving faith (Col 2:12).
- State the nature and cause of the condition of spiritual death in Colossians 2:13.
- Recognize how Paul uses the images of being made alive by forgiveness of transgressions, the sign nailed to the cross, and a military parade in Colossians 2:14-15 to illustrate how God made believers alive with Christ; and explain the relationship between justification and dying and rising with Christ.

Assignments

For each paragraph of Colossians covered in this lesson follow this three-step procedure:

Step 1:

    (a) Read this passage of Colossians.

    (b) Make a structural diagram of the passage on the worksheet provided.

    (c) Summarize the results in an outline and theme statement.

    (d) Compare your conclusions with those in the answer section.

Step 2:

    Examine the details of the paragraph. Record your observations, interpretations, and applications on the worksheet.

Step 3:

    (a) Read the commentary on this passage of Colossians.

    (b) Answer the questions in the lesson.

    (c) Pay special attention to the *Important Facts to Remember*.

Topic 1: Made Full by Dying and Rising with Christ (Col 2:9-12)

In the previous paragraph, Paul exhorts the Colossians to continue in the teachings about Christ they received in the beginning and warns them regarding the deceptive claims of the false teachers. Now in Colossians 2:9-12, he begins a doctrinal explanation of why they should reject these claims. It is because of who Christ is and what he accomplished for them through his death and resurrection

Begin your study by reading Colossians 2:9-12. Then read the Worksheet on Colossians 2:9-12. Copy it in your Life Notebook and complete step 1 of the "Assignments." Check your conclusions by comparing them with the Answer Section for Colossians 2:9-12. Next, complete step 2 by recording on the same worksheet your detailed observations, interpretations, and applications. For the third and final step, carefully read the Commentary on Colossians 2:9-12. Then answer the following questions, taking special note of the *Important Facts to Remember*.

Worksheet for Colossians 2:9-12

⁹ FOR

in him all the fullness of deity lives in bodily form,

¹⁰ AND

you have been filled in him,

> who is the head over every ruler and authority.

¹¹ In him you also were circumcised—

> not, however, with a circumcision performed by human hands
>
> but by the removal of the fleshly body
>
> that is, through the circumcision done by Christ.

¹² Having been buried with him in baptism,

you also have been raised with him

> through your faith in the power of God,
>
>> who raised him from the dead.

Commentary on Colossians 2:9-12
B. The Gospel Explained—Colossians 2:9-15

In the last paragraph (Col 2:6-8) Paul introduced the main part of the body of the letter (Col 2:6– 4:6). There he exhorted the Colossians to continue to walk in the path of the gospel that they received in the beginning and not to allow false teaching to take them captive. Now in Colossians 2:9-15 he explains further why they should be on guard against the deceptive teaching. He does this by reminding them of all that God has already done for them through Christ. This doctrinal exposition of the saving blessings of the gospel is the theological heart of the body of the letter.

1. Redemption as Dying and Rising with Christ—Colossians 2:9-12.

Paul begins this explanation by reminding the Colossians that all the fullness of deity dwells in Christ and that, as a result, God made them "full" when they were united with Christ at the time of conversion. This filling means that they have been circumcised spiritually by sharing in Christ's death and burial. As a result, God has also raised them up with Christ to new life.

Verse 9

For. This word introduces an explanation of why they should continue steadfastly in the path of Christ and not allow anyone to lead them astray. Paul's strategy here is to remind the Colossians of all that God has already given them in Christ and how this surpasses by far those things the false teachers claim to offer.

in him all the fullness of deity lives in bodily form. Paul begins by reminding them that Jesus Christ, the author of their salvation, is God incarnate. This statement picks up the thought of Colossians 1:19 and expands it. That passage explains how it was God's decision that all of his fullness should dwell in Christ so that through his death on the cross he could accomplish the work of reconciliation. God's fullness is the divine nature itself. This fullness came to dwell in Christ in the event of the incarnation when the eternal Son of God took to himself a body of flesh (Col 1:22; Jn 1:14). Now in Colossians 2:9, Paul describes what God did by causing his fullness to dwell in Christ, i.e., to make Christ's death a continuing reality for us.

The word "bodily" means in physical form. It emphasizes that the fullness of the divine nature continues to dwell in the resurrected and glorified body of Christ. The incarnation did not cease with Christ's death. Furthermore, as Paul goes on to explain in Colossians 2:10, it is because all the fullness of deity dwells in the risen Christ that believers "have been filled in him."

Verse 10

And. In this context "and" means "and, as a result."

and you have been filled in him. Because all the fullness of deity dwells in Christ, those who are united to him by faith are themselves made full. But in what sense have they been filled? First, it cannot mean that they are now full of all the fullness of deity just as Christ is. Christ is unique. The incarnation cannot be reproduced in others. Second, it does not mean they have already **experienced** the fullness of salvation. The salvation process (i.e., our sanctification) will be complete only when Christ returns (see Col 1:5; 2:7; 3:4).

Colossians 2:10a is a response to the "fine-sounding" arguments of the false teachers. The false teachers were telling the Colossians that their relationship with God was deficient; and only if they become Jews, keep the Jewish law, and achieve heavenly visions, can they truly be made full. Paul's purpose here is to assure the Colossians this is not so. Because all the fullness of deity dwells in Christ, nothing can be lacking in the salvation he brings. Nothing needs to be added to it by following the practices of the false teachers.

who is the head over every ruler and authority. Another reason the Colossians can rest assured that nothing is lacking in their salvation is that Christ is head over every ruler and authority. As Paul explained in Colossians 1:16, 20, angelic beings were created by Christ in the beginning, and through his death on the cross those who rebelled against God were subjugated (or "pacified"; see the comments on Col 1:20). "Head" in this context simply indicates Christ's supreme authority over these beings. It does not mean they are members of his body, the church. This is a different concept and image altogether.

Next in Colossians 2:11-15, Paul explains in detail the nature of the saving acts by which God made the Colossians "full." They have been made full through their union with Christ in his death, burial, and resurrection.

Verse 11

In him you also were circumcised—not, however, with a circumcision performed by human hands. The words "not . . . by human hands" describe something done directly by God without human agency. Paul is referring to the moral and spiritual transformation that Christians experience in conversion. In Romans 2:29, he calls it the circumcision of the heart. The image of a circumcised heart comes from the Old Testament (Deut 10:16; 30:6; Jer 4:4). In the Bible, circumcision ordinarily refers to the removal of the male foreskin. But the term was also used figuratively for the removal of a covering—a foreskin as it were—from something. That which was covered was said to be uncircumcised. For example, a man who had difficulty speaking, as though his lips were covered by a foreskin, was said to have uncircumcised lips (Ex 6:12). Someone who had difficulty hearing, as though his ears were covered, was said to have uncircumcised ears. Jeremiah used this image to describe the spiritual deafness of those who refused to listen to the word of God (Jer 6:10).

The case is similar with an uncircumcised heart. For the Hebrews, the heart was the organ of emotion, thought, and will, the very core of the person. It was with the heart that one understood God's word and responded to him in faith, love, and service. The person whose heart was uncircumcised refused to respond to God in this way. Instead, he was stubborn and rebellious (Jer 9:26; Acts 7:51; 28:27). It was as though a covering over his heart prevented him from relating properly to God. Like uncircumcised lips and uncircumcised ears, the uncircumcised heart is impaired and defective. To circumcise the heart means to remove this covering. The result is a heart that has become dedicated and responsive to God. It now functions properly, as God intended.

This type of heart problem was all too common in ancient Israel. But the prophets foretold a permanent cure in the future age of salvation. In Deuteronomy 30:6, Moses tells of the coming day when God will reconcile his rebellious people to himself by forgiving their sins and circumcising their hearts. This promise of a transformed heart appears again in Jeremiah and Ezekiel except the image is changed somewhat. In Jeremiah 31:31-34, God promises to make a new covenant with his people in which he will write his law upon their hearts. In Ezekiel 36:26-28, he promises to remove their heart of stone and to replace it with a living heart. "And I will put My Spirit within you and cause you to walk in My statutes . . . so you will be My people and I will be your God" (NASB).

Paul is saying here in Colossians 2:11a that this long-promised blessing has come at last. It has come to all who have embraced the gospel of Jesus the Messiah. They have become heirs of the salvation promised through Moses and the Prophets. They are the people of God's new covenant. What then is the need for physical circumcision? The Jews insisted that it is necessary for salvation. But it is no longer physical circumcision but the circumcision of the heart that marks one as a member of God's people.

What is this moral and spiritual transformation that God has produced in the Colossians? Paul referred to it earlier in Colossians 1:21-22. Only he used the broader term reconciliation rather than circumcision. Formerly they were alienated from God, hostile in mind, doing evil deeds (Col 1:21). But God reconciled them to himself and made them his covenant people. He forgave their sins and transformed their hearts so that they are now able to love and serve him. This was accomplished "through Christ's death in his body of flesh" (Col 1:22). Now in Colossians 2:11, Paul has returned to this subject in order to explain it in more detail. God accomplishes this transformation—this circumcision of the heart—by causing them to share in the death of Christ, as the remainder of Colossians 2:11 explains.

but by the removal of the fleshly body. This spiritual circumcision consists in the removal of the body of flesh. Physical circumcision consists in the removal of a small piece of flesh; spiritual circumcision means removal of the entire body of flesh. But what is this "fleshly body" that is stripped off? It is not the sinful nature or the old man. "Fleshly body" is simply an expression for the physical body. Recall that Paul used it in Colossians 1:22 to describe the physical death that Christ suffered on the cross. Stripping off the fleshly body is a figurative expression for physical death in which the body is pictured as a garment that is put off in death (see 2 Cor 5:2-4).

But Christians, of course, do not die physically in conversion. Paul is referring here to the spiritual death they experience when they are united with Christ in his death for them in which he stripped off his fleshly body (see Rom 6:2-6). Thus, Colossians 2:11b describes the Colossians' spiritual death with Christ using the language of his physical death for them. We see a similar expression in Galatians 2:20 where Paul declares, "I have been *crucified* with Christ" (emphasis added). He uses the language of Christ's physical death (crucifixion) to describe his spiritual death with Christ. Here in Colossians 2:11b, Paul identifies this spiritual death with the circumcision made without hands. He interprets this spiritual death later in Colossians 3:9 as the stripping off of "the old man." As we will see in our study of Colossians 3:9, this expression refers to the unconverted individual as a member of Adam's fallen race. In conversion, this "old man" dies with Christ and is raised up with him as a "new man."

that is, through the circumcision done by Christ. These words clarify the meaning of the previous line. "The circumcision done by Christ" is the circumcision that Christ endured in his death as the stripping off of his body of flesh. Christians were circumcised spiritually because in conversion they were united with Christ in his circumcision—that is, in his death for them. They were circumcised in his circumcision. They died in his death.

To summarize, in Colossians 2:11 Paul assures the Colossians that God has made them heirs of the salvation he promised long ago through Moses and the Prophets: he has circumcised their hearts. This circumcision exists in their union with Christ in his atoning death for them. Paul's explanation of this transformation continues in Colossians 2:12 with the statement that they were also buried and raised with Christ. As we will see, burial with Christ belongs to the concept of dying with Christ, and resurrection with him follows as the inseparable result of dying with him. Thus, Paul can summarize the experience of salvation at the time of conversion as dying and rising with Christ. Our task now is to explore briefly what it means that Christians have died and risen with Christ.

Special Explanation: The Meaning of Dying and Rising with Christ

Our death and resurrection **with** Christ must be understood in relation to his death and resurrection **for** us. God accomplished the work of redemption through Christ's death and resurrection for us. God applies to us the benefits of this redemption at the time of conversion. This is our death and resurrection with Christ. Therefore, our explanation must begin with the meaning of Christ's own death and resurrection.

Redemption Accomplished: Christ's Death and Resurrection for Us

God created Adam to be holy and upright and to live eternally in fellowship with him. Adam's sin instead brought alienation and death. And since God had appointed Adam to serve as the representative of the race descended from him, his disobedience brought the entire human race under the reign of sin and death. Christ came as a new Adam to restore what was lost through the first Adam. As Adam brought condemnation and death to the race descended from him, so Christ brings justification and life to a new race made up of all who accept him (Rom 5:18).

Christ accomplished this work of redemption through his death and resurrection. Since sin brought Adam's race under condemnation and death, Christ identified himself with us in our unredeemed condition and went to the cross to bear the penalty of death for our sins—as our representative and substitute. Although he was sinless, God pronounced on him the verdict of guilty (condemnation) for the sins we had committed, and sentenced him to die the death we deserve (Isa 53:5–6; 2 Cor 5:21). Christ experienced God's holy wrath on the cross. For the first time, he experienced separation from God—the personal alienation from him that is the condition common to all who are unredeemed (Mt 27:46).

However, his death paid the penalty for those sins as an atoning sacrifice. Since Christ's sacrifice perfectly atoned for the sins of all mankind, God raised him up to new life and bestowed on him the immortal existence that God intended for man from the beginning. This was an act of new creation in which Christ, as the first to rise, became the Adam of a new–redeemed human race, its founder and head. In this way, it can be seen that in the events of his death and resurrection Christ experienced in himself the reversal of the Fall. The stage is now set for understanding our death and resurrection **with** Christ.

Redemption Applied: Our Death and Resurrection with Christ

As our Redeemer, Christ pioneered the path of deliverance from death and alienation from God. By traveling this path himself, he opened the way for others. This is God's method of redemption. To put it simply: Christ traveled this path, and in conversion he takes us *with him*. This means that at the time of conversion God applies to us the benefits of Christ's death and resurrection by making us partakers of these saving events. There are two aspects to this. The first is legal in nature and concerns our justification and associated forgiveness. The second is moral in nature and concerns our ability to walk in new life (sanctification). We will begin with the legal aspect.

    A. The Legal Aspect: Justification.

    When a person responds in faith to the gospel, God considers him in a legal sense to have suffered the penalty of death for his sins in the person of Christ, his representative. [To clarify, it is Christ's suffering and death that pays the penalty for our sins. He has taken our place in bearing the punishment we deserved, so that we do not have to be punished]. When a person responds in faith to the gospel, the benefit of Christ's substitutionary death is applied to him. God grants him complete forgiveness of all sins he has ever committed, and God *justifies* him. Justification means that God declares him "not guilty" (Deut 25:1; 2 Chron 6:23). And since God raised Christ from the dead, he also makes alive (spiritually) everyone whom he includes in this verdict. They are "raised with Christ." He restores them to the eternal life of fellowship with himself that he intended for man from the beginning.

    This method of redemption was foreshadowed in the sin offering of the Old Testament. When an Israelite sinned, his relationship with God was broken, and he was deserving of death. Through the sacrifice of an animal, however, his relationship with God could be restored. The animal served as the man's substitute and representative in judgment before God—to pay the penalty of death. Before slaying the animal, the man would lay his hand on its head. This symbolized his identification with the animal in its death (Lev 1:4). Thus, the death of the animal was counted as the death of the man himself (the man was acknowledging by this that he deserved the death). And so by participating in the animal's death, the man passed through the judgment of death and entered again into the life of a renewed relationship with God

B. The Moral Aspect: Sanctification.

God not only removes the guilt of our sins and restores us to life, he also renews us morally so that we may walk in new life (Rom 6:4).

Through his deliverance from the judgment of death and his resurrection to life, Christ pioneered the path from the old creation to the new. In our death and resurrection with him, we experienced a similar passage from the old to the new. Our "old man" (all that we were before our salvation) was crucified with Christ, enabling us to begin living the life of a "new man" in Christ (Col 3:9-10). This means, first of all, an inward transformation. God circumcised our calloused and fallen hearts and gave us a new ability to love and serve him (Deut 30:6; Col 2:11). This was the start of a process in which God is renewing us to his image (Col 3:10).

Second, it means transference to a new realm, as it were, and to a new Lord. We died to the world (Gal 6:14), to sin (Rom 6:11), and to the law (Rom 7:6). Thus, we no longer belong to "this present evil age" (Gal 1:4) which is the world (Col 2:20), but to the heavenly kingdom of Christ (Col 1:13; Col 3:1-3). We are no longer enslaved to sin but serve a new master (Rom 6:22). We are no longer bound by the old sin-producing law but are joined to Christ and serve in the new way of the Spirit (Rom 7:5-6). We have been transferred from the fallen race of Adam to the redeemed race of Christ (Col 1:18; Col 3:11).

Yet, the application of redemption remains incomplete. We have experienced the beginning of the new life, but not its fullness. We still live in the midst of the old fallen creation in our unredeemed bodies. Redemption will only be complete when Christ returns and we receive resurrection bodies (Rom 8:23). In the meantime, we must walk by faith, living out the reality of our new life in Christ in the midst of a fallen world. Nevertheless, the decisive event has already happened: our death and resurrection with Christ. In that event, we experienced forgiveness and reconciliation to God, the circumcision of the heart, transfer to the life of the new creation—the reversal of the Fall.

Verse 12

Having been buried with him in baptism. In Colossians 2:11, Paul explained that the Colossians were circumcised spiritually when they were united with Christ in his death. Now he reminds them that they were also buried with him. Burial with Christ is not an aspect of redemption distinct from dying with Christ. A burial marks a death. It confirms that the one buried has truly died and passed out of this world. To be buried with Christ, therefore, simply underscores the fact of our death with him.

Paul mentions baptism here because water baptism symbolized burial—and, therefore, also death—with Christ. Through this symbolic act, the one coming to Christ expressed publicly his faith in the gospel and what this means for him. By going down under the water, he proclaimed his acceptance of God's verdict of condemnation on his sins and his identification with the One who bore in himself the judgment of death for those sins. In this way, he died with Christ. And as such, he was laid with Christ in his tomb.

you also have been raised with him through your faith in the power of God who raised him from the dead. Baptism also symbolized resurrection with Christ. As Christ rose from the dead on the third day and came forth from his tomb, so the convert rose up out of the water, symbolizing the start of a whole new life. He has received God's verdict of acquittal. His sins are forgiven. He has been reconciled to God. He has passed from the old fallen existence into the immortal life of the new creation. As an "old man," he died and was buried. In an act of new creation, God raised him up as a "new man" in Christ.

QUESTION 1

What is the meaning of the statement in Colossians 2:10 that Christians have been *made full* in Christ?

   A. They have already experienced the fullness of salvation.
   B. They have been filled with the Holy Spirit.
   C. They have been filled with the knowledge of God's will.
   D. There is nothing lacking in the salvation Christ brings.
   E. They have been filled with the fruit of righteousness.

QUESTION 2

Explain briefly the Old Testament background of the circumcision of the heart and how this relates to Colossians 2:11.

QUESTION 3

The expression "fleshly body" refers to the physical body. The stripping off of the fleshly body in Colossians 2:11 describes the believer's spiritual death with Christ using the language of his physical death for us. Paul does, however, interpret this spiritual death later in Colossians 3:9 as the stripping off of the "old man"—a reference to our old fallen existence in Adam. *True or False?*

QUESTION 4

After Christ died for our sins, the Father was satisfied with his atoning work and therefore raised him from the dead. *True or False?*

QUESTION 5

When a person responds in faith to the gospel, God considers him in a _____ sense to have suffered the penalty of death for his sins in the person of Christ, his representative.

QUESTION 6

God raises believers with Christ to new life because he has _____ them on the basis of faith in Christ and his finished work.

QUESTION 7

Which of the following does **not** happen to the believer at the time of conversion through dying and rising with Christ?

   A. The circumcision of the heart
   B. Reconciliation
   C. Justification
   D. Entry into the life of the new creation
   E. Transfer from the fallen race of Adam to the redeemed race of Christ
   F. The fullness of redemption (i.e., the redemption of our bodies)

QUESTION 8

Explain briefly the symbolism of water baptism and its relationship to saving faith.

QUESTION 9

Assume that you receive a letter from a Christian friend who has heard you are taking a course on Colossians. He writes to ask if you can help him understand the concept of dying and rising with Christ, since it often appears in Colossians. He has always found this concept profound but also something of a mystery. After all, Christ died and rose again long ago and far away. How can someone die and rise *with* him? Your friend states that he has often dreamed of going to a Bible college or seminary just so he could understand this difficult concept. So he asks if you would you be able to explain it to him.

Your assignment is to write a letter in reply. Try to explain it in your own words. You may find the summary in the *Important Facts to Remember* section helpful. Perhaps you could even add an illustration of your own. Alternatively, you may do this as a role-playing exercise. Find someone to play the role of the inquiring friend and explain it in person. The purpose of this exercise is to help clarify your own understanding. Be prepared to discuss this assignment in the next meeting of your group.

QUESTION 10

Did the commentary's explanation of dying and rising with Christ give you any new insight into the nature of our salvation? If so, explain briefly. What parts of this concept do you still find unclear?

Important Facts to Remember About Colossians 2:9-12

1. All believers have been *made full* in Christ (Col 2:10). This means there is nothing lacking in the salvation that Christ brings. God made them full through their union with Christ in his death and resurrection (Col 2:11-12).

2. The circumcision made without hands (Col 2:11) fulfills the ancient promise that God would transform the hearts of his people to love and serve him (Deut 30:6; Ezk 36:26-28); Jer 31:31-34). God's act of circumcising us is our union with Christ in his death.

3. The meaning of our death and resurrection with Christ:

    - Redemption accomplished: Christ's death and resurrection for us.

    - God created man to live eternally in fellowship with him, but Adam's sin brought alienation and death.

    - Christ came as a new Adam to restore what was lost through the first Adam. He accomplished this through his death and resurrection.

    - He identified himself with us in our unredeemed condition, he was condemned, and suffered the penalty of death for our sins as our representative and substitute.

    - Because his death paid sin's penalty, God was satisfied with the atonement for sins that Christ had made at the cross, and therefore raised him from the dead.

    - This was an act of new creation in which Christ experienced the reversal of the Fall and the restoration of the immortal existence that God intended for man from the beginning.

    - As the first to rise, Christ became the Adam of the new redeemed human race.

4. Redemption applied: our death and resurrection with Christ

    - At conversion God made us partakers with Christ of the redeeming events that he experienced as our representative.

    - God considered us in a legal sense to have suffered the penalty of death for our sins in the person of Christ our representative and substitute (we died with Christ).

    - Satisfied with what Christ did on the cross, God therefore justifies those who place their faith in Christ (raising them with Christ to new life)

    - Through our death with Christ, God circumcised our rebellious hearts and gave us a new ability to love and serve him.

    - Like Christ we passed from the old creation to the new. The "old man" (what we were before knowing Christ) has been crucified with Christ, so that we do not have to obey its dictates. Hence, we can and should put on the "new man" who is being renewed to God's image.

    - The application of redemption remains incomplete. We are still being renewed. It will only be complete when Christ returns and we receive resurrection bodies.

5. Water baptism symbolizes death, burial, and resurrection with Christ. Going down under the water symbolizes death and burial. Coming up again symbolizes resurrection.

6. Water baptism by itself does not result in salvation. It was the means by which the early Christians expressed publicly their faith in Christ. Since those who responded in faith to the gospel were quickly baptized, the act of faith and water baptism were looked upon as simply two parts of a single experience.

Topic 2: Made Alive with Christ (Col 2:13-15)

We have seen that Colossians 2:9-15 is a doctrinal exposition of the nature of Christian salvation through the death and resurrection of Christ. It is the theological heart of the letter. In the first paragraph of this important section Paul states his basic point. Christians have been made full in Christ. The false teachers have nothing that can add to this salvation. Paul explains this fullness in terms of our union with Christ in his death, burial, and resurrection. In Colossians 2:13-15 he carries this explanation forward by explaining the nature of our resurrection with Christ and the role of his death in securing it. God made us alive with Christ by forgiving our sins through his death on the cross for us.

Begin your study by reading Colossians 2:13-15. Then turn to the Worksheet on Colossians 2:13-15. Copy it in your Life Notebook and complete step 1 of the "Assignments." Check your conclusions by comparing them with the Answer Section for Colossians 2:13-15. Next, complete step 2 by recording on the same worksheet your detailed observations, interpretations, and applications. For the third and final step, read the Commentary on Colossians 2:13-15. Read it carefully, and then answer the following questions.

Worksheet for Colossians 2:13-15

¹³ And even though you were dead in your transgressions,

and in the uncircumcision of your flesh,

he nevertheless made you alive with him,

having forgiven all your transgressions.

¹⁴ He has destroyed what was against us,

a certificate of indebtedness expressed in decrees opposed to us.

He has taken it away

by nailing it to the cross.

¹⁵ Disarming the rulers and authorities,

he has made a public disgrace of them,

triumphing over them by the cross.

Commentary on Colossians 2:13-15

We have seen that Colossians 2:9-15 is a doctrinal exposition of the nature of Christian redemption through the death and resurrection of Christ. This is the theological heart of the letter. In the first paragraph of this important section, Paul states his basic point. Christians have been made full in Christ. The false teachers have nothing that can add to this salvation. Paul then explains this fullness in terms of our union with Christ in his death, burial, and resurrection. In Colossians 2:13-15, he carries this explanation forward by explaining the nature of our resurrection with Christ and the role of his death in securing it. God made us alive with Christ having forgiven our sins through his death for us.

Verse 13

And even though you were dead. This statement repeats the last word of the previous verse ("dead") in order to draw a comparison: As Christ was dead and God raised him to new life, so you yourselves were also dead spiritually and God made you alive with Christ. This comparison points us back to the statement of Colossians 1:18 that Christ is the firstborn from the dead. Christ was the first to rise, and those who are united to him by faith follow with him in his victory over death and his entry into the life of the new creation. They are raised spiritually at the moment of faith, and they will be physically resurrected at the "coming" of Christ (cf. 1 Cor 15:22-23).

What does it mean that the Colossians were previously dead? It does not mean that a special part of them, called their human spirit, was dead. To be spiritually dead means that one has not yet been "regenerated" (made spiritually alive) and does not have the indwelling Holy Spirit. As a result, one is unable to understand spiritual truth or properly respond to God. The human spirit is dead to God even though it is very much alive to other influences. The meaning is seen in Colossians 1:21. Before conversion, the Colossians were alienated from God and hostile in mind, doing evil deeds. To be alienated from God means to be separated from him, excluded from his fellowship. To be dead spiritually is to be alienated from God. The same condition is described in Colossians 1:13 as being a prisoner in the dominion of darkness.

in your transgressions and in the uncircumcision of your flesh. This line states the reason for their state of death. Transgressions are violations of God's law. They are sins. The uncircumcision of their flesh refers, first of all, to their bodily condition as Gentiles. But this was merely an outward symbol of their inward state. The true reference is to their sinful hearts, demonstrated particularly by their hostility toward God prior to conversion (see Col 1:21). Death, in other words, is the consequence of sin. It is the condition of all who are under the judgment of God.

he nevertheless made you alive with him. As God made Christ alive when he raised him from the dead, so also has he made alive these Colossian believers. (In this context, to raise and to be made alive mean the same thing.) This line is the theme statement of the paragraph. The remaining verses all serve to explain how God made them alive with Christ. We need to bear this in mind as we proceed through Colossians 2:14-15.

having forgiven all your transgressions. This line explains in general terms how God made us alive. Our problem with sin brought us under the condemnation of God. It alienated us from him. It caused our spiritual death. The solution is forgiveness. As sin brought death, so the forgiveness of sin brings life—eternal life in a restored relationship with God.

Verse 14

He has destroyed what was against us, a certificate of indebtedness expressed in decrees opposed to us. Paul now elaborates how God forgave us and made us alive by use of an illustration from first-century culture. A "certificate of indebtedness" was an accounting term ordinarily used of a record of **debt**—a certificate of debt in which the debtor promised to repay the amount recorded.

By drawing on this image, Paul is saying the following about Christians. In our state of spiritual death, we were like those indebted to God for our sins. All our earthly sins were written on the indictment. This record of sin was the chief witness against us. It was "against us and stood opposed to us" because on it all our transgressions of God's ordinances were listed. But God blotted it out, declaring us not guilty—acquitted of all charges. Therefore, he made us alive. We have passed out of the realm of death and into the realm of eternal life, never to be judged for our sins again. We see the same basic teaching on the lips of Jesus in John 5:24: Whoever "hears my message and believes the one who sent me has eternal life and will not be condemned, but has crossed over from death to life" (see also Jn 3:18).

He has taken it away by nailing it to the cross. This final line of Colossians 2:14 states the means by which God was able to blot out our record of sin. He did it by nailing our "certificate of indebtedness" to the cross. There is a large amount of truth in these few words, and we must now study them in more detail. Christ was tried and condemned before a Roman judge (although he was innocent). The punishment was death by crucifixion. In keeping with Roman practice, a sign was nailed to the cross announcing the crime for which he was being punished. It read "The King of the Jews" (Mk 15:26). This indicated the crime of rebellion against the Roman emperor. But Paul is saying here that the true reason for which Jesus suffered was the transgressions recorded on the record of sin against us. In the words of Isaiah 53:6, God "laid on him the iniquity of us all" and thus he suffered the penalty of death as our representative and substitute. He was condemned for our record of sin and suffered the penalty of death in our place. Thus, it is because Christ discharged the penalty due to us that God can blot out the record of sin that was against us—declaring us not guilty.

Verse 15

Disarming the rulers and authorities, he has made a public disgrace of them, triumphing over them by the cross.

The main point of Col 2:15 is to highlight the victory that Christ won at the cross when he died for our sins, and to indicate the defeat that this meant for his spiritual enemies. To emphasize the greatness of this victory and the importance of the result, Paul weaves in an additional image. It is the image of a triumphal procession—a Roman military parade in celebration of a great victory. In this parade, the conquering general would ride in a chariot at the head of his army while leading before him as captives the defeated enemies. In this parade, these enemies would have previously been stripped of their weapons ("disarming the rulers and authorities"). These enemies, however, are not mere earthly soldiers, but *angelic* rulers and authorities (Satan's agents) that stood opposed to Christ. The purpose of making a public spectacle of these conquered enemies was to proclaim the glory and power of the victor.

This is how Paul illustrates Christ's ascension to heaven. It was like a triumphal procession celebrated in honor of Christ's victory over the powers in which he "made a public disgrace of them triumphing over them by the cross." This public display proclaims the power and glory of Christ and the greatness of his victory. It marks the beginning of the new creation. Christ, as God's agent in reconciling all things to himself (Col 1:20), has re-asserted his lordship over the fallen and rebellious creation (Col 1:16, 20; 2:10). He has broken the power of sin and death. He has opened the way of redemption.

We are now able to give a complete answer to what it means that God has made us alive with Christ (Col 2:13). It means that at the time of conversion God extended to us the verdict of acquittal (the forgiveness of our sins). Thus, he granted us entry into new life. We have been raised with Christ. Like Christ, God delivered us from the realm of death and the dominion of the powers and authorities and transferred us into the realm of heavenly, eternal life. This, of course, does not mean that we have ascended to heaven as Christ did. We still live on planet Earth. Instead, we should understand this transfer in the light of what Paul wrote earlier in Colossians 1:13. God rescued us out of the dominion of darkness and transferred us into the kingdom of his beloved Son.

We now, therefore, belong to Christ's heavenly kingdom. We will not experience the fullness of the kingdom and this new life until he returns and transforms our bodies to be like his. Nevertheless, God has already made us citizens of this heavenly kingdom and made us alive with a heavenly and resurrected type of life. We are no longer dead—alienated from God. He has brought us into the relationship with himself that he intended from the beginning. This is eternal life indeed (Jn 17:3).

Finally, we should recall that Paul's words in Colossians 2:13-15 along with Colossians 2:9-12 come in response to the threat posed by the false teachers. The way to eternal life, they claimed, was to become a Jew and keep the law of Moses. And for the super-spiritual, brief experiences of that life can be achieved even now in the form of visionary journeys to heaven. In response Paul is saying this: what God has given Christians is far better. The coming of Christ has fulfilled the hope of Judaism. The age of salvation has begun. Already God has fulfilled his promise to circumcise the hearts of his people. And since the Gentile-born Colossians have received this blessing, this means they already belong to God's people, the community of salvation. Moreover, God has justified them and made them alive with Christ. The eternal life of the age to come has begun, and they eagerly await its fullness at Christ's return. Therefore, says Paul, do not be taken captive by the claims of these Jews. In Christ, you have been made full (Col 2:9, 10).

QUESTION 11

Explain briefly the nature and cause of spiritual death mentioned in Colossians 2:13.

QUESTION 12

Which of the following lines from Colossians 2:13-15 best expresses the theme of this paragraph?
- A. You yourselves also were dead.
- B. God made you alive with Christ.
- C. He blotted out the record of sin.
- D. On that cross Christ stripped the powers and authorities.
- E. He led the powers as captives in his triumphal procession.

QUESTION 13

According to Col 2:13, which of the following statements correctly describes God's forgiveness of our sins?

A. All our sins are forgiven, provided that we have first undergone water baptism.
B. All our sins are forgiven up until the moment we believe, but afterwards only those we confess to God.
C. All our sins our forgiven, meaning all that we will ever commit, both before and after believing the gospel message.
D. All our sins are forgiven, provided that we do not commit the unpardonable sin.

QUESTION 14

In ordinary usage, "record of sin" was an accounting term for a certificate of debt. The Jews, however, also used these words for the written record for a man's sins that would serve as the indictment against him at the final judgment. *True or False?*

QUESTION 15

The background of "nailing a record" is the Roman practice of posting a sign at public executions to announce the crime for which the condemned was being punished. *True or False?*

QUESTION 16

The statement that on the cross Christ stripped from himself the powers and authorities means that he stripped from himself their _____.

QUESTION 17

What image does Paul use in Colossians 2:15 to describe Christ's resurrection and ascension to heaven?

A. The coronation of a king
B. A welcoming celebration for a returning dignitary
C. A wedding procession
D. A harvest celebration
E. A military parade
F. A victory parade for an Olympic athlete

QUESTION 18

How does the image of nailing a "certificate of indebtedness" to a cross help you understand how God looks upon your sin?

QUESTION 19

Paul's question in Rom 8:33, "Who will bring any charge against God's elect?" receives an extended answer in Colossians 2:13-15. What confidence does this passage give you about the certainty of your salvation? How can it help you respond to feelings of guilt and the fear that Satan has a rightful basis for accusing you before God? Record your response in your Life Notebook.

QUESTION 20

Consider how you could use the image of the judgment seen in Colossians 2:13-15 to explain the gospel to a non-Christian. In your Life Notebook, write a brief outline of a gospel presentation in which you first picture the plight of the unsaved as that of a person on trial before God for his earthly sins. Then use the message of Colossians 2:13-15 to explain the solution that God offers to all who believe.

QUESTION 21

What truths do you find in the two paragraphs covered by this lesson (Colossians 2:9-15) that belong in your course *What Every Christian Should Know About Salvation*?

Important Facts to Remember About Colossians 2:13-15

1. To be dead spiritually means to be alienated from God (Colossians 1:21). This state of death is the consequence of sin—both outward transgressions and inner hostility to God.

2. For the one who believes upon Christ, however, they are no longer spiritually dead but made alive with Christ (Col 2:13-14). Paul uses the example of a "certificate of indebtedness" to illustrate how this comes about:

    -The indictment is the record of sin "which was against us."

    - This indictment was nailed to the cross, meaning that Christ died for all our sins.

    - God's verdict of not guilty is his act of blotting out the record of sin (signifying the forgiveness of our sins).

    - The result of the verdict is passage from death to eternal life.

3. Paul makes use of a Roman victory parade to illustrate Christ's triumph over his spiritual enemies (Col 2:15)

The point is that the victory has been won, and the enemies of Christ (demonic angels) have been defeated. They were not able to stop God's plan of salvation, and they are now shown to be the losers. On the cross Christ accomplished everything that was necessary for us to be forgiven and have eternal life. We who believe are now spiritually alive.

Lesson 8 Self Check

QUESTION 1

What does it mean in Colossians 2:10 that Christians have been *made full* in Christ?
- A. They have been filled with joy.
- B. They have been filled with the Holy Spirit.
- C. There is nothing lacking in the salvation Christ brings.
- D. They have been filled with the fruit of righteousness.
- E. They have been filled with the knowledge of God's will.
- F. They have experienced the fullness of the end time salvation.

QUESTION 2

In the Old Testament, circumcision was used as a metaphor for the cleansing of that which was defiled *True or False?*

QUESTION 3

When a person responds in faith to the gospel, God considers him in a _____ sense to have suffered the penalty of death for his sins in the person of Christ, his representative.

QUESTION 4

Which of the following Old Testament events or practices foreshadowed God's redemption as dying and rising with Christ?
- A. The sin offering
- B. The Passover celebration
- C. The Exodus from Egypt
- D. The sacrifice of Isaac
- E. The redemption of the firstborn
- F. The flood and Noah's ark

QUESTION 5

Water baptism was the means by which the early Christians expressed publicly their faith in Christ at the time of conversion. *True or False?*

QUESTION 6

To be dead spiritually (Col 2:13) means that a part of our inner being called our spirit is without life. *True or False?*

QUESTION 7

In ordinary usage the term translated "record of sin" referred to the written record of a person's _____.

QUESTION 8

The background to the nailing of the record of sin to the cross in Colossians 2:14 is found in the Romans practice of posting a sign at public executions stating the crime for which the condemned was being punished. *True or False?*

QUESTION 9

What image does Paul use in Colossians 2:15 to describe Christ's resurrection and ascension?

   A. A wedding procession
   B. A parade for a victorious Olympic athlete
   C. A welcoming parade for a returning dignitary
   D. A military parade
   E. The coronation of a king
   F. A harvest festival

QUESTION 10

God makes believers alive with Christ because at the time of conversion he pronounces upon them a verdict of _____ .

Lesson 8 Answers to Questions

WORKSHEET FOR COLOSSIANS 2:9-12

```
Answer for Colossians 2:9-12

Why follow Christ?
    ⁹ FOR (explanation: why follow Christ and not the false teachers)
    in him all the fullness of deity lives in bodily form, (1ˢᵗ part of explanation)
    ¹⁰ AND (result)
    you have been filled in him, (2ⁿᵈ part of explanation)

Explanation made full
    (description of Christ) who is head over every ruler and authority.
    ¹¹ In him you also were circumcised—(explanation of "made full," 1ˢᵗ part)
        not, however, with a circumcision performed by human hands
            (description of action: "were circumcised")
        but by the removal of the fleshly body
        that is, through the circumcision done by Christ.
    ¹² Having been buried with him in baptism,
        (explanation of "made full," 2ⁿᵈ part)
    (additional explanation)
    you also have been raised with him (explanation of "made full," 3ʳᵈ part)
        through your faith in the power of God, (means of action)
            (description of God) who raised him from the dead.
```

Textual Outline of Colossians 2:9-12.
I. Why follow Christ? (Col 2:9-10)
    A. The fullness of deity dwells in him. (Col 2:9)
    B. Result: God has made full those in Christ. (Col 2:10a)
    C. Christ is head over all powers. (Col 2:10b)
II. Explanation of "made full" in Christ (Col 2:11-12)
    A. Circumcised in him (Col 2:11)
    B. Buried with Christ (Col 2:12a)
    C. Raised with Christ (Col 2:12b-d)

Theme Statement for Colossians 2:9-12.
The Colossians were "made full" in Christ when they were circumcised in him, buried, and raised with him.

QUESTION 1
    D. There is nothing lacking in the salvation Christ brings.
QUESTION 2: *Your answer should be similar to the following:*
In the Old Testament, circumcision was used as a metaphor for the removal of a covering or blockage. That which was covered was said to be uncircumcised. Someone whose lips were uncircumcised spoke with difficulty, as though his lips were covered. Someone with uncircumcised ears was unable to hear, as

though his ears were covered. Someone whose heart was uncircumcised was stubborn and rebellious against God, as though his heart was covered. To circumcise such a heart means to remove this covering so that the person can respond to God in love and obedience as he intended. Moses and the prophets told of a day when God would circumcise the hearts of his people. That day has arrived, says Paul. Christians have become heirs of this promise.

QUESTION 3: False [The expression "fleshly body" in Colossians 2:11 refers to the sinful nature. Thus "the stripping off of the body of flesh" describes the removal of the sinful nature at conversion.]

QUESTION 4: True

QUESTION 5: legal

QUESTION 6: *Your answer should be one of the following:*
justification, acquittal

QUESTION 7
F. The fullness of redemption

QUESTION 8: *Your answer should be similar to the following:*
Water baptism symbolizes death, burial, and resurrection with Christ. It therefore symbolizes the application of the saving benefits of Christ's death and resurrection to the believer at the time of conversion. Going down under the water symbolizes death and burial with Christ. In this act the one coming to Christ expresses his acceptance of God's verdict of condemnation on his sins and his identification with Christ in his death to bear the divine judgment for those sins. Rising up out of the water symbolizes that God has pronounced on him a verdict of acquittal and therefore raised him up with Christ to a new and immortal life. Since baptism symbolizes salvation in this way, the early Christians used it as a means of expressing publicly their faith in Christ at the time of conversion.

QUESTION 9: *Your answer*

QUESTION 10: *Your answer*

WORKSHEET FOR COLOSSIANS 2:13-15

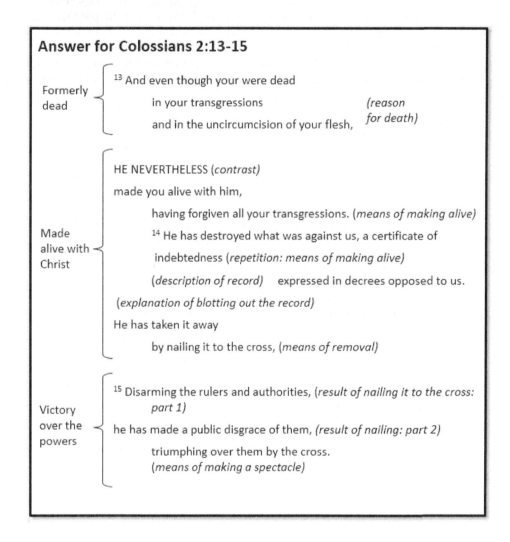

Textual Outline of Colossians 2:13-15.
I. Formerly dead (Col 2:13a,b)
    A. The Colossians were dead. (Col 2:13a)
    B. Reason for death: Trespasses and uncircumcision (Col 2:13b)
II. Made alive with Christ (Col 2:13c-14)
    A. God made them alive with Christ. (Col 2:13c)
    B. The means: Forgiveness (Col 2:13d)
    C. The means: Blotting out the record of sin through the cross (Col 2:14)
III. Victory over the powers (Col 2:15)
    A. Christ stripped from himself the powers. (Col 2:15a)
    B. He made a public spectacle of them. (Col 2:15b)
    C. The means: he led them as captives in his triumphal procession. (Col 2:15c)

Theme Statement for Colossians 2:13-15.
God made us alive with Christ by forgiving our sins.

QUESTION 11: *Your answer should be similar to the following:*
Spiritual death is the condition of all those outside of Christ. It is the condition of alienation from God described in Colossians 1:21, and imprisonment in the dominion of darkness mentioned in Colossians 1:13. The cause is sin: both inward hostility toward God and outward actions. This state of death is God's judgment on sin.

QUESTION 12
    B.   God made you alive with Christ.

QUESTION 13
    C. All our sins our forgiven, meaning all that we will ever commit, both before and after believing the gospel message.

QUESTION 14: True

QUESTION 15: True

QUESTION 16: dominion

QUESTION 17
    E.   A military parade

QUESTION 18: *Your answer should be similar to the following:*

If we could imagine all of our sins being listed out on a written record, this could be likened to the image of a "certificate of indebtedness." We owe God, as it were, for these sins. Yet we do not have the means to repay God for all the sins we have done. In ancient times a paper was nailed to the cross of a criminal being crucified, listing the sin(s) for which he was being punished. Because Christ died in our place—thereby paying the debt we owed—our "certificate of indebtedness" has now been cancelled out. It has been nailed to the cross, meaning that God has forgiven us and no longer holds our sin against us. The debt has been fully paid.

QUESTION 19: *Your answer*
QUESTION 20: *Your answer*
QUESTION 21: *Your answer*

Lesson 8 Self Check Answers

QUESTION 1
   C. There is nothing lacking in the salvation Christ brings.
QUESTION 2: False
QUESTION 3: legal
QUESTION 4
   A. The sin offering
QUESTION 5: True
QUESTION 6: False
QUESTION 7: debt
QUESTION 8: True
QUESTION 9
   D. A military parade
QUESTION 10: *Your answer should be one of the following:* justification, acquittal, or not guilty

Lesson 9: The False Teaching—Colossians 2:16-23

To set the stage for this lesson, we begin with a brief review. Recall that in Colossians 1:24-2:5 Paul explained his reason for writing. God commissioned him to proclaim the gospel among the Gentiles. The goal of his mission is to bring every believer to maturity in Christ. Next, in Colossians 2:6-8 Paul introduced the section of the letter (Col 2:6-4:6) that is most directly concerned with fulfilling this purpose. In this pivotal introduction, he exhorts the Colossians to continue to walk in accordance with the message of Christ they received in the beginning and not allow themselves to be taken captive by deceitful teaching.

What follows in Colossians 2:9-4:6 is a fresh exposition of that message they received in the beginning, but with special attention to the deceptive teaching. This exposition falls into two parts—one doctrinal, the other application based. Lesson 8 contains the doctrinal section (Col 2:9-15). This section focuses on the blessings of salvation that come to all at conversion. It shows the superiority of these blessings to what the deceptive teaching claimed to offer. Through their union with Christ in his death, burial, and resurrection, God has blotted out their sins, circumcised their hearts, and granted them eternal life.

This brings us to the application-based section. This section also falls into two parts. The first is Colossians 2:16-3:4. Here Paul applies the truths set forth in the doctrinal section to the specific claims of the false teachers. The second part, Colossians 3:5-4:6, applies these truths to the Christian life in general. The subject of lesson 9 is the application to the false teaching in Colossians 2:16-23.

Christ fulfilling the Ceremonial Law was covered in Topic 1, based on Colossians 2:16-17. This first application focuses on the Old Testament requirements regarding diet and special days. The Jews were condemning the Colossian believers for not keeping these requirements. Ignore this criticism, writes Paul. Such ceremonial practices merely foreshadowed what the Messiah would bring. Now that he has come, they are obsolete.

Topic 2 covers Colossians 2:18-19. Here Paul responds to those who boasted of heavenly visions. These private mystical experiences, they claimed, lead to the most advanced spiritual state. Not so, says Paul. Their visions are false; the product of their own minds. The true spiritual growth comes through a relationship with Christ and through sharing in the life of his body, the church.

Colossians 2:20-23 is the subject of Topic 3. In the third paragraph, Paul exposes the folly of those who seek visions of heaven through ceremonial practices involving "unsparing treatment of the body." These practices are not "heavenly" but of the world and enslave all who belong to it. Dying with Christ freed believers from this bondage, since those who die no longer belong to the world. These practices appear to be wise and heavenly-minded, but they only serve to gratify the flesh.

Lesson Outline

Topic 1: Christ Fulfills the Ceremonial Law (Col 2:16-17)

Topic 2: Those Who Claim to Have Visions (Col 2:18-19)

Topic 3: Liberated from Ceremonial Rules (Col 2:20-23)

Lesson Objectives

When you have completed this lesson, you should be able to:
- Explain why Christians do not need to keep the ceremonial laws of the Old Testament.
- Summarize the claims of the false teachers regarding their visions and defend the view that "the humility and worship of angels" in Colossians 2:18 means the humility and worship that angels perform.

- Identify the source of these visions; and discuss how connection to Christ and his body is the true path to spiritual maturity.
- Explain how dying with Christ has freed believers from "elemental spirits of the world."
- Contrast the reasons the Jewish mystics engaged in "unsparing treatment of the body" with Paul's evaluation of this practice.
- Identify three basic elements in Paul's defense of the faith in Colossians 2:9-23.

Assignments

For each paragraph of Colossians covered in this lesson follow this three-step procedure:

Step 1:

(a) Read this passage of Colossians.

(b) Make a structural diagram of the passage on the worksheet provided.

(c) Summarize the results in an outline and theme statement.

(d) Compare your conclusions with those in the answer section.

Step 2:

Examine the details of the paragraph. Record your observations, interpretations, and applications on the worksheet.

Step 3:

(a) Read the commentary on this passage of Colossians.

(b) Answer the questions in the lesson.

(c) Pay special attention to the *Important Facts to Remember*.

Topic 1: Christ Fulfills the Ceremonial Law (Col 2:16-17)

Paul has now completed his doctrinal exposition of the nature of our redemption through Christ's death and resurrection. He has demonstrated the superiority of this salvation to what the Jews of Colossae were promoting. Christ fulfills the hope of Judaism. The age of salvation has begun. In him, Christians have been made full. Nothing is lacking in the salvation he brings. Paul's next task is to show how these truths apply to the specific claims of the false teachers. He begins in Colossians 2:16-17 with their claim that it is necessary to keep the ceremonial laws of the Old Testament regarding diet and special days. Not so, says Paul. Christ has fulfilled the ceremonial law. It now belongs to the past.

Begin your study by reading Colossians 2:16-17. Then read the Worksheet on Colossians 2:16-17. Copy it in your Life Notebook and complete step 1 of the "Assignments." Check your conclusions by comparing them with the Answer Section for Colossians 2:16-17. Next, complete step 2 by recording on the same worksheet your detailed observations, interpretations, and applications. For the third and final step, carefully read the Commentary on Colossians 2:16-17. Then answer the following questions, taking special note of the *Important Facts to Remember*.

Worksheet for Colossians 2:16-17

¹⁶ THEREFORE,

do not let anyone judge you with respect to food or drink,

or in the manner of a feast,

new moon,

or Sabbath days—

¹⁷ these are only the shadow of the things to come,

BUT

the reality is Christ!

Commentary on Colossians 2:16-17
C. The Gospel Applied—Colossians 2:16-4:6

Paul has now completed his doctrinal exposition of the nature of our redemption through Christ's death and resurrection. He has demonstrated the superiority of this salvation to what the Jews of Colossae were promoting. Christ fulfills the hope of Judaism. The age of salvation has begun. In him, Christians have been made full. Nothing is lacking in the salvation he brings. Now in Colossians 2:16 Paul turns to the practical implications of these truths: How should they conduct their lives as a result? He answers this question in two extended sections, Colossians 2:16-3:4 and Colossians 3:5-4:6. The first applies these truths to the claims of the deceptive teaching. The second applies them to the Christian life in general.

1. The Gospel Applied to the False Teaching—Colossians 2:16-3:4

a. Christ Fulfills the Ceremonial Law—Colossians 2:16-17

Paul's application of the doctrinal truths of Colossians 2:9-15 to the false teaching unfolds in four paragraphs. This first responds to the claim that these Christians must keep the ceremonial laws of the Old Testament regarding diet and special days. Not so, says Paul. Christ has fulfilled these ceremonial laws. They now belong to the past.

Verse 16

Therefore. This word introduces a conclusion drawn from the explanation of Colossians 2:9-15. The Jews were telling these young Christians that the way to salvation is to become a Jew and to keep the law of Moses. Paul explained in those verses how Christ has fulfilled the hope of Judaism. The salvation the Jews seek is already present for all who are united with Christ in his death and resurrection. God has already pronounced on them the verdict of the last judgment. With Christ, they have already entered the life of the age to come. Therefore, Paul warns, do not listen to those who condemn you for not keeping the Jewish law. It belongs to the age of promise, not the age of fulfillment.

do not let anyone judge you with respect to food or drink, or in the matter of a feast, new moon, or Sabbath days. The Jews of Colossae were telling these Gentile-born Christians that if they wish to be a part of God's people and to inherit salvation, they must first become Jews and live like Jews. This means—in addition to being circumcised (see Col 2:11)—they must keep all the rules of the Old Testament and Judaism regarding food and drink. They must also keep all of the special holy days of the Jewish calendar: the annual festivals such as the Passover, the Day of Atonement and the Feast of Tabernacles, as well as the monthly new moon celebrations and the Sabbath day. The Jews were condemning them for failing to do these things. They were saying, "How can you claim to believe the Scriptures and expect God to save you, if you fail to do the most basic things he requires of his people?"

Such arguments must have created doubts in the minds of some of the Colossian believers. And with the doubts, there came the temptation to submit to these ceremonial laws. Thus, Paul is saying to the congregation, do not listen to these criticisms. Do not let anyone lead you away from the path of the gospel.

Verse 17

these are only the shadow of the things to come, but the reality is Christ! Paul now explains the point of the conclusion he is drawing from Colossians 2:9-15. God has made the Colossians heirs of the salvation he promised his people through the Scriptures of the Old Testament. God intended these ceremonial practices to be educational. They are symbols meant to illustrate the future salvation the Messiah would bring. They can be compared to the shadow of a man walking with the sun behind him. The shadow travels ahead of the him. It signals his approach and reveals his basic shape. But it is not the man himself (compare Heb 10:1).

QUESTION 1

The first word of Colossians 2:16 is "therefore." It introduces a conclusion from what passage?

  A. Colossians 2:1-15

  B. Colossians 2:8

  C. Colossians 2:9-15

  D. From the entire argument of the letter up to this point

QUESTION 2

Why does Paul conclude that Christians do not need to keep the Old Testament regulations regarding diet and special days?

QUESTION 3

Even though God does not require Christians to keep the ceremonial laws of the Old Testament, Paul urges them to do so anyway in the hope of winning their Jewish neighbors to Christ. *True or False?*

QUESTION 4

Some Christians today insist that believers should still keep certain aspects of the Old Testament ceremonial law. Sometimes this relates to food. More often it concerns the Sabbath day. Some of the cults of Christianity, the Mormons for example, also insist on keeping some of these practices. How would you explain to a young believer that God does not require him to keep the Sabbath as it was required of the Old Testament saints? What is the proper role of the Sabbath, the Lord's day (Jn 20:1, Jn 20:9; Acts 20:7)? Record your answer in your Life Notebook.

QUESTION 5

This question concerns the very nature of application itself. In Colossians 2:9-15 Paul explains to the Colossians the nature of their redemption through Christ. In Colossians 2:16-17 he begins to apply these truths to their specific circumstances. This approach to application provides us with an example to follow in our own lives. We see two basic principles at work here:

- *Exhortations should be based on biblical truths.* In other words, commands and exhortations should be accompanied by an explanation of the biblical reason behind such action. They should be presented as applications to biblical truth.
- *Apply the biblical truth to the specific circumstances of your audience.* Paul knew that the Colossians were tempted to keep the Jewish ceremonial laws because the Jews said this is necessary for salvation. Therefore, in Colossians 2:16-17 Paul applies the more general truths of redemption (Col 2:9-15) to this specific issue.

Consider your own ministry in the light of these two principles. Can you think of an instance recently (such as a sermon) where you followed both principles? Can you think of ways to apply these principles more consistently in the future?

Important Fact to Remember About Colossians 2:16-17

The ceremonial laws of the Old Testament foreshadowed the salvation Christ would bring. Now that he has come, their purpose is fulfilled. There is no longer a need to do these things.

Topic 2: Those Who Claim to Have Visions (Col 2:18-19)

In this paragraph, Paul continues the application to the false teaching that he began in Colossians 2:16-17. There he was responding to the claim that it is necessary to keep the ceremonial laws of Judaism. Now in Colossians 2:18-19, he responds to the claim of the Jewish mystics that the fullness of spiritual attainment comes through heavenly visions. Paul again warns the Colossians to ignore this claim. These are not true visions. They are merely the product of the human mind. Moreover, it is not the Christians but the Jews who are missing out on the fullness of spiritual attainment. This is because they have failed to take hold of their own promised Messiah. It is only in a vital relationship with him and through the mutual ministry of the body of which he is the head that one can experience the spiritual growth that is from God.

Begin your study by reading Colossians 2:18-19. Then read the Worksheet on Colossians 2:18-19. Copy it in your Life Notebook and complete step 1 of the "Assignments." Check your conclusions by comparing them with the Answer Section for Colossians 2:18-19. Next, complete step 2 by recording on the same worksheet your detailed observations, interpretations, and applications. For the third and final step, carefully read the Commentary on Colossians 2:18-19. Then answer the following questions, taking special note of the *Important Facts to Remember*.

Worksheet for Colossians 2:18-19

[18] Let no one who delights in humility and the worship of angels pass judgment on you.

That person goes on at great lengths about what he has supposedly seen,

BUT

he is puffed up with empty notions by his fleshly mind.

[19] He has not held fast to the head

    from whom the whole body,

    supported and knit together through its ligaments and sinews,

    grows with a growth that is from God.

Commentary on Colossians 2:18-19

1. The Gospel Applied to the False Teaching—Colossians 2:16-3:4 (Continued)

b. The Problem with Visions—Colossians 2:18-19

This paragraph continues the application to the false teaching that began in Colossians 2:16-17. Paul was responding to the claim that it is necessary to keep the ceremonial laws of Judaism. Now in Colossians 2:18-19, he responds to the claim of the Jewish mystics that the fullness of spiritual attainment comes through heavenly visions. Again, Paul warns the Colossians to ignore this claim. These are not true visions. They are merely the product of the human mind. Moreover, it is not Christians but Jews who are missing out on the fullness of spiritual attainment. This is because they have failed to take hold of their own promised Messiah. It is only in a vital relationship with him and through the mutual ministry of the body of which he is the head that one can experience the spiritual growth that is from God.

Verse 18

Let no one who delights in humility and the worship of angels pass judgment on you. Paul now draws a second conclusion from his explanation of Colossians 2:9-15. The basic point of this conclusion is the same as that of Colossians 2:16: Because of the salvation God has already given you, do not be deceived by someone who says you must do additional things to gain salvation. Only here in Colossians 2:18, Paul directs this conclusion to the claims of an elitist group within the Jewish synagogue. These Jews claimed they could experience the joys of the future salvation even now in the present through visionary journeys to heaven. Such visions, they claimed, are only granted to those who engage in strict bodily disciplines and maintain a high degree of ceremonial purity. They boasted of their superior experiences of salvation and condemned the Colossian Christians as disqualified from such experiences. Only the most holy and disciplined Jews can qualify. We learn from Colossians 2:20-23 that some of these young Christians were tempted to seek visions of their own by submitting to these practices. Thus Paul warns: Do not be deceived. What God has already granted you is far superior to what these people claim to achieve.

The phrase "delights in the humility and worship of angels" begins a brief description of the kind of person who is condemning them. It is the most important statement in the letter for identifying the false teachers. It is also the most difficult to interpret. For this reason it has been the subject of considerable discussion among Bible scholars. The key question is this: What is the "worship of angels"? Is it the worship that angels **receive**? Or is it the worship that angels **perform**? In other words, does this verse tell us that the false teachers worshiped angels? Or does it tell us they took delight in the worship performed by angels, which they saw in their visions and sought to imitate in their own lives? The common understanding among earlier generations of Bible scholars was that the false teachers worshipped angels. Indeed, a number of scholars still believe this. But more recent research into the nature of Judaism in Paul's day, together with a fresh examination of his argument in Colossians suggests that the "worship of angels" here may refer to worship performed by angels. In Lesson 1, we gave the following reasons for this conclusion.

1. Nothing else in the letter indicates that the false teachers worshipped angels.

2. Aside from their visions and their "unsparing treatment of the body" (Col 2:23) everything else in the letter clearly points to the conclusion that the false teachers were Jews. And we know from history that Jews did not worship angels.

3. Is it possible then that the false teachers were pagans who worshipped angels but also kept the food laws of the Old Testament along with the Sabbath, the annual

festivals, and the new moon celebration (see Col 2:16-17)? There is no historical evidence that such a group ever existed.

4. There was, however, a movement among the Jews known as Merkabah mysticism whose practices fit the description of Colossians 2:18. These Jews practiced fasting and other kinds of severe bodily discipline in order to attain visions in which they claimed to enter the heavenly temple, to see the angels and to join them in their worship before the throne of God. As a scriptural basis for these claims, they pointed to Ezekiel's vision of the heavenly chariot (*merkabah*) in Ezekiel 1:4-28.

It is therefore reasonable to believe that Paul's warning here is directed against Jews in this movement. There was a large Jewish community in Colossae, and these Jewish mystics could have formed a small elitist group within that community. They boasted of their visions of the angelic worship of God in heaven and condemned the Christians as disqualified from having such advanced spiritual experiences.

This understanding goes a long way toward explaining why this teaching was so dangerously attractive to these young Christians. For what could be more desirable in principle than a deeper experience of worshipping God? On the other hand, if the false teachers had worshipped angels, we may ask what these Christians would have found attractive about such a clear violation of the first commandment—"You shall have no other gods before Me" (Deut 5:7, NASB). And, indeed, would not Paul have warned them strongly on this very point? The best explanation may simply be that the false teachers did not worship angels. At issue was their delight in the worship that angels perform. They sought to look upon the angels in their worship in the heavenly temple, to join with them and then to imitate this angelic form of worship in their earthly lives.

This brings us to a second question. If the "worship of angels" means the worship performed by angels, then what is "the humility and worship of angels"? First of all, we can conclude that if the "worship of angels" is the worship that angels perform, then the humility of angels must be understood similarly. It is a type of humility that angels perform. What then is this angelic "humility," and what does it mean that the false teachers took delight in it?

The term *humility* in this context refers to the self-abasement of fasting (see Col 2: 23, "false humility achieved by an unsparing treatment of the body"). In the Old Testament to fast meant to humble oneself (Ps 35:13; Isa 58:3). Therefore, the term *humility* was often used among the Jews of Paul's day as a reference to the practice of fasting. For example, the Day of Atonement, the one day of the year in which God required his people to fast (Lev 16:29), was sometimes called the Day of Fasting and sometimes the Day of Humility. For those Jewish mystics who sought heavenly visions, fasting was an essential activity. They would fast for days to prepare themselves. They believed this was a requirement for gaining visionary entry into heaven because the angels themselves do not eat. If they wished to join the angels in their place of worship, they must imitate the angels. They must imitate the humility of angels. In actual fact, their fasting along with other techniques such as chanting prayers helped to produce a trance-like state which they identified as a heavenly vision.

That person goes on at great lengths about what he has supposedly seen. This line continues the description of the kind of person who was condemning the Colossian Christians. It explains how these Jewish mystics encountered (or claimed they encountered) the angelic practices they imitated. The Greek text simply says, "He saw these things when entering." Because the Colossians already knew what these Jews taught, this abbreviated statement would have been perfectly understandable. They understood that the "seeing" of these angels took place in a vision. They also understood that these visions took the form of a journey in which the traveler entered heaven, the place where the angels worshipped before the throne of God (Isa 6:1-3; Rev 4:1-11). Indeed, we know from the later writings of the Merkabah mystics that "entering" was one of the special terms they used to refer to a heavenly journey.

but. This word introduces a statement that contrasts sharply with the previous line.

he is puffed up with empty notions by his fleshly mind. Paul now gives his own evaluation of the judgmental attitude and superior claims of these Jews. First of all, their visions are false. They claim to be lifted up to heaven in visions as a result of their "humility." In reality they have only been puffed up with conceit by their minds of flesh. (Compare the similar evaluation of the false prophets of Jeremiah's day in Jer 14:14; 23:16.) The phrase "by his fleshly mind" is a Hebrew expression that Paul has carried over into Greek. Similar expressions appear in the Old Testament and later Jewish writings: "eyes of flesh" (Job 10:4), "arm of flesh" and "hand of flesh." In each context, the word "flesh" refers not so much to what is sinful as to what is merely human. And since it is human, it is weak, mortal and earthly, unlike that which is *spirit* and therefore of God. Paul's point is to identify the source of these so-called visions as simply the earth-bound minds of these men. They are not true visions of heaven. And since their visions are false, there is no basis for the superior attitude of these Jews or for their special religious practices. So ignore them.

Verse 19

He has not held fast to the head. This line begins a second part of Paul's evaluation of those who claim a superior spiritual status because of their so-called visions. They are seeking spiritual advancement in the wrong place and in the wrong way. True spirituality is found in a relationship with Christ, the Messiah, the head of God's people. The Messiah was promised to Israel, to the Jews (Rom 9:4-5). He was their coming King. But these Jews failed to take hold of their King when he came (Jn 1:11). They have rejected what should have been theirs.

By describing Christ as "the head," Paul takes up an image he introduced earlier in Colossians 1:18. Christ is the head of the body, the church. In this context, Paul presents the church as the redeemed people of God's new creation (see the comments on Col 1:18). Christ became the founder and head of this new people by virtue of his resurrection from the dead. But why does Paul take up this image of Christ and his body again here in Colossians 2:19? The Jews were telling the Colossians they were excluded from membership in the people of God. They were also excluded from the advanced spirituality of the elite among them who experience heavenly visions. Not so, says Paul. They are the ones who are excluded. They have excluded themselves by rejecting Christ. To be a part of God's people and to draw near to him in a special relationship is not based on keeping rules about food and drink, religious festivals, ceremonial purity or having visions of angels. What matters is taking hold of Christ. All who do this, whether Jew or Gentile, become heirs of the salvation God promised in the Old Testament. He raises them up with Christ and makes them members of his new redeemed people—the people of which Christ is the founder and head. They become members of his body and sharers in the true spiritual growth.

The remainder of the verse explains the nature of this spiritual growth that comes from taking hold of Christ. This instruction regarding spiritual growth also serves as a warning to any Christian who was tempted to seek spiritual advancement apart from the body through heavenly visions.

from whom the whole body. This line assumes a certain understanding of the way the human body works—namely that the head is the *governing* member of the body. The body is completely dependent upon the head. It determines everything that takes place within the body—particularly its growth. And so, it is on the spiritual level between Christ and his body, the church. Those who take hold of him become members of this body and share in its Christ-directed growth.

This statement contains two principles that have direct application for any Christian who was tempted to join the false teachers in their quest for heavenly visions. The first is that true spiritual advancement is only found through a vital connection with Christ, as a part of his body. It cannot be found in heavenly visions.

The second principle is that spiritual growth is about **the whole body**. The body is composed of individual members and each is to grow spiritually, but not in isolation from the other members. As with the members of a physical body, each individual is to function and grow as a part of the whole—in connection with and dependence upon one another, under the direction of the head (Eph 4:16). The quest for heavenly visions, on the other hand, is a quest for purely individual spiritual experience and advancement. Any Christian who sought such experiences would be isolating himself from the rest of the body. Not only would he fail to achieve the spiritual growth he sought (see Col 2:18d), he would also cause harm to the whole body by turning aside from the role assigned to him by the head for promoting the growth of the body. This point will become clearer in the final line of this verse.

supported and knit together through its ligaments and sinews. This final line describes the means of the body's growth. Under the direction of the head, the body is enabled to grow through the proper functioning of its ligaments and sinews. Joints are places of contacts between bones, which are held together by ligaments and sinews. The word translated "ligaments" means a bond—something that joins two or more things together (Col 3:14; Eph 4:3). It was used as a medical term for what we today call ligaments and tendons: bands of tissue that bind the joints together, attach muscles and hold organs in place. The joints and ligaments are the means by which the various parts of the body are bound together to become a unified whole. Without them our physical bodies would collapse and waste away. And so it is with the body of which Christ is the head. Only as its various members are bound together in mutual dependence can it become a unified whole and therefore function and grow as God intended under the direction of the head.

What then do the ligaments and sinews of this image represent? What is it that holds the church together in this way? Is it the Holy Spirit? Is it love? Is it specially gifted individuals such as pastors and teachers? Or is the reference to all believers? To see the ligaments and sinews as specially gifted members of the body who perform the ministry of "connecting" is attractive since it is consistent with other statements by Paul about differing ministries within the one body (see especially Eph 4:11-12, 16; Rom 12:4-8; 1 Cor 12:12-30). On the other hand, since there is nothing else in Colossians about such specially gifted members, it seems doubtful that we can discover them here. In fact, to give any specific answer to our question is probably to read more into the illustration than is actually there. It seems better to interpret it as a simple comparison or analogy. As the various members of a physical body are bound together by its ligaments and sinews into a unified whole, and this enables the whole to function and grow under the direction of the head, so it is with the body of Christ. Thus, spiritual growth is about the whole body. Individual believers grow in much the same way that the individual members of a physical body grow. They grow not in isolation from one another but only as they are bound together in relationships of mutual dependence and interaction within the body.

This concept of spiritual growth is the very opposite of what the false teachers advocated with their emphasis on individual mystical experiences. Paul's illustration, therefore, includes a warning: To join in their quest for heavenly visions would be to tear yourself from the ligaments that bind you to other believers in the body. The result would be harm to the body, since the growth of the whole is affected, and harm to yourself, since growth is not found apart from the body.

with a growth that is from God. A previous line states that the growth of the body comes from Christ, the head. Now we are told that it comes from God. What this means is simply that Christ is the agent or mediator of God's activity. We saw this concept set forth

> earlier in very broad terms in Colossians 1:15-20 where Paul describes Christ as God's agent in both creation and redemption (or new creation).
>
> To say that this growth is from God is also to say that this manner of spiritual advancement is the one God designed and ordained for his people. This is the growth that is from God—not the so-called growth that comes from private mystical experiences.

QUESTION 6

Summarize briefly the claims of the false teachers regarding their visions.

QUESTION 7

Give four reasons why the "worship of angels" in Colossians 2:18 should be understood as the worship that angels perform, rather than the worship that angels receive.

QUESTION 8

The humility of angels refers to the great courtesy and meekness they display toward one another. *True or False?*

QUESTION 9

Jews in Paul's day used the term *humility* to refer to the practice of _____.

Lesson 9: The False Teaching—Colossians 2:16-23

QUESTION 10

The phrase "the head" in Colossians 2:19 refers to which of the following?
- A. Church members
- B. Church leaders
- C. Christ
- D. Colossian Jews
- E. Colossian Christians
- F. Colossian Jews and Christians

QUESTION 11

The word "fleshly" in Colossians 2:18 refers not so much to what is sinful as to what is merely human. *True or False?*

QUESTION 12

The image of Christ as the head of the body in Colossians 2:19 assumes a certain understanding of the way the human body works—namely that the head is the _____ member of the body.

QUESTION 13

According to the commentary, what do the joints and ligaments represent in the image of the church as the body of Christ?
- A. The Holy Spirit
- B. Love
- C. All believers
- D. Specially gifted individuals such as pastors and teachers

QUESTION 14

According to Colossians 2:19, the body of Christ grows as it is supported by its joints and ligaments. Explain briefly Paul's point in this image, and how it relates to the false teaching.

QUESTION 15

Imagine the following situation. Someone in your congregation, perhaps a new arrival, announces that as a result of fasting he had a vision. In this vision, he saw angels worshipping God in heaven. He claims it was the most deeply moving spiritual experience of his life. He now feels closer to God because he has learned to worship him the way the angels do. Others within the congregation now want to experience the same thing. They believe they cannot reach the highest level of spirituality until they do. This man has offered to teach them how to achieve such visions. How would you respond to this situation—especially in light of Colossians 2:18-19?

QUESTION 16

In Colossians 2:19, Paul emphasizes that spiritual growth is about *the whole body*—meaning the whole congregation. Through the individual members being bound together in relationships of mutual dependence into a united whole, the whole body is enabled to grow under the direction of Christ.

- Can you give an example from your own experience of how this principle works?
- What have you observed when individual Christians and entire congregations are not properly supported and held together in this way?
- Evaluate your own church in relation to this principle. What can you do to promote the operation of this principle of spiritual growth?

Important Facts to Remember About Colossians 2:18-19

1. The Jewish mystics claimed to have experienced visions in which they entered the heavenly temple and looked upon the angels in their worship of God (Col 2:18).

2. These Jews sought to imitate the religious practices of these angels in their daily lives. This included fasting, which they called "humility." Fasting, they claimed, was an essential requirement for entering heaven.

3. Paul makes two criticisms of these mystics (Col 2:18d-19):

    -Their visions are not genuine but merely the product of their own minds.

    -They have failed to take hold of Christ, the Messiah promised to Israel. It is only in a vital relationship with him and through the mutual ministry of the body of which he is the head that one can experience the spiritual growth that is from God.

Topic 3: Liberated from Ceremonial Rules (Col 2:20-23)

In Colossians 2:20-23 Paul continues his response to those who boasted of heavenly visions. In order to be holy enough to enter heaven in a vision, they claimed one must keep many additional ceremonial rules and regulations including fasting. Do not be deceived, says Paul. Such rules are a form of bondage. They enslave all who belong to the world. Dying with Christ freed you from these things. This is because those who died with Christ no longer belong to the world. So do not start living as though you still did. Moreover, these teachings are not of God, but of men. And although they appear to be wise and heavenly minded, they only serve to gratify the self-seeking desires of the flesh.

Begin your study by reading Colossians 2:20-23. Then read the Worksheet on Colossians 2:20-23. Copy it in your Life Notebook and complete step 1 of the "Assignments." Check your conclusions by comparing them with the Answer Section for Colossians 2:20-23. Next, complete step 2 by recording on the same worksheet your detailed observations, interpretations, and applications. For the third and final step, carefully read the Commentary on Colossians 2:20-23. Then answer the following questions, taking special note of the *Important Facts to Remember*.

Worksheet for Colossians 2:20-23

20 If you have died with Christ

to the elemental spirits of the world,

why, do you submit to them as though you lived in the world,

   21 "Do not handle! Do not taste! Do not touch!"

22 These are all destined to perish with use,

founded as they are on human commands and teachings.

23 Even though they have the appearance of wisdom

   with their self-imposed worship and false humility,

   achieved by an unsparing treatment of the body—

a wisdom with no true value—

they in reality result in fleshly indulgence.

Commentary on Colossians 2:20-23

1. The Gospel Applied to the False Teaching—Colossians 2:16-3:4 (Continued)

c. Liberated from Ceremonial Rules—Colossians 2:20-23

This is the third paragraph of Paul's application of the doctrinal truths of our salvation in Colossians 2:9-15 to the claims of the false teachers. In the first paragraph (Col 2:16-17) he responded to their claim that if the Colossians hoped to be saved, they must keep the ceremonial laws of Judaism. Not so, says Paul. Christ has fulfilled the ceremonial law.

In the next paragraph (Col 2:18-19) he responded to those who boasted of heavenly visions of the angelic worship and sought to imitate these angelic practices in their daily lives. This, they claimed, led to the most advanced spiritual state. Not so, says Paul. Their visions are false, the product of their own earthly minds. The true spiritual growth comes through a relationship with Christ and through sharing in the life of his body, the church.

Now in Colossians 2:20-23 Paul continues his response to those who boasted of heavenly visions. In order to be holy enough to enter heaven in a vision, they claimed, one must keep many additional ceremonial rules and regulations including fasting. Do not be deceived, says Paul. Such rules are a form of bondage. They enslave all who belong to the world. Dying with Christ freed you from these things. This is because those who died with Christ no longer belong to the world. So do not start living as though you still did. These teachings are not of God, but of men. And although they appear to be wise and heavenly minded, they only serve to gratify the self-seeking desires of the flesh.

Verse 20

If you have died with Christ. Paul's explanation of salvation in Colossians 2:9-15 centers around the fact that Christians have died and risen with Christ. As we saw, dying and rising with Christ results in transfer out of the old fallen existence in Adam and into the new creation in Christ. Dying means the end of the old existence; rising means the start of the new. In this paragraph, Paul points out the implication of this transfer out of the old existence. In the next paragraph, he will do the same in regard to their transfer into the new existence.

to the elemental spirits of the world. This line describes a result of the Christian's death with Christ. This phrase is usually translated with the word "to" instead of "from". This is in keeping with other statements by Paul regarding the believer's death to sin (Rom 6:2), to the law (Rom 7:4) and to the world (Gal 6:14). Translated in this way, the meaning is that death has ended the believer's relationship to "the elemental spirits of the world." The word "to" here could also be translated "from." As in Colossians 2:18, Paul is using abbreviated language. In this context, "from" is short for "released from" or "freed from" (compare Rom 7:6). It indicates that death freed the believer from the authority or control of these elements. The two statements mean basically the same thing. The difference is simply one of emphasis. The word "from" emphasizes the fact of a previous state of bondage and the freedom from this state that dying with Christ effected.

This statement in Colossians 2:20 raises three questions. (1) What are "the elemental spirits of the world"? (2) In what ways were the Colossians formerly bound by these "elemental spirits"? (3) How did dying with Christ set them free?

First, as we saw in our study of Colossians 2:8, Paul uses this expression to describe ceremonial rules and practices. In ordinary Greek usage it referred to **physical** things. The "elements" are the basic building blocks of which all things are composed. Paul uses it for ceremonial practices—both Jewish and pagan—because they are concerned with physical, earthly things, unlike the gospel which is concerned with spiritual, heavenly matters. In this sense all religions outside of Christ keep their followers in a state of bondage under ceremonial rules and regulations. In Galatians 4:1-3 Paul compares this state of bondage to the conditions of an under-aged child who is heir to his father's estate, but is ruled by guardians and managers until the date set by his father. Until that time the child has no more freedom than a slave. But when that date arrives, he is set free to enjoy the full privileges of a mature son. And so it is with the Christian (Col 2:4-7). Formerly, we were in bondage under "the elemental spirits of the world." But in the fullness of time, God sent his Son to redeem us from that bondage and to adopt us as mature sons and heirs.

How then does the Christian's death with Christ free him from this state of bondage under "the elemental spirits of the world"? Paul's line of reasoning is based on the common sense understanding that a person who dies departs from this world (Jn 13:1; 1 Tim 6:7). And since only those who live in the world are subject to "the elemental spirits of the world," to depart from the world results in freedom. But in what sense does one who dies with Christ depart from the world? Obviously, it is in the theological and not the physical sense. The world in this context refers to the present fallen world where sin, death, and the law reign (Rom 5:14, 21; 7:6). "This present evil age" is another way of expressing it (Gal 1:4). It stands in contrast to the kingdom of God and the new creation. Dying with Christ transfers the believer from the one dominion to the other. They no longer belong to this world but to the heavenly kingdom of Christ (Col 1:13). We are citizens of heaven living on earth (Phil 3:20. We are in the world but not of it (Jn 17:15).

Paul uses a similar line of reasoning in Romans 6 and 7 to explain how dying with Christ freed us from the dominion of sin and the law. As death frees a slave from his master, so dying with Christ freed us from sin so that we now serve a new Master (Rom 6:6-20). As death frees a married woman from the legal bond that tied her to her husband, so dying with Christ freed us from the law, so that we could be joined to another and serve him in the new way of the Spirit (Rom 7:1-6). "The elemental spirits of the world" (ceremonial rules) are simply one aspect of the law. Dying with Christ freed us from the dominion of that old way of life. The time for the earthly and unspiritual regime of ceremonial rules and practices has passed. The time for a heavenly and spiritual relationship with God has come. Like the child who finally comes of age, we have passed into the freedom of a mature relationship.

Paul's argument in this verse must be seen in relation to the claims of the Jewish mystics. They sought visionary journeys to **heaven**. The **world** is what they sought to leave behind. Their ceremonial rules, they claimed, are heavenly in nature. They are practiced by angels and required of all who wish to worship with them. On the contrary, says Paul. These practices—concerned as they are with material, earthly things—are of this world. Indeed, they enslave all who belong to it. Christians, on the other hand, have been liberated from such things. Dying with Christ transferred them out of the world.

why do you submit to them as though you lived in the world? Dying with Christ freed the Colossians from the bondage they knew as Gentiles under their old pagan religious rules and regulations. Believers have been freed to serve God in the new way of the Spirit (Rom 7:6). It would then be foolish to return to that old servitude by submitting to these kinds of things all over again.

The question "why do you submit" to its ordinances could mean that some of the Colossians had actually begun to practice these Jewish regulations. Yet, Paul's earlier statements of confidence and praise toward the Colossians for their steadfastness in the faith suggest this is not the case (Col 1:23; 2:5). His introduction to the present section in Colossians 2:6-8 can serve as our guide to the meaning of Colossians 2:20. There he exhorts the Colossians to continue in the path they have been traveling since the beginning (Col 2:6-7). He then warns them against being taken captive by a deceptive teaching (Col 2:8). This warning should be seen as an introductory statement for his evaluation of this teaching in Colossians 2:16-3:4. It seems best then to interpret Paul's question here in Colossians 2:20 simply as a specific development of his general introductory warning in Colossians 2:8. In other words, we should see Colossians 2:20 more as a **warning** aimed at those who are in danger of being deceived into doing this rather than as a **rebuke** to those who are already doing it. If we interpret it this way, then Paul is saying this: "You who are tempted to do this, why would you submit to such things, since to do so would be to return to something from which Christ set you free?"

Verse 21

"Do not handle! Do not taste! Do not touch!" These are examples of the kind of ceremonial rules from which Christ freed them and to which the Jews would have them return. They are "the elemental spirits of the world" that keep those who belong to the world in a state of bondage. Taboos regarding touch and taste in order to avoid ceremonial impurity summarize much of the purity laws of the Judaism of Paul's day. Moreover, strict ceremonial purity including fasting was an essential requirement for gaining visionary entry into the heavenly temple in order to look upon and join the angels in their worship of God. Or so these Jewish mystics claimed. If one must be pure to enter the earthly temple, how much more so to enter the temple of heaven?

Verse 22

These are all destined to perish with use. These practices all concern material things ("elemental spirits of the world") that pass away in time as they are used. This is particularly the case with food. It perishes in the act of eating and digesting it. Such things are therefore of no real importance compared to the spiritual and eternal realities of the gospel.

founded as they are on human commands and teachings. In addition, Paul writes, these taboos were not established by God, as the false teachers claimed. They are from **people**. The phrase, "human commands and teachings," is based on Isaiah 29:13. Jesus quoted this text in regard to the way the Pharisees had added a multitude of extra rules to God's commands. But in doing so they had actually set aside his word (Mt 15:6-9; Mk 7:5-9). Recall that earlier in Colossians 2:8, Paul referred to this Jewish practice of adding to God's commands as "according to human traditions."

Verse 23

Even though they have the appearance of wisdom with their self-imposed worship and false humility achieved by an unsparing treatment of the body. The words "worship" and "humility" (referring to fasting) are repeated here from Colossians 2:18. The Jews claimed they were imitating the angels in their form of worship which they saw in visions. These practices have the appearance of wisdom. Fasting and other forms of strict bodily denial appear to be the actions of a very spiritual and heavenly-minded person. But it is an appearance only—one that is "empty, deceitful" (Col 2:8). God never required such things of his people, nor did he authorize them. These are made-up, self-imposed practices.

The second half of the verse introduces a contrast to what is said in the first half. The contrast is between the appearance of these practices and what they amount to in actual fact.

a wisdom with no true value. The Jewish mystics strove to keep all of their self-imposed rules of ceremonial purity including fasting and other forms of denying the natural desires of the body for one simple reason. They believed these practices were of great value. They believed that they led to an advanced experience of God and therefore also to a more exalted standing in the eyes of their fellow Jews.

This manner of thinking can be seen particularly in regard to fasting. We know that some Jews of Paul's day believed that being full of food energized the passions of the body, especially sexual desires. Fasting, therefore, was taught as a way of suppressing these desires. And thus, they claimed it promoted purity of heart. Fasting, moreover, was seen as an act of humility and contrition before God. By fasting the worshipper laid aside his pride and self-centeredness in order to express whole-hearted devotion to God.

No doubt the Jewish mystics of Colossae were saying the same kind of thing. They fasted and treated their bodies with severity (imitating the angels) in order to join in the heavenly worship with purified hearts as well as purified bodies. But Paul is telling the Colossians to see these false claims for what they are. There is no real value to this "unsparing treatment of the body." It does not promote purity of heart. It promotes the very opposite. It gratifies the flesh.

they in reality result in fleshly indulgence. The words "fleshly indulgence" stand in contrast to the phrase "unsparing treatment of the body" in the first half of the verse. The Greek word translated "indulgence" was commonly used for being filled or satisfied with food. The word "flesh" was commonly used to refer to the body or the material of which the body is made. In such cases, nothing bad or sinful was intended. Paul uses it in this way in Colossians 1:22 where he refers to Christ's death in his "body of flesh" (similar uses appear in Col 1:24; 2:1, 5, 11). But he can also use "flesh" in a bad sense. He exhorts the Romans to "put on the Lord Jesus Christ, and make no provision for the flesh to arouse its desires" (Rom 13:14). Similarly, he tells the Galatians to "live by the Spirit and you will not carry out the desires of the flesh" (Gal 5:16). He then describes the works of the flesh as "sexual immorality, impurity, depravity, idolatry, sorcery, hostilities," and so forth (Gal 5:19). In each of these passages, the flesh refers to fallen human nature—man in his sin apart from the redeeming grace of God and the sanctifying work of the Holy Spirit.

This is also Paul's meaning here in Colossians 2:23. The false teachers' attempt to promote spiritual purity and heavenly worship by not satisfying the natural desires of the body for food was actually promoting sin. It was satisfying the sinful desires of fallen human nature for self-exaltation. Their self-imposed religious practices result in self-centered pride and self-righteousness. These are the works of the flesh.

Observations on Paul's Defense of the Faith in Colossians 2:9-23

In Colossians 2:8 Paul warned the Colossians to be on guard so that no one takes them captive through a hollow and deceptive teaching. Each paragraph since then (Col 2:9-23) must be seen in relation to this warning. In each paragraph Paul shows these young believers what is hollow and deceptive about the teaching. His purpose throughout is to safeguard them from capture and thereby to keep them walking in the path of Christ. Paul's defense of the faith in these verses is one of our earliest examples of Christian *apologetics* (from the Greek word meaning defense). And since it comes from the pen of an inspired writer, and since the need for defending the faith is as great in our day as it was in Paul's, we should pause here to observe his apologetic method.

While his basic method can be summed up in the words "Do not be deceived," we can identify at least three elements in it.

> 1. *He understood the teaching.* The first element in any defense of the faith must be an accurate understanding of the opposing doctrine. Paul obviously understood this one quite well. He was born and raised as a Jew and educated as a rabbi. No doubt he was familiar with Jewish visionary mysticism before his conversion. But aside from how he gained his understanding of the deceptive teaching that threatened the Colossians, the point is that he possessed it. And it was this understanding that enabled him to expose what was false about it and to show how the gospel is superior.
>
> 2. *He showed the superiority of the gospel.* The deceptive teaching offered an alternative way of salvation. Its message was: Do these things and the blessings of salvation become possible. In response, Paul's strategy was to explain that

> what Christ already accomplished for believers is superior to what these people claimed to offer. In response to their claim regarding the necessity of circumcision, Paul explains how Christians have already received the circumcision of the heart. In response to their claim regarding the dietary laws and holy days of Judaism, he explains that these were but the shadow of which Christ is the substance. In response to the Jewish promise of eternal life for those who keep the law of Moses, Paul explains how believers have already received the verdict of the last judgment and entered into eternal life. In response to their claim that spiritual advancement comes from private mystical experiences, Paul explains that true spiritual advancement comes only through a vital connection with Christ and being a part of his body, the church.
>
> *3. He exposed the true nature of the teaching.* In addition to showing how the gospel provides what the false teachers only claim to offer, Paul points out the emptiness of their other claims. Their visions are not real but just the products of their own minds. Their special ceremonial practices are not of heaven but the world. They are not of God but of men. And their "unsparing treatment of the body" are of no value in promoting purity of heart and heavenly worship—they simply gratify the desires of the flesh.
>
> Paul's defense of the faith in Colossians then involved three key elements: an understanding of the deceptive teaching, showing the superiority of the gospel and exposing the teaching's true nature. This method worked with the church of Colossae, and God has given it to us as an example to follow.

QUESTION 17

In Colossians 2:20, the phrase "If you have died with Christ" means we are no longer part of the old fallen existence in Adam and are now part of the _____ in Christ.

QUESTION 18

Paul uses the expression "elemental spirits of the world" as a designation for ceremonial practices because they are concerned with physical, earthly things rather than spiritual, heavenly matters. *True or False?*

QUESTION 19

What image does Paul use in Colossians to illustrate the way that believers were previously in bondage under "elemental spirits of the world."

A. A wife bound by law to her husband
B. A slave bound to his master
C. A child ruled by guardians
D. A soldier who must obey his superiors
E. A prisoner of war

QUESTION 20

"The world" in Colossians 2:20, refers to the present fallen world where sin, death, and the law reign. Another expression for it is "this present evil _____."

QUESTION 21

What common sense understanding provides the basis for Paul's conclusion that believers no longer belong to the world because they died with Christ?

QUESTION 22

The question, "Why do you submit to the elemental spirits of the world" in Colossians 2:20 reveals that some of the Christians in Colossae had already begun to submit to the rules and regulations of the false teachers *True or False?*

QUESTION 23

What spiritual value did the Jewish mystics claim to find in their "severe treatment of the body" (including fasting), and what does Paul say was the actual effect of these practices?

QUESTION 24

What are the three basic elements of Paul's defense of the faith that we observed in Colossians 2:9-23?

QUESTION 25

Colossians 2:20-23 reveals an important insight into fallen human nature. Human sinfulness can manifest itself in many different ways. It can manifest itself in very obvious actions such as drunkenness and sexual immorality. Or, as we see in this passage, it can manifest itself in more subtle ways such as an unscriptural kind of religiousness. This can include fasting and other forms of self-denial, as well as keeping various rituals, rules, taboos and holy days that God does not require. These types of things have the appearance of wisdom, as Paul explains in Colossians 2:23, but they only serve to gratify the flesh. Record your response in your Life Notebook.

1. Have you observed this type of fleshly, unscriptural religiousness in non-Christians?
2. What do you think is their motivation for doing these things?
3. Why are some Christians tempted to start these types of practices?
4. Have you experienced this temptation yourself?
5. What are some things you could do for those you minister to keep them from falling prey to this temptation?

QUESTION 26

In Colossians 2:9-23, we see an excellent example of how to respond to a deceptive teaching that threatens a congregation. We identified three elements in Paul's defense of the faith:

1. He had an accurate understanding of their beliefs and practices.
2. He explained the nature of Christian salvation in relation to the false teaching. He showed how the salvation that Christ provides is superior to what these false teachers were claiming to offer.
3. He exposed the true nature of their teachings. He showed that their claims are false and how they offer no real solution to man's spiritual problems.

Paul's apologetic method provides us with a model to follow when seeking to prevent those in our care from being taken captive by a deceptive teaching. Answer the following questions in regard to a false teaching that is a problem where you live. Record your answer in your Life Notebook.

- How can you get an accurate understanding of this teaching?
- What is its central claim regarding the nature of salvation? How can you show that the salvation Christ provides is superior?
- How can you expose what is false and deceptive about this teaching?

QUESTION 27

What truths do you find in the three paragraphs covered by this lesson (Col 2:16-23) that belong in your course *What Every Christian Should Know About Salvation*?

Important Facts to Remember About Colossians 2:20-23

1. In ordinary Greek usage "the elemental spirits of the world" referred to physical things. Paul used it as a general designation for ceremonial rules and practices—Jewish and pagan. This is because ceremonial practices are concerned with physical, earthly things, unlike the gospel which is concerned with spiritual, heavenly matters.
2. All religions outside of Christ keep their followers in a state of bondage under "the elemental spirits of the world"—their ceremonial rules and regulations.
3. Dying with Christ liberated believers from this bondage. It removed them from "the world" (this present evil age) and transferred them, in a theological sense, to a new dominion. They now

belong to the new creation; to Christ's heavenly kingdom, and they serve in the new way of the Spirit.

4. For Christians to submit to non-Christian ceremonial rules would be foolish, since it would mean returning to the bondage from which Christ set them free (Col 2:20).

5. The Jewish mystics believed that severe treatment of the body (including fasting) suppressed the passions of the body and promoted purity of heart and undistracted devotion to God. In this they sought to be like the angels. In fact, says Paul, while these practices appear wise and heavenly minded, they only serve to gratify the self-seeking desires of "the flesh" (fallen human nature).

6. Paul's defense of the faith in Colossians 2:9-23 a three-part method that Christians today can follow when responding to a false teaching: (a) understand the teaching, (b) show the superiority of the gospel, (c) expose the true nature of the teaching.

Lesson 9 Self Check

QUESTION 1

The ceremonial practices of the Old Testament were _____ meant to illustrate the future salvation the Messiah would bring.

QUESTION 2

The point of Paul's exhortation in Colossians 2:16, to let no one sit in judgment on you regarding food and drink, etc., was to urge the Colossians to go ahead and keep these rules, even though God does not require it, just to maintain peace with their Jewish neighbors in the hope of winning them to Christ. *True or False?*

QUESTION 3

Which of the following was **not** one of the claims of the false teachers regarding their visions?

   A. They experienced the joys of the future salvation even now in the present time.

   B. They saw the angels worshipping God in the heavenly temple.

   C. To qualify for such a vision, one must fast as the angels do.

   D. To qualify for such a vision, one must become celibate like the angels.

   E. To qualify for such a vision, one must maintain the ceremonial purity that angels do.

QUESTION 4

Which of the following is **not** one of the reasons given in the commentary for concluding that the "worship of angels" in Colossians 2:18 refers to the worship angels perform?

   A. Nothing else in the letter indicates that the false teachers worshipped angels.

   B. The false teachers were clearly Jews, and the Jews of Paul's day did not worship angels.

   C. Among the Jews of Paul's day, there was a movement called Merkabah mysticism that sought visions of the angelic worship in heaven.

   D. On the wall of the synagogue of Colossae, archaeologists have discovered carved images that show Jews worshipping with angels.

   E. If the Colossians were being tempted to worship angels, surely Paul would have warned them very strongly against such a clear violation of the First Commandment.

QUESTION 5

When Paul identifies the mystic's "fleshly mind" as the source of the visions described in Colossians 2:18, he is emphasizing that a *sinful* mind—rather than one that is merely human—produced these visions. *True or False?*

QUESTION 6

The image of Christ as the head of the body in Colossians 2:19 assumes a certain understanding of the way the body works—namely that the head is the _____ member of the body.

QUESTION 7

Since the expression "the elemental spirits of the world" refers to physical things, Paul uses it to describe ceremonial practices because they are concerned with physical, earthly things rather than spiritual, heavenly matters. *True or False?*

QUESTION 8

When Paul concludes that dying with Christ has freed believers from "the elemental spirits of the world," his line of reasoning is based on the common sense understanding that a person who dies departs from the _____.

QUESTION 9

Which of the following was **not** a motive for "unsparing treatment of the body" which the Jewish mystics practiced?

   A. To suppress the passions of the body
   B. To atone for their sins
   C. To join in the angelic worship in heaven
   D. To promote purity of heart
   E. To become ceremonial pure

QUESTION 10

Which of the following is **not** one of the three basic elements of Paul's defense of the faith that we observed in Colossians 2:9-23?

   A. He understood the deceptive teaching
   B. He exposed what was false about it
   C. He challenged the opponents to public debate
   D. He showed the superiority of the gospel

Lesson 9 Answers to Questions

WORKSHEET FOR COLOSSIANS 2:16-17

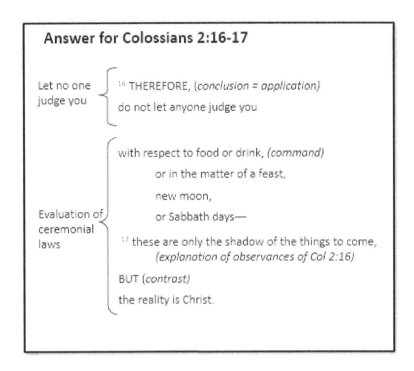

Textual Outline of Colossians 2:16-17
I. Conclusion: Let no one judge you for not keeping the ceremonial law. (Col 2:16)
    A. Command: Let no one judge you. (Col 2:16a)
    B. The basis of judgment: Failure to keep Old Testament ceremonial laws (Col 2:16b)
II. Evaluation of the ceremonial laws (Col 2:17)
    A. They foreshadowed Christ's coming. (Col 2:17a)
    B. The reality is found in Christ. (Col 2:17b)

Theme Statement for Colossians 2:16-17.
The Colossians should allow no one to condemn them for failing to observe the Old Testament ceremonial laws, since these merely foreshadowed what Christ would bring.

QUESTION 1
    C. Colossians 2:9-15
QUESTION 2: *Your answer should be similar to the following:*
These ceremonial rules were symbols intended to illustrate the future salvation the Messiah would bring. Since this salvation has now arrived, the rules are obsolete.

QUESTION 3: False [The Jews of Colossae were telling these Gentile-born Christians that if they wish to be a part of God's people and to inherit salvation, they must first become Jews and live like Jews. This means—in addition to being circumcised (see Col 2:11)—they must keep all the rules of the Old Testament and Judaism regarding food and drink. They must also keep all of the special holy days of the Jewish calendar: the annual festivals such as the Passover, the Day of Atonement and the Feast of Tabernacles, the monthly new moon celebrations and the Sabbath day. Such arguments must have created doubts in the minds of some of the Colossian believers. And with the doubts, there came the temptation to submit to these ceremonial laws. Thus, Paul is saying to the congregation, "Do not listen to these criticisms." "Do not let anyone lead you away from the path of the gospel."]

QUESTION 4: *Your answer*

QUESTION 5: *Your answer*

WORKSHEET FOR COLOSSIANS 2:18-19

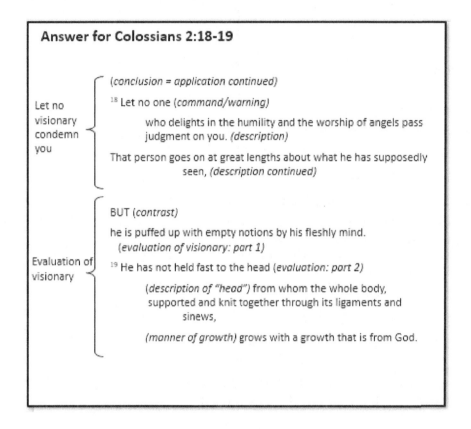

Textual Outline of Colossians 2:18-19

I. Let no visionary condemn you. (Col 2:18a-c)
    A. The command: Let no one condemn you. (Col 2:18a)
    B. Description of the visionary (Col 2:18b-c)
        1. He delights in the humility and worship of angels. (Col 2:18b)
        2. He saw these things in a heavenly vision. (Col 2:18c)
II. Evaluation of the visionary (Col 2:18d-19)
    A. His visions are false. (Col 2:18d)
    B. He has failed to take hold of Christ, the head. (Col 2:19)

Theme Statement for Colossians 2:18-19.
Let no visionary condemn you since his visions are false, and the true spiritual growth comes through a relationship with Christ and sharing in the life of his body.

QUESTION 6: *Your answer should be similar to the following:*
They claimed they could experience the joys of the future salvation even now in the present through visions in which they enter the heavenly temple, see the angels, and join them in their worship of God. In order to experience such visions, it was necessary they claimed, to engage in strict bodily disciplines, including fasting, and to maintain a high degree of ceremonial purity.

QUESTION 7: *Your answer should be similar to the following:*
Nothing else in the letter indicates that the false teachers worshipped angels. Aside from their visions (Col 2:18c), and "unsparing treatment of the body" (Col 2:23), everything else in the letter clearly points to the conclusion that the false teachers were Jews. We know from history that the Jews of Paul's day did not worship angels; there is no historical evidence of a pagan group that worshipped angels but also kept the Jewish ceremonial rules mentioned in Colossians. There was, however, a Jewish movement known as Merkabah mysticism that fits the description of the false teachers of Colossae. They engaged in severe bodily disciplines in order to believe they achieved visionary journeys to heaven in which they joined the angels in their worship in the heavenly temple.

QUESTION 8: False [The term humility in this context refers to the self-abasement of fasting (see Col 2: 23, "false humility achieved by an unsparing treatment of the body"). In the Old Testament to fast meant to humble oneself (Ps 35:13; Isa 58:3). Therefore, the term humility was often used among the Jews of Paul's day as a reference to the practice of fasting.]

QUESTION 9: fasting

QUESTION 10
  C. Christ

QUESTION 11: True [As indicated in the Commentary, "flesh" or "fleshly" is a Hebrew word that Paul has carried over into the Greek. Similar expressions appear in the Old Testament and later Jewish writings: "eyes of flesh" (Job 10:4), "arm of flesh" and "hand of flesh." In each context, the word flesh refers not so much to what is sinful as to what is merely human. And since it is human, it is weak, mortal and earthly, unlike that which is spirit and therefore of God. Paul's point is to identify the source of these so-called visions as simply the earth-bound minds of these men.]

QUESTION 12: governing

QUESTION 13
  C. All believers

QUESTION 14: *Your answer should be similar to the following:*
As the various members of a physical body are bound together by its joints and ligaments into a unified whole that enables it to function and grow under the direction of the head, so it is with the body of which Christ is the head. Thus, spiritual growth is about the whole body. Individual believers grow in much the same way that the individual members of a physical body grow—not in isolation from one another, but only as they are bound together in relationships of mutual dependence. If a Christian were therefore to seek spiritual advancement by joining the false teachers in their quest for individual mystical experiences, he would be isolating himself from the rest of the body—torn, as it were, from the ligaments that bind him to the other members. The result would be harm to the body, since the growth of the whole body is affected, and harm to himself since growth is not found apart from the body.

QUESTION 15: *Your answer*

QUESTION 16: *Your answer*

WORKSHEET FOR COLOSSIANS 2:20-23

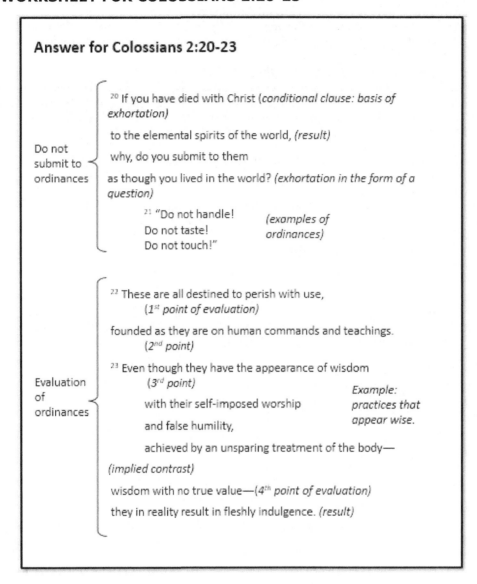

Textual Outline of Colossians 2:20-23
I. Do not submit to worldly ordinances. (Col 2:20-21)
    A. Basis of exhortation (Col 2:20a-b)
        1. They died with Christ. (Col 2:20a)
        2. The result: Freedom from the elements of the world (Col 2:20b)
    B. Exhortation (Col 2:20c-21)
        1. They must no longer submit to the world's ordinances. (Col 2:20c-d)
        2. Examples of such ordinances (Col 2:21)
II. Evaluation of the ordinances (Col 2:22-23)
    A. They concern things destined to perish with use. (Col 2:22a)
    B. They are based on human teachings. (Col 2:22b)
    C. They appear to be wise, but are not. (Col 2:23a-b)
    D. They only gratify the flesh. (Col 2:23c)

Theme Statement for Colossians 2:20-23
Because dying with Christ freed the Colossians from the elements of the world, they must not follow the religious practices of the false teachers.

QUESTION 17: new creation
QUESTION 18: True
QUESTION 19
    C. A child ruled by guardians
QUESTION 20: age
QUESTION 21: *Your answer should be similar to the following:*
A person who dies departs from this world.
QUESTION 22: False [It is better to see the question, "Why do you submit to" its ordinances? in Colossians 2:20, as a warning to those who are tempted to submit to ordinances rather than as a rebuke to those who are already doing it. This is in keeping with the warning in Colossians 2:8 to be on guard so that you do "not to allow anyone to captivate you." Since this verse acts as an introduction to this section, we should allow it to guide our interpretation of Colossians 2:20.]
QUESTION 23: *Your answer should be similar to the following:*
These Jews believed that severe treatment of the body suppressed the passions of the body and promoted purity of heart and undistracted devotion to God. Paul says it has no such value. It only serves to gratify the self-seeking desires of fallen human nature ("the flesh").
QUESTION 24: *Your answer should be similar to the following:*
The three elements are as follows: (a) Paul understood the deceptive teaching; (b) he showed the superiority of the gospel; and (c) he exposed the true nature of the teaching.
QUESTION 25: *Your answer*
QUESTION 26: *Your answer*
QUESTION 27: *Your answer*

Lesson 9 Self Check Answers

QUESTION 1: *Your answer should be one of the following:*
symbols, shadows

QUESTION 2: False

QUESTION 3
    D. To qualify for such a vision, one must become celibate like the angels.

QUESTION 4
    D. On the wall of the synagogue of Colossae, archaeologists have discovered carved images that show Jews worshipping with angels.

QUESTION 5: False

QUESTION 6: governing

QUESTION 7: True

QUESTION 8: world

QUESTION 9
    B. To atone for their sins

QUESTION 10
    C. He challenged the opponents to public debate

Unit Three Exam

QUESTION 1

In Colossians 2:1-5, Paul explains that the specific purpose of his letter is to bring the readers to maturity in Christ. *True or False?*

QUESTION 2

In Colossians 2:1, Paul mentions how hard he was striving for the believers of Colossae and nearby towns. Which of the following was **not** a part of Paul's striving?

- A. His letter to them
- B. His concern regarding the false teaching
- C. His anxieties over the persecution they faced
- D. His prayers for them

QUESTION 3

To truly understand "the knowledge of the mystery of God, namely, Christ" (Col 2:2) means to have a thorough understanding of God's plan of salvation through Christ, including how to live according to it. *True or False?*

QUESTION 4

The Jews of Paul's day taught that "the treasures of wisdom and knowledge" are in _____.

QUESTION 5

In the ancient world, the expression "absent in body, present in spirit" was often used to describe a writer's presence through his _____.

QUESTION 6

Which of the following is **not** true of the paragraph Colossians 2:6-8?

- A. Paul repeats the theme and purpose of the letter.
- B. It displays striking similarities with Colossians 1:9-10.
- C. It introduces the final major section of the body of the letter, Colossians 2:6-4:6.
- D. It summarizes the saving benefits of Christ's death and resurrection.

QUESTION 7

When Paul mentioned in Colossians 2:6 how the Colossians "received Christ Jesus", he was referring to the teaching about Jesus that they received. *True or False?*

QUESTION 8

What does it mean in Colossians 2:10, that Christians have been *made full* in Christ?

    A. They have been filled with joy.

    B. They have been filled with the Holy Spirit.

    C. There is nothing lacking in the salvation Christ brings.

    D. They have been filled with the knowledge of God's will.

    E. They have experienced the fullness of the end–time salvation.

QUESTION 9

In the Old Testament, circumcision was used as a metaphor for the cleansing of that which was defiled. *True or False?*

QUESTION 10

When a person responds in faith to the gospel, God considers him in a _____ sense to have suffered the penalty of death for his sins in the person of Christ, his representative.

QUESTION 11

Which of the following Old Testament events or practices foreshadowed God's redemption as dying and rising with Christ?

    A. The sin offering

    B. The Passover celebration

    C. The Exodus from Egypt

    D. The sacrifice of Isaac

    E. The redemption of the firstborn

    F. The flood and Noah's ark

QUESTION 12

Water baptism was the means by which the early Christians expressed publicly their faith in Christ at the time of conversion. *True or False?*

QUESTION 13

To be dead spiritually (Col 2:13), means that a part of our inner being called our *spirit* is without life. *True or False?*

QUESTION 14

In ordinary usage, the term translated "record of sin" referred to the written record of a person's _____.

QUESTION 15

The historical background of the nailing of the record of sin to the cross in Colossians 2:14 is found in the Romans' practice of driving a nail through a person's certificate of debt to show that the debt has been paid in full. *True or False?*

QUESTION 16

What image does Paul use in Colossians 2:15 to describe Christ's resurrection and ascension?

A. A wedding procession
B. A parade for a victorious Olympic athlete
C. A welcoming parade for a returning dignitary
D. A military parade
E. The coronation of a king
F. A harvest festival

QUESTION 17

God makes believers alive with Christ because at the time of conversion he includes them in the verdict of _____ that he pronounced on Christ.

QUESTION 18

The ceremonial practices of the Old Testament were _____ meant to illustrate the future salvation the Messiah would bring.

QUESTION 19

Which of the following was **not** one of the claims of the false teachers regarding their visions?

A. They could experience the joys of the future salvation even now in the present.
B. They were able to see the angels worshipping God in the heavenly temple.
C. To qualify for such a vision, one must fast as the angels do.
D. To qualify for such a vision, one must become celibate like the angels.
E. To qualify for such a vision, one must maintain the ceremonial purity that angels do.

QUESTION 20

Which of the following is **not** one of the reasons given in the commentary for concluding that the "worship of angels" in Colossians 2:18 refers to the worship that angels perform?

A. Nothing else in the letter indicates that the false teachers worshipped angels.
B. The false teachers were clearly Jews, and Jews did not worship angels.
C. The Jewish movement, Merkabah mysticism, sought visions of the angelic worship.
D. Wall carvings at the synagogue of Colossae, recently uncovered by archaeologists, display scenes of angels worshipping God.
E. If the Colossians were being tempted to worship angels, surely Paul would have warned them very strongly against such a clear violation of the first commandment.

QUESTIONS 21

Paul describes the source of these visions as the visionary's own "fleshly mind" because he wished to emphasize that these visions are not of God but merely the mortal, earthly human mind. *True or False?*

QUESTION 22

In the image of the church as the body of Christ in Colossians 2:19, the joints and ligaments represent (according to the commentary) specially gifted members of the congregation who perform the ministry of "connecting." *True or False?*

QUESTION 23

When Paul concludes that dying with Christ has freed believers from "elemental spirits of the world," his line of reasoning is based on the commonsense understanding that anyone who dies departs from the _____.

QUESTION 24

Which of the following was **not** a motive for the false teachers' "unsparing treatment of the body"?
   A. To suppress the passions of the body
   B. To join in the heavenly worship
   C. To promote purity of heart
   D. To atone for their sins
   E. To become ceremonially pure

QUESTION 25

A primary element in Paul's defense of the faith seen in Colossians 2:9-23 is that of showing the _____ of the gospel.

Unit 3 Exam Answers

QUESTION 1: True
QUESTION 2
   C. His anxieties over the persecution they faced
QUESTION 3: True
QUESTION 4: heaven
QUESTION 5: letter
QUESTION 6
   D. It summarizes the saving benefits of Christ's death and resurrection.
QUESTION 7: True
QUESTION 8
   C. There is nothing lacking in the salvation Christ brings.
QUESTION 9: False
QUESTION 10: legal
QUESTION 11
   A. The sin offering
QUESTION 12: True
QUESTION 13: False
QUESTION 14: debt
QUESTION 15: False
QUESTION 16
   D. A military parade
QUESTION 17: *Your answer should be one of the following:*
acquittal, justification
QUESTION 18: *Your answer should be one of the following:*
symbols, shadows
QUESTION 19
   D. To qualify for such a vision, one must become celibate like the angels.
QUESTION 20
   D. Wall carvings at the synagogue of Colossae, recently uncovered by archaeologists, display scenes of angels worshipping God.
QUESTIONS 21: True
QUESTION 22: False
QUESTION 23: world
QUESTION 24
   D. To atone for their sins
QUESTION 25: superiority

Unit Four: The Gospel Applied to the Christian Life

In the previous unit, you studied the entire second chapter of Colossians. The three lessons of this final unit will cover chapters 3 and 4.

In Lesson 10, you will examine Colossians 3:1-11. In the first of these two paragraphs, (Col 3:1-4) Paul completes his application of the gospel to the false teachers by exhorting the Colossians to true heavenly-mindedness. The second paragraph, (Col 3:5-11) begins the application to the Christian life in general. Paul exhorts these young believers to walk in accordance with what God has made them as "new men" in Christ by putting to death all the sins that remain of their former lives as pagans.

You will study Colossians 3:12-21 in Lesson 11 where Paul continues his application of the gospel to the Christian life. He urges them to put on the Christ-like virtues of the new man (Col 3:12-14), to live in peace with one another, to be thankful, and to do all in the name of Christ (Col 3:15-17). Since the gospel must be lived out within the home, Paul also includes instructions regarding the relationship of husbands and wives (Col 3:18-19) and that of parents and their children (Col 3:20-21).

Lesson 12 covers Colossians 3:22-4:18. Here you will examine Paul's instructions regarding the relationship of slaves and masters (Col 3:22-4:1), his concluding exhortations concerning prayer (Col 4:2-4), and the relationship of Christians to those outside the faith (Col 4:5-6). You will also do an overview of the closing section of the letter, Colossians 4:7-18. This includes Paul's final instructions, personal greetings from his co-workers, and a closing benediction (Col 4:7-18).

Unit Outline

Lesson 10: Set Your Minds on Things Above—Colossians 3:1-11

Lesson 11: Walk as "New Men"— Colossians 3:12-21

Lesson 12: Serve Christ; Closing Instructions—Colossians 3:22-4:18

Unit Objectives

When you have completed this unit, you should be able to:
- Discuss the nature of the believer's heavenly life in Colossians 3:1-4.
- Recognize how to apply the truth of the gospel to relationships within Christian households, the church, and with those outside the faith.
- Understand the circumstances surrounding Paul's letter to the Colossians as displayed in Colossians 4:7-18.

Lesson 10: Set Your Minds on Things Above—Colossians 3:1-11

In Lesson 9, you studied the first three paragraphs of Paul's application of the truth of the gospel to the claims of the false teachers, explained in Colossians 2:9-15. In Colossians 2:16-17, he explains how it is no longer necessary to keep the ceremonial laws of Judaism. Christ has fulfilled the hope of Judaism which the law foreshadowed. In Colossians 2:18-19, Paul explains how true spiritual growth comes through Christ and the life of his body— the church, and not through the private mystical experiences of so-called heavenly visions. Finally, in Colossians 2:20-23, Paul exposes the folly of those who seek heavenly visions through ceremonial practices and "unsparing treatment of the body." These things have nothing to do with heaven. They are of the world, and they enslave all who belong to it. Dying with Christ liberated Christians from this kind of bondage by removing them from this world. The fourth and final paragraph of Paul's response to the claims of the false teachers appears in Colossians 3:1-4. This passage together with Colossians 3:5-11 is the subject of the present lesson.

Topic 1 covers Colossians 3:1-4. Here Paul explains true heavenly-mindedness in contrast to the misguided claims of the false teachers. Because Christians have been raised with Christ, they already belong to the realm above. They should therefore set their minds on the things above by seeking to live for Christ as they wait for the day of his return when they will be transformed to be like him.

Putting off the ways of the old man is Topic 2 which covers Colossians 3:5-11. This paragraph marks the start of Paul's more general application of the gospel to the Christian life. He begins this instruction by urging the Colossians to put to death all the sinful ways that characterized their former lives as pagans. God has made them "new men" in Christ, and so they must walk accordingly. They must be what they are.

Lesson Outline

Topic 1: The True Heavenly-Mindedness—Colossians 3:1-4

Topic 2: Put Off the Ways of the Old Man—Colossians 3:5-11

Lesson Objectives

When you have completed this lesson, you should be able to:
- Recognize the relationship between the realm above and being raised with Christ.
- Contrast what Paul meant by "Keep thinking about things above" with what the Jewish mystics meant by this slogan; define "things on the earth" in Colossians 3:2.
- Discuss the meaning of the statements, "your life is hidden with Christ" and Christ "is your life."
- Explain what it means that believers will be revealed with Christ in glory.
- Explain what it means to "put to death whatever in your nature belongs to the earth" (Col 3:5).
- Recognize the importance of putting away the sins of the old life.
- Explain how believers have stripped off the old man and put on the new; and discuss the nature of the renewal of the new man.

Assignments

For Colossians 3:1-4, follow the three-step procedure outlined below.

Step 1:

    (a) Read this passage in Colossians.

    (b) Make a structural diagram of the passage on the worksheet provided.

    (c) Summarize the results in an outline and theme statement.

    (d) Compare your conclusions with those in the answer section.

Step 2:

    (a) Examine the details of the paragraph.

    (b) Record your observations, interpretations, and applications on the worksheet.

Step 3:

    (a) Read the commentary on this passage of Colossians.

    (b) Answer the questions following the commentary.

    (c) Pay special attention to the *Important Facts to Remember*.

Because Colossians 3:5-11 is an unusually lengthy paragraph, make two copies of the worksheet. Do the structural diagram of step 1 on one and the detailed analysis of step 2 on the other.

Topic 1: The True Heavenly-Mindedness—Colossians 3:1-4

Paul's theme in this paragraph is the true heavenly-mindedness. For the false teachers, heavenly-mindedness meant seeking visions of heaven through "unsparing treatment of the body." However, for Christians it begins with the understanding that they already belong to the realm above, because they have been raised with Christ. Therefore, they should seek to walk in accordance with this new reality by seeking to live for him as they await the full possession of their resurrection life when he is revealed from heaven at his coming.

Begin your study by reading Colossians 3:1-4. Then read the Worksheet on Colossians 3:1-4. Copy it in your Life Notebook and complete step 1: a structural diagram, outline, and theme statement. You can check your results by comparing them with the Answer Section for Colossians 3:1-4. Next, complete step 2 by recording on the worksheet your detailed observations, interpretations, and applications. For step 3, carefully read the Commentary on Colossians 3:1-4. Then answer the questions, taking special note of the *Important Facts to Remember*.

> **Worksheet for Colossians 3:1-4**
>
> ¹THEREFORE,
>
> if you have been raised with Christ,
>
> keep seeking the things above,
>
> > where Christ is, seated at the right hand of God.
>
> ²Keep thinking about things above, not things on the earth,
>
> ³FOR
>
> you have died
>
> AND
>
> your life is hidden with Christ in God.
>
> > ⁴When Christ (who is your life) appears,
>
> then you too will be revealed in glory with him.

Commentary on Colossians 3:1-4

1. The Gospel Applied to the False Teaching—Colossians 2:16-3:4 (Continued)

d. The True Heavenly Mindedness—Colossians 3:1-4

In the extended section of Colossians 2:16-3:4, Paul applies the truths of salvation explained in Colossians 2:9-15 to the false teaching. In our study of Colossians 2:16-23, we saw the negative side of this application. Now in Colossians 3:1-4 we see the positive side. Because the Colossians were raised with Christ they now belong to the realm above. Therefore, they should set their minds on the things above, as they await the day of Christ's appearance from heaven when they will be revealed with him in glory.

Verse 1

Therefore. This word makes a logical connection with Colossians 2:20. There Paul argues that since believers died with Christ, they no longer belong to the world, and therefore they should not continue to live as though they did. But by saying they no longer belong to (literally "live in") the world, Paul has in mind that they belong to another realm—namely heaven, the realm which is above. This is the result of their resurrection with Christ. "Therefore," writes Paul, since you no longer belong to the world but to the realm above, live in accordance with this new reality: keep seeking the things above.

if you have been raised with Christ. The Colossians were raised with Christ in conversion, and this spiritual event was symbolized in water baptism (Col 2:12). To have been raised with Christ means to have suffered the judgment of death for sin in the person of Christ our representative, to receive God's verdict of justification, and thereby to enter eternal life. This saving event involves a transfer. Those who have been raised with Christ are transferred out of the old fallen existence in Adam in this sin-determined world and into the life of the new creation. And although believers still live physically on the earth, the new life they possess by virtue of their resurrection with Christ is a heavenly kind of life. They no longer belong to this world (Col 2:20), but to the realm above. They are citizens of heaven living on earth.

keep seeking the things above. Because the Colossians now belong to the realm above (namely heaven) they must keep seeking the things above. The words "keep seeking the things above" were actually a slogan of the false teachers. These exact words are found in the writings of other ancient Jewish mystics. On the lips of the Colossian mystics it was an exhortation to seek heavenly visions through severe treatment of the body and self-imposed ceremonial practices (Col 2:23). But Paul turns the slogan around on them. In actual fact, they are seeking **earthly** things. Their practices are concerned with the things of the earth—food and drink, special days, rules about handling or touching certain objects. These are "the elemental spirits of the world." Instead, Paul urges the Colossians to engage in **true** heavenly mindedness. The true heavenly mindedness begins with the understanding that Christians—unlike these Jewish mystics—already possess heavenly life and belong to the realm above. (Notice once again Paul's apologetic strategy of showing the superiority of the gospel.) Therefore, says Paul, live in accordance with what you already are in Christ. Essentially this means seeking to live for Christ. As we will see later, this involves following the exhortations of Colossians 3:5-17.

where Christ is, seated at the right hand of God. This description of the realm above belongs to Paul's explanation of why they should keep seeking the things above. It is because the one with whom they were raised is there. He is their Redeemer, the author of their new life. The fact that he is seated at God's right hand recalls the description of the enthronement of the Messiah in Psalm 110:1. This reminds them of his victory over the powers and authorities (Col 1:13; 2:15) and that he is Lord over all. Most important, it reminds them that he is **their** Lord and King. Thus, seeking the things above is an activity that is centered on Christ. It means seeking to live for him and in accordance with the new life that he brings.

Verse 2

Keep thinking about things above, not things on the earth. Here Paul repeats the exhortation of Colossians 3:1, except he changes the wording and then strengthens it by adding the contrast between things above and earthly things. This contrast does not mean that what is physical is evil (earthly things) and what is spiritual is good (things above). Instead the contrast is between their old life of sin in the fallen creation, and the redeemed life of the new creation to which they now belong. Paul is not telling them to turn away from the legitimate use and enjoyment of God's creation here on earth. Nor is he telling them to cease being concerned with the ordinary responsibilities of life. Earthly things describe the sinful ways of the old man (Col 3:5-8) and the kind of ceremonial rules that

Paul describes in Colossians 2:20 as bondage under "the elemental spirits of the world." Setting the mind on things above means turning away from that old way of life and living for him who is seated at God's right hand.

Verse 3

For. This word introduces an additional explanation of why the Colossians should set their minds on things above and not earthly things. This explanation has three parts. (1) You died with Christ, (Col 3:3a). (2) Your new life is hidden with Christ in God, (Col 3:3b). (3) You will be revealed with Christ at his coming, (Col 3:4)

you have died. Paul begins this explanation by repeating for the sake of emphasis what he said wrote earlier in Colossians 2:20: The Colossians died with Christ. This means they no longer belong to the "world." Death removed them from it. And thus, as those who no longer belong to the world, they must no longer set their minds on earthly things.

And. In this context, the word "and" indicates *result*. Dying with Christ results in resurrection with him to new life. The two are inseparable.

Your life is hidden with Christ in God. Because they died with Christ, they also rose with him to a new and heavenly kind of life. But what does it mean that this new life is **hidden** with Christ in God? Paul's point is not that this life is hidden because it belongs to the inner, unseen person of the heart as opposed to the outward, visible person of the body (2 Cor 4:16-18). Rather it is hidden because it is located with Christ who is enthroned in heaven at God's right hand (Col 3:1). Since Christ is hidden, our life is hidden.

This statement must be seen in connection with what Paul said earlier in Colossians 1:5 regarding "the hope laid up for you in heaven." The fullness of our salvation, which includes the redemption of our bodies, remains in the future. Yet it is certain and secure because it is presently laid up in heaven. In this sense, it is ours already. But the full experience and possession of it is not. We will receive it when Christ returns in glory. What is now hidden will then be revealed. A proper understanding of this truth leads to godly Christian conduct (Col 1:4), to setting one's mind on things above. This is Paul's essential point here in Colossians 3:3-4. He has taken up this topic again in order to show how it relates to our new resurrection life.

To illustrate this truth, consider the image of a safe-deposit box that is kept in a bank vault. A person with valuable possessions such as jewelry can deposit them in this box for safe-keeping. There are four elements in this image. The first is the **bank** itself with its vault. The second is the **deposit** that is kept in the vault in the safe-deposit box. The third is the **depositor** who entrusts what is his to the bank. And finally, there is the **banker**. He is the trustee or guardian of the deposit—responsible for safeguarding it and restoring it to the depositor at the proper time.

In this illustration, Christians are the depositors and our resurrection life is the deposit. The bank is the bank of heaven, and Christ, together with God the Father, represents the banker who safeguards our deposit. Our resurrection life was placed on deposit for us at the time of conversion, and we will receive it from Christ in full when he comes from heaven.

This explanation, however, leaves out one important element. Our experience of this new life does not remain **completely** in the future. We have already begun to experience it now in the present—at least in a partial way. As we have seen, God's act of making us alive with Christ (Col 2:13) means first of all that he has forgiven our sins and reconciled us to himself. He has circumcised our hearts and transferred us to the new creation. This is a present experience of the eternal life which is salvation. Yet the fullness of this new life, which involves the redemption of our bodies, awaits the future. It is laid up for us in heaven—hidden with Christ. We experience it now only in preliminary and partial form. This present experience is but a foretaste and pledge of what we will experience when

Christ returns. Believers must, therefore, recognize the true nature of their present lives in Christ and set their minds on things above, not on earthly things, as they await that day. "For in hope we were saved. Now hope that is seen is not hope, because who hopes for what he sees? But if we hope for what we do not see, we eagerly wait for it with endurance." (Rom 8:24-25).

Verse 4

When Christ (who is your life) appears. This hidden condition is only temporary. It will come to an end when Christ is revealed from heaven at his second coming. This is the only direct reference to Christ's return in all of Colossians.

In Colossians 3:3, Paul explains that the fullness of our resurrection life remains in heaven, hidden with Christ in God. We illustrated this concept using the image of a bank in which Christ is the banker—the guardian and trustee of our resurrection life. Now in Colossians 3:4, Paul identifies this hidden life with Christ himself. He is "your life." This tells us in what sense Christ is the guardian and trustee of our life and in what sense it lies prepared for us in heaven.

It means we are not to think of what is laid up in heaven in terms of a great quantity of a substance called resurrection life—with a specific portion reserved for each believer. Nor are we to think of a great storage room filled with "imperishable" garments—resurrection bodies—that we will put on at Christ's return (1 Cor 15:53). Instead, we are to think of Christ—the resurrected and exalted Christ. In other words, Christ is not only the banker, he is also *the deposit*. Paul's meaning is this: As our Redeemer, the risen Christ possesses this life in its fullness, and at his return he will impart it to those who belong to him by transforming them to be like him. Or to state it more simply, *Christ is the possessor and giver of life*. We see the same basic truth expressed in the following well-known passages. (NASB)

- I am the resurrection and the life. The one who believes in Me will live even if he dies. John 11:25.

- I am the way, the truth, and the life. No one comes to the Father except through Me. John 14:6.

- Because I live, you will live also. John 14:19.

- He who has the Son has the life. 1 John 5:12.

The essential point in each of these passages is that Christ is the center of God's saving activity. Salvation is in Christ. Life—resurrection life—comes to us because of him.

Here in Colossians 3:4, Paul's focus is on the resurrection life which Christ has secured for believers. While they now experience a foretaste of this life, the fullness of it remains a future hope. Paul's point is to assure the Colossians of the certainty of this hope. Indeed, it is already theirs in the sense that it is laid up for them, as it were, in the bank of heaven, with Christ as its guardian and trustee. But this deposit is none other than Christ himself. He is our life. As the firstborn from the dead, he possesses this life in its fullness, and the day is coming when he will grant us this life in all its fullness by transforming us to be like him. This event will take place when Christ is revealed from heaven.

then you too will be revealed in glory with him. On that day when Christ is revealed from heaven in his glory, so also will the true but previously hidden nature of our lives be revealed with him. Prior to his return, Christians experience resurrection life in a partial and preliminary form. They do not yet possess the resurrection body itself. To be revealed

> in glory with him means we will be made like Christ in his glorious bodily existence. That which is now ours in hope because we belong to Christ, will then become ours in actual experience. He "will transform these humble bodies of ours into the likeness of his glorious body" (Phil 3:21). On that day, our redemption will be complete (Rom 8:23). We will inherit the fullness of salvation. This is the hope of glory (Col 1:5, 27). This hope is a final reason Christians should not set our minds on earthly things but on the things above.

QUESTION 1

Believers belong to the realm above because they were raised with Christ. *True or False?*

QUESTION 2

Which of the following statements was used as a slogan by the false teachers?
- A. Put to death your earthly members.
- B. Set not your minds on earthly things.
- C. Seek the things above.
- D. Let your life be hidden with God.
- E. He who ascends to God will be revealed with him in glory.

QUESTION 3

Explain briefly how and why Paul turns the slogan in Question 2 into an exhortation to believers.

QUESTION 4

Paul exhorts believers in Colossians 3:2 not to set their minds on earthly things because what is physical (earthly things) is evil and what is spiritual (things above) is good. *True or False?*

QUESTION 5

In the statement of Colossians 3:3, "For you died and your life is hidden with Christ in God," the word *and* indicates _____.

Lesson 10: Set Your Minds on Things Above--Colossians 3:1-11

QUESTION 6

Which of the following statements best explains the meaning of the statement, "Your life is hidden with Christ in God?"

- A. As those who have died are now hidden in the earth, so those who have died with Christ are now hidden in him.
- B. Our true life is hidden because it belongs to the inner unseen person of the heart.
- C. Each believer has a double which is his true spiritual self who lives in heaven with Christ.
- D. The fullness of our resurrection life lies prepared for us in heaven with Christ.
- E. The world knows neither Christ nor Christians, and Christians do not even clearly know one another.

QUESTION 7

The commentary on Colossians 3:3 uses the image of a bank to illustrate what it means that the believer's life is "hidden with Christ." In this illustration, Christ represents the banker, and our resurrection life represents the _____.

QUESTION 8

Explain what Paul means in Colossians 3:4 when he says that Christ "is your life."

QUESTION 9

Consider the fact that your life is hidden with Christ, that he is in fact your life, and that you will one day be revealed with him in glory. What are some ways that this understanding can make a difference in the way you look at yourself and others? How can this understanding make you more heavenly minded? Record your answers in your Life Notebook.

QUESTION 10

What truths do you find in Colossians 3:1-4 that should be included in your course, *What Every Christian Should Know About Salvation*?

Important Facts to Remember About 3:1-4

1. When God raises believers to new life with Christ, he transfers them out of the old fallen existence of this sin-determined world and into the new existence of the heavenly realm. Thus, while they still live physically on the earth, they no longer belong to this world but to the realm above.

2. On the lips of the false teachers, the slogan, "Seek the things above" was an exhortation to seek heavenly visions through severe treatment of the body and self-imposed ceremonial practices.

3. As a part of his apologetic strategy of showing the superiority of the gospel, Paul used this slogan to urge the Colossians to *true* heavenly-mindedness.

4. The command to set your minds on things above and not on earthly things in Colossians 3:2 does not mean that what is physical is evil. The phrase "whatever in your nature belongs to the earth" in this context refers to the practices of man in the fallen creation (Colossians 3:5-8) and bondage under "elemental spirits of the world" (Colossians 2:20-23).

5. The statement "your life is hidden with Christ in God" in Colossians 3:3 means that the full experience of salvation, which includes the redemption of the body, remains in the future. However, it is certain and secure because it is "laid up for you in heaven" (Col 1:5). To illustrate, our resurrection life (although we experience a foretaste of it now) is like a valuable possession that has been placed in a bank for safe-keeping with Christ himself as the guardian.

6. The statement that Christ "is your life" means (to continue our illustration) that not only is Christ the guardian of our resurrection life, he is also the deposit itself. As our Redeemer, the risen Christ possesses this life in its fullness, and at his return, he will impart it to those who are his by transforming them to be like him.

7. To be revealed with Christ in glory means that the fullness of our resurrection life which was previously hidden with him—laid up, in the bank of heaven—will be revealed when Christ himself is revealed from heaven at his coming. This *revelation* of believers in glory will consist of Christ transforming their mortal bodies into the likeness of his glorious body.

Topic 2: Put off the Ways of the Old Man— Colossians 3:5-11

In Colossians 3:1-4, Paul urged the Colossians to set their minds on things above and not on earthly things because they have died and risen with Christ. But how exactly does one do this? Paul begins his answer to this question in Colossians 3:5-11 by addressing the negative side of it. They must put to death and put off all that remains of their former lives as pagans. This is appropriate because in conversion they put off the "old man," and God remade each of them into a "new man" in Christ. Thus they must live in accordance with what God has made them.

Begin your study by reading Colossians 3:5-11. Then read the Worksheet for Colossians 3:5-11. Copy it in your Life Notebook and complete step 1: a structural diagram, outline and theme statement. You can check your results by comparing them with the Answer Section for 3:5-11. Next, read the Worksheet for Colossians 3:5-11 (refer to this Article placed earlier in the lesson) again. Copy it in your Life Notebook and use it to complete step 2 with your detailed observations, interpretations, and applications. For step 3, carefully read the Commentary on Colossians 3:5-11. Then answer the questions, taking special note of the *Important Facts to Remember*.

Worksheet for Colossians 3:5-11

⁵SO,

put to death whatever in your nature belongs to the earth:

    sexual immorality,

    impurity,

    shameful passion,

    evil desire,

    and greed,

        which is idolatry.

⁶Because of these things the wrath of God is coming on the sons of disobedience.

⁷You also lived your lives in this way at one time,

    when you used to live among them.

⁸BUT

now, put off all such things as

    anger,

    rage,

    malice,

    slander,

    abusive language from your mouth.

⁹Do not lie to one another,

SINCE

you have put off the old man with its practices,

¹⁰AND

have been clothed with the new man,

    that is being renewed in knowledge

        according to the image of the one who created it.

¹¹Here there is neither Greek nor Jew,

    circumcised or uncircumcised

    barbarian, Scythian, slave or free,

BUT

Christ is all and in all.

Commentary on Colossians 3:5-11

2. The Gospel Applied to the Christian Life—Colossians 3:5–4:6

In this extended section from Colossians 3:5–4:6 Paul continues making application to the important doctrinal exposition of Colossians 2:9-15. In the previous section, Colossians 2:16–3:4, he directed his applications to the claims of the false teachers. Now in Colossians 3:5–4:6 they are directed to the Christian life in general. The central point is that Christians must conduct their lives in accordance with what God has made them as his redeemed people. Paul's purpose in writing to the Colossians, as we saw in Colossians

1:9-10, is that they might understand God's saving will so that they might walk in accordance with it.

a. Put off the ways of the Old Man—Colossians 3:5-11

In Colossians 3:5-17, Paul unpacks the meaning of his exhortation in Colossians 3:2, "Keep thinking about things above, not things on the earth." In Colossians 3:5-11 he develops the negative side with the command to put to death and to put off the sins of the past. Colossians 3:10-11 are actually transitional to Colossians 3:12-17 where he develops the positive side.

Verse 5

So. With this word, Paul introduces a conclusion drawn from the preceding paragraph. Since the Colossians died with Christ and no longer belong to the earth, they should put to death all that remains of that old earthly sinful way of life.

put to death whatever in your nature belongs to the earth. The words "in your nature" refer to the physical parts of the human body, such as eyes, mouth, hands, feet (see 1 Cor 12:15-17). This exhortation therefore sounds like a call for the kind of severe treatment of the body that the false teachers practiced, and which Paul condemns in Colossians 2:23 as actions that simply gratify the flesh. But the sins listed in the second part of Colossians 3:5 make it clear that what Paul has in mind is quite different from what these people practiced. They sought spiritual experiences of heaven by their severe bodily disciplines. Their slogan was, "Seek the things above by putting to death your earthly members." In Colossians 3:1-4 Paul explained the true heavenly mindedness. Now in Colossians 3:5, he explains the true method of putting to death one's earthly members. This, says Paul, is the true path to spiritual progress.

Paul's actual meaning is that Christians should put an end to the **sinful use** of their bodily members. The underlying idea is that our bodily members are the instruments by which we act—for good or for evil. We must therefore place our members in the service of God and not of sinful desires.

The command in Colossians 3:5 reveals the tension that exists in the life of all Christians. We have died and risen with Christ, yet we continue to exist in the same unredeemed bodies whose members were the instruments of sin in our pre-Christian days. Paul's exhortation, moreover, assumes that the old sinful desires represented by the sins of Colossians 3:5b remain alive and active within believers, and that the possibility remains for them to carry out these desires. The Christian's bodily members are therefore the place of contention between the claims of the old existence and the new. Thus, Paul is urging these new Christians never again to allow their earthly members to be the instruments of those old fallen ways. Instead, they must place their earthly members in the service of their heavenly Lord.

We see a fuller explanation of this concept in Romans 6. Because dying with Christ has freed Christians from sin's dominion over their bodies (Rom 6:6), they must never again allow sin to reign in their mortal bodies so that they obey its desires. Instead Paul exhorts them: "Present yourselves to God as those alive from the dead and your members as instruments of righteousness to God" (Rom 6:13b, (NASB).

Sexual immorality. This list of sins in Colossians 3:5b focuses on sexual sins and covetousness. "Sexual immorality" refers to every kind of improper sexual conduct (see for example Lev 18:6-23). The fact that sexual immorality appears at the top of this list and other such lists (1 Cor 10:5-11; 6:11; Gal 5:19-21; Eph 5:3) reflects the seriousness with which it was viewed. Sexual sin, Paul writes, is especially harmful because the immoral person uniquely sins against his or her own body. For this reason, Paul warns in 1 Corinthians 6:18, "Flee sexual immorality."

Impurity, shameful passion. The term "impurity" frequently appears with "sexual immorality" (Gal 5:19; 2 Cor 12:21; Eph 5:3) in the sense of sexually immoral conduct. Thus, it is not used here to refer to an additional kind of conduct but to underscore the warning against immorality. The same is true with the words "shameful passion" in this text. The Greek word actually means passion. But in this context the reference is to passion of a sexual nature, and so "shameful passion" is the proper translation here.

Evil desire. The fourth sin probably has a wider reference than improper sexual desire in the light of the following sin "greed." This admonition calls to mind the tenth command, "You shall not covet" (Deut 5:21; NASB). This sin is fundamental in nature, since it concerns not concrete actions but the thoughts and feelings from which these actions arise (see Rom 7:7-8). The death of such activities of the mind comes by fixing the mind on the things above.

and greed which is idolatry. The final sin, "greed," is set off from the other four by the explanation, "which is idolatry." The Greek word translated "greed" means a desire to have more. It can also be translated "covetousness." Thus, since greed and covetousness are basically the same thing, and since "evil desire" (the fourth sin) includes coveting, the sin of greed as a special form of "evil desire." Greed is that special form of evil desire that is nothing less than idolatry. Idolatry is not just the worship of false gods in the form of idols. It is giving to anything the devotion and service that rightly belong to God. The greedy person makes a portion of God's creation into an object of worship. Such a person therefore violates the second commandment as well as the first (Deut 5:7-8; compare Mt 6:24).

Verse 6

Because of these things, the wrath of God is coming on the sons of disobedience. This statement emphasizes the seriousness of these sins. Such sins deserve the wrath of God. Indeed, in the future he will pour out his wrath in judgment on those who live this way. Paul's aim here is not to warn the Colossians that if they persist in these sins they will lose their salvation. Rather he does it to remind them of what would have happened to them if they had not embraced the message of the gospel. He also does it to emphasize the importance and necessity of putting to death what remains of their old way of life.

Verse 7

You also lived your lives in this way at one time, when you used to live among them. Here Paul reminds the Colossians that their lives were once given over to these sins. They deserved the wrath of God. But he says this to emphasize that a great change has taken place. They are no longer living that kind of life. God is doing a work of transformation in them—a work in which he has assigned them an active role. He has rescued them and transferred them to the new order. Their task is now to put to death and to put off all that remains of that old sinful way of life.

Verse 8

But. This word indicates a contrast between that old, former way of life, and their present life with its obligation to put off those old practices.

Now put off all such things. Paul now introduces a second list of five sins that also characterized the Colossians' lives before conversion. With the first list, he used the image of "put to death" (Col 3:5). Now he uses the image of removing clothing. They are to put off those old sins as they would put off old and filthy articles of clothing. But putting to death and putting off are not two separate actions. They are simply two different images that describe the same action.

As anger, rage, malice. This list of sins deals with attitudes and actions that often destroy human relationships—particularly anger and the speech that accompanies it. Anger is first on the list probably because of the great harm that it causes. While there is such a thing as righteous anger, the Bible has almost nothing positive to say about human anger (Prov 22:24; Mt 5:22; Jas 1:19-20). Rage is a form of anger. It is the emotional outburst of anger. Malice is the deliberate and wicked intention to do harm. It is usually the result of anger.

Slander, abusive language from your mouth. Malice often accomplishes this harm through slander. Slander is evil speech against someone. It consists of giving misleading or false reports about someone with the intention of causing harm to their reputation. Malice is also expressed through abusive speech. This is speech that is used as a club to inflict pain and injury on someone. The Greek word refers to language that is foul and obscene. Abusive speech is often foul.

Verse 9

Do not lie to one another. A third sin of speech is lying. The addition of the phrase "to one another" emphasizes the social nature of this sin. The church is to be a community of mutual trust, support, and love. Lying destroys such trust. It poisons relationships.

since. This word introduces an explanation of why they should put off these sins.

you have put off the old man with its practices. They should do these things because of the transformation that took place in their lives at conversion. Paul's use of the language of Genesis 1:27 in the next verse (see below: Col 3:10c) shows that "the old man" and "the new man" must be understood with reference to Adam, the first man. (The Hebrew word *Adam* means "man.") Thus, in the expression "the old man," the word "man" refers to Adam; the word "old" refers to the old fallen creation. The old man is therefore the unconverted person as a member of Adam's fallen race—belonging to the old fallen creation, having a heart hardened towards God and living a life of sin. At the time of conversion, the old man dies. He is crucified with Christ (Rom 6:6; Gal 2:20). As Christ's death was the removal of the fleshly body (Col 2:11), so the convert's death with Christ means the putting off of his old existence in Adam together with the sinful practices that characterized that old life. Thus, because God brought that old life to an end, believers must be diligent to walk in accordance with what he has made them.

Verse 10

And. This word introduces a second part of this explanation of why the Colossians should put off those sins of the old life.

have been clothed with the new man. They not only put off the old man when they died with Christ, they also put on the new man when they rose with him. In the expression "the new man," the word "new" refers to the new creation; the word "man" refers to Christ as the Adam of this new creation. The new man is therefore the converted person as a member of the redeemed race of Christ and belonging to the new creation. God has forgiven his sins, circumcised his heart and granted him eternal life. At the time of conversion, the convert, as the old man, died and was raised to new life as the new man. He has died and risen with Christ.

As the image of putting off a garment reflects the idea of death as the putting off of the earthly body, so the image of putting on a new garment reflects the idea of the new immortal body that is put on in resurrection (1 Cor 15:54). Thus, as Christ in his resurrection put on a new body and entered the life of the new creation, so the believer when he was raised with Christ put on the new existence in Christ. He put on the new man. And because believers put on the new man in this way, Paul exhorts them in Colossians 3:12-14 to walk accordingly by putting on the virtues of the new man.

Our interpretation that the old man is dead and the believer is now a new man must face an important objection. If the old man is truly dead, and the new man was raised in his place, how can Paul write in Ephesians 4:22-24 that believers must lay aside the old man and put on the new? How can they lay aside what is already crucified and buried with Christ? How can they put on what has already been put on in their resurrection with Christ? This exhortation seems to imply that the old man is not yet dead, and the new man is not yet raised. This, however, is not the case. Paul is simply saying that believers must not go on living as though they were still "old men." The old man died, and in an act of new creation God re-made each believer into a new man by raising him to new life with Christ. Therefore, they must become in actual practice what God has already made them. This requires laying aside all that remains of that old manner of life and putting on Christ-like virtues. This is what Paul meant in that context by laying aside the old man and to putting on the new.

We can illustrate this point by imagining a conversation between two men waiting in line at a health clinic to receive an injection. One says he has always been fearful of needles and wants to leave. His friend replies, "Don't be a child." The friend is saying in effect, "You are no longer a child, so do not act like one. Lay aside the child. You are a man, so be what you are." In the same way, Paul is saying to the believer, "You are no longer an old man, so do not act like one. Lay aside the old man. You are a new man in Christ, so be what you are."

that is being renewed. The new man is new because he belongs to the new creation. But the fact that he is being renewed shows that the work of redemption (new creation) is not yet complete. Each Christian is undergoing a process of moral and spiritual renewal that will only be complete at Christ's return (Col 3:4). The passive verb "being renewed" indicates that this process is the work of God. However, it includes the active efforts of the believer to lay hold of the truth of his death and resurrection with Christ and to respond in faith by actively putting off the sins of the past and putting on Christ-like virtues (see Col 3:12-14).

in knowledge according to. These words also express the goal of this process of renewal. In the Fall, men lost the true knowledge of God. Their minds descended into ignorance and moral darkness (Eph 4:18). Conversion means a return to the knowledge of God. But this return is not complete with conversion. The entire Christian life involves a continual growth in the knowledge of God, his will, and how to walk in accordance with it. In Romans 12:2, Paul describes this process as "the renewing of your mind."

the image of the one who created it. This statement identifies the pattern and goal of this process of renewal. The words are taken from Genesis 1:27. This text tells the story of how Adam and Eve were created as the image of God. Because of Adam's disobedience, the image of God in man was tarnished and distorted. Paul draws on this story because he wishes to communicate that redemption is a new act of creation in which God is progressively renewing believers to the image he intended men to possess from the beginning. What was lost in the beginning, is being restored in the present.

But there is more to this explanation. Christ, in his resurrection, is the image of God in his fully renewed and perfected form (Col 1:15). As the new Adam, he is the pattern for God's work of re-creating men in his image. Therefore, this process of renewal is the process of being made like Christ. It is the process of being conformed to the image of God's Son (Rom 8:29; 2 Cor 3:18).

Verse 11

Here there is neither Greek nor Jew, circumcised or uncircumcised, barbarian, Scythian, slave or free. This re-creation and renewal of the believer as the new man has an important bearing on the **unity** of the church. Because believers have been raised with Christ and transferred to the new creation and the new human race, the old distinctions that separate people into different social, religious, or cultural groups no longer count for anything. The Jews divided the human race into Jew and Greek (or Gentile). The terms "circumcised" and "uncircumcised" describe this same distinction. The Greeks divided society into Greeks and non-Greeks, whom they called barbarians. Scythian was a term of contempt that referred to the most uncivilized of all the barbarians. The society of Paul's day was also divided between slave and free, with slaves making up one third of the population.

But in the society of the new creation, the new human race, there is only one kind of person: the new man. In the days of Adam before the Fall, there were no divisions in the human race. In the new creation, this original unity is being restored. The exhortations of Colossians 3:12-17 should be seen in this light. As members of the new humanity, Christians have the responsibility to put on those Christ-like virtues that break down the old barriers and promote harmony within the church: compassion, kindness, humility, gentleness, patience, forgiveness, love, and mutual submission to the rule of Christ.

But Christ is all and in all. Christ himself is the perfect example of the principle of unity within the church. Their common relationship to him surpasses and overrides all other distinctions. For those who have risen with him, he is all that matters in every relationship of life.

QUESTION 11

Explain briefly the meaning of Paul's exhortation in Colossians 3:5, "put to death whatever in your nature belongs to the earth."

QUESTION 12

The statement in Colossians 3:6, "Because of these things the wrath of God is coming on the sons of disobedience" warns the Colossians that if they persist in the sins of their old life, they will lose their salvation. *True or False?*

QUESTION 13

Putting to death and putting off are not two different kinds of actions required for two different kinds of sin, but simply two different images that describe the same action. *True or False?*

QUESTION 14

Giving false or misleading reports about someone with the intention of causing harm to that person's reputation is called _____.

QUESTION 15

The Greek word translated "_____" means a desire to have more.

QUESTION 16

Which of the following best defines the "old man"?

A. Adam

B. The fallen Adamic nature within each of us

C. A believer

D. The unconverted person as a member of Adam's fallen race

QUESTION 17

Explain briefly how believers have put off the old man and put on the new.

QUESTION 18

When will the process of renewal described in Colossians 3:10 be complete?

A. When the believer dies and goes to heaven.

B. When the believer reaches spiritual maturity.

C. When the believer is filled with the Holy Spirit.

D. When the believer makes Christ Lord of every area of his life.

E. When the believer is transformed to be like Christ at his return.

QUESTION 19

The statement in Colossians 3:11 that in the case of the new man "there is neither Greek or Jew, etc." means that in the church, the society of the new creation, the original _____ of the human race is being restored.

QUESTION 20

Consider the concept seen in Colossians 3:5 and in Romans 6 regarding our bodily members as the instruments by which we act for good or for evil. Dying with Christ freed us from sin's dominion over our bodies. Therefore, we must no longer allow our members to be used in the service of sinful desires. Instead we must place them in the service of God.

Think of ways you can apply this to specific situations in your personal life and ministry. Take for example, anger and rage mentioned in Colossians 3:8. What kinds of things cause you to become angry with family members? How can this concept help you not to give way to anger the next time it begins to rise? Another example could be sexual immorality mentioned in Colossians 3:5. How could you use this concept to counsel a new convert who has turned from an immoral past but still struggles with the desire to return to that old way of life? Record your answer in your Life Notebook. Be prepared to discuss your answer in the next group meeting.

QUESTION 21

Consider the distinctions listed in Colossians 3:11 that divided the society of ancient Colossae. Every society has divisions of this kind. Rewrite Colossians 3:11 and replace the divisions that Paul lists with the divisions that exist in your society. Do these old distinctions also create barriers within individual churches or between churches? How can the truths of Colossians 3:10-11 help to overcome these barriers and promote unity? Record your answer in your Life Notebook.

QUESTION 22

What truths do you find in Colossians 3:5-11 that should be included in your course *What Every Christian Should Know About Salvation*? Notice especially the answers it supplies to the questions, *What happens to a person at conversion?* and *How should Christians conduct their lives?*

Important Facts to Remember About Colossians 3:5-11

1. In Colossians 3:5-11, Paul begins to apply the truth of our redemption to the Christian life in general. Because we have died and risen with Christ, we must put an end to all that remains of our old fallen way of life.

2. The unusual exhortation, "put to death whatever in your nature belongs to the earth" (Col 3:5), means we should put an end to the *sinful use* of our body. Instead, we should put them in the service of our heavenly Lord (compare with Rom 6:13).

3. The "old man" refers to the unconverted person as a member of Adam's fallen race and belonging to the old fallen creation.

4. The "new man" refers to the believer as a member of the redeemed race of Christ, the new Adam, and belonging to the new creation.

5. The change of identity takes place in conversion by dying and rising with Christ. The person coming to Christ dies, as the old man, and is raised to new life as the new man. Paul describes this event in Colossians 3:9-10 as putting off the old man and putting on the new man.

6. Because the believer is no longer an old man but a new man, he must walk accordingly by putting off his old sinful ways and putting on Christ-like virtues. Paul describes this in Ephesians 4:22-24 as laying aside the old man and putting on the new man.

7. The work of redemption is not complete at conversion. Each Christian is undergoing a process of spiritual renewal (Col 3:10) that will only be complete at Christ's return (Col 3:4). This renewal is the work of God, but it includes our active efforts in the obedience of faith.

8. The goal of this process is to be made like Christ. As the new Adam, he is the pattern for God's work of re-creating men in his image (Rom 8:29 and 2 Cor 3:18).

9. In the redeemed race of the new creation (which is the church) the original unity of the human race is being restored. Christ is our example of the principle of unity (Col 3:11).

Lesson 10 Self Check

QUESTION 1

Believers already belong to the realm above. *True or False?*

QUESTION 2

Which of the following statements served as a slogan for the false teachers?
- A. Put to death your earthly members.
- B. Seek the things above.
- C. Set not your minds on earthly things.
- D. Let your life be hidden with God.
- E. He who ascends to God will be revealed with him in glory.

QUESTION 3

The phrase "belongs to the earth" refers to the sinful ways of the "old man" and the ceremonial practices by which the false teachers sought heavenly visions. *True or False?*

QUESTION 4

Which of the following best explains the meaning of the statement, "Your life is hidden with Christ in God?"
- A. As those who have died are now hidden in the earth, so those who have died with Christ are now hidden in him.
- B. Our true life is hidden because it belongs to the inner unseen person of the heart.
- C. Each believer has a double which is his true spiritual self who lives in heaven with Christ.
- D. The world knows neither Christ nor Christians, and Christians do not even distinctly know one another.
- E. The fullness of our resurrection life lies prepared for us in heaven with Christ.

QUESTION 5

In the commentary on Colossians 3:3-4 the image of a bank was used to illustrate what it means that the believer's "life is hidden with Christ." In this illustration, Christ represents the banker but the statement in Colossians 3: 4 that he "is your life" indicates that he is also the _____.

QUESTION 6

Paul's exhortation in Colossians 3:5 to "put to death whatever in your nature belongs to the earth" means to put to death the sinful use of our bodily members. *True or False?*

QUESTION 7

The statement in Colossians 3:6, "the wrath of God is coming on the sons of disobedience" warns the Colossians that if they persist in their old sinful ways they will lose their salvation. *True or False?*

QUESTION 8

In the expression "the old man," the word "man" carries a reference to _____.

QUESTION 9

Which of the following statements is **not** true regarding the renewal of the new man?

A. It is the work of God.
B. It is a process.
C. It begins at the time of conversion.
D. Its object is to conform us to the image of Christ.
E. It will be complete when we die and go to heaven.
F. It includes the active efforts of the believer.

QUESTION 10

The statement in Colossians 3:11 that in the case of the new man "there is neither Greek nor Jew, circumcised or uncircumcised, etc." means that in the church, the society of the new creation, the original _____ of the human race is being restored.

Lesson 10 Answers to Questions

WORKSHEET FOR COLOSSIANS 3:1-4

Answer for Colossians 3:1-4

Seek the things above:
- ¹ THEREFORE, *(conclusion = application)*
- if you have been raised with Christ, *(conditional clause: basis of command)*
- keep seeking the things above, *(command)*
- where Christ is, seated at the right hand of God. *(description of "above")*
- ² Keep thinking about things above, not things on the earth, *(command repeated)*

Explanation: why seek things above:
- ³ FOR *(explanation)*
- you have died *(1st part of the explanation)*
- AND *(result = 2nd part of explanation)*
- your life is hidden with Christ in God. *(3rd part of the explanation)*
- ⁴ When Christ (who is your life) appears, *(time of revealing)*
- then you too will be revealed in glory with him.

Textual Outline of Colossians 3:1-4
I. Conclusion: Seek the things above. (Col 3:1-2)
    A. Basis of command: You were raised with Christ. (Col 3:1a)
    B. Command: Seek the things above. (Col 3:1b-c)
    C. Command repeated: Set your mind on things above. (Col 3:2)
II. Explanation: Why seek the things above (Col 3:3-4)
    A. They died. (Col 3:3a)
    B. Their lives are hidden with Christ. (Col 3:3b)
    C. They will be revealed with Christ. (Col 3:4)

Theme Statement for Colossians 3:1-4
The Colossians should seek the things above, since their life is now hidden with Christ and they will be revealed with him in glory at his coming.

QUESTION 1: True
QUESTION 2
    C. Seek the things above.
QUESTION 3: *Your answer should be similar to the following:*
For the false teachers, the slogan "keep seeking the things above" was an exhortation to seek heavenly visions through severe treatment of the body and self-imposed ceremonial practices. But these activities, says Paul, belong to the world (Col 2:20-23). Those who do them are really seeking earthly things. Paul therefore uses the words, "keep seeking the things above" to exhort believers to the true heavenly-mindedness. This begins with the understanding that Christians—unlike the Jewish mystics—already

possess heavenly life and belong to the realm above. Thus, true heavenly-mindedness means seeking to live for Christ, the One through whom they have received this life. Paul makes use of the false teachers' slogan in this way in order to show the superiority of the gospel.

QUESTION 4: False [The contrast in this verse is not between a physical world (earthly things) that is evil and a spiritual world (things above) that is good. Instead it is the contrast between the Colossians' old life of sin in the fallen creation and the redeemed life of the new creation to which they now belong. God's creation here on earth is good, and believers should use and enjoy it in ways that God intended.]

QUESTION 5: result

QUESTION 6

   D. The fullness of our resurrection life lies prepared for us in heaven with Christ.

QUESTION 7: deposit

QUESTION 8: *Your answer should be similar to the following:*

In Colossians 3:3, Paul states that the life which Christians now possess as a result of their death with Christ "is hidden with Christ in God." And since Christ is in heaven, seated at God's right hand (Col 3:1), this means their life is hidden there too. This state of affairs is what Paul described earlier in Colossians 1:5 as "the hope laid up for you in heaven," This hope is the fullness of the resurrection life, which includes the redemption of the body and which believers will receive at Christ's return. It lies prepared for us in heaven like a treasured possession that has been placed in a bank and of which Christ is the guardian. Thus, in Colossians 3:4 when Paul identifies this deposit (our resurrection life) as Christ himself, he is telling us in what sense Christ is the guardian of our life and in what sense it lies prepared for us in heaven. That Christ "who is your life" means that as our Redeemer, he possesses this life in its fullness and at his return he will impart it to all who belong to him by transforming you to be like him.

QUESTION 9: *Your answer*

QUESTION 10: *Your answer*
WORKSHEET FOR COLOSSIANS 3:5-11

Worksheet for Colossians 3:5-11

Put to death earthly ways
⁵SO, *(conclusion = application)*
put to death whatever in your nature belongs to the earth: *(command)*
    sexual immorality,   *(examples of "earthly members")*
    impurity,
    shameful passion,
    evil desire,
    and greed
        which is idolatry. *(explanation of greed)*

Explanation of these ways
⁶Because of these things the wrath of God is coming on the
    sons of disobedience. *(explanation of sins - 1st part)*
⁷You also lived your lives in this way at one time,
    (explanation of sins - 2nd part)
    when you used to live among them. *(time of action)*

Put off these sins
⁸BUT *(contrast)*
now, put off all such things as *(command)*
    anger,   *(examples of "these things")*
    rage,
    malice,
    slander,
    abusive language from your mouth.

Explanation: Why put off these sins
⁹Do not lie to one another, *(command)*
SINCE *(explanation: why put off these sins)*
you have put off the old man with its practices, *(1st reason)*
¹⁰AND *(additional explanation)*
have been clothed with the new man, *(2nd reason)*
    that is being renewed in knowledge *(description of new man)*
        according to the image of one who created it.
        (description of renewal)
¹¹Here there is neither Greek nor Jew, *(description of new man)*
    circumcised or uncircumcised
    barbarian, Scythian, slave or free,
  BUT *(contrast)*
  Christ is all and in all.

Textual Outline of Colossians 3:5-11
I. Conclusion: Put to death earthly ways. (Col 3:5)
    A. The command to put to death (Col 3:5a)
    B. List of sins to put to death (Col 3:5b)
II. Explanation of these ways (Col 3:6-7)
    A. They incur God's wrath. (Col 3:6)
    B. Formerly the Colossians walked in these ways. (Col 3:7)
III. Put off these sins. (Col 3:8-9a)

      A. The command to put off (Col 3:8a)
      B. List of sins to put off (Col 3:8b)
      C. Special command: Do not lie. (Col 3:9a)
  IV. Explanation: Why put off these sins (Col 3:9b-11)
      A. First reason: The Colossians have put off the old man. (Col 3:9b)
      B. Second reason (Col 3:10-11)
          1. They have put on the new man. (Col 3:10a)
          2. Description of the new man (Col 3:10b-11)

Theme Statement for 3:5-11
The Colossians must rid themselves of the sinful ways of their former life, because in conversion they put off the old man and put on the new.

QUESTION 11: *Your answer should be similar to the following:*
It means to put to death the sinful use of our bodily members. Instead of using them as instruments of sin, we should put them in the service of Christ, our heavenly Lord.

QUESTION 12: False [It reminds them of what would have happened to them if they had not placed their faith in Christ. Thus, it emphasizes the seriousness of sin and the importance of putting to death what remains of their old way of life.]

QUESTION 13: True

QUESTION 14: slander

QUESTION 15: greed

QUESTION 16
    D. The unconverted person as a member of Adam's fallen race

QUESTION 17: *Your answer should be similar to the following:*
Putting off the old man and putting on the new describes the believer's death and resurrection with Christ at the time of conversion. As Christ put off his mortal body in death (Col 2:11) and put on a transformed body in resurrection, so also the believer by sharing with Christ in his death and resurrection put off the old man (the old fallen existence in Adam) and put on the new man (the new redeemed existence in Christ, the new Adam). This means the believer is no longer an old man but a new man. Paul's exhortation in Ephesians 4:22 to lay aside the old man does not mean believers are still "old men" but that they must walk in accordance with what God has made them. They must be what they are by laying aside all that remains of that old manner of life.

QUESTION 18
    E. When the believer is transformed to be like Christ at his return.

QUESTION 19: unity

QUESTION 20: *Your answer*

QUESTION 21: *Your answer*

QUESTION 22: *Your answer*

Lesson 10 Self Check Answers

QUESTION 1: True

QUESTION 2
    B. Seek the things above.

QUESTION 3: True

QUESTION 4
    E. The fullness of our resurrection life lies prepared for us in heaven with Christ.

QUESTION 5: deposit

QUESTION 6: True

QUESTION 7: False

QUESTION 8: Adam

QUESTION 9
    E. It will be complete when we die and go to heaven.

QUESTION 10: unity

Lesson 11: Walk as "New Men"— Colossians 3:12-21

In Lesson 10, you concluded your study of Paul's application of the gospel to the false teaching (Col 3:1-4) and began his application to the Christian life in general (Col 3:5-11). The subject of Colossians 3:1-4 is true heavenly-mindedness. Because Christians have died and risen with Christ, they now belong to the realm above — the new creation. They should therefore set their minds on things above and not earthly things. But how specifically does one do this? The following paragraphs of Colossians can be seen as an answer to this question. In Colossians 3:5-11, Paul takes up the negative side of the answer. Paul states it is by putting to death and putting off all the sinful ways that belonged to their former lives as pagans. They are to walk as *new men* in Christ, because this is what God has made them. This lesson examines the positive side of the answer in Colossians 3:12-21.

Topic 1 covers Colossians 3:12-14. Here Paul describes the Christ-like virtues of the new man that the Colossians are to put on; such as compassion, kindness, forgiveness, and love.

Colossians 3:15-17 and the idea of Christ being everything is the subject of Topic 2. He continues by encouraging them to live in peace, to exhort one another in the message of the gospel, and to do all in the name of Christ.

In Topic 3 marriage is the subject of Colossians 3:18-19. In this passage, Paul shifts his focus to the relationship of husbands and wives. He exhorts wives to submit to their husbands and husbands to love their wives.

Topic 4 covers Colossians 3:20-21. Here, Paul turns to a second relationship in the Christian household—that of children and parents. Children are to obey their parents, and fathers in particular must not provoke their children.

Lesson Outline

Topic 1: Put on the Ways of the "New Man" (Col 3:12-14)

Topic 2: Let Christ Be All (Col 3:15-17)

Topic 3: The Duties of Wives and Husbands (Col 3:18-19)

Topic 4: The Duties of Children and Parents (Col 3:20-21)

Lesson Objectives

When you have completed this lesson, you should be able to:
- Discuss the nature of the virtues that believers are to put on (Col 3:12).
- Explain the special importance of forgiveness and love. (Col 3:13-14).
- Explain why peace should prevail in the church (Col 3:15).
- Recognize the importance of thanksgiving in the Christian life (Col 3:16-17).
- Discuss how to "Let the word of Christ dwell in you richly" (Col 3:16).
- State what it means to do everything in the name of the Lord Jesus (Col 3:17).
- Summarize the duties of husbands and wives toward one another (Col 3:18-19).
- Summarize the duties of parents and children toward one another (Col 3:20-21).

Assignments

For each paragraph of Colossians covered in this lesson follow this three-step procedure:

Step 1:

    (a) Read this passage of Colossians.

    (b) Make a structural diagram of the passage on the worksheet provided.

    (c) Summarize the results in an outline and theme statement.

    (d) Compare your conclusions with those in the answer section.

Step 2:

    (a) Examine the details of the paragraph. Record your observations, interpretations, and applications on the worksheet.

Step 3:

    (a) Read the commentary on this passage of Colossians.

    (b) Answer the questions following the commentary.

    (c) Pay special attention to the *Important Facts to Remember*.

Topic 1: Put on the Ways of the "New Man" (Col 3:12-14)

In Colossians 3:5-11, Paul exhorted these new believers to put off the sinful ways of their pagan past, because when they became Christians, they put off the old man (the fallen existence in Adam) and put on the new man (the new existence in Christ). Since they are *new men*, they must no longer walk and dress as *old men*. They must be as God intended. Now in Colossians 3:12-14, Paul carries forward this thought by exhorting them to put on the Christ-like virtues of the new man.

Begin your study by reading Colossians 3:12-14. Then read the Worksheet for Colossians 3:12-14. Copy it in your Life Notebook and complete step 1 of the Assignments section. Check your conclusions by comparing them with the Answer Section for Colossians 3:12-14. Next, complete step 2 by recording on the same worksheet your detailed observations, interpretations, and applications. For the third and final step, carefully read the Commentary on Colossians 3:12-13. Then answer the questions, taking special note of the *Important Facts to Remember*.

Worksheet for Colossians 3:12-14

¹²THEREFORE,

  as the elect of God, holy and dearly loved,

clothe yourselves with a heart of

      mercy,

      kindness,

      humility,

      gentleness, and

      patience,

¹³bearing with each other,

  AND

forgiving one another,

if someone happens to have a complaint against anyone else.

Just as the Lord has forgiven you, so you also forgive others.

¹⁴And to all these virtues, add love,

which

is the perfect bond.

Commentary on Colossians 3:12-14

2. The Gospel Applied to the Christian Life—Colossians 3:5–4:6 (Continued)

b. Put on the Ways of the New Man—Colossians 3:12-14

As we have seen in the lengthy section that begins with Colossians 3:5 and goes through Colossians 4:6, Paul applies the truth of the gospel to the Christian life in general. His overall theme is that believers are to walk in accordance with what God has made them as his redeemed people (see Col 1:9-10). In Colossians 3:5-9a, Paul lists the kinds of sin that characterized their former lives as pagans. They must diligently put off all of those old ways, because in conversion they put off the old man (the old existence in Adam), and they put on the new man (the new existence in Christ). Now in Colossians 3:12-14, Paul begins to describe the positive way of life and the virtues of the new man which they must put on.

Verse 12

Therefore. This word introduces a conclusion drawn from the previous verse. Because the Colossians are now "new men" they must put on the qualities of the new man. In other words, they are to live out the new reality of what God has made them in Christ.

as the elect of God, holy and dearly loved. Formerly these Colossian believers were pagans. They were alienated from God, hostile in mind and subject to his wrath. Now, however, he has made them his chosen people, holy and dearly loved. This description is drawn from Deuteronomy 7:6-7. It is the language of the covenant that God used concerning his people, Israel. In this way, Paul once again reminds the Colossians that contrary to the claims of the Jewish false teachers, they now belong to God's people (see Col 1:12; 2:11). And since they are his people, they must "be what they are." A poor child who is adopted into the family of a king must now dress as a prince. Even so, those who are transferred into the covenant people of God must now dress as "new men." They must clothe themselves in godly virtues.

clothe yourselves with a heart of mercy. The word "clothe" pictures the virtues in this verse as articles of apparel. This image of putting on new garments corresponds to the earlier image of putting off the old garments of sin in Colossians 3:8. Both images are linked to the fact that in conversion the believer put off the old man and put on the new (Col 3:9-10). In this way, Paul calls on believers to be what they are. Since in conversion they put on the new man and are now God's people, they must live accordingly. They must put on the virtues of the new man. The virtues that follow are all qualities displayed by God or Christ. God's aim is to conform us to his image in Christ. Each of these virtues relates to our relationship to our fellow man, particularly those within the body of Christ.

The Greek expression here could be translated "heartfelt compassion" or "mercy." Jesus said, "Be merciful, just as your Father is merciful" (Lk 6:36). In the Old Testament, compassion is often contrasted with anger. Thus, it is appropriate that as anger was first on the list of sins to be put off in Colossians 3:8, so compassion is first on the list of virtues to be put on. Anger hardens the heart. Compassion describes a heart that is soft and merciful toward others. This biblical notion of compassion can be illustrated from the Old Testament. The Hebrew word for compassion is based on the word that means womb. Compassion is the feeling a mother and father have for their child (Ps 103:13).

Kindness, humility. The word *kindness* is used several times by Paul to describe God's gracious actions toward sinners. Salvation itself is said to be the manifestation of God's kindness and love for mankind (Tit 3:4). Since believers have experienced God's kindness in salvation, they should be kind to one another. To be kind is to be gracious and forgiving, treating others as God has treated us (Eph 4:32).

We have already encountered the word "humility" twice in this letter (Col 2:18, 23). In both cases, it referred to a practice of the false teachers: the self-abasement of fasting. In this context, however, Paul uses it to refer to the Christian virtue of humility. The word itself means literally "lowliness of mind." The opposite is to be "high of mind" (Rom 12:16), which means to be haughty in mind, conceited, proud. The meaning of humility is perhaps best illustrated from Philippians 2:3. Here Paul contrasts humility with selfish ambition and vanity. Humility is expressed by being concerned for the welfare of others (Phil 2:4) and treating them as more important than oneself. Paul then points to Christ in Colossians 3:6-9 as the supreme example of this attitude.

Gentleness, and patience. In ancient Greek, the word translated *gentleness* described a mild and friendly composure that did not give way to anger or bitterness over unpleasant people or circumstances. It was often used of a person in whom both strength and gentleness were combined. It therefore carried the notion of self-control. Thus, it was considered a quality of the ideal king (compare Mt 21:5). In the New Testament, it is seen first of all as a quality that Christ displayed in his earthly ministry (Mt 11:29; 21:5; 2 Cor 10:1). It is also a fruit of the Spirit (Gal 5:23). Gentleness is associated with a peaceful nature, forbearance, humility, and love (1 Cor 4:21; Jas 1:19-21; 3:13, 17). It was with gentleness that the erring brother should be restored (Gal 6:1), opponents in the church corrected (2 Tim 2:25; Tit 3:2), and the gospel shared with unbelievers (1 Pet 5:15).

The word "patience" means literally to be slow to anger, to be long-suffering—in contrast to being short-tempered. Patience can be expressed as steadfastness in the face of suffering. We see this for example in the case of Job (Jas 5:10). It can also be expressed as forbearance in relationships with others. In this context, Paul's emphasis is on relationships within the church. The ultimate example of patience in this regard is the patience that God demonstrated toward us (Rom 2:4; 1 Tim 1:16). This is the basis and the model for the patience we should express toward one another.

Verse 13

bearing with one another. Patience is expressed by bearing with each other. This exhortation reminds us that all of these virtues concern the Christian's relationship with others. God's design for the believer is to live in a community with others—the community of the church. The ability to be patient and forbearing with others is essential to harmony within the church. The expression "bearing with" suggests tolerance toward things that irritate us in others. This includes not only their personal shortcomings but also the cultural, social, and religious differences that Paul mentioned in Colossians 3:11.

and forgiving one another. Patience is also expressed through forgiveness. The ability to forgive lies at the heart of the Christian life. It can mean the difference between success and failure in Christian relationships. Forgiveness is the very test of the reality of our Christianity.

if someone happens to have a complaint against anyone else. This line states a condition. Paul is saying, "By commanding this, I am not referring to any specific situation. I am not accusing anyone of sin or of withholding forgiveness. Only, if such a situation should exist, then by all means, forgive the one you have a grievance against."

Just as the Lord has forgiven you, so you also forgive other. Paul now explains why believers should forgive each other. It is because of the forgiveness we have received through the cross (Col 1:22; 2:13). Since the word "Lord" is consistently used in Colossians as a designation for Christ (Col 1:3, 10; 2:6; 3:17, 24), we should recognize the same meaning here. But since elsewhere in Colossians God the Father is the one who forgives, we must understand this reference to Christ in terms of what he accomplished as the Father's agent or mediator in salvation ("in Christ God was reconciling the world to himself" 2 Cor 5:19). In the parallel statement of Ephesians 4:32, Paul instructs believers to forgive "just as God in Christ also forgave you." This divine act of forgiveness provides not only the basis for mutual forgiveness within the church but also the pattern or model. The Lord's gracious act of forgiving us serves as the model for how we should forgive one another. In this regard, we are to be imitators of God and Christ (Eph 5:1-2).

Verse 14

And to all these virtues add love. Love is the crowning virtue. It is the greatest and the sum of all the virtues (1 Cor 13:13). In Romans 13:9-10, we read that all of God's commandments are summed up in the single command to love one another. Similarly, in Galatians 5:14, Paul states that "the whole law can be summed up in a single commandment." Jesus also taught that in regard to human relationships, love is the greatest commandment, and he gave it to his disciples as "a new commandment" (Jn 13:34; 1 Jn 3:23).

which is the perfect bond. The reason to add love, Paul writes, is that it is a bond—a bond that unites the church and produces maturity. This explanation echoes two earlier statements in Colossians regarding the role of love in spiritual growth. In Colossians 2:2, Paul states that the purpose of his efforts for his readers is that their hearts might be **knit together** by love so that they may attain maturity in Christ. The other passage is Colossians 2:19 where Paul pictures the church as the body of which Christ is the head. To paint this picture, he takes up the unusual word translated "knit together" earlier in Colossians 2:2 to describe how the ligaments bond or hold together the diverse parts of the body and enable it to grow. It is evident that these ligaments represent the binding power of love expressed through each member. In returning to this theme once again in Colossians 3:14, Paul uses the word translated "ligament" in Colossians 2:19 to describe love as the **bond** that produces maturity. The repetition of this principle regarding love demonstrates its central importance. Love is the essential virtue for each believer to "put on" so that the church as a body can be bound together in harmony and enabled to grow to maturity.

QUESTION 1

By describing the Colossian Christians as "the elect of God, holy and dearly loved" (Col 3:12), Paul is reminding them once again of something he has already said. What is it? Explain briefly.

QUESTION 2

The word translated "mercy" in Colossians 3:12 is related to the Hebrew word for flower, which like the compassionate heart, is both soft and fragrant. *True or False?*

QUESTION 3

The word translated "humility" means literally _____ of mind.

QUESTION 4

According to the commentary, which of the following terms carries with it the notion of self-control?

    A. Compassion
    B. Kindness
    C. Humility
    D. Gentleness
    E. Patience

QUESTION 5

According to the commentary, the instruction, "Just as the Lord has forgiven you, so you also forgive others." (Col 3:13), means that as we forgive others the Lord will also forgive us. *True or False?*

QUESTION 6

The Bible describes _____ as the perfect bond.

QUESTION 7

What kinds of things do you find irritating in other Christians (see Col 3:13a)? Is there one particular person or group that you find especially irritating? What do you think others might find irritating about you? How can the knowledge that God has forgiven each of us and made us "the elect of God, holy and dearly loved" help you "to bear with" these fellow Christians? Record your response in your Life Notebook.

QUESTION 8

Is there someone (particularly a fellow Christian) against whom you have a grievance? How should you respond to this grievance as a Christian? If you have not done so already, ask the Lord's enabling grace to forgive this person from your heart.

Important Facts to Remember About Colossians 3:12-14

1. Because God has made us his holy people, we should walk accordingly by putting on the godly virtues of compassion, kindness, humility, gentleness, patience, forgiveness and love.

2. The Lord's act of forgiveness toward believers is the basis and model for mutual forgiveness within the church.

3. Love is the greatest and the sum of all the virtues. As believers display this virtue toward one another, the church is bound together in harmony and enabled to grow to maturity (Col 3:14).

Topic 2: Let Christ Be All (Col 3:15-17)

In the previous paragraph, Paul exhorted the Colossians to be as God intended by putting on the Christ-like virtues of the new man; compassion, kindness, humility, gentleness, patience and love. Now in Colossians 3:15-17, he gives four additional exhortations that further define how to live out the new reality of what God has made them. They are to live in peace with one another, to give thanks, to let the message of Christ dwell among them richly, and to do all in the name of the Lord Jesus.

Begin your study by reading Colossians 3:15-17. Then read the Worksheet on Colossians 3:15-17. Copy it in your Life Notebook and complete step 1 of the Assignments section. Check your conclusions by comparing them with the Answer Section for Colossians 3:15-17. Next, complete step 2 by recording on the same worksheet your detailed observations, interpretations, and applications. For the third and final step, carefully read the Commentary on Colossians 3:15-17. Then answer the questions, taking special note of the *Important Facts to Remember*.

Worksheet for Colossians 3:15-17

¹⁵Let the peace of Christ be in control in your hearts

(FOR

you were in fact called as one body to this peace),

AND

be thankful.

¹⁶Let the word of Christ dwell in you richly,

    teaching and exhorting one another with all wisdom,

    singing psalms, hymns, and spiritual songs,

        all with grace in your hearts to God.

¹⁷AND

    whatever you do in word or deed,

do it all in the name of the Lord Jesus,

    giving thanks to God the Father through him.

Commentary on Colossians 3:15-17

2. The Gospel Applied to the Christian Life—Colossians 3:5–4:6 (Continued)

c. Let Christ Be All—Colossians 3:15-17

In this paragraph, Paul continues his exhortations regarding how to walk as "new men." In Colossians 3:12-14, his exhortations centered on the Christ-like virtues of the new man. Now in Colossians 3:15-17, his focus shifts to other aspects of the life of the congregation. The four exhortations of this passage can be summed up in the words, "Let Christ be all."

Verse 15

Let the peace of Christ be in control in your heart. What is the peace that Christ gives? It is the peace with God that Christ gave us through his death on the cross (Col 1:20-22). Thus, Paul is saying let that peace that Christ established between you and God be the ruling principle in all your relationships in the church. The lives of God's people should correspond to the grace he has given them.

(for you were in fact called as one body to this peace). Paul's explanation is: because God placed us in a body, it follows that he has called us to peace. Thus, Paul illustrates the concept of peace by drawing on the image of the church as the body of Christ. As the members of a body (head, hands, feet, and so forth) are at peace with each other—there is harmony and unity of purpose and action—so the members of the church should live in harmony, unity, and peace.

And be thankful. Not only are we to live in peace with our fellow believers, but our lives are to be characterized by thanksgiving to God, that is, by praise. When believers are unified in their praise to God, there is peace and harmony. Complaining and criticizing should be replaced by a common attitude of thanksgiving. Finally, notice how often in this letter Paul mentions the giving of thanks. It appears three times in the first two chapters (in Col 1:3, 12; 2:7). He mentions it twice more in the present paragraph—verses 15 and 17. A sixth mention appears in Colossians 4:2. Clearly Paul did this to emphasize the special importance of thanksgiving in the Christian life.

Verse 16

Let the word of Christ dwell in you richly. This is yet another exhortation in this paragraph. The message of Christ is the message of the gospel. It includes the words and actions of Christ himself recorded in the gospel accounts. It also refers to other doctrinal teachings that Epaphras delivered to the Colossians at the time of their conversion. This message is to **dwell** among them. By using the word "dwell" Paul pictures the congregation as a house in which the message of Christ has a continuing presence—not as a guest but as the Master of the house. The exhortation is to allow the message to have its way with them by giving careful attention to it, by submitting to its authority and applying it in their daily lives. The word "richly" (abundantly) describes the manner of this indwelling. This message is to be abundantly active in their lives. In Colossians 1:6, Paul spoke of how the gospel first came to them and how it has been bearing fruit and growing among them since the day of their conversion. Now in Colossians 3:16, he is telling them to let the gospel continue producing this abundant harvest among them.

teaching and exhorting one another with all wisdom. This line explains how to let the message of Christ dwell among them. Recall that in Colossians 1:28 Paul said that his ministry consists of instructing and teaching all those he leads to Christ with the goal of bringing them to maturity. Now he is saying that the church as a body is to carry on this ministry of nurture toward one another. This is a key principle of spiritual growth. The message of the gospel is a means of spiritual growth. Believers have a responsibility to teach and encourage one another regarding the meaning and application of the message of salvation revealed.

singing psalms, hymns, and spiritual songs, all with grace in your hearts to God. One way to carry out the admonition of letting the message of Christ dwell among them richly is through songs. An example of such a song is Colossians 1:15-20. As we saw earlier, this passage is often called the Colossian hymn. An important observation in this verse is that good Christian songs are not only a way to praise God but a way to teach and encourage fellow worshippers. This means that such songs must express biblical truth.

Psalms, hymns, and spiritual songs refer to different types of songs that are sung in worship to God. Psalms are the hymns to God that were sung by the people of the Old Covenant. They are recorded in the book of Psalms and still have a place in Christian worship today. The word "psalm" is based on a word that means to pluck with the fingers, which is what one does when playing a stringed instrument. Originally the psalms were sung to the accompaniment of musical instruments (Ps 6:1).

Hymns and spiritual songs do not necessarily refer to two completely different types of songs. Although the first suggests a more formal song, while the second something more spontaneous. More important than the type of song is the attitude of the heart with which it is sung. The phrase "with grace in your hearts" indicates that this singing should be both sincere and robust. It also should be done with joy and gratitude to God. And we should sing these songs with a view to "teaching and exhorting one another with all wisdom."

> *Verse 17*
>
> **And whatever you do in word or deed.** In this section, Paul has been giving various instructions regarding how to live out the new reality of what God has made us in Christ. Now he gives a sweeping exhortation that both sums up these previous exhortations and introduces those that follow. Everything without exception—every thought, word, and deed—is to be done "in the name of the Lord Jesus Christ."
>
> **Do it all in the name of the Lord Jesus.** What does it mean to do something in the name of the Lord Jesus? To do something in the name of another means to act as that person's **representative**. Paul's meaning is that everything we do should be done as a Christian and to glorify Christ. We are, in a sense, his representatives. As Christians, we should make no real separation between the sacred and the secular—between work, play, or church. Each of us is a Christian twenty-four hours a day. This is our identity. Our attitude in this matter is based on both the doctrine of creation and the doctrine of redemption. Through Christ, God created all things. And he placed us within his creation to honor and serve him as his redeemed people. Therefore, all of our activities are to be done as Christians. Our eating and drinking, our conversations, the time we spend with our families, and so forth. All is to be done under the lordship of Christ.
>
> **giving thanks to God the Father through him.** As all of life is to be lived in the name of the Lord Jesus, so our continual accompanying activity is to be one of thanksgiving to God the Father through our Lord Jesus Christ. This constitutes a total world and life view.

QUESTION 9

Briefly explain why, according to Colossians 3:15, peace and harmony should prevail in the church.

QUESTION 10

Which of the following is shown to have special importance in the Christian life because it is mentioned so frequently in Colossians?

- A. Witnessing
- B. Tithing
- C. Giving thanks
- D. Singing
- E. Meditation on Scripture

QUESTION 11

The message of Christ that the Colossians are to let dwell among them richly (Col 3:16) is the message of the _____.

QUESTION 12

According to Colossians 3:16, Paul's goal of bringing everyone to maturity in Christ by teaching and admonishing every convert is also to be the goal of the church as a body. *True or False?*

QUESTION 13

In what passage of Colossians (which is sometimes called "the Colossian hymn") does Paul teach that Christian songs are a way to praise God and to teach and encourage fellow worshippers?

- A. Colossians 1:9-14
- B. Colossians 1:15-20
- C. Colossians 1:24-28
- D. Colossians 2:9-15
- E. Colossians 3:15-17

QUESTION 14

The word "_____" is based on the word that means to pluck with the fingers.

QUESTION 15

State briefly what it means to do something in the name of another (Col 3:17).

QUESTION 16

Why do you think giving thanks is such an important part of the Christian life (Col 3:15-17)? Consider the trials, disappointments, and failures you have experienced in the past year. Take a moment to thank God for his grace and love toward you in the midst of these situations.

Lesson 11: Walk as "New Men"—Colossians 3:12-21

QUESTION 17
Consider the principle that the church grows spiritually as its members teach and admonish one another regarding the message of the gospel (Col 3:16). Have you seen this type of teaching and admonishing happening among the members of your church? Can you think of ways to encourage more of it? One way is through singing hymns that teach and celebrate the truths of our salvation (Col 3:16c). Name three hymns that you believe are especially effective for this purpose.

Important Facts to Remember About Colossians 3:15-17

1. Peace should prevail in the church because (a) Christ has given us peace with God, and (b) God called us to peace by making us members of one body (Col 3:15).

2. Paul mentions the practice of giving thanks in three different exhortations in Colossians 3:5-17 as well as four other times in Colossians. This demonstrates its special importance in the life of the Christian.

3. The church grows spiritually as the members teach and admonish one another regarding the message of salvation through Christ. One way to do this is through songs of praise (Col 3:16).

4. The command to do all in the name of the Lord Jesus (Col 3:17) means that everything we do should be done under the lordship of Christ.

Topic 3: The Duties of Wives and Husbands (Col 3:18-19)

In Colossians 3:15-17 Paul applies the truth of the gospel to the life of the congregation as a whole. Now in Colossians 3:18, he moves from the general to the specific—from the congregation as a whole to the individual households that make up the congregation. How is this new reality of redemption to be lived out in the home? Paul begins with the marriage relationship. Wives are to submit to their husbands, and husbands in turn are to love their wives.

Begin your study by reading Colossians 3:18-19. Then read the Worksheet on Colossians 3:18-19. Copy it in your Life Notebook and complete Step 1 of the Assignments section. Check your conclusions by comparing them with the Answer Section for Colossians 3:18-19. Next, complete Step 2 by recording on the same worksheet your detailed observations, interpretations, and applications. For the third and final step, carefully read the Commentary on Colossians 3:18-19. Then answer the questions, take special note of the *Important Facts to Remember about Colossians 3:18-19*.

Worksheet for Colossians 3:18-19

¹⁸ Wives, submit to your husbands,

as is fitting in the Lord.

¹⁹ Husbands, love your wives

AND

do not be embittered against them.

Commentary on Colossians 3:18-19

2. The Gospel Applied to the Christian Life—Colossians 3:5–4:6 (Continued)

d. Duties of the Domestic Life—Colossians 3:18–4:1

The gospel must be applied to every aspect of the Christian life. Paul now shifts his comments from relationships within the church to relationships within the household. In the following three paragraphs, he deals with the mutual responsibilities within three types of relationships: wives and husbands, children and parents, and slaves and masters.

    (1) The Duties of Wives and Husbands—Colossians 3:18-19

Paul begins with the most basic relationship in the home—that of the husband and wife. Wives are to submit to their husbands, and husbands are to love their wives.

Verse 18

Wives, submit to your husbands. The word translated "submit" means to take a **subordinate** position in relation to another. God ordained marriage as a unique partnership between a man and a woman. And within this partnership, he appointed the husband to be the leader and entrusted him with the authority that is essential to his task. In the same way, God appointed the wife to follow her husband's leadership and submit to his authority.

Does this submission include obedience? Some have reasoned that since the wife is told to submit, whereas children and slaves are told to obey, there must be a difference between submission and obedience. Thus they conclude that while wives must submit to their husbands, they need not necessarily obey them. But this is a misreading of the text. The word "submit" is simply a broader term than "obey." We can see this in 1 Peter 3:1, where Peter instructs wives to be submissive to their husbands. Later in 1 Peter 3:6, he illustrates submission by pointing to Sarah who **obeyed** Abraham, calling him lord. Submission therefore includes obedience.

Does this mean that a wife should submit to her husband in the same way that a slave submits to his master or a child submits to his parents? No. The nature of the relationship shapes the nature of the submission.

as is fitting in the Lord. This statement explains why wives should submit to their husbands. Paul is not saying submit only as is it is fitting—that is, if and when it is fitting. Instead, he is saying that God ordained marriage, and this is the way he designed it to be. It is fitting for the wife to submit to her husband. In this way, she also shows trust and obedience to God.

Verse 19

Husbands, love your wives. The responsibility that God laid upon the husband is to love his wife. The best commentary on this command is perhaps the one Paul provides in Ephesians 5:25-33. Here he holds up Christ as the example of love: "Husbands, love your wives just as Christ loved the church and gave himself up for her." In Colossians itself we find an excellent prescription for how husbands should love their wives in the exhortations of Colossians 3:12-14. As a new man in Christ, the husband should display toward his wife the qualities listed in these verses: compassion, kindness, gentleness, forgiveness, humility, and patience. This should involve putting her needs and interests above his own. He can also express his love by giving her sound leadership of which to submit.

and do not be embittered against them. Paul balances this positive command to husbands to love their wives with a negative command: Do not be harsh with them. Loving one's wife means being gentle and not harsh. But why does Paul single out the sin of harshness? It is because husbands might have a tendency to be harsh with their wives. They could express this harshness through unkind words, anger, and impatience. Thus, Paul is spelling out a way for husbands to express love toward their wife. It is through gentleness and patience.

QUESTION 18

The word "submit" means to take a _____ position in relation to another.

QUESTION 19

Some claim that submission in Colossians 3:18 does not necessarily include obedience, since in Colossians 3:18-20 only children and slaves are told to obey. How would you respond to this interpretation?

QUESTION 20

As wives are called by God to submit to their husbands, so husbands are called by God to love their wives and not to become embittered against them. *True or False?*

QUESTION 21

Which of the following passages provides the clearest teaching on the command in Colossians 3:19 for husbands to love their wives?

- A. Colossians 3:12-14
- B. Romans 7:1-6
- C. Galatians 5:16-26
- D. Ephesians 5:25-33
- E. Song of Solomon 1
- F. 1 Timothy 3:1-7

QUESTION 22

What are some specific situations where a wife finds it difficult to submit to her husband? What are some things a husband can do to make it easier for his wife to submit to his leadership?

QUESTION 23

What are some specific situations where a husband is tempted to be harsh and unloving toward his wife? What are some things a wife can do to make it easier for her husband to express the proper love toward her?

QUESTION 24

Who do you know who are Godly examples of a husband and wife whose marriage serves as a role model for young couples in your church?

Important Facts to Remember About Colossians 3:18-19

1. God ordained marriage and entrusted the husband with the stewardship of authority over his wife. She should therefore submit to his leadership, which includes obeying him.

2. In this position of leadership and authority, the husband should love his wife in a Christ-like manner as explained more fully in Ephesians 5:25-33.

Topic 4: The Duties of Parents and Children (Col 3:20-21)

How are believers to live out the reality of their redemption within the Christian household? This is the question Paul addresses in Colossians 3:19-4:1. In Colossians 3:19-20, he instructs husbands and wives regarding their duties toward one another. Now in Colossians 3:21-22, the topic is the duties of parents and children. Children are to obey their parents in everything, while the parents—the father in particular since he is the ultimate authority in the home—must not provoke the children and cause them to become discouraged.

Begin your study by reading Colossians 3:20-21. Then read the Worksheet on Colossians 3:20-21. Copy it in your Life Notebook and complete step 1 of the Assignments section. Check your conclusions by comparing them with the Answer Section for Colossians 3:20-21. Next, complete step 2 by recording on the same worksheet your detailed observations, interpretations, and applications. For the third and final step, carefully read the Commentary on Colossians 3:20-21. Then answer the questions, taking special note of the *Important Facts to Remember*.

> **Worksheet for Colossians 3:20-21**
>
> ²⁰ Children, obey your parents in everything,
>
> FOR
>
> this in pleasing in the Lord.
>
> ²¹ Fathers, do not provoke your children,
>
> SO
>
> they will not become disheartened.

Commentary on Colossians 3:20-21

2. The Gospel Applied to the Christian Life—Colossians 3:5–4:6 (Continued)

d. Duties of the Domestic Life—Colossians 3:18-4:1 (Continued)

    (2) The Duties of Children and Parents—Colossians 3:20-21

Having instructed husbands and wives regarding their mutual duties within the household, Paul now turns to their relationship with their children. Children are to obey their parents in everything, while the parents—the father in particular since he is the ultimate authority in the home—must not provoke them and cause them to become discouraged.

Verse 20

Children, obey your parents in everything. This address is to children within the church whose parents are Christians. Children are those who are still in the process of growing up. Paul is not addressing adult offspring here. Adults also have duties toward their parents such as providing financial support when they are in need (Mt 15:4-6). They are to honor their parents in this way and others, but not necessarily by obeying them. Paul is writing here to children in regard to their duty to obey.

As God ordained the family and gave the husband authority over his wife, he also gave parents authority over their children. He entrusted them with their care, upbringing, and instruction. This exhortation reflects the fifth commandment: Honor your father and your mother (Ex 20:12; compare Eph 6:1). Children express faith and serve God by obeying their parents and submitting to their instruction. It is the duty of parents to guide, direct, and exercise authority over them and to do so in a wise and responsible manner. They have a stewardship, a God-given responsibility, toward their children.

> **for this is pleasing in the Lord.** God is pleased when children obey their parents. Alternatively, God is displeased when they disobey. The relationship of children to their parents illustrates the relationship of the believer to God: he is our heavenly Father. We must help our children to understand their relationship to God, by modeling this pattern while they are young and in the home.
>
> *Verse 21*
>
> **Fathers, do not provoke your children.** This command applies to both parents, but Paul addresses fathers because the father is the ultimate authority in the home. Fathers are responsible ultimately for making decisions and seeing that the child obeys. But the father must exercise his authority wisely, not foolishly. He must not provoke the child with harsh commands, always finding fault, or nagging.
>
> **So.** This word introduces a statement of purpose that explains why fathers should not provoke their children.
>
> **they will not become disheartened.** A provoking type of behavior on the part of the parent will incite the child to anger and frustration. He will become exasperated and discouraged. Fathers must use their authority in ways that encourage. They must be wise and gentle leaders of their children, whose aim, as Paul writes in Ephesians 6:4, is to "raise them up in the discipline and instruction of the Lord."

QUESTION 25

The command in Colossians 3:20 for children to obey their parents is not directed to adult offspring but to those who are still growing up. *True or False?*

QUESTION 26

The exhortation for children to obey their parents reflects the _____ commandment of the Ten Commandments.

QUESTION 27

Explain briefly why the exhortation of Colossians 3:21 ("Fathers, do not provoke your children") is directed to fathers only and not also to the mothers.

QUESTION 28

Which passage (mentioned in the commentary) expresses what should be the aim of fathers with their children?

- A. 2 Timothy 2:22
- B. Ephesians 6:4
- C. Titus 2:6
- D. Romans 14:19
- E. Ephesians 5:18

QUESTION 29

What are some things (other than threats of punishment) that parents can do to motivate their children to obey them and thus please the Lord?

QUESTION 30

Assume you are the parent of a seven–year–old child. The child has an annoying habit or immature pattern of behavior that needs to stop (choose something from your experience). How could you direct this child into the proper kind of behavior without provoking him or her to anger and causing discouragement?

Important Facts to Remember About Colossians 3:20-21

1. Children express faith and serve God by obeying their parents. Parents are responsible to exercise authority over their children wisely.
2. Fathers have the ultimate authority in the home. They must see that their children learn obedience, yet without provoking them to anger and causing discouragement.

Lesson 11 Self Check

QUESTION 1

Paul's description of the Colossian Christians as God's chosen people, holy and dearly loved in Colossians 3:12 is based on the description of Israel in the Old Testament book of _____.

QUESTION 2

According to the commentary, the instruction, "Just as the Lord has forgiven you, so you also forgive others." (Col 3:13) means that the Lord's act of forgiving us is the basis and model for mutual forgiveness in the church. *True or False?*

QUESTION 3

Which of the following does the commentary describe as the sum of all the virtues?

- A. Compassion
- B. Kindness
- C. Humility
- D. Gentleness
- E. Forgiveness
- F. Love

QUESTION 4

The exhortation, "Let the peace of Christ be in control in your heart" (Col 3:15) refers to the feelings of peacefulness that the Holy Spirit produces in the heart when one is walking in a manner pleasing to the Lord. *True or False?*

QUESTION 5

Which of the following is shown to have special importance in the Christian life because it is mentioned so frequently in Colossians 3:15-17?

- A. Meditation on Scripture
- B. Singing
- C. Witnessing
- D. Teaching
- E. Giving thanks
- F. Tithing

QUESTION 6

To do something in the name of another means to act as that person's _____.

QUESTION 7

The word translated "submit" in Colossians 3:18 means to take a _____ position in relation to another.

QUESTION 8

As Sarah is mentioned in the commentary as a model of how wives are to submit to their husbands, so _____ is mentioned as a model of how husbands are to love their wives.

QUESTION 9

The command in Colossians 3:20 for children to obey their parents is directed to adult offspring as well as to those who are still growing up. *True or False?*

QUESTION 10

Which of the following passages (according to the commentary) expresses what should be the aim of fathers with their children?

    A. Romans 14:19
    B. Ephesians 4:6
    C. Ephesians 6:4
    D. 2 Timothy 2:26
    E. Titus 2:5

Lesson 11 Answers to Questions

WORKSHEET FOR COLOSSIANS 3:12-14

Answer for Colossians 3:12-14

Put on virtues:
- ¹²THEREFORE, *(conclusion = application)*
- as the elect of God, holy and dearly loved, *(description of those addressed)*
- clothe yourselves with a heart of *(command)*
  - mercy, *(what to put on)*
  - kindness,
  - humility,
  - gentleness and
  - patience,

Forbear and Forgive:
- ¹³bearing with one another, *(command)*
- AND *(additional command)*
- forgiving one another
- if someone happens to have a complaint against anyone else. *(condition of action)*
- Just as the Lord has forgiven you, so you also should forgive others. *(explanation = example)*

Put on love:
- ¹⁴And to all these virtues, add love *(additional command)*
- WHICH *(explanation)*
- is the perfect bond.

Textual Outline of Colossians 3:12-14
I. Conclusion: Put on Christ-like virtues. (Col 3:12)
    A. Description of those addressed (Col 3:12a)
    B. The command: Put on Christ-like virtues. (Col 3:12b)
II. Forbear and forgive. (Col 3:13)
    A. The commands: Bear with and forgive each other. (Col 3:13a-b)
    B. Condition of these actions: When grievances occur (Col 3:13c)
    C. Explanation: Follow the Lord's example. (Col 3:13d)
III. Put on love. (Col 3:14)
    A. The command: Put on love. (Col 3:14a)
    B. Explanation: This produces maturity. (Col 3:14b)

Theme Statement for Colossians 3:12-14
Because they have put on the new man, the Colossians must put on Christ-like virtues.

QUESTION 1: *Your answer should be similar to the following:*
This statement, in Colossians 3:12, is based on God's description of Israel, his covenant people in Deuteronomy 7:6-7. By applying this same language to the formerly pagan Colossian Christians, Paul is reminding them that, contrary to the claims of the Jewish false teachers, they now belong to God's people.

QUESTION 2: False [The word translated "mercy", which can also be translated "compassion," is related to the Hebrew word for womb. Compassion is the feeling a mother and father have for their child.]

QUESTION 3: lowliness

QUESTION 4
  D. Gentleness

QUESTION 5: False [It means that the Lord's forgiveness of us is both the basis and the example for mutual forgiveness within the church.]

QUESTION 6: love

QUESTION 7: *Your answer*

QUESTION 8: *Your answer*

WORKSHEET FOR COLOSSIANS 3:15-17

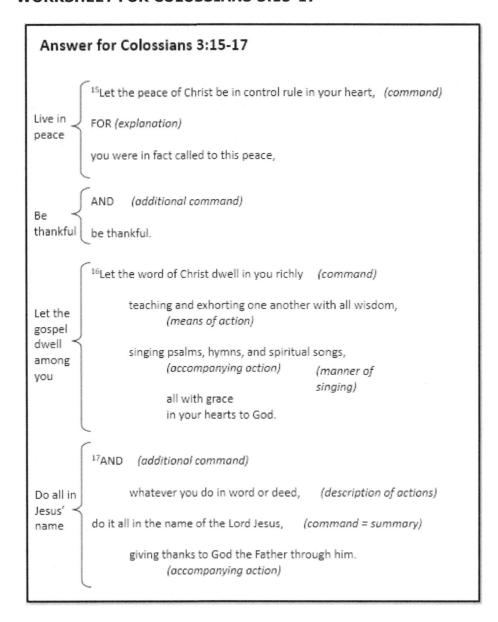

Textual Outline of Colossians 3:15-17
I. Live in peace. (Col 3:15a-b)
    A. The command: Live in peace. (Col 3:15a)
    B. Explanation: You were called to peace. (Col 3:15b)
II. Be thankful. (Col 3:15c)
III. Let the gospel dwell among you. (Col 3:16)
    A. The command: Let the gospel dwell among you. (Col 3:16a)
    B. The means: By teaching and admonishing one another (Col 3:16b)
    C. Accompanying action: Singing to God (Col 3:16c)
IV. Do all in Jesus' name. (Col 3:17)
    A. The command: Do all in Jesus' name. (Col 3:17a,b)
    B. Accompanying action: Giving thanks to the Father (Col 3:17c)

Theme Statement for Colossians 3:15-17
The Colossians must live in peace, be thankful, let the gospel dwell among them, and do all in Jesus' name.

QUESTION 9: *Your answer should be similar to the following:*
Firstly, peace and harmony should prevail in the church because Christ has given us peace with God and our lives should correspond to the grace we have received. Secondly, it is evident that he has made us members of one body. As the members of a physical body must act in harmony with one another so also must the members of the church, which is the body of Christ.

QUESTION 10
    C. Giving thanks

QUESTION 11: gospel

QUESTION 12: True

QUESTION 13
    B. Colossians 1:15-20

QUESTION 14: psalm

QUESTION 15: *Your answer should be similar to the following:*
To do something in the name of another means to act as that person's representative.

QUESTION 16: *Your answer*

QUESTION 17: *Your answer*

WORKSHEET FOR COLOSSIANS 3:18-19

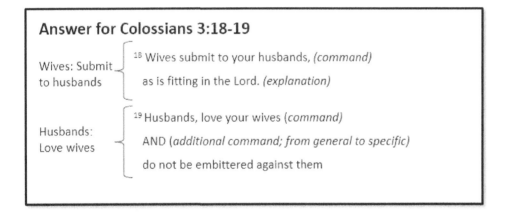

Textual Outline of Colossians 3:18-19
I. Wives must submit to their husbands. (Col 3:18)
    A. The command to submit (Col 3:18a)
    B. The reason: It is fitting in the Lord. (Col 3:18b)
II. Husbands must love their wives. (Col 3:19)
    A. The command to love (Col 3:19a)
    B. More specific command: Do not be harsh. (Col 3:19b)

Theme Statement for Colossians 3:18-19
Wives are to submit to their husbands, while husbands are to love their wives.

QUESTION 18: subordinate

QUESTION 19: *Your answer should be similar to the following:*
In 1 Peter 3:1, Peter instructs wives to be submissive to their husbands, and then illustrates this with Sarah's obedience to Abraham. Submission therefore includes obedience. Wives, however, submit in a

different way than children do to their parents or slaves do to their masters. The nature of the relationship shapes the nature of the submission.

QUESTION 20: True

QUESTION 21
    D. Ephesians 5:25-33

QUESTION 22: *Your answer*

QUESTION 23: *Your answer*

QUESTION 24: *Your answer*

WORKSHEET FOR COLOSSIANS 3:20-21

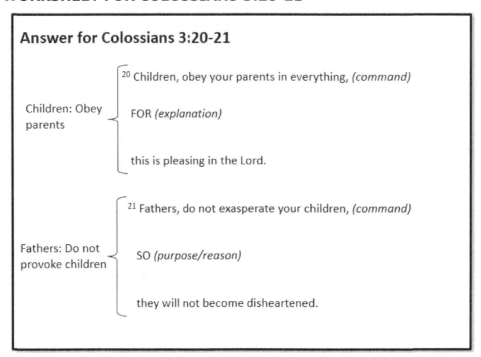

Textual Outline of Colossians 3:20-21
I. Children must obey their parents. (Col 3:20)
    A. The command to obey (Col 3:20a)
    B. Explanation: This pleases the Lord. (Col 3:20b)
II. Fathers must not provoke their children. (Col 3:21)
    A. The command not to provoke (Col 3:21a)
    B. Reason: To avoid discouraging them (Col 3:21b)

Theme Statement for Colossians 3:20-21
Children must obey their parents, while fathers must not provoke their children.

QUESTION 25: True

QUESTION 26: fifth

QUESTION 27: *Your answer should be similar to the following:*
While the exhortation of Colossians 3:21 certainly applies to mothers, fathers are addressed because Paul recognizes the father as the ultimate authority in the home. He therefore bears the ultimate responsibility for the child's obedience.

QUESTION 28
   B. Ephesians 6:4
QUESTION 29: *Your answer*
QUESTION 30: *Your answer*

Lesson 11 Self Check Answers

QUESTION 1: Deuteronomy
QUESTION 2: True
QUESTION 3
    F. Love
QUESTION 4: False
QUESTION 5
    E. Giving thanks
QUESTION 6: representative
QUESTION 7: subordinate
QUESTION 8: Christ
QUESTION 9: False
QUESTION 10
    C. Ephesians 6:4

Lesson 12: Serve Christ and Closing Instructions—Colossians 3:22-4:7-18

In Lesson 11, you examined Paul's application of the gospel to the Christian life in general contained in Colossians 3:12-21. As previously studied, his overall theme in the extended section which we labeled "The Gospel Applied to the Christian Life" (Col 3:5-4:6), is that Christians should live in accordance with what God has made them. They should walk as *new men*. Thus, in Colossians 3:12-14, Paul exhorts the Colossians to put on the Christ-like virtues of the *new man*, and in Colossians 3:15-17 to live in peace, to be thankful, and to do all in the name of Christ.

Walking as *new men* also involves relationships within the household. Husbands should love their wives, and wives should submit to their husbands (Col 3:18-19). Similarly, children are to submit to their parents, and fathers are not to provoke their children (Col 3:20-21). In the present lesson, you will complete your study of these exhortations regarding how to walk as *new men*. The lesson concludes with an overview of Paul's closing greetings and instructions in Colossians 4:7-18.

Topic 1 covers Colossians 3:22-4:1. In this passage, Paul addresses the question of how Christian slaves should conduct themselves toward their masters, and how Christian masters should treat their slaves. Slaves are to obey their masters as service to Christ, their heavenly master. Similarly, masters must treat their slaves justly knowing that they too have a master in heaven.

Colossians 4:2-4 and the subject of prayer are the subjects covered in Topic 2. Paul exhorts the Colossians to be persistent in prayer, then includes a specific request that they pray for him in his mission of proclaiming the gospel.

Conduct toward non-Christians Colossians 4:5-6 is covered in Topic 3. This passage focuses on relationships with non-Christians. In their encounters with those outside the church, Paul counsels the Colossians to act with wisdom and to speak graciously and thoughtfully.

Topic 4 covers Colossians 4:7-18, the closing section of the letter to the Colossians. Paul ends with a series of personal greetings from his co-workers and final instructions for his readers. These closing statements give us many helpful insights in the circumstances surrounding the letter.

Lesson Outline

Topic 1: The Duties of Slaves and Masters (Col 3:22–4:1)

Topic 2: Pray Persistently (Col 4:2-4)

Topic 3: Act Wisely toward Non-Christians (Col 4:5-6)

Topic 4: Closing Greetings and Instructions (Col 4:7-18)

Lesson Objectives

When you have completed this lesson, you should be able to:
- Summarize the duties of slaves and masters toward one another, and recognize how the principles involved apply to Christians in the workplace today.
- Discuss Paul's instructions regarding persistent prayer in Colossians 4:2, and recognize the relevance of Paul's request in Colossians 4:2-4 for missionaries today.
- Understand how, according to Colossians 4:5-6, Christians should act and speak with non-Christians.
- Identify Paul's co-workers; explain how he repeats the theme of the letter in the closing section; identify the letter "from Laodicea"; discuss the circumstances of Paul's letter to the Colossians as they are reflected in Colossians 4:7-18.

Assignments

Follow the three-step procedure outlined below for each of the paragraphs of Colossians covered in this lesson, except for Colossians 4:7-18.

Step 1:

    (a) Read this passage of Colossians.

    (b) Make a structural diagram of the passage on the worksheet provided.

    (c) Summarize the results in an outline and theme statement.

    (d) Compare your conclusions with those in the Answer section.

Step 2:

    (a) Examine the details of the paragraph. Record your observations, interpretations, and applications on the worksheet.

Step 3:

    (a) Read the commentary on this passage of Colossians.

    (b) Answer the questions following the commentary.

    (c) Pay special attention to the *Important Facts to Remember*.

Topic 1: The Duties of Slaves and Masters (Col 3:22–4:1)

In this special address to slaves and masters within the Christians household, Paul admonishes those who are slaves to embrace the gospel by obeying their masters out of reverence for Christ, their heavenly master. Likewise, the earthly masters are to treat their slaves justly and fairly keeping in mind that they too have a master in heaven. In this way, Paul Christianizes the slave-master relationship.

Begin your study by reading Colossians 3:22-4:1. Then read the Worksheet on Colossians 3:22-4:1. Copy it in your Life Notebook and complete step 1 of the Assignments section. Check your conclusions by comparing them with the Answer Section for Colossians 3:22-4:1. Next, complete step 2 by recording on the same worksheet your detailed observations, interpretations, and applications. For the third and final step, carefully read the Commentary on Colossians 3:22-4:1, then answer the questions taking special note of the *Important Facts to Remember*.

Worksheet for Colossians 3:22-4:1

²²Slaves, obey your earthly masters in every respect;

> not only when they are watching—
>
> like those who are strictly people-pleasers—
>
> but with a sincere heart
>
> fearing the Lord.

²³Whatever you are doing, work at it with enthusiasm,

> as to the Lord and not for people,

²⁴BECAUSE

you know that you will receive your inheritance from the Lord as the reward.

Serve the Lord Christ.

²⁵FOR

the one who does wrong will be repaid for his wrong,

AND

there are no exceptions.

⁴:¹Masters, treat your slaves with justice and fairness,

BECAUSE

you know that you also have a master in heaven.

Commentary on Colossians 3:22-4:1

2. The Gospel Applied to the Christian Life—Colossians 3:5–4:6 (Continued)

d. Duties of the Domestic Life—Colossians 3:18–4:1 (Continued)

    (3) The Duties of Slaves and Masters—Colossians 3:22–4:1

This brings us to the third and final relationship within the household; that of slaves and masters. Slavery was very common in the ancient Roman Empire. It was a fundamental and accepted part of that society. In Paul's day, one person out of every three in Greece and Italy was a slave. However, by that time the main source of slaves was no longer capture in warfare or piracy. Instead they were born to slave owners. Slaves were considered a part of the owner's household and were trained to perform some useful task. Many did simple household jobs such as cooking, cleaning, gardening, and caring for children. Others, however, worked as craftsman, merchants, and teachers. Many slaves enjoyed better living conditions than free laborers. Some people even sold themselves into slavery in order to gain these benefits. Moreover, slavery was usually not for life. A slave could expect to be freed after ten to twenty years of service. While some masters were cruel and unjust, most treated their slaves well. A good owner would treat his slaves similar to the way he treated his children. Nevertheless, slavery was **slavery**. The slave was the property of the master and had no rights under Roman law. Thus, in 1 Corinthians 7:21, Paul advises slaves to become free if they can.

As with the other two relationships discussed in this section, the theme here is submission. Slaves are to obey their earthly masters in everything as service to Christ. The masters are to use their authority responsibly by treating their slaves justly and fairly since they too—masters as well as slaves—have a master in heaven. In this way, Paul Christianizes the slave-master relationship by bringing it under the lordship of Christ.

Verse 22

Slaves, obey your earthly masters in every respect. Because the slave was the property of his master, it was assumed in that society that he owed complete obedience to the master. Yet in Colossians 3:11, Paul wrote that in the society of the new creation, the new human race to which Christians now belong, the old distinctions that divide society no longer count for anything. Christ is all in all. There is neither Greek nor Jew, slave nor free. Their common relationship with him surpasses and overrides all other distinctions. How then does this new relationship with Christ affect the way a slave responds to his owner (particularly a Christian owner) in the day-to-day affairs of life? Should it free him from the honor and obedience normally expected of slaves? No, says Paul. It should make him a better slave: honest and hard working—as service to the Lord rather than to men. As Paul explains elsewhere, Christian slaves who respond in this way embrace the gospel. The world is watching to see how this new teaching works in daily life. Slaves who live for Christ testify to the truth of the gospel. They make it more attractive (Tit 2:10; 1 Tim 6:1). The same is true in principle for all believers who serve under the authority of a boss.

not only when they are watching - like those who are strictly people-pleasers. The remainder of this verse explains how slaves should obey. Paul begins by telling them how **not** to obey. This line points to a common problem with slaves. Indeed, it is a common problem with all workers, including children working in the home. The problem is with service that is done only for the sake of appearance. It is going through the outward motions of work without a corresponding inner commitment of the heart. The motive is to win favor in a dishonest way. The slave is trying to make the master think he is working hard and doing a good job, when in fact, he is not. Do not be that kind of a worker, says Paul.

but with a sincere heart, fearing the Lord. By way of contrast, Paul now explains the proper manner and motivation for obedience. The manner is "with a sincere heart." These words reflect the common Old Testament expression "morally upright," "integrity" or "uprightness" (Ps 32:11, 1 Chr 29:17, Deut 9:5). The heart is the inner core of the man, the seat of his will, emotions and thought. It determines his attitude and conduct. "With a sincere heart" means a heart that is honest and truthful, not deceptive, but straightforward and upright. The efforts of such people flow from an inner commitment to do the job and to do it well.

The motivation for working in this manner is "reverence for the Lord"—literally the fear of the Lord. In the Old Testament, the fear of the Lord is frequently given as the reason to walk in his ways and avoid evil. "He whose walk is upright fears the Lord" (Prov 14:2, NIV). The "fear of the Lord" is the response of the believing heart to the revelation of God's awesome power, majesty, and holiness. It manifests itself in trust and obedience to his word. The Lord in this context is Christ (see Col 3:24). "For in him all the fullness of deity lives in bodily form" (Col 2:9). Thus, obedience to the earthly master is to be done out of reverence for Christ, the heavenly Lord and master.

Finally, we should note that Paul uses the same Greek word in this paragraph for the earthly "master" and the heavenly "Lord." The word is *kyrios*. It is used twice for the earthly master and five times for the heavenly master.

Verse 23

Whatever you are doing, work at it with enthusiasm, as to the Lord and not for people. This exhortation supports and clarifies the exhortation of Colossians 3:22. The word "enthusiasm" corresponds to "a sincere heart" in Colossians 3:22. It refers to a full commitment or wholeheartedness that flows from the inner man. In contrast is the halfhearted attitude of dragging one's feet, resenting the job, and the master who commanded it. The slave is to work in this manner because he is doing it for the Lord and not just the earthly master. In other words, service to the earthly master is in fact service to the heavenly master. This does not mean that the earthly master stands in the place of Christ as his representative. It simply means that the slave is to do his work as though he were doing it for Christ himself and not just for the master. In this way, the slave is making specific application of Paul's exhortation earlier in Colossians 3:17: "And whatever you do in word or deed, do it all in the name of the Lord Jesus."

Verse 24

Because. This word introduces an explanation of why slaves should obey the exhortation of Colossians 3:22-23. It is because there will be a future reward for those who do (Col 3:24) and punishment for those who do not (Col 3:25).

you know that you will receive your inheritance from the Lord as the reward. Ordinary masters used rewards to motivate their slaves to work better. They would offer such things as better food, better clothing, and better shoes. But the owner would not offer to give his slaves a share in the inheritance of his estate. This was reserved for his children. Indeed, such a thing was not permitted under Roman law. But Paul is encouraging these slaves to think of themselves at all times as slaves of Christ. He is their true master. He too offers a reward, but unlike an earthly master the reward is an inheritance. The inheritance is the hope laid up in heaven mentioned earlier in Colossians 1:5 (see also Col 1:27; 3:4; Eph 1:14; 1 Pet 1:4). They will receive it when Christ returns in glory. They are slaves of Christ, but through him they also have been adopted as sons and daughters of God (Rom 8:15-17). Thus, with all believers they can look forward to this future inheritance.

Serve the Lord Christ. This command follows as a conclusion. So then, says Paul, since you can look forward to this future reward from Christ, work wholeheartedly for him. In all that you do for your earthly master, look upon Christ as your true master and do it as service to him.

Verse 25

For. Paul now introduces an additional word of explanation regarding their service to Christ as their true master. Earthly masters not only rewarded their slaves for good service, they also punished them for wrongdoing. The same is true in principle with service to Christ. Therefore, Paul now adds this warning: "For anyone who does not serve Christ as master in this way but does wrong, that person will be repaid for the wrong he has done."

the one who does wrong will be repaid for his wrong. Paul states this warning in the form of a general principle. There are two aspects to the principle. The first is that the punishment will fit the wrong that was done (see Ex 21:23-25). It will be neither more than the slave deserves nor less. This is justice. The second is that the punishment will be certain. Since the heavenly master is neither limited in his knowledge of the slave's action nor in his ability to repay him for his wrongdoing, the punishment will be certain. Thus,

> Paul warns these Christian slaves that if they do not serve Christ as master but persist in wrongdoing, he will punish them in a way that is both just and certain.
>
> But to what kind of punishment is Paul referring? Is he saying they will lose their inheritance? No. This would be a contradiction of what he said earlier. Salvation is by grace through faith, and Paul is not expressing doubt as to whether or not these slaves are truly saved. Instead we must assume he is speaking of punishment appropriate to Christians. There are two kinds. The first is the corrective discipline that God applies to us as his children (see Heb 12:7-11). The second will take place at the judgment seat of Christ where each believer will "receive what is due him for the things done while in the body, whether good or bad" (2 Cor 5:10, NIV). In either case God deals with us as members of his family. Nevertheless, the warning of punishment must not be taken lightly. It is part of the motivation for faithful service to the master.
>
> **and there are no exceptions**. Paul closes this admonition to slaves with a final principle regarding the kind of punishment they can expect for wrongdoing. God is no respecter of persons. He does not show partiality in judgment (Rom 2:11). To do so would be unjust (Lev 19:15; Jas 2:9). They can expect perfect fairness from him. It is interesting to note that Paul repeats this same principle in his warning to masters in Ephesians 6:9. Therefore, the point applies equally to Christian slaves and to Christian masters. Christ is the Lord of both. So, when it comes to wrongdoing, he will deal with both by the same standard. With the Lord, there are no exceptions and there is no favoritism.
>
> *Verse 1*
>
> **Masters, treat your slaves with justice and fairness**. Paul now deals briefly with the duty of Christian masters (such as Philemon) to their slaves. Slaves were the property of their masters and had no rights. The master could treat them as he wished. He could be a harsh tyrant, or he could treat them well. Paul exhorts the masters to treat them justly and fairly. The word "justice" refers to that which is right—that which is in accord with certain requirements of justice. In this context, it means what is right in the sight of God (compare Acts 4:19). The word "fairness" refers to even-handed, impartial treatment. Masters are not to show favoritism but to treat all their slaves equally according to the same standards of justice. Paul is not telling the masters to free their slaves but to rule them wisely—with justice and even-handedness.
>
> **Because**. Having stated their duty, Paul now explains why they should do this.
>
> **you know that you also have a master in heaven**. The reason given to masters for fair treatment of their slaves is basically the same as the reason given to slaves for obeying their earthly masters. Both slave and master are slaves of the one heavenly master. While their duties toward one another are different, both owe obedience to the heavenly master. Thus, earthly masters have a model for their behavior. It is Christ himself. They must treat their slaves with the same justice and fairness that they hope to receive from their master in heaven.

QUESTION 1

Which of the following statements is **true** regarding slaves in Paul's day?

- A. A slave could rarely expect to be freed.
- B. Slaves had the same rights as free people under Roman law.
- C. Slaves did only menial, unskilled, labor.
- D. Slaves were advised by Paul to do their work with a deep inner commitment of the heart.
- E. Most slaves in Paul's day in the Roman Empire were born into slavery.

QUESTION 2

In Colossians 3:11, Paul writes that in the church, the society of the new creation, the old distinctions such as slave and free are no longer valid. Explain briefly how this new reality should affect the relationship of a Christian slave to his Christian owner in the day-to-day affairs of life.

QUESTION 3

The phrase "with a sincere heart" in Colossians 3:22 reflects what Old Testament expression?

- A. Clean heart
- B. Circumcised heart
- C. Upright in heart
- D. Understanding heart
- E. Undivided heart

QUESTION 4

Explain briefly the meaning of the expression "fearing the Lord."

QUESTION 5

The Greek word _____ is used twice in Colossians 3:22-4:1 for the earthly master and five times for the heavenly master.

QUESTION 6

The statement that the slave should do his work "as to the Lord" means the earthly master stands in the place of Christ as his representative. *True or False?*

QUESTION 7

In Colossians 3:25, Paul warns that "For the one who does wrong will be repaid for his wrong, and there are no exceptions." While this warning is directed toward slaves, the principle applies equally to Christian masters. *True or False?*

Lesson 12: Serve Christ and Closing Instructions—Colossians 3:22-4:7-18

QUESTION 8

Paul's exhortation to masters (Col 4:1) to treat their slaves justly and fairly was his way of telling them they ought to free their slaves. *True or False?*

QUESTION 9

Unlike the relationships mentioned in Colossians 3:18-21, slavery has almost completely disappeared from the world. Nevertheless, the principles of the passage remain valid today for the relationship of bosses to those who work under their authority. Consider Paul's exhortation to slaves in Colossians 3:23, "Whatever you are doing, work at it with enthusiasm, as to the Lord and not for people." How can you apply this verse in the tasks that you have ahead of you this week in your job?

QUESTION 10

If you are in a position of authority over others (a boss), what are some ways that you have tried to treat them fairly and justly? Is there something more you can do in this regard? How does the knowledge that you have a master (boss) in heaven help in this regard? Record your response in your Life Notebook.

Important Facts to Remember About Col 3:22-4:1

1. Christ is Lord of all. All Christians should therefore look upon themselves as slaves of Christ, their heavenly master, and do their work as service to him.

2. For those under the authority of a boss, this means working with sincerity and enthusiasm.

3. For those who are bosses, this means treating those under them justly and fairly, as they themselves wish to be treated by their heavenly master.

> **Worksheet for Colossians 4:2-4**
>
> ²Be devoted to prayer,
>
> > keeping alert in it with thanksgiving.
>
> ³At the same time pray for us too,
>
> THAT
>
> God may open a door for the message,
>
> SO THAT
>
> we may proclaim the mystery of Christ,
>
> > for which I am in chains.
>
> ⁴Pray that I may make it known as I should.

Topic 2: Pray Persistently (Col 4:2-4)

In this passage, Paul exhorts the Colossians to pray persistently, with alertness and thanksgiving. In particular, he asks (writing from his prison cell) they pray for him as he seeks to fulfill the commission God has given him to proclaim the gospel.

Begin your study by reading Colossians 4:2-4. Then read the Worksheet on Colossians 4:2-4. Copy it in your Life Notebook and complete step 1 of the Assignments section. Check your conclusions by comparing them with the Answer Section for Colossians 4:2-4. Next, complete step 2 by recording on the same worksheet your detailed observations, interpretations, and applications. For the third and final step, carefully read the Commentary on Colossians 4:2-4. Then answer the questions, taking special note of the *Important Facts to Remember*.

> ## Commentary on Colossians 4:2-4
>
> **2. The Gospel Applied to the Christian Life—Colossians 3:5–4:6** (Continued)
>
> e. Concluding Exhortations—Colossians 4:2-6
>
> These final two paragraphs bring to a conclusion the section of the letter in which Paul applies the message of the gospel to the Christian life in general (Col 3:5-4:6). The central message of this entire section is that Christians should walk in accordance with what God has made them as his redeemed people. To review, in Colossians 3:5-17, Paul addressed

the entire church regarding the need to put off the ways of their old fallen existence in Adam and to put on the Christ-like ways of the new man. In Colossians 3:18-4:1, Paul explains how believers should relate to one another within the Christian household; addressing first husbands and wives, then parents and children and finally masters and slaves. Now in these closing exhortations of Colossians 4:2-6, he once more addresses the entire church. The final topics are prayer (Col 4:2-4) and the believer's relationship to non-Christians (Col 4:5-6). One deals with the inner, hidden life of our communication with God, the other with the outward life of where we meet the world.

(1) Pray persistently—Colossians 4:2-4

In this paragraph, Paul exhorts the Colossians to pray persistently, with alertness and thanksgiving. And in particular, he asks that they intercede for him in his God-given task of proclaiming the gospel.

Verse 2

Be devoted to prayer. Prayer is a vital part of our new life. God rescued us out of darkness (Col 1:13) and alienation from him (Col 1:21-22) and brought us into a personal relationship with himself. Prayer is central to this new relationship. Through prayer we pour out our grateful praise before his throne, we confess our sins, make requests for our needs, and intercede for others. Thus, Paul exhorts these young believers to live lives of consistent and persistent prayer.

The Greek word translated "be devoted" could also translate "continue steadfastly." It is based on the root verb that means to be strong. Prayer is not always easy. It requires effort—both physical and emotional. It can lead to weariness. Moreover, our petitions can seem to go unanswered, and there is the temptation to become discouraged and to give up. Don't be overcome by these things, says Paul. Be persistent in prayer. This exhortation echoes what Jesus taught about persistent prayer (Lk 11:5-8; 18:1-8).

keeping alert in it with thanksgiving. Prayer should not be done in a dull, careless, way. We should be spiritually alert and on guard. First, be alert to the temptations and spiritual dangers that we face. Prayer is of great importance in guarding our hearts from the assaults of the world, the flesh, and the devil (1 Pet 5:8). Secondly, we should be alert to our needs, the needs of others, and to the promises and the will of God.

Alert prayer should also include thanksgiving to God for all of his blessings through Christ. As we recall God's past blessings, and as we praise him for these things, our faith is strengthened to persist in our present prayers.

Verse 3

At the same time pray for us too. Paul now moves from the general to the specific: When you pray, pray also for us. He began this letter with an account of his persistent prayers for the Colossians (Col 1:3, 9). Now in this concluding section, he requests that they pray for him and his fellow workers. These missionaries are no longer in need of our prayers. Yet all Scripture is profitable (2 Tim 3:16), and Paul's request contains an application-based principle that is valid today regarding prayer for those involved in the difficult task of proclaiming the gospel.

That. Here Paul introduces the **content** of his prayer.

God may open a door for the message. Paul uses this figure of an open door elsewhere to denote an opportunity for effective evangelism (1 Cor 16:9; 2 Cor 2:12). Notice that his request is not specifically for release from prison. While the prayer for God to open a door could easily be seen as such a request, we know that for Paul, prison sometimes provided opportunity for missionary work (Phil 1:12-13; Acts 28:30-31). Liberty, on the other hand, did not automatically guarantee such open doors (1 Cor 16:8-9). The important point to observe is that Paul states his request not in terms of his personal freedom but in terms of his mission. Nevertheless, it is reasonable to believe that he thought of this "open door" as one that included his freedom. Indeed, his personal letter to Philemon assumes that Philemon is praying for a speedy release: "At the same time also, prepare a place for me to stay, for I hope that through your prayers I will be given back to you" (Phm 22).

So that. These words introduce the **purpose** for which Paul desires an open door.

We may proclaim the mystery of Christ. Recall that in the opening section of the body of this letter Paul explained how God commissioned him with the task of proclaiming the mystery of Christ, which is the gospel (Col 1:25-27). Paul labors and strives to fulfill this task (Col 1:28-29). Indeed, he has written this letter for the purpose of discharging this duty with the Christians of Colossae and Laodicea (Col 2:2). Now, in these closing exhortations he seeks to enlist them in this ministry of proclamation by praying for him and his co-workers. Implied in this request for participation with him in his ministry is an expression of **confidence** that they will take to heart what he has written to them about the gospel and not turn away to the false teaching.

for which I am in chains. For the first time in the letter, Paul mentions that he is writing from prison. It is because of his work of proclaiming the gospel of Christ that he was arrested and placed there.

Verse 4

Pray that I may make it known. Here Paul repeats for the sake of emphasis the reason he desires an open door for the message. He is saying essentially the same thing here as in Colossians 4:3, only he restates his purpose in order to underscore the true nature of his mission. The verb translated "make it known" means to manifest, reveal, disclose. Paul used this verb earlier in Colossians 1:26 in regard to the mystery which was previously hidden, but has now been **disclosed** to the saints. As we saw earlier, the word "saints" in this context refers to a select group of saints—the apostles. God disclosed the mystery of the gospel to the apostles and entrusted them with the task of disclosing it to the world. Paul's special commission was to make it known among the Gentiles. Thus, in closing he reminds the Colossians of this special commission and asks for their earnest prayers that he might faithfully fulfill it.

as I should. This final statement emphasizes that since it is God who commissioned Paul with this task, it is a duty and necessity. The chains that bind him in prison now provide the picture by which he illustrates this obligation: As I am bound by chains here in this prison (Col 4:3), even so am I bound by duty to fulfill the commission God gave me to proclaim the gospel (see 1 Cor 9:16-17).

QUESTION 11

Summarize in a single sentence the central message of Colossians 3:5-4:6.

QUESTION 12

The Greek word translated "be devoted" in Colossians 4:2 is based on the root verb that means to be _____.

QUESTION 13

Paul's prayer request to "open a door for the message" did not include a request to be released from prison. *True or False?*

QUESTION 14

Paul's request for the Colossians to participate in his ministry of proclaiming the mystery of Christ by praying for him contains an expression of _____ that they will take to heart what he has written to them in this letter and not turn aside to the false teaching.

QUESTION 15

What precisely is "the mystery of Christ" in Colossians 4:3-4 that Paul desired to make known?

A. The rapture of the church
B. The gospel
C. The fact that Christ indwells all believers, Jew and Gentile alike
D. The mystery of the incarnation of Christ as both fully God and full man
E. The mystery of the "one flesh" union between Christ and the Church

QUESTION 16

What are some specific ways you can apply the exhortations of Colossians 4:2 to your life? Would it help to keep a regular prayer list, or even to write your prayers in a prayer journal?

QUESTION 17

How can you apply the principle seen in Colossians 4:3 regarding the need to pray for missionaries like Paul? What value do you see in motivating a congregation to pray for a specific missionary or team of missionaries? Record your response in your Life Notebook.

Important Facts to Remember about Colossians 4:2-4

1. We should pray persistently, alertly, and with thanksgiving.
2. Paul exhorted the Colossians to participate with him in his ministry through their prayers. Believers today should do the same with their own "Paul."

Topic 3: Act Wisely toward Non-Christians (Col 4:5-6)

In this application section, Paul has been instructing the Colossians on how to walk as new men. He has written about their relationship with God, their relationships with one another within the church, and their relationships within the household. Now, last but not least, he addresses their relationship with those outside the church. Some of their fellow townsmen will be curious about the Christian's faith. Others will be suspicious or even hostile. Some will be genuinely interested and attracted. In every encounter with your non-Christian neighbors, writes Paul, seek to live out the gospel. This means conducting yourselves with wisdom and speaking graciously in every encounter.

Begin your study by reading Colossians 4:5-6. Then read the Worksheet on Colossians 4:5-6. Copy it in your Life Notebook and complete step 1 of the Assignments section. Check your conclusions by comparing them with the Answer Section for Colossians 4:5-6. Next, complete step 2 by recording on the same worksheet your detailed observations, interpretations, and applications. For the third and final step, carefully read the Commentary on Colossians 4:5-6. Then answer the questions, taking special note of the *Important Facts to Remember*.

Worksheet for Colossians 4:5-6

⁵Conduct yourselves with wisdom toward outsiders,

    making the most of the opportunities.

⁶Let your speech always be gracious, seasoned with salt,

SO THAT

you may know how you should answer everyone.

Commentary on Colossians 4:5-6

2. The Gospel Applied to the Christian Life—Colossians 3:5–4:6 (Continued)

e. Concluding Exhortations—Colossians 4:2-6 (Continued)

    (2) Act wisely toward non-Christians—Colossians 4:5-6

In this final paragraph, Paul calls upon the Colossians to act with wisdom in all their dealings with unbelievers. Society in the first century was both curious and suspicious of Christians. Some were all too willing to believe slanderous rumors about them. Paul therefore calls upon the Colossians to live out the gospel before the watching world in a way that both removes suspicion and provides opportunity for sharing the reason for the hope that is within them.

Verse 5

Conduct yourselves with wisdom toward outsiders. According to the Old Testament, wisdom is not simply knowledge of what is true and right but **skill** in living in accordance with it. Specifically, it is skill in living according to God's Word. Paul's meaning here is basically the same. We should relate his exhortation to the purpose of his letter set out in Colossians 1:9-10. His purpose is for his readers to come to a mature knowledge of God's plan of salvation so that they might walk in a manner worthy of the Lord. From Colossians 3:5–4:1, Paul focused specifically on what it means for Christians to walk worthy of the Lord in their daily lives. This is what it means to live wisely. Now in this closing exhortation, Paul makes specific application of this wise way of life to their dealings with those outside the church. By conducting themselves wisely with non-Christians they will remove suspicions, testify to the reality of the gospel, and glorify the name of Christ.

making the most of the opportunities. Wise conduct toward non-Christians includes "making the most of the opportunities." The Greek text says literally, "redeeming the time" (see also Eph 5:16). The image is that of the marketplace. "Time" refers to the opportunities that time offers. To redeem or buy up these opportunities means to make full use of them. Each Christian encounters special opportunities in his contact with non-Christians for living out the gospel and thus doing what is pleasing to the Lord. We should make the most of these opportunities when they arise and while they last. A very important example is the opportunity we have when we speak with non-Christians. This is the topic of the next verse.

Verse 6

Let your speech always be gracious, seasoned with salt. Wise conduct toward those outside the church means speaking with them graciously. "Words from a wise man's mouth are gracious" (Eccl 10:12, NIV; see also Prov 22:11). Gracious speech is speech that is pleasant, attractive, beneficial. To illustrate, Paul likens the Christian's speech to a meal served to a non-Christian. As a cook adds salt to food to improve the taste, so Christians should add graciousness to their speech to improve the attractiveness. This salt of graciousness is the character of the new man described in Colossians 3:12-14: kindness, humility, gentleness, etc. When these qualities flavor a Christian's speech—regardless of the topic—they display the attractiveness and life-changing reality of the gospel.

So that. These words introduce an intended result. By learning to speak graciously to non-Christians in all circumstances, the believer will come to know how to respond properly when the opportunity arises to share his faith.

you may know how you should answer everyone. Seeking to live out the gospel in the midst of the world leads to opportunities for witness. The word "answer" indicates that believers will be asked (or challenged) by their non-Christian neighbors and associates about their new faith. Your response should always be gracious, says Paul. Whether the person is suspicious or merely curious, hostile or genuinely interested; respond graciously. You should treat each person differently depending on his or her needs. But graciousness with each will add attractiveness and persuasiveness to your words (see 1 Pet 3:15).

QUESTION 18

According to the Old Testament, wisdom is not simply the knowledge of what is true and right, but _____ in living in accord with this knowledge.

QUESTION 19

The translation of "making the most of the opportunities" is based on an image drawn from what sphere of activity?

A. Farming
B. Cooking
C. Athletic competition
D. Metal working
E. The marketplace
F. Warfare

QUESTION 20

Paul states in Colossians 4:6 that the Christian's speech should always be "gracious, seasoned with salt." Explain briefly this image of speech being seasoned with graciousness.

QUESTION 21

Which of the following terms best defines the quality of graciousness that makes the Christian's speech attractive and pleasant?

A. Humor
B. Eloquence
C. Kindness
D. Common sense
E. Intelligence
F. Tolerance

QUESTION 22

In your current season in life, what opportunities for ministry are open now that will later close? An example would be the opportunities that parents have for contact with the parents of their children's friends and with their children's teachers.

QUESTION 23

The speech of Christians should always be gracious (Colossians 4:6). Some are more gracious than others. Think of someone you know who is a model in this regard. What specifically do you find pleasant, attractive and beneficial about talking with this person? What would a non-Christian find attractive? In what ways can this person's example help you to add the salt of graciousness to your conversations—particularly with non-Christians?

Important Facts to Remember About Colossians 4:5-6

1. Wise conduct toward non-Christians means living in a manner worthy of the Lord (see Col 1:9-10).
2. Our speech with non-Christians should always be gracious (attractive)—manifesting the qualities of the new man described in Colossians 3:12-14.

Topic 4: Closing Greetings and Instructions (Col 4:7-18)

Paul has completed the substance of his message to the Colossians and now concludes in customary fashion with personal greetings and final instructions. This closing section has four parts. It begins with a commendation of the men who will deliver the letter (Col 4:7-9). This is followed by personal greetings from Paul and six co-workers who are presently with him (Col 4:10-15). Paul then adds instructions regarding an exchange of letters with the Laodiceans and an exhortation to Archippus (Col 4:16-17). He ends with a greeting in his own handwriting, a request to remember his imprisonment, and a benediction (Col 4:18).

Unlike the other topics in this lesson, there are no worksheets to complete for Colossians 4:7-18. Your assignment is to do only step 3 of the three-step procedure for this passage. Begin by reading Colossians 4:7-18. Then carefully read the Commentary on Colossians 4:7-18, and then answer the questions, taking special note of the *Important Facts to Remember*.

Commentary on Colossians 4:7-18
V. The Closing Section—Colossians 4:7-18

Paul has completed the body of his letter. Now in this final section, he brings the letter to a close with various greetings, final instructions, and a brief benediction. While perhaps not as rich in spiritual content as earlier sections, these closing verses provide us with many valuable insights into the circumstances of the Colossians and the identity of Paul's co-workers.

A. Paul's Representatives—Colossians 4:7-9

Verse 7

Tychicus. This letter to the Colossians was delivered by Tychicus, another member of Paul's missionary team. He was a native of the Roman province of Asia (where Colossae lies), probably from the city of Ephesus (Acts 20:4). He later accompanied Paul on his last journey to Jerusalem. Later still, we see Paul sending him to take over an assignment from Titus in Crete (Tit 3:12) and another from Timothy in Ephesus (2 Tim 4:12) so that these men might rejoin Paul. During his present journey to deliver this letter to Colossae, he carried at least two other letters. One was for Philemon in Colossae. A second was for the Laodiceans. We will consider the identity of this letter to the Laodiceans in the comments on Colossians 4:16 below.

a dear brother, faithful minister, and fellow slave in the Lord, will tell you all the news about me. With this threefold description, Paul expresses his confidence in

Tychicus. Paul uses the same words to describe Epaphras in Colossians 1:7. He is saying that Tychicus is a man of the same quality as Epaphras. You can trust him just as you have trusted Epaphras.

Verse 8

I sent him to you for this very purpose, that you may know how we are doing and that he may encourage your hearts. Paul now gives two reasons for sending this trusted fellow worker. The first is to bring news of Paul's circumstances. Such news could have been written in a letter, but apparently, Paul wanted it conveyed in person. Since Tychicus was a close companion and fellow worker, he was the right man to provide this information.

The second reason is that Tychicus might encourage (strengthen) their hearts. Recall that in Colossians 2:2, Paul tells the Colossians that the purpose of his hard work for them—and indeed the purpose of this letter—is to encourage their hearts. They needed the encouragement in the face of the deceptive teaching so that they could gain understanding and confidence in the truth of the gospel. This was necessary so that they could walk in accordance with it and progress toward maturity. Therefore, Tychicus is present in Colossae to reinforce the message of the letter itself. He is there to add his own ministry of encouragement with the goal of strengthening them in the faith and bringing them to maturity in Christ.

Verse 9

I sent him with Onesimus, the faithful and dear brother, who is one of you. They will tell you about everything here. Tychicus was accompanied by the slave, Onesimus. He belonged to Philemon in whose house the Colossian church met. He had previously run away, perhaps to Ephesus, where he encountered Paul who led him to Christ. Paul is now returning Onesimus to his master. In a separate letter carried by Tychicus, Paul appeals to Philemon to forgive Onesimus. Paul mentions none of this, however, here in his letter to the Colossians. Instead, Onesimus is simply commended to them as "the faithful and dear brother" who is a member of their congregation. Moreover, he is there on a mission. Paul has made him a partner with Tychicus in this task of informing the Colossians about Paul's situation in Ephesus.

B. Personal Greetings—Colossians 4:10-15

Verse 10

Aristarchus, my fellow prisoner, sends you greetings. In this section, Paul sends personal greetings from himself and six of his fellow workers in Ephesus. The first three are Jewish Christians. Aristarchus was from the city of Thessalonica (Acts 19:29; 20:4). After his ministry with Paul in Ephesus, he traveled with him to Jerusalem and from there to Rome (Acts 20:2). He is described here as sharing Paul's imprisonment in Ephesus. The word translated "prisoner" is a military term meaning "prisoner of war." In this brief way, Paul identifies Aristarchus as a fellow soldier of Christ, suffering in the service of his Lord.

As does Mark, the cousin of Barnabas. The second greeting comes from Mark (also known as John), a native of Jerusalem (Acts 12:12, 25). The fact that he is identified here by his relationship to Barnabas tells us the Colossians knew who Barnabas was. He and Paul had founded the churches of Galatia, a region 200 miles (320 km) to the east, several years before during Paul's first missionary journey (Acts 13:2-14:27). Thus, they knew Barnabas by reputation. Mark had also been on this journey, at least in the beginning. But because he turned back (Acts 13:13), Paul refused to allow him to come on their second journey (Acts 15:37-40). Barnabas, however, saw potential in his young cousin and took him on a separate mission. From this statement in Colossians, we may conclude that Mark prospered under Barnabas' patient instruction, since Mark is now seen as a trusted member of Paul's team (see also 2 Tim 4:11). Later in his life he composed the gospel of Mark.

(about whom you received instructions; if he comes to you, welcome him). This brief statement concerns a possible visit by Mark to Colossae in the near future. But for what purpose we are not told. One theory is that he was traveling to join Peter in his missionary work east of Colossae. We know from 1 Peter 5:13, that Mark later worked very closely with Peter (he refers to Mark as "my son"). The fact that Peter addressed his letter (1 Pet 1:2) to Christians in a wide territory that included Colossae suggests that he had once ministered among these people. Does Colossians 4:10, therefore, concern Mark's transfer (perhaps temporarily) from Paul's missionary team to Peter's? And was the instruction about him an explanation of Mark's new assignment and a request for hospitality for this traveling missionary, should he pass through their town? Perhaps. In any event, this short statement in Colossians 4:10 opens a small window for us on the comings and goings of missionaries in Paul's day that we would not otherwise know about.

Verse 11

And Jesus who is called Justus also sends greetings. The third greeting is from Jesus Justus. The name Jesus was actually common among Jews of this period (Acts 13:6). It is the Greek form of the Hebrew name Joshua. His family name, Justus, is given here to distinguish him from others with this name. Unlike Aristarchus and Mark, this man is mentioned nowhere else in Scripture.

In terms of Jewish converts, these are the only fellow workers for the kingdom of God, and they have been a comfort to me. Paul now further identifies these three men as converts from Judaism (literally "from the circumcision"; compare Col 3:11). In fact, they are the only Jewish believers to join him in his work there in Ephesus, and by doing so they have become a comfort to him.

The word translated "comfort" refers to the relief of pain. It was used in regard to emotional pain—such as sorrow over the death of a loved one. It was also used of medicines for relief of physical pain. The pain Paul suffered was emotional. The source of his pain was his fellow Jews. In Romans 9:2-3, he writes of the "great sorrow and unceasing anguish" in his heart because the Jews, as a people, had rejected their Messiah. In addition, Paul experienced great hostility and persecution at the hands of these Jews (Acts 17:13; 21:27-28; 2 Cor 11:24; 1 Thess 2:14-16). In the midst of this opposition Paul found special joy and encouragement in the presence of these three Jewish co-workers, Aristarchus, Mark, and Jesus Justus.

Finally, it is worthwhile to observe that Paul describes these men as "fellow workers for the kingdom of God." He often describes his friends and companions as fellow workers (Rom 16:3; 2 Cor 8:23; Phil 4:3; 1 Thess 3:2). Only here, however, does he describe the work they perform as "for the kingdom of God." What does it mean to work for the kingdom of God?

Simply stated, it is the work of the gospel. The evangelist Phillip preached "the good news about the kingdom of God" (Acts 8:12). Paul also preached the kingdom of God (Acts 20:25, 28, 31). And their message was a continuation of "the gospel of the kingdom" that Jesus preached (Mt 4:23, Lk 4:43). Strictly speaking, the kingdom of God is something future. It will only be established on earth in its fullness when Christ returns in glory (Mt 25:31-34). Nevertheless, as we read in Colossians 1:12-14, there is a present aspect to the kingdom. Even now when a person accepts the message of God's forgiveness through Christ, he becomes a subject of the kingdom. He becomes a citizen of the kingdom in its heavenly form (2 Tim 4:18), and an heir to the fullness of the kingdom in its future earthly form.

To work for the kingdom of God, therefore, means to work for the advancement of the kingdom. This is done by proclaiming this message of forgiveness and by nurturing those who believe so they might become mature followers of Christ, the King. This summarizes the ministry of Paul and his co-workers (see Col 1:28).

Verse 12

Epaphras, who is one of you and a slave of Christ, greets you. Now in Colossians 4:12-14, Paul sends greetings from the three non-Jewish members of his missionary team. The first is Epaphras, mentioned earlier in Colossians 1:7. It was through him that the Colossians first heard the message of the gospel. As Paul's representative, he had established the church there and nurtured it through its early stages. He had returned from Colossae to inform Paul of the condition of the church and to seek advice regarding the false teaching that threatened to take captive these young believers. During this visit, however, he himself had been arrested and imprisoned (Phm 23). Like Onesimus in Colossians 4:9, Paul identifies Epaphras as a member of their congregation (one of you). In Colossians 1:7, Paul commended Epaphras as our dear fellow servant who is a faithful minister of Christ. Now in closing, he commends Epaphras again. He is a servant of Christ. In this way, Paul again assures the Colossians of his high regard for Epaphras.

He is always struggling in prayer on your behalf. Paul now moves from the general to the specific. He has just described Epaphras as a servant of Christ. A specific example is the way he prays for them. The word "always" and phrase "in prayer" call to mind what Paul wrote in the opening paragraphs of this letter regarding his prayers for the Colossians: "We always give thanks to God . . . when we pray for you" (Col 1:3); we "have not ceased praying for you" (Col 1:9). This seems to refer to a regular time of prayer in which Paul and his co-workers gathered to thank God for his work of grace in the congregations they had established and to pray for their spiritual welfare.

Paul testifies here to the great concern that Epaphras manifests for the Colossians in these times of prayer. He *struggles* on their behalf. Paul has used this term twice already to describe his own efforts in ministry. In Colossians 1:28-29, he told how he labors and struggles to present everyone mature in Christ, and indeed it is to this end that he is now struggling for the Colossians (Col 2:1-2). As we saw in connection with Colossians 1:29, the word "struggles" originally meant to compete in an athletic contest (such as a wrestling match). But it came to be used in a figurative way for any kind of struggle or conflict. Thus, Paul is telling the Colossians of the urgency and energy with which Epaphras intercedes for them. He wrestles for them in prayer. By using the same term that Paul used to describe his own intense labor, he is recognizing Epaphras as a true kindred spirit in ministry.

so that you may stand mature and fully assured in all the will of God. This line states the content of Epaphras' prayer. Although the wording is somewhat different, it is the same thing Paul prays for the Colossians in Colossians 1:9. God's will in this context refers to his overall plan of salvation as revealed in the gospel (see the comments on Col 1:9). Epaphras is, therefore, praying that God will bring them to a full and confident understanding of all that he has done for them, what he will do in the future, and how he desires them to live as a result. To have this understanding and to walk in accordance with it is what it means to be mature in Christ (see the comments on Col 1:28c). It is also the best defense against the "arguments that sound reasonable" of the deceptive teaching (Col 2:4). As God brings these young believers to maturity in Christ, they will be able to stand firm against those who would seek to take them captive (Col 2:8).

Finally, we should observe that this prayer repeats once again the theme and purpose of the letter. We first saw this expressed in Colossians 1:9-10 with Paul's prayer for the Colossians to be filled with the knowledge of God's will. We saw it again in Colossians 1:28-29 where he explains that the goal of his ministry is to present everyone mature in Christ. It appears again in Colossians 2:1-2 where he speaks of struggling to bring the

Colossians to the "riches that assurance brings in their understanding." An echo from each of these statements can be heard in Colossians 4:12. This is Paul's way of giving a concluding summary of his purpose in writing to the Colossians. It is the very thing that Epaphras prays for them so fervently. It is for God to bring them to maturity in Christ.

Verse 13

For I can testify that he has worked hard for you and for those in Laodicea and Hierapolis. Paul now adds this additional word of explanation about Epaphras' ministry of prayer. Paul has not simply heard about it from someone else; he is an eyewitness. They prayed together regularly. Indeed, they were living together in the same prison. Paul is reminding the Colossians that Epaphras is still on the job for them. He is still serving them as a pastor. He is not there physically to do the work of preaching, teaching, and admonishing, but intercessory prayer is a vital part of the work of ministry. And so Epaphras' ministry toward them continues even now. He labors strenuously in prayer. No doubt, he planned to return to Colossae as soon as he was released from prison. (Recall that Paul himself intended to go to Colossae upon release, according to Phm 22.)

Finally, we should observe that Epaphras prays not only for the believers in Colossae but for those in the neighboring towns of Laodicea and Hierapolis as well. It is from this statement that we draw the conclusion that his missionary work included these other two towns (see also Col 2:1).

All three towns were located in the Lycus River valley. This valley has the shape of a wedge that points eastward. It is sixteen miles (26 km) wide at its base in the west, twenty-six miles (42 km) long and narrows to one mile (1.6 km) at its eastern tip where the river descends into it. This valley is a gateway from the low-lying coastal region of the west to the great central plateau of Asia Minor. Foothills and high cliffs surround it. Snowcapped mountains are visible in the distance. Through the valley and along the river ran the great Eastern Highway, the major trade route between the port of Ephesus and the interior, stretching all the way to the Euphrates valley. Laodicea, the largest and wealthiest of the three towns (Rev 4:17), was located in the middle of the valley at a major crossroads. Hierapolis was six miles (9.7 km) to the north on the edge of the valley and clearly visible from Laodicea. Colossae, the oldest and smallest of the three, was twelve miles (19.3 km) up river from Laodicea at the narrow eastern tip of the valley.

Verse 14

Our dear friend Luke the physician and Demas greet you. The other two non-Jewish men among Paul's co-workers to send greetings are Luke and Demas. Luke later wrote the gospel of Luke and the Acts of the Apostles. Thus, two of the four gospel writers, Luke and Mark, were with Paul at this time. We learn from the "we" and "us" statements in Acts that Luke accompanied Paul on his second and third missionary journeys as well as his trip to Rome (Rom 16:10-17; 20:5-21; 27:1-28). Only from this verse in Colossians, however, do we learn that he was a medical doctor. In Paul's final imprisonment, as he awaited death, only Luke was with them (2 Tim 4:11). Luke was obviously one of Paul's most steadfast and devoted companions. The term "dear friend" informs us of Paul's affection for him.

No word of commendation is given Demas, although in Philemon 24 he is mentioned along with Luke as Paul's fellow worker. The only other mention of Demas is in 2 Timothy 4:10. There we read that he deserted Paul at a time when Paul still needed a lot of help.

Verse 15

Give my greetings to the brothers and sisters who are in Laodicea and to Nympha and the church that meets in her house. After sending greetings from his six co-workers, Paul now asks the Colossians to convey his greetings to Christians in the neighboring area. Is the church in Nympha's house the church of Hierapolis? Probably not. The mention of Laodicea both before (Col 4:15a) and after (in Col 4:16) the mention of this church suggests it was also connected to Laodicea. Either all of the "brothers and sisters who are in Laodicea" met in Nympha's house or a significant portion of them. The Greek text will support either interpretation.

Whichever view we take (the Colossians themselves knew exactly what Paul meant), the important observation to make here is that the earliest Christians met in homes (see also Phm 2; 1 Cor 16:19; Rom 16:5). They had no special buildings called churches. Such buildings only came into use about two centuries later. The congregation itself was the church. (The Greek word translated "church" means assembly or congregation; see Acts 19:39, 41.) In some cities, such as Colossae, the entire church was small enough to meet in a single home. But where the church was large, more than one home was required. This was certainly the case in Jerusalem—probably also in Rome, Corinth, and Ephesus. In these places the house churches served as more manageable circles of worship and service within the larger body of the citywide church.

C. Final Instructions—Colossians 4:16-17

Verse 16

And after you have read this letter, have it read to the church of Laodicea. Paul closes with two brief instructions. The first concerns the reading of this letter and another one in the possession of the Laodiceans. The word "read" in this context means to read aloud in public. This letter would have been read aloud to the entire congregation during one of their regular gatherings for worship in the house of Philemon (compare Acts 15:30; 1 Thess 5:27). But the contents of the letter also had direct application to the church in Laodicea. No doubt the deceptive teaching was a threat there as well. Therefore, Paul instructs the Colossians to have someone take the letter (or a copy of it) without delay to Laodicea and to read it there to the assembled church. When this person returned to Colossae, it is likely he would bring with him the letter that is the subject of the final line of this verse.

In turn, read the letter from Laodicea as well. This statement indicates that Paul was sending a separate letter to the Laodiceans. Tychicus would leave it there on his way to Colossae. Thus, Paul instructs them to read this letter once it has been forwarded on to them from Laodicea.

What was this letter to the Laodiceans? There are two possibilities. The first is that it is a lost letter. Surely in his long career as a missionary Paul wrote more letters than the thirteen preserved in the New Testament. Only those that were inspired were included in the Bible. And yet, Paul's instruction for it to be read to the entire congregation indicates that it was indeed an important and valuable letter.

The other possibility is that this letter was not lost. It may be the one we know as the Letter to the Ephesians. According to this theory, Ephesians was not written to a single congregation. Instead, Paul wrote it as a general letter of instruction with the intention of circulating it among all the churches he and his missionary team had planted in the province of Asia (including Ephesus) during his long stay in Ephesus. It came to be known as the Letter to the Ephesians (the words "in Ephesus" in Eph 1:1 do not appear in many early Greek manuscripts) because Ephesus was the chief city of this province.

There is considerable evidence to support this theory:

    (a) No individuals are addressed in Ephesians.

    (b) No advice is given regarding any particular situation.

(c) The teaching is very wide-ranging.

(d) The parallels with Colossians in subject matter and in actual wording suggest that these two letters were written at about the same time.

(e) Both Colossians and Ephesians were delivered by Tychicus (Eph 6:22; Col 4:7).

(f) The earliest testimony we have from the ancient church (around AD 150) identifies Ephesians as the letter from Laodicea. This theory fits the facts so well that it should be accepted as the more likely interpretation.

Verse 17

And tell Archippus, "See to it that you complete the ministry you received in the Lord." After giving the Colossians instructions about the exchange of letters, Paul comes to his second and final matter of instruction. The Colossians are to exhort one of their members to show diligence in fulfilling the ministry he has been given. This instruction presents something of a puzzle to the modern-day reader. Who was Archippus? What was his ministry? And why does Paul choose to exhort him in this way?

According to Philemon 2, Archippus belonged to the household of Philemon and his wife, Apphia—in whose home the Colossian congregation met. He may have been their son. Paul refers to him there as "our fellow soldier." One of Paul's favorite images of the Christian minister and his work is that of a soldier (see 2 Tim 2:3). By describing Archippus in this way, Paul is saying that his ministry there in Colossae made him Paul's comrade-in-arms. They are fellow soldiers in the Christian warfare.

While we cannot know for certain the exact nature of the ministry that Archippus received, we can make a reasonable guess. The Greek word translated "received" was often used of someone who took over a task or office from someone else. Epaphras had previously carried the responsibility of teaching and preaching among the churches of the Lycus Valley. This verse suggests that when he departed for Ephesus to consult with Paul, it was Archippus who took over this responsibility.

If this is correct, then in Colossians 4:17 we see Paul exhorting Archippus to be diligent in fulfilling this ministry. Since the church had appointed Archippus to this task, it was more appropriate for Paul to direct his exhortation to him through them. In this way, Paul puts his stamp of approval on their appointment. But does this exhortation have the tone of a rebuke? Does it imply some lack of diligence? There is no need to interpret it in this way. Paul's charge to Timothy in 2 Timothy 4:1-5 has a similar tone. It is formal and solemn, but it is certainly not a rebuke. Likewise, Paul's message to Archippus reflects the seriousness of the task before him. It also reveals a genuine concern for Archippus and for those under his care that he will fulfill this difficult assignment successfully.

D. Farewell and Benediction—Colossians 4:18

Verse 18

I, Paul, write this greeting by my own hand. It was Paul's custom to dictate his letters to a companion and then to add a personal note at the end in his own handwriting (see 1 Cor 16:21; Gal 6:11-18; 2 Thess 3:17-18; Phm 19; Rom 16:22). This final note added a personal touch to the letter and served to confirm that it was a genuine letter from Paul (see 2 Thess 2:2; 3:17). A signature at the end of a typed letter today functions in much the same way.

Remember my chains. In this brief and final exhortation, Paul calls upon the Colossians to bear in mind that he is now a prisoner for the sake of the gospel. But what exactly is he asking them to do? His appeal could include many things, but we should understand it first of all as a request for prayer on his behalf: "In your prayers before God, remember me in my imprisonment." This underscores his request in Colossians 4:3 for new opportunities for proclaiming the gospel. But the Colossians would also pray for sustaining grace in this time of suffering and for a speedy release (see Phm 22).

We may also hear in this exhortation a final effort to underscore the message of the letter: "Remember that it is because of my ministry on your behalf and others like you that I am in chains. Therefore, honor me by taking to heart what I have written here and apply it to your lives" (Col 1:24, 28-29; 2:1-2).

Grace be with you. Paul ends his letter as it began: with a prayer of blessing for God's grace (see Col 1:2). Grace is God's undeserved favor toward sinners. He has revealed it most clearly in his gift of salvation through Christ. God also acts in grace to enable us to grow in Christ and to walk in a manner pleasing to him. Seen from this point of view, grace has been the subject of the entire letter. But even more than that, Paul intended the letter to be a means of grace in their lives—a means of causing them to progress to maturity in Christ. And now in closing, he offers this brief prayer of benediction that God will continue to sustain and enable them by his grace.

QUESTION 24

Match the description with the correct name.

Description	Name
I was with Paul in his final imprisonment	Barnabas
Paul and I founded the churches of Galatia	Archippus
I took over the ministry of Epaphras	Nympha
I delivered Paul's letter to the Colossians	Tychicus
Church met in my house	Luke

QUESTION 25

Match the description with the correct name.

Description	Name
I was a runaway slave	Mark
I established the church in Laodicea	Epaphras
I set out with Paul on his first missionary journey	Aristarchus
My first name is the Greek form of the Hebrew name Joshua	Onesimus
I am a Jewish Christian from the town of Thessalonica	Justus
I deserted Paul when he needed me	Demas

QUESTION 26

Paul included a series of personal greetings near the end of this epistle to:
- A. Provide specific instructions regarding certain individuals
- B. Keep the Colossians informed about the ministry of other people
- C. Keep the Colossians informed about his own ministry
- D. To share greetings from other people to the Colossians
- E. Provide encouragement to the readers of this epistle
- F. All of the above statements are true

QUESTION 27

The pain Paul felt was caused by hostility from the Jews not the Gentiles. *True or False?*

QUESTION 28

Explain briefly how Paul repeated the theme of the letter in his closing greetings.

QUESTION 29

Match the description with the correct town.

Description	Town
This town sits on a high cliff overlooking the Lycus Valley	Colossae
The oldest and smallest of the three towns of the Lycus Valley	Laodicea
The largest and wealthiest of the three towns	Hierapolis

QUESTION 30

In Colossians 4:16 Paul mentions a letter that would be coming soon to the Colossians from Laodicea. By what name do some people believe this letter is known by today?
- A. Laodiceans
- B. Philemon
- C. Galatians
- D. Ephesians
- E. Philippians
- F. Hebrews

QUESTION 31

How should we understand Paul's message to Archippus in Colossians 4:17 to attend to the ministry he received in the Lord that he may discharge it fully?

A. As a mild rebuke

B. As a sharp rebuke

C. As a solemn charge but not a rebuke

D. As a commendation for agreeing to take over the ministry of Epaphras

QUESTION 32

In Paul's closing appeal, "Remember my chains" (Col 4:18), we can hear a final effort to underscore the message of the letter. *True or False?*

Important Facts to Remember About Colossians 4:7-18.

1. Tychicus, Paul's co-worker; and Onesimus, Philemon's recently converted runaway slave, delivered Paul's letter to the Colossians.

2. Paul sends greetings from his three Jewish co-workers Aristarchus, Mark, and Justus.

3. In the greeting from Epaphras, Paul repeats once again the theme of the letter. Epaphras always prays for the Colossians that they "may stand mature and fully assured in all the will of God." (Col 4:12). This prayer echoes earlier expressions of the theme in Col 1:9-10, in Colossians 1:28-29, and Colossians 2:1-2.

4. The greeting to the brothers in Laodicea and to Nympha and the church that meets in her house (Col 4:15) informs us of the church in Laodicea.

5. The letter that was coming "from Laodicea" mentioned in Colossians 4:16 is perhaps the letter that Paul circulated among all the churches of that area, and which we know today as Ephesians.

6. Archippus may have been the son of Philemon. If so, then he took over the responsibility of preaching and teaching among the churches of the Lycus Valley when Epaphras departed. Paul's message to him in Colossians 4:17 is not a rebuke but a solemn charge to be diligent in fulfilling this difficult and important assignment.

7. In Paul's closing exhortation, "Remember my chains" (Col 4:18), we can hear a final effort to underscore the message of the letter: "It is because of my ministry for you and others that I am in chains. Take to heart, therefore, what I have written and apply it to your lives."

Lesson 12 Self Check

QUESTION 1
Which of the following statements is **true** regarding slaves in Paul's day?
- A. A slave could rarely expect to be freed.
- B. Slaves had the same rights as free people under Roman law.
- C. Slaves did only menial, unskilled, labor.
- D. Slaves were advised by Paul to do their work with a deep inner commitment of the heart.
- E. Most slaves in Paul's day in the Roman Empire were born into slavery.

QUESTION 2
The Greek word _____ is used twice in Colossians 3:22-4:1 for the earthly master and five times for the heavenly master.

QUESTION 3
Paul's exhortation to masters in Colossians 4:1 to treat their slaves justly and fairly was his way of telling them they ought to free their slaves. *True or False?*

QUESTION 4
The Greek word translated "be devoted" in Colossians 4:2 is based on the root verb that means to be _____.

QUESTION 5
Paul's prayer request for an open "door for the message" in Colossians 4:3 included a request for a speedy release from prison. *True or False?*

QUESTION 6
In the original Greek, the phrase translated "making the most of the opportunities" (Col 4:5) is based on a proverb about farming. It said that for a farmer to have a good harvest he must do everything at the right time. *True or False?*

QUESTION 7
Which of the following best defines the quality of graciousness that makes the Christian's speech attractive and pleasant?
- A. Humor
- B. Eloquence
- C. Kindness
- D. Common sense
- E. Intelligence
- F. Open mindedness and tolerance toward the religious beliefs of others

QUESTION 8

In which verse of the closing section does Paul repeat the theme of the letter?

- A. Colossians 4:7
- B. Colossians 4:10
- C. Colossians 4:12
- D. Colossians 4:13
- E. Colossians 4:17

QUESTION 9

In Colossians 4:16, Paul mentions a letter that was coming to the Colossians from Laodicea. Today we recognize that this may be the letter to the _____.

QUESTION 10

How should we understand Paul's message to Archippus in Colossians 4:17 to attend to the ministry he has received in the Lord that he may discharge it fully?

- A. As a mild rebuke
- B. As a sharp rebuke
- C. As a solemn charge but not a rebuke
- D. As a commendation for agreeing to take over the ministry of Epaphras

Lesson 12 Answers to Questions

WORKSHEET FOR COLOSSIANS 3:23-4:1

Answer for Colossians 3:22–4:1

Slaves: Obey your masters
- ²²Slaves, obey your earthly masters in every respect, *(command)*
  - not only when they are watching— *(manner of action)*
  - like those are strictly people pleasers—
  - but with a sincere heart and
  - fearing the Lord.
- ²³Whatever you are doing, work at it with enthusiasm, *(command)*
  - as to the Lord and not people, *(manner of action)*
- ²⁴BECAUSE *(explanation)*
  - you know that you will receive your inheritance from the Lord as the reward.
  - Serve the Lord Christ. *(command repeated)*
- ²⁵FOR *(explanation)*
  - the one who does wrong will be repaid for his wrong,
- AND *(additional explanation)*
  - there are no exceptions.

Masters: Treat slaves fairly
- ⁴:¹Masters, treat your slaves with justice and fairness, *(command)*
- BECAUSE *(explanation)*
  - you know that you also have a master in heaven.

Textual Outline of Colossians 3:22-4:1
I. Slaves must obey their masters. (Col 3:22-25)
    A. They must obey with sincerity and reverence for the Lord. (Col 3:22)
    B. They must work wholeheartedly, as service to the Lord. (Col 3:23)
    C. Explanation: The Lord will reward you. (Col 3:24a)
    D. Command repeated: Serve the Lord. (Col 3:24b)
    E. Explanation: Wrongdoers will be repaid. (Col 3:25)
II. Masters must treat their slaves fairly. (Col 4:1)
    A. Command: Treat slaves fairly. (Col 4:1a)
    B. Explanation: You have a master in heaven. (Col 4:1b)

Theme Statement for Colossians 3:22-4:1
Slaves must obey their masters, while masters must treat their slaves fairly.

QUESTION 1
   D. Slaves were advised by Paul to do their work with a deep inner commitment of the heart.
QUESTION 2: *Your answer should be similar to the following:*
This new reality does not free the slave from the honor and obedience normally expected of slaves toward their masters. Instead, it should make him a better slave: honest and hardworking, as service to the Lord, rather than to men. Slaves who live for Christ in this way embrace the gospel.
QUESTION 3
   C. Upright in heart
QUESTION 4: *Your answer should be similar to the following:*
The fear of the Lord is the response of the believing heart to the revelation of God's awesome power, majesty, and holiness. It manifests itself in trust and obedience to his Word.
QUESTION 5: kyrios
QUESTION 6: False [It simply means that the slave is to do his work as though he were doing it for Christ himself and not just for the earthly master. This is a specific application to the exhortation of Colossians 3:17 to do everything in the name of the Lord Jesus.]
QUESTION 7: True
QUESTION 8: False [He is simply telling the masters to rule their slaves wisely—with justice and even-handedness.]
QUESTION 9: *Your answer*

QUESTION 10: *Your answer*
WORKSHEET FOR COLOSSIANS 4:2-4

Answer for Colossians 4:2-4

Pray persistently
- ²Be devoted to prayer, *(command)*
  - keeping alert in it with thanksgiving. *(accompanying activity)*
- ³At the same time pray for us too, *(command/ request)*

  THAT *(content of prayer)*

  God may open a door for the message,

  SO THAT *(purpose of open door)*

  we may proclaim the mystery of Christ,
  - for which I am in chains. *(explanation)*

Prayer request for Paul's ministry
- ⁴Pray that I may make it known as I should. *(command/ request repeated)*

Textual Outline of Colossians 4:2-4.
I. Pray persistently. (Col 4:2)
    A. The command to pray persistently (Col 4:2a)
    B. Accompanying activity: Alertness and thanksgiving (Col 4:2b)
II. Prayer request for Paul's ministry (Col 4:3-4)
    A. The request (Col 4:3)
        1. The request: An open door for their message (Col 4:3a,b)
        2. Purpose: To proclaim the mystery of Christ (Col 4:3c)
        3. Explanation: Paul is in prison for doing this. (Col 4:3d)
    B. Request repeated (Col 4:4)
        1. The request: To make known the mystery (Col 4:4a)
        2. Explanation: This is Paul's duty. (Col 4:4b)

Theme Statement for Colossians 4:2-4.
Paul exhorts the Colossians to persistent prayer, and particularly for his ministry of proclaiming the gospel.

QUESTION 11: *Your answer should be similar to the following:*
The central message of Colossians 3:5–4:6 is that Christians should walk in accordance with what God has made them as his redeemed people.

QUESTION 12: strong

QUESTION 13: False [While Paul states his request in terms of his mission and not his personal freedom, it is reasonable to believe that he thought of this open door as one that included his freedom. Confirmation of this can be seen in Paul's letter to Philemon where he assumes that Philemon is praying for his release (Phm 22).]

QUESTION 14: confidence

QUESTION 15
  B. The gospel

QUESTION 16: *Your answer*

QUESTION 17: *Your answer*

WORKSHEET FOR COLOSSIANS 4:5-6

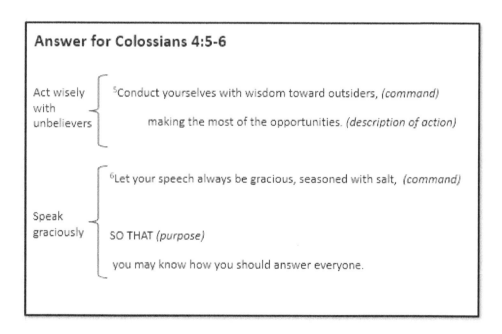

Textual Outline of Colossians 4:5-6
I. Act wisely with unbelievers. (Col 4:5)
    A. The command to act wisely (Col 4:5a)
    B. Description of action: Make the most of opportunities. (Col 4:5b)
II. Speak graciously with unbelievers. (Col 4:6)
    A. The command to speak graciously (Col 4:6a)
    B. Purpose: To be able to make the best response (Col 4:6b)

Theme Statement for Colossians 4:5-6
In their relations with unbelievers, the Colossians must act wisely and speak graciously.

QUESTION 18: skill

QUESTION 19
    E. The marketplace

QUESTION 20: *Your answer should be similar to the following:*
Paul compares the Christian's speech to a meal served to a non-Christian. As the cook adds salt to the food to improve the taste, so the Christian should add graciousness to his speech to improve the attractiveness.

QUESTION 21
    C. Kindness

QUESTION 22: *Your answer*

QUESTION 23: *Your answer*

QUESTION 24

Description	Name
I was with Paul in his final imprisonment	Luke
Paul and I founded the churches of Galatia	Barnabas
I took over the ministry of Epaphras	Archippus
I delivered Paul's letter to the Colossians	Tychicus
Church met in my house	Nympha

QUESTION 25

Description	Name
I was a runaway slave	Onesimus
I established the church in Laodicea	Epaphras
I set out with Paul on his first missionary journey	Mark
My first name is the Greek form of the Hebrew name Joshua	Justus
I am a Jewish Christian from the town of Thessalonica	Aristarchus
I deserted Paul when he needed me	Demas

QUESTION 26:
    F. All of the above statements are true

QUESTION 27: True

QUESTION 28: *Your answer should be similar to the following:*
In sending greetings from Epaphras, (Col 4:12), Paul mentions how Epaphras is always striving for the Colossians in prayer that they "may stand mature and fully assured in all the will of God." This prayer summarizes the theme and purpose of the letter. We see it first expressed in Paul's prayer (Col 1:9-10) for the Colossians to be filled with the knowledge of God's will (his plan of salvation) that they might walk in accordance with it. We see it again in Colossians 1:28 where Paul states that the goal of his ministry (and therefore the goal of this letter) is to bring every believer to maturity in Christ. It appears again in Colossians 2:1-2 where Paul tells how he strives to bring his readers " all the riches that assurance brings in their understanding" so that they might continue to stand firm and not be seduced by the arguments of the false teachers "that sound reasonable". An echo of each of these passages can be found in Colossians 4:12.

QUESTION 29

Description	Town
This town sits on a high cliff overlooking the Lycus Valley	Hierapolis
The oldest and smallest of the three towns of the Lycus Valley	Colossae
The largest and wealthiest of the three towns	Laodicea

QUESTION 30
    D. Ephesians

QUESTION 31
    C. As a solemn charge but not a rebuke

QUESTION 32: True

Lesson 12 Self Check Answers

QUESTION 1
   D. Slaves were advised by Paul to do their work with a deep inner commitment of the heart.
QUESTION 2: kyrios
QUESTION 3: False
QUESTION 4: strong
QUESTION 5: False
QUESTION 6: False
QUESTION 7
   C. Kindness
QUESTION 8
   C. Colossians 4:12
QUESTION 9: Ephesians
QUESTION 10
   C. As a solemn charge but not a rebuke

Unit Four Exam

QUESTION 1

Which of the following statements served as a slogan for the false teachers?

    A. Put to death your earthly passions.

    B. Seek the things above.

    C. Set not your minds on earthly things.

    D. Let your life be hidden with God.

    E. He who ascends to hidden places will be revealed in glory.

QUESTION 2

Paul exhorts believers in Colossians 3:2 not to set their minds on earthly things because what is physical (earthly things) is evil and what is spiritual (things above) is good. *True or False?*

QUESTION 3

Which of the following statements best explains the meaning of the statement, "Your life is hidden with Christ in God"?

    A. As those who have died are now hidden in the earth, so those who have died with Christ are now hidden in him.

    B. Our true life is hidden because it belongs to the inner, unseen person of the heart.

    C. Each believer has a double which is his true spiritual self who lives in heaven with Christ.

    D. The world knows neither Christ nor Christians, and Christians do not even know clearly one another.

    E. The fullness of our resurrection life lies prepared for us in heaven with Christ.

QUESTION 4

In the commentary on Colossians 3:3-4, the image of a bank was used to illustrate what it means that the believer's "life is hidden with Christ." In this illustration, Christ represents the banker but the statement in Colossians 3:4 that he "is your life" indicates that he is also the _____.

QUESTION 5

The exhortation to "put to death whatever in your nature belongs to the earth" pictures our "earthly members" as sins that make up the body of the earthly "old man." *True or False?*

QUESTION 6

The Greek word translated _____ means a desire to have more.

QUESTION 7

In Ephesians 4:22-24, Paul writes that believers must lay aside the old man and put on the new. This does not mean that they are still "old men" and not yet "new men" but that they must be what they are. *True or False?*

QUESTION 8

Which of the following statements is **not** true regarding the renewal of the new man?

A. It is the work of God.
B. It is a process.
C. It begins at the time of conversion.
D. Its object is to conform us to the image of Christ.
E. It will be complete when we die and go to heaven.
F. It includes what Paul calls "the renewing of your mind" in Romans 12:2.

QUESTION 9

The statement in Colossians 3:11 that in the case of the new man "there is neither Greek nor Jew . . ." means that in the church, the society of the new creation, the original_____ of the human race is being restored.

QUESTION 10

According to Colossians 3:!2, we are to "clothe ourselves" with which of the following?

A. Mercy
B. Kindness
C. Humility
D. Gentleness
E. Patience
F. All of the above responses are true

QUESTION 11

The biblical instruction "Just as the Lord has forgiven you, so you also forgive others." (Col 3:13), means that as we forgive others the Lord will also forgive us. *True or False?*

QUESTION 12

In what passage of Colossians (which is sometimes called "the Colossian hymn") does Paul teach that Christian songs are a way to praise God and to teach and encourage fellow worshipers?

A. Colossians 1:9-14
B. Colossians 1:15-20
C. Colossians 1:24-28
D. Colossians 2:9-15
E. Colossians 3:15-17

QUESTION 13

To do something in the name of another means to act as that person's _____.

QUESTION 14.

The word "submit" means to take a _____ position in relation to another.

Unit 4 Exam

QUESTION 15

Which of the following portions of Scripture provides the clearest additional teaching on the command in Colossians 3:19 for husbands to love their wives?

    A. Colossians 3:12-14
    B. Romans 7:1-6
    C. Galatians 5:16-26
    D. Ephesians 5:25-33
    E. Song of Solomon
    F. 1 Timothy 3:1-7

QUESTION 16

The command in Colossians 3:20 for children to obey their parents is not directed to adult offspring but to those who are still growing up. *True or False?*

QUESTION 17

The command in Colossians 3:21 for fathers not to provoke their children is directed to fathers only, because mothers tend to be very gentle with children and no such admonition is needed. *True or False?*

QUESTION 18

The statement in Col 3:23 that the slave should do his work "as to the Lord" means the earthly master stands in the place of Christ as his representative. *True or False?*

QUESTION 19

Choose the best interpretation of the instruction for masters to treat their slaves justly.

    A. Masters should treat their slaves in accordance with Roman law.
    B. They should free all of their Christian slaves.
    C. They should treat their slaves according the Old Testament laws regarding slaves.
    D. They should treat their slaves according to what is right in the eyes of God.

QUESTION 20

Paul's request in Colossians 4:3 for the Colossians to participate in his ministry of proclaiming the mystery of Christ by praying for him contains an expression of _____ that they will take to heart what he has written to them in this letter and not turn aside to the false teaching.

QUESTION 21
What precisely is "the mystery of Christ" in Colossians 4:3-4 that Paul desired to make known?
   A. The rapture of the church
   B. The gospel
   C. The fact that Christ indwells all believers, Jew and Gentile alike
   D. The mystery of the incarnation of Christ as both fully God and fully man
   E. The mystery of the "one flesh" union between Christ and the Church

QUESTION 22
The statement "Let your speech always be gracious, seasoned with salt" (Col 4:6) pictures the Christian's speech with the non-Christian as a meal served to a guest with the salt of graciousness added to improve the taste. *True or False?*

QUESTION 23
Which of the following best defines the quality of graciousness that makes the Christian's speech attractive and pleasant?
   A. Humor
   B. Eloquence
   C. Kindness
   D. Common sense
   E. Intelligence
   F. Open mindedness and tolerance toward the religious beliefs of others

QUESTION 24
In which verse of the closing section does Paul repeat the theme of the letter?
   A. Colossians 4:7
   B. Colossians 4:10
   C. Colossians 4:12
   D. Colossians 4:13
   E. Colossians 4:17

QUESTION 25
In Colossians 4:16 Paul mentions a letter that was coming to the Colossians from Laodicea. Today we recognize that this may be the letter to the _____

Unit 4 Exam Answers

QUESTION 1
  B. Seek the things above.
QUESTION 2: False
QUESTION 3
  E. The fullness of our resurrection life lies prepared for us in heaven with Christ.
QUESTION 4: deposit
QUESTION 5: False
QUESTION 6: greed
QUESTION 7: False
QUESTION 8
  E. It will be complete when we die and go to heaven.
QUESTION 9: unity
QUESTION 10
  F. All of the above responses are true
QUESTION 11: False
QUESTION 12
  B. Colossians 1:15-20
QUESTION 13: representative
QUESTION 14.: subordinate
QUESTION 15
  D. Ephesians 5:25-33
QUESTION 16: True
QUESTION 17: False
QUESTION 18: False
QUESTION 19
  D. They should treat their slaves according to what is right in the eyes of God.
QUESTION 20: confidence
QUESTION 21
  B. The gospel
QUESTION 22: True
QUESTION 23
  C. Kindness
QUESTION 24
  C. Colossians 4:12
QUESTION 25: Ephesians

Made in the USA
Coppell, TX
27 October 2024

39226211R00184